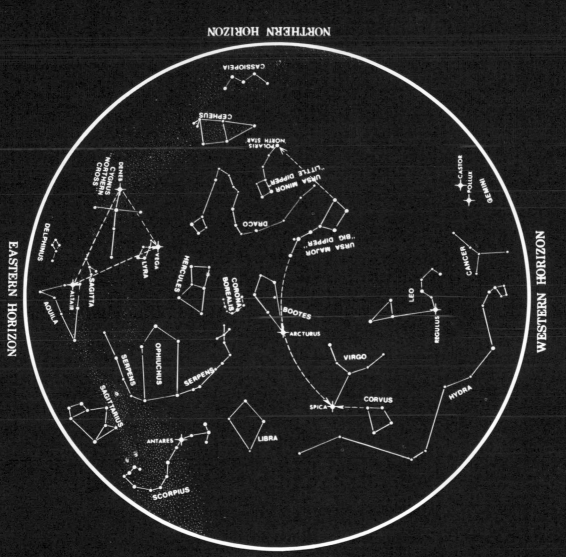

NORTHERN HORIZON

EASTERN HORIZON

WESTERN HORIZON

SOUTHERN HORIZON

THE NIGHT SKY IN JUNE

Griffith Observer star charts,
Griffith Observatory, Los Angeles

^{THE}ASTRONOMERS

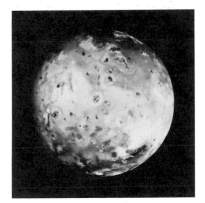

Io. (NASA photograph.)

Anglo–Australian Telescope. (Photograph by Dr. David Malin, courtesy of the Anglo–Australian Telescope Board.)

THE ASTRONOMERS

Donald Goldsmith

Companion Book to the
PBS Television Series

ST. MARTIN'S PRESS   NEW YORK

Director of Manufacturing: Karen Gillis
Production Editor: David Stanford Burr
Designer: Glen Edelstein

Library of Congress Cataloging-in-Publication Data

Goldsmith, Donald.
    The astronomers / Donald Goldsmith.
        p.   cm.
    ISBN 0-312-05380-0
     1. Astronomy—Popular works. 2. Astronomers—Biography—Popular works. 3. PBS television series (Television program) I. Title.
    QB44.2.G63   1991
    520—dc20   90–49205
                                            CIP

First Edition: April 1991

10 9 8 7 6 5 4 3 2 1

To my daughter Rachel
—and to all who wonder at the stars

Contents

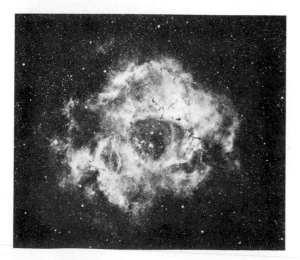

Rosette Nebula. (Photograph courtesy of National Optical Astronomy Observatories.)

Arecibo radio telescope. (Photograph courtesy of National Astronomy & Ionosphere Center.)

Edwin Hubble. (Hale Observatories photograph.)

Acknowledgments

Andromeda galaxy. (Lick Observatory photograph.)

IN WRITING THIS book, I have received generous assistance from a host of friends, acquaintances, colleagues, co-workers, and others who have kindly helped me onward. I hope that the result will not disappoint them, but whether or not it does, their help has not passed unremembered. I would like to record the names of many who assisted with this project, hoping that those whom I may have overlooked will forgive my carelessness.

The PBS television series "The Astronomers" was made possible by a generous grant to KCET-TV, the public-television station in Los Angeles, by the W. M. Keck Foundation. I would like to enter a special note of appreciation to Mr. Howard B. Keck, the foundation's chairman, to Judge David Thomas, the chairman of the foundation's Southern California Committee, and to Mrs. Joan DuBois, the project officer, for their roles in helping to support astronomy in this way.

Of course, no program on astronomy would be possible without the research and the direct assistance of professional astronomers, many of whom gave generously of their time to the television film crews and also aided my efforts to write about them and their work. In this connection I would like to thank Evgeny Alekseyev, David Allen, Dave Alsop, Halton Arp, Don Backer, John Bahcall, Valery Barsukov, Sasha Basilevsky, Gibor Basri, Eric Becklin, Steve Beckwith, Charles Beichman, Peter Bender, Hans Bethe, Leo Blitz, Nancy Boggess, Stuart Bowyer, Vladimir Braginsky, Andre Brahic, Russell Cannon, Pat Cassen, Catherine Cesarsky, Chip Cohen, Judy Cohen, Marshall Cohen, Stirling Colgate, John Conway, Marc Davis, Eugene DeGeus, Imke DePater, Mark Dickinson, George Djorgovski, John Dobson, Mike Dopita, Alan Dressler, Ron Drever, Richard Epstein, David Evans,

Edith Falgarone, George Field, Alex Filippenko, Andrew Fraknoi, Ian Gatley, Tom Geballe, Margaret Geller, Dan Gezari, Mark Giampapa, Gary Gibbons, Owen Gingerich, Peter Goldreich, Paul Goldsmith, Jesse Greenstein, Leonid Grishschuk, Puragra Guhathakurta, Alan Guth, Mike Hauser, Carl Heiles, John Huchra, Andy Ingersoll, Dan Jaffe, Torrence Johnson, Richard Joyce, Ivan King, Bob Kirshner, Ed Krupp, Shri Kulkarni, Andrew Lange, Dave Latham, John Leibacher, Ken Libbrecht, Phil Lubin, Roger Lynds, David Malin, Richard Manchester, Steve Maran, Bruce Margon, Laurence Marschall, John Mather, Toshio Matsumoto, Dave Morrison, Norm Murray, Jerry Nelson, Colin Norman, Benjamin Peery, Richard Perley, Malcolm Perry, Tom Phillips, Sterl Phinney, Richard Porcas, Carolyn Porco, Bill Press, Tom Prince, Tony Readhead, Paul Richards, Vera Rubin, Bernard Sadoulet, Carl Sagan, Ed Salpeter, Anneila Sargent, Wallace Sargent, Maarten Schmidt, François Schweizer, Dave Schramm, Nick Scoville, Brad Smith, George Smoot, Larry Soderblom, Steve Soter, Hy Spinrad, Jason Spyromiliou, Gary Steigman, Ed Stone, Jill Tarter, Rich Terrile, Silvia Torres-Peimbert, Scott Tremaine, Neil Turok, Tony Tyson, Tiziana Venturi, Rochus Vogt, Robert Wagoner, Joseph Weber, Rai Weiss, Jack Welch, Arno Witzel, Stan Woosley, Judy Young, Ben Zuckerman, and most of all Ken Brecher, Kevin Krisciunas, Toby Owen, and Kip Thorne, who gave more time and assistance than they bargained for.

The team of science advisors who helped with the making of the television series played a special role in answering a host of questions, not only from myself but from a dozen people involved in the project; they also met to discuss our plans and reviewed what we produced. Chaired by Edward Stone, this team included Roger Blandford, David DeVorkin, Joseph Miller, Mark Morris, Frank Shu, Joseph Silk, David Stevenson, and Virginia Trimble, all of whom helped me as well as the series.

Among those working at astronomical and scientific institutions who helped with this book, I would like to thank George Alexander, Ron Brashear, Richard Dreiser, Shaun Hardy, and David Seidel.

A large number of people worked on the television series and thus aided me in creating this book. It would take a chapter (which my editor insisted on saving for another work) to describe this process and to show how we interacted. I shall content myself with listing the titles of those who worked on the series. These include: Phylis Geller, KCET's Vice President of National Programming; Blaine Baggett, the Executive Producer of the television series; the Series Producer, Peter Baker; the Producers of the individual programs (with whom I was co-writer for each program), Linda Feferman, James Golway, Julio Moline, David Oyster, and Chris Wiser; the Associate Producers, Patricia Colvig, Liliana Cruz, Suzanne Marong, and Susan Racho; the Production Manager, Jeanne O'Brien; the Production Accountant, Casey Spira; the

Jupiter's Great Red Spot. (NASA photograph.)

Production Assistants, Maria Crean and Cynthia Woodard; the Film Editors, Lillian Benson, Jack Reifert, David Saxon, and Vincent Stenerson, and their Assistant Editors, Chris Capp, Nina Kawasaki, Sara King, Ken Luebbert, and Sheryl Riley; the Sound Editor, Erica Pflaum; the Visual-Effects Coordinator, Michael Van Himbergen; the Storyboard Artist, John Nelson; the Production Runners, Joel Morales and Bill Ward; and the PBS Television Interns, Keiann Collins, Andrew Crane, George Hawkins, Vivian Mesa, Trina Mortley, Mellisa Olen, and Elizabeth Hong Yang.

Beyond KCET, I am especially grateful to the special-effects designers and artists, computer experts with artistic souls, with whom I worked to produce explanatory visual effects for the series, some of which appear as stills in this book. John Grower, Jeff Kleiser, Diana Walczak, and Erica Walczak of Kleiser/Walczak Construction Company; Joan Collins, Mike Gunning, Michael Rivero, Andrew Rosen, Keith Schindler, Steve Sidley, Vicki Sidley, Mark Sorell, Jean-Jacques Tremblay, and Steve Wright of Sidley/Wright Company; and David Lipman, John Ornelas, Ron Sabatino, Carl Sims, and John Whitney, Jr., of Digital Animation Laboratory—all showed patience and willingness to work hard beyond the call of contract. I am grateful to the film crews with whom I was on location for their patience in dealing with my inquiries and special needs, and I want to thank H. J. Brown, Bob Eber, Tom Evans, John Parentau, Peter Pilafian, Scott Sakamoto, Ernie Shinagawa, and especially Petur Hliddal and Paul Goldsmith (the "other Paul Goldsmith"—because my brother Paul Goldsmith is an astronomer) for showing me their ropes.

All these and more deserve my thanks. I could not have spent a year and a half commuting to and from my home in Berkeley without the aid and comfort of my friends Victor and Marjorie Garlin, Jo Powe and Tom McGuire, Merrinell Phillips, Arlene Prunella and Pascal Debergue, and Scott Davis. Crystal Stevenson and Marjorie Garlin have put up with a lot from me in order to execute the line art in this book; David Oyster, a friend since "Cosmos" days, who first brought me into this project, has never failed to provide key insight about making science documentaries; Liliana Cruz provided able assistance with the fact-checking and photo research; and Laurie Sieverts Snyder and Sally Weare secured excellent photographs of astronomers. My daughter Rachel has once again proven tolerant of my faults beyond the call of family.

My editor at St. Martin's Press, Michael Sagalyn, has

demonstrated his familiar verve and acumen in dealing with the manuscript of this book, and the Assistant Editor, Ed Stackler, has also proven a fount of intriguing suggestions. My publishers, who labored long and hard on *The Astronomers,* share my hopes for its success. I feel amply rewarded by having had the chance to increase my knowledge of astronomy—and of the men and women who have brought us an ever-increasing understanding of the cosmos.

Preface

Spiral galaxy M 81. (Lick Observatory photograph.)

The Astronomers has grown from the PBS television series of the same name, for which I was the science editor and the co-writer (in collaboration with the producers of the individual programs). The book can be read as a "companion" to "The Astronomers," in which case chapters 1–3 present material in the first program, chapters 9 and 10 cover the second, 4 and 5 deal with the third, chapters 13 and 14 with the fourth program, chapters 6, 7, and 8 with the fifth, and chapters 11 and 12 with the final program. The book can also be read on its own, as an introduction to modern astronomy with emphasis on the men and women who strive to advance our knowledge of the universe. It does not aim at encyclopedic coverage of the world of astronomy, but it does attempt to present the high points of recent discoveries in astronomy, as well as to forecast some of the discoveries expected in the near future.

Like the television series, this book offers a view into the lives of the astronomers who perform the research that yields discoveries. Since I was trained as a professional astronomer and worked hard as a researcher until I strayed onto the path of popularization, many of the astronomers whom I interviewed are friends and acquaintances. This was both a blessing and a curse: I could talk to them more easily than most who seek to explain what they do, but I found myself reluctant to expose any weak spots in their personalities. Fortunately I didn't find anything seriously wrong, and readers who search for an exposé of the "truth behind the official version" of astronomical reality will find slim pickings here.

I hope that this book can and will be read with interest and enjoyment by anyone who is interested in astronomy. To those of us who teach astronomy and write books on the subject, a great regret (shared by science teachers everywhere) remains—the fact that many adults have had such negative experiences as children with science education that they approach any information on the subject with what may charitably be called diffidence. With this book I seek to do my part to tip the balance in a direction favorable to science, which not only deserves attention (as all admit) but in addition offers the great pleasure of learning both scientific facts and the way that we came to believe those facts to be true. In an uncertain world this is no small feat. May astronomy prosper so long as, and to the extent that, it satisfies the public's desire to separate fact from fantasy, and may this book find its readers among those who delight in both—and in knowing the difference.

—Donald Goldsmith
Berkeley/Los Angeles
Spring/Summer 1990

Saturn. (NASA photograph.)

The summit of Mauna Kea. (Courtesy of Dr. Dale Cruikshank and the University of Hawaii).

1. Under the Dome of Heaven

IN THE CENTER of the Pacific Ocean, on the Big Island of Hawaii, the world's greatest astronomical observatory perches atop the dormant volcano Mauna Kea. Rising six miles from the ocean floor and nearly three miles above the ocean surface, Mauna Kea and its neighbor, Mauna Loa, form the bulk of the island of Hawaii. Astronomers have seized the opportunity that the volcanic heights offer: spectacular views of the heavens from above the clouds. On Mauna Kea astronomers are now completing the world's largest telescope, and are planning to construct even more advanced instruments to probe further into the universe.

Mauna Kea's merits as an observatory site became clear to astronomers during the early 1960s, when surveys revealed the astonishing transparency of the skies over the summit. The possibilities interested an astronomical potentate, Gerard Kuiper of the University of Arizona's Lunar and Planetary Laboratory, who had discovered the fifth moon of Uranus and the second moon of Neptune. Kuiper knew the excellence of the solar observatory on Haleakala, Maui's 10,000-foot peak, and saw that Mauna Kea could provide even better viewing conditions. He therefore encouraged continued testing of the site. The study revealed that Mauna Kea's additional height often frees it from the clouds that shroud Haleakala.

Astronomers describe conditions of still, clear air as photometric, meaning suitable for photometry—the exact measurement of the brightnesses of objects. Under less-than-photometric conditions, measurements made on a given night cannot be properly compared with those made on another night, or even with measurements made earlier that evening. A typical year on Mauna Kea has close to 175 photometric nights. This unusually high frequency of clear conditions, combined with the high altitude that keeps most of the atmospheric water vapor below the summit, make Mauna Kea an outstanding observatory location. Such excellence extends not only to conventional (optical) observations, but also to the measurement of invisible types of radiation from space such as infrared (heat) radiation.

An observatory on a mountain requires a road that gives access to the summit. In 1964, Kuiper persuaded the governor of Hawaii and the president of the University of Hawaii to agree that the state would build a highway to an observatory that the university would help to operate. By July, work on the observatory had proceeded to the point where a dedication ceremony seemed appropriate; by the end of that year, the astronomers saw that they had found a new Mecca. During the twenty-five years since then, Mauna Kea has drawn professional astronomers as pollen attracts bees. As part of the arrangements among astronomical institutions that have created the large telescopes, the University of Hawaii's astronomers receive large amounts of observing time at each instrument. This situation has led many astronomers to make the ultimate sacrifice: exchanging their stressful lives in the crowded cities of the continental United States for the balmy climate of Honolulu, where the University of Hawaii's campus is located. From the university's Institute for Astronomy, the hardy astronomers commute to their "observing runs," each a few days long, atop Mauna Kea (Color Plate 1).

Astronomers are not the only ones drawn to the summit. Every tourist who rents a car on this island receives a contract that states in bold print: "Do not take this vehicle on the 'saddle road' [the narrow, winding, and poorly asphalted road between the two giant volcanos]." A few renters, seeking the full Hawaii experience, disregard this suggestion. Some drivers turn off at the high point of the saddle, where an even narrower road to the north winds up to an altitude of nearly two miles. There the tourist encounters a group of wooden buildings that blend rather handsomely with the lava-made slopes. This is Hale Pohaku (House of Stone), where the Mauna Kea Observatory has offices, dormitories, construction barracks, a library, and an eating facility—in short, everything an astronomer needs to prepare for a night at the summit and to recover afterward. No one spends twenty-four hours at the summit: The air is so thin that even experienced observers find their judgment impaired. At that altitude, simply climbing a flight of stairs can be fatiguing in the extreme. The astronomers drive upward at dusk and descend before sunrise, passing their nights at the observatory summit, and their days farther down at Hale Pohaku, 9,200 feet above sea level, where they try to sleep past noon and eat at least two full meals to prepare for the next night's endeavors.

At Hale Pohaku the tourist can read, in letters much larger than those on the car rental contract, that only authorized persons may proceed further on what becomes an eight-mile-long dirt road suitable only for four-wheel-drive vehicles. The occasional foolhardy tourist takes this as a challenge, and a small fraction of such souls manage to reach the top—quite an impressive feat in an automobile tuned for sea-level driving. The top of Mauna Kea is 13,800 feet above sea level. The actual summit, holy ground to the native Hawaiians, remains free from roads and telescope domes, which do quite well at sites a few hundred feet lower. One arrives after an ascent of nearly a mile in altitude, passing the surprisingly large Lake Waiau along the way. The barren terrain seems more representative of the moon than one of Earth's lushest islands. In winter, snow often blankets the peak and on occasion covers the entire mountaintop, so Mauna Kea has the only ski area in the state. An organization in Oahu, where most Hawaiians live, waits for news of good snow conditions and then sends groups of skiers.

No one visits the observatory without feeling the altitude. At the summit, the air pressure falls to about 60 percent of its sea-level value, straining the lungs and heart of anyone who grew up in a place lower than the lofty city of La Paz, Bolivia. Astronomers who find themselves at the observatory's telescopes during the daytime often pause to observe the drunken stagger of unauthorized visitors who emerge from their vehicles, people who seem to expect a reward for their arduous journey. Some astronomers have strange stories to tell: of the female graduate student who insisted on swimming in Lake Waiau without a bathing suit, or of the observatory employee who formed the fixed intention to don scuba equipment and then ski down the cinders into the lake's 20-foot depths.

Mauna Kea may be a great astronomical site on most nights, but when things turn bad there they can turn truly bad. The most common type of storm brings winds that howl at 100 miles per hour or more, and the summit has many other different types of inclement weather. On one day in August 1982, an astronomer at the summit noted sunshine, rain, sleet, hail, and freezing fog in succession. Weather aside, the effect of extreme altitude on how an astronomer thinks causes certain problems. Some of the astronomers, experienced observers at lower altitudes, arrive with an ego problem: "I've observed on mountains around the world— I'm ready for this." They are not. One engineer, 37 years old, died at the summit of an apparent heart attack a few hours after the start of his observing run. Most of the institutions that run the different telescopes have a stringent policy: If you feel weird (imperfectly defined), you descend to Hale Pohaku—or all the way to sea level—until you feel better. High altitude impairs your judgment in a way well known to those who have studied it: You can no longer deal with new input data, nor carry on with whatever activity you happened to be engaged in when the light in your brain grew dim. This makes it essential to delineate an observing plan before ascending to the summit; otherwise, you and your observing partner can have endless arguments about the best way to proceed—arguments that reveal themselves as trifling once lower altitudes are regained.

If an astronomer happens to combine a temporary loss of judgment with a four-wheel-drive, "I-can-go-anywhere" feeling, serious trouble tends to arise. Many of the astronomers who drive the summit road acquire modest or definite overconfidence as they maneuver their four-wheel-drive vehicles with abandon, speeding up and down the volcano as if possessed by cosmic furies. On at least one occasion, two French astronomers caught by the four-wheel-drive spirit and adversely affected by the high altitude attempted to set a speed record for the descent. At the 11,000-foot level they skidded over the edge of the washboard road and wrecked their observatory's $30,000 vehicle.

During the 1960s, as plans for the Mauna Kea Observatory became reality, astronomers accepted these hazards eagerly. They saw that in addition to its clear skies, the observatory site offered an additional benefit: It lies at a latitude just over 20 degrees north, almost as far south as Mexico City. Astronomers know well that they cannot see all the stars in the skies from a given location on our rotating planet, because some stars lie too far to the south (for Northern Hemisphere observers) or to the north (for Southern Hemisphere observers) ever to rise above the horizon. But observatories closer to the equator can observe a larger fraction of the skies as the spinning Earth revolves about the sun during the course of a year. Technically, a site exactly on the equator might allow an astronomer to view the entire sky, but our atmosphere prevents useful observations from being made all the way down to the horizon, and at the equator some of the stars (those almost directly above the Earth's north and south poles) barely rise above the northern or southern horizon (Figure 1). Mauna Kea does as well as any observatory, and better than nearly all, in allowing the widest possible view of the skies.

The 1970s and 1980s brought the construction of ever-larger telescopes at the summit: first the University of Hawaii's 88-inch reflector, then the Canada-France-Hawaii 142-inch reflector, and finally, in an advance that removed any doubt about the astronomical center of gravity on this planet, the mighty Keck Telescope, whose 400-inch-diameter complex of mirrors will be double the size of the Palomar Mountain telescope's single mirror.

In addition to these enormous optical instruments, half a dozen smaller telescopes complement the large ones at Mauna Kea, and four highly specialized instruments observe the heavens in certain types of radiation with wavelengths longer than the wavelengths of visible light—what scientists call infrared and submillimeter radiation. Though the water vapor in our atmosphere blocks nearly all the infrared and submillimeter radiation that reaches the Earth, some of these waves *do* penetrate to the summit of Mauna Kea when viewing conditions are especially dry (Figure 2).

Figure 1. An observatory in the Northern Hemisphere cannot observe objects close to the "south celestial pole," the point directly above the Earth's south pole, because such objects never rise above the horizon. (Drawing by Crystal Stevenson.)

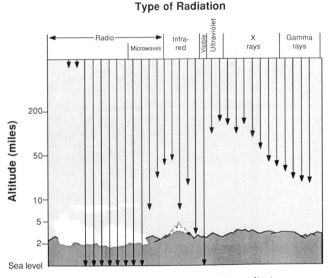

Figure 2. Different types of electromagnetic radiation penetrate to different altitudes before being blocked by the Earth's atmosphere. Only visible light and certain types of radio waves can penetrate all the way to sea level. (Drawing by Marjorie Baird Garlin.)

The Many Types of Electromagnetic Radiation

Light waves are one type of electromagnetic radiation. Other types are radio waves, submillimeter, infrared, ultraviolet, x rays, and gamma rays. Nearly everything that we know about what lies beyond Earth—nearly all the information that we have gained about the cosmos—has come to us in one form of radiation or another.

All of these types of electromagnetic radiation consist of streams of massless particles called *photons*. Photons always travel at the speed of light, 186,000 miles per second. We can imagine each photon as a sort of cosmic tadpole, wiggling through space, flailing its tail in a regular, rhythmic oscillation as it travels. The photon's *frequency* measures the number of times the tail oscillates each second, and the *wavelength* measures the distance the photon travels while its "tail" moves back and forth once (Figure 3). Higher frequencies imply shorter wavelengths, since with more oscillations per second (a larger frequency), the photon travels less distance (a shorter wavelength) during each individual oscillation.

What we call visible light is the type of electromagnetic radiation that we can see. Our eyes perceive dif-

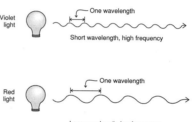

Figure 3. Each photon has a characteristic wavelength (distance between wave crests) that defines the nature of that photon. For visible light, violet has the shortest wavelengths and red, the longest. (Drawing by Crystal Stevenson.)

ferences in wavelength and frequency as differences in the *color* of visible light. Red light has the longest wavelengths and smallest frequencies of all the radiation our eyes can detect. In contrast, violet light has the shortest wavelengths and highest frequencies. But the entire span of visible light from red through violet covers only a tiny portion of the spectrum of all types of electromagnetic radiation. Our eyes evolved to detect the type we call visible light because our environment is especially rich in this sort of radiation.

Photons possessing different frequencies and wave-

A TRIP TO THE MOUNTAINTOP

A visitor to the observatory must pause, as all astronomers do, at Hale Pohaku, 4,600 feet below the summit of Mauna Kea. A stay at the lower level of at least two hours is recommended by those who supervise visits to the observatory. The body needs a chance to adjust to the stress that high altitudes place on the heart and mind. The altitude, already a significant factor at nearly two miles high, affects people in different ways. Some cannot form words crisply, and must speak much more slowly than usual, while others prattle on at speeds undreamt of at sea level.

On a typical good afternoon, an observer on the sunny veranda at Hale Pohaku can look over the clouds that swell above the saddle between the volcanos and see the giant bulk of Mauna Loa, and a hundred miles beyond, the empty Pacific. The primary purpose of Hale Pohaku is to provide food and sleep. Some astronomers find the high altitude conducive to 14 to 16 consecutive hours of rest, while others, unlucky souls, obtain a full night's sleep only with difficulty, if at all. The 57 rooms at the site's three dormitories resemble those in the spartan dormitory of a boarding school, with one difference that is common to all observatories: The rooms all contain well-fitted dark blinds and shades that allow scientists to sleep past noon after a hard night's work.

When an astronomer visits an observatory, the first order of business is to shift from a daytime to a nighttime mode of operation. Here food plays an important role: If you want your body to sleep, you may find it useful to eat a meal a few hours before you repose. The cafeteria at Hale Pohaku accepts and acts on this principle and has food in abundance ready in the wee hours for astronomers who descend from the summit hungry. Astronomers' unusual eating habits are part of the lore of the field. A favorite story (because it recalls Americans' concern for one another) recounts the time when two astronomers who finished their night's work at Yerkes Observatory, located not in Hawaii but in the far reaches of the Wisconsin lakes district, drove to a local greasy-spoon diner at dawn. One of them wanted a beer, but the waitress simply refused to let him ruin his system, despite his repeated explanation that this "breakfast" would in fact be his dinner.

lengths produce different effects upon the objects they encounter. The photons that make up radio waves have the longest wavelengths and lowest frequencies and are particularly effective at penetrating seemingly solid walls. They therefore prove useful for carrying television and radio broadcasts. Submillimeter waves have wavelengths somewhat shorter and frequencies somewhat greater than those of radio waves. The types of radiation between radio and submillimeter, called "microwaves," has proven immensely useful in modern kitchens, because when we place food in their path the microwave photons strike water molecules in the food, cause the molecules to dance rapidly, to produce friction and . . . hot food.

Infrared radiation consists of photons with even shorter wavelengths and higher frequencies than the photons that comprise submillimeter radiation. We often call infrared "heat radiation" because our bodies tend to perceive infrared as heat. Military personnel are interested in infrared radiation. Hundreds of millions of dollars and years of effort have gone into the design and manufacture of detectors that distinguish the infrared radiation that are emitted by humans and their equipment from the infrared emitted by trees, rocks, and the ground.

Astronomers likewise eagerly seek to observe the universe in infrared, but they face a difficulty (also experienced by the military): Our atmosphere blocks many wavelengths of infrared and allows others to pass only grudgingly—that is, the air "absorbs" most infrared. Water vapor in the atmosphere causes most of this absorption, because water molecules are especially effective in blocking infrared. Hence high-altitude observatories, aircraft, rockets, and satellites play crucial roles in infrared observations of the universe.

Ultraviolet comes on the other side of visible light in the spectrum. Ultraviolet radiation consists of photons with shorter wavelengths and higher frequencies than those of visible light. Because most stars emit ultraviolet, this type of electromagnetic radiation would offer a fine way to observe the universe, were it not for the protective envelope of our atmosphere, which prevents almost all ultraviolet from reaching the Earth's surface.

The sun, like most stars, emits great amounts of ultra-

Fittingly enough, that astronomer now holds the record for the greatest number of observing nights at Mauna Kea—and has a beer anytime he chooses.

From the stop at Hale Pohaku, the visitor typically continues upward to the summit in a four-wheel-drive vehicle with a Mauna Kea expert. One of these is Kevin Krisciunas of the Joint Astronomy Centre, headquartered at Hilo, the large city of the Big Island. The Joint Astronomy Centre is an organization funded by Canada, Holland, and Britain (hence the spelling of *Centre*) that operates the United Kingdom Infrared Telescope (UKIRT) and the James Clerk Maxwell Telescope (JCMT) on the summit. Krisciunas, a slim, laconic man who loves to compose astronomically oriented lyrics for old Gilbert and Sullivan songs, was trained at Lick Observatory in California and has flown to high altitudes aboard the Kuiper Airborne Observatory to make infrared measurements. To Krisciunas, a trip to the summit forms part of the workday routine, though he is quick to point out that one *never* gets used to the altitude; believing that you do is one of the signs of reduced perception.

Krisciunas will happily take a visitor from dome to dome, showing off the specialized telescopes that each contains, culminating with a view of the Keck Telescope ("always call it the mighty Keck," he says), which is still under construction, though partial operation began as 1990 drew to a close. Even experienced astronomers who think they are immune to impressions based on size find the Keck Telescope amazing. All large reflecting telescopes have a prime focus cage, a metal framework suspended high above the main mirror, in which an observer rides to make certain types of delicate observations. Since the prime focus cage blocks light from reaching the mirror, only the largest telescopes can use them. The biggest telescopes have mirrors that are large enough for the light blocked by the cage to be just a small fraction of the total incoming light. The Keck Telescope is so immense that the diameter of its prime focus cage exceeds the size of the primary mirror found in all but the six largest telescopes on Earth.

The Keck Telescope's mirror, the key to its abilities, has four times the surface area and four times the light-gathering power of the 200-inch reflector at Palomar Mountain. The secret of the telescope's construction, the only reason that astronomers can build this new instrument to enlarge our horizons, lies in its new approach to gathering and focusing light. This mirror does not consist of a single piece of glass, as the mirrors of almost all the

violet. If we had "ultraviolet eyes" and rose above the atmosphere, we would see a galaxy sprinkled with bright points of light. Since life on Earth has evolved beneath our blanket of air, which filters out nearly all ultraviolet, most forms of life—humans included—cannot stand much ultraviolet radiation. The Earth's atmosphere acts as a filter, with ozone molecules in its upper layers that block nearly all the ultraviolet that reaches our airy veil. Regrettably, human activities are steadily reducing the amount of ozone in the atmosphere, so that the amount of protection diminishes with each passing year. From a purely astronomical viewpoint, the atmospheric ultraviolet filter so important to human health actually hinders observation. Astronomers therefore require satellites above the atmosphere that observe the cosmos in ultraviolet. The same holds true for radiation of still shorter wavelengths and higher frequencies: x rays and gamma rays. These types of radiation pose even greater dangers to humans, but astronomical objects emit relatively little gamma and x radiation, and our atmosphere blocks it too.

Named in the days when these "rays" were utterly mysterious, x rays proved to be a high-energy type of electromagnetic radiation. All photons carry some energy, which the photons can deposit in the matter they encounter, as infrared radiation does when it causes sunburn, or as visible light does when it strikes the retina of a human eye. A photon's energy or ability to penetrate matter increases as its frequency increases, so each x-ray photon carries far more energy than a photon of visible light. This fact allows x rays to penetrate human flesh (but not teeth or bone) and thus to produce photographs of the human skeleton or teeth.

Of all types of electromagnetic radiation, gamma rays have the shortest wavelengths, the highest frequencies, and the greatest amounts of energy per photon. On Earth, few natural sources of x rays or gamma rays exist, but we have learned how to produce gamma rays artificially. As we shall see in a later chapter, cosmic gamma rays arise only in scenes of immense violence.

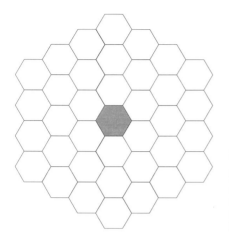

Figure 4. The 400-inch mirror of the Keck Telescope consists of 36 hexagonal segments. The 37th hexagon, in the center, is left open in order for the light collected by the mirror to be reflected downward through the mirror to instruments behind it. (Drawing by Crystal Stevenson.)

world's other great telescopes do, but instead is a honeycomb of 36 individual pieces of glass, working together as no set of mirrors ever has before (Figure 4).

No telescope mirror can perform its basic function of focusing light to create an image—an image that can be studied and magnified in various ways—unless the surface of the mirror is smooth. And what is smoothness in a mirror? To an astronomer, smoothness means that the reflector must not deviate from its desired shape by more than a fraction of the wavelength of the light that the mirror focuses. The desired shape is that of a *paraboloid,* a surface curved so perfectly that it reflects all incoming parallel rays of light to a single point, called the focus. This allows a detector mounted at the focus to receive all the light that reaches the telescope from a distant source. In addition, a mirror placed near the focus can reflect light from the focus downward through an opening in the center of the honeycombed main mirror. Additional mirrors then may reflect the beam into a separate room, where instruments too large or too delicate to be mounted above the main mirror can analyze the messages of star light. To make the Keck Telescope's mirror, astronomers had to create a paraboloidal reflecting surface 33 feet across. Their task was analogous to creating a near-perfect dome for a football stadium whose shape matches a perfect paraboloidal curve to within one one-hundredth of the thickness of a human hair.

In fact, the relatively "easy" part of the Keck Telescope was the creation of a near-perfect mirror surface. The difficult part would be to *hold* that surface within the specified tolerance as the telescope moves, an absolute necessity if the telescope is to observe objects in different parts of the sky. Gravity complicates matters. The mirror will be deformed slightly by its own weight, so astronomers must find design and engineering solutions to the problem of keeping a movable mirror in perfect shape. Previous large telescopes solved the problem by brute force: They employed reflective glass sufficiently strong to keep any deformation below the level that would ruin the telescope's ability to focus light waves.

But astronomers well knew that the 200-inch diameter of the Palomar Mountain Telescope represents a mirror close to the practical limit. The total amount of material in a mirror increases in proportion to the *cube* of the mirror's diameter, so a mirror twice as wide as the 200-inch would weigh eight times as much. For the Keck Telescope, an astronomer named Jerry Nelson provided the solution. Since no single mirror could do the job, Nelson suggested that the 400-inch diameter could be achieved with multiple mirrors, each of them capable of resisting deformation. But in order for the assemblage of reflectors to function as a single, integrated mirror, they must be held in alignment just as precisely as a single mirror's surface. How could this ever be done?

Nelson realized that the solution was *interactive optics*—a mirror system that continuously responds to the changes in the surface produced by gravity. In the Keck Telescope, each of the 36 hexagonal mirror segments rests on supports that are designed to minimize gravitational distortion (Figure 5). But the key to success lies in the fact that along each line where two mirrors meet, two sensors continually monitor any deviations from a perfect match. The sensors communicate with a computer that calculates the exact changes needed to restore alignment, and activates adjusting rods behind each hexagonal segment. The rods continually move the edges of each of the mirror segments backward and forward through distances up to one one-hundredth of an inch. Thus the Keck Telescope mirror achieves the goal of maintaining a nearly perfect paraboloid not by conquering gravity but by adjusting to it.

Because the mirrors must be adjusted on time scales of about one one-thousandth of a second, the Keck Telescope would have been an impossible proposition before advances in computer technology that occurred during the 1980s. Building the mighty Keck has been a challenge, but one that astronomers seem to have met successfully. Fabrication of the 36 individual mirror segments was a challenge for the optical technicians. Each segment spans more than 70 inches (and hence represents a good-sized telescope

Figure 5. The support system for the 36-segment main mirror of the Keck Telescope must allow each of the segments to be adjusted continuously, in order to correct for the slight changes in gravitational stress upon the mirror segments as the telescope moves. (Photograph courtesy of California Association for Research in Astronomy.)

mirror in itself) but is only 3 inches thick, in order to minimize the total weight of the mirror. The entire mirror will weigh no more than that of the 200-inch on Palomar Mountain, despite having four times the latter's light-collecting area.

To help reduce any distortion of their amazing mirror, the Keck Telescope astronomers have made plans to minimize, so far as possible, another source of deformation: temperature change. All artificial sources of heat, such as computers, are located in a separate part of the building, and the dome that contains the great instrument has an enormous cooling system, so that during the daytime the temperature will not rise significantly above its nighttime level. Thus when the dome opens at sunset, the telescope should not require—as other telescopes do—time for its mirror to adjust to the cool of the evening.

During 1989 and 1990, the structural steel for the telescope frame and then the mirror segments made the ocean journey to a port on Hawaii's west coast and were trucked up the mountain for installation. By the winter of 1991, with 9 of its 36 segments in place, the Keck Telescope already had a reflecting area equal to that of the 200-inch; from then on, even as the remaining segments were being installed, the telescope ranked as the world's mightiest. (The 236-inch reflector in the Caucasus Mountains of the Soviet Union, whose mirror exceeds that of the Palomar Mountain Telescope, has never yielded much useful data, apparently because of poor engineering.) Although plans exist for still larger telescopes, the Keck Telescope should for many years open new vistas to astronomy—vistas that draw special benefit from the high altitude and favorable weather conditions of Mauna Kea.

NIGHT ON BALD MOUNTAIN

Astronomical observatories much older than Mauna Kea, such as the Palomar Mountain and Lick Observatories in California, pioneered the use of mountain sites that provided dark skies and atmospheric clarity. These observatories, a mile or so above sea level, are easy places for astronomers to work, offering clear air and ready access. The Mauna Kea Observatory, on a mountaintop more than three times as high as Lick Observatory, is different. When night falls on Mauna Kea, the sky above you and the tightness in your chest give the sense that you might well have been left on another planet. If the moon has not risen, you can often see the faint *zodiacal light*—the glow of sunlight reflected by countless dust particles strewn throughout our solar system. If the moon is up, you can't see the zodiacal light. But you can see the *milky way,* a luminous band across the sky that contains the bulk of our galaxy's stars. At the summit, bright stars such as Sirius and Canopus seem to have been wired into high-voltage sockets, and the faintest objects—ones that astronomers learn about but rarely see— suddenly sparkle from within constellations such as Orion and Canis Major.

After this bracing look at the heavens, imagine that you are a scientist who has been invited to tour the facilities. You climb into the four-wheel-drive vehicle that an astronomer friend has lent you, and set off on a tour of the Mauna Kea telescope domes. Though the structures are only a few hundred yards apart, they are far too widely spaced to encourage a nighttime walk at high altitudes. You would likely survey the scene with a sense of awe, while wondering whether this is really the right place to master a stick shift and the right time to learn the pattern of unlit dirt roads. One faint consolation is that a basic knowledge of the constellations will keep you from getting lost in the greater scheme of things. On every clear night of the year, the Big Dipper—the most prominent part of the constellation Ursa Major—will stand out above the Pacific Ocean's northward roll to Alaska. "Follow the Drinking Gourd," you may say to yourself, repeating the line from the song of the underground railroad, telling slaves to follow the Big Dipper north to freedom.

The northern ridge of telescopes includes three giant domes, which contain the 142-inch Canada-France-Hawaii reflector, the University of Hawaii's 88-inch reflector, and the UKIRT infrared telescope. Until the Keck Telescope began operation, the lord of the mountain was the "CFHT," the Canada-France-Hawaii Telescope, run by a consortium of astronomers from Canada, France, and the United States. The CFHT incorporated the best in modern (but pre-Keck) telescope design: a single mirror, almost 12 feet across, ground to a parabolic shape; a framework to support this mirror; the prime focus cage above it; secondary mirrors to reflect beams of light to specialized instruments, and a computer-controlled guidance system that allows the telescope to track selected objects across the sky as the Earth turns.

Time on any of the telescopes is precious, and doubly so for a telescope as large as the CFHT. On a typical fall evening, a visiting scientist could find a three-part observing session in progress, extending from late afternoon to dawn. The session began with observations of Venus, an object sufficiently bright to be studied profitably in daylight and dusk. Observing Venus on that night were Tobias Owen from the State University of New York at Stony Brook and his longtime collaborator, Catherine DeBergh from France. They were searching for evidence of a special kind of water in Venus's atmosphere—water that contains not ordinary hydrogen but deuterium, a rare isotope of hydrogen. Owen and DeBergh used an instrument called a spectrograph to measure the amount of deuterium-laden water vapor on Venus by studying the sunlight reflected by the planet's surface. Owen and DeBergh hoped to confirm or disprove the popular theory that Venus once had oceans. These bodies of water would have evaporated when the sun heated the planet's atmosphere, causing a tremendous greenhouse effect and raising the temperature close to 1,000 degrees Fahrenheit.

Once the Earth's rotation had caused Venus to disappear below the horizon, other astronomers planned to use the CFHT to study the composition of the interstellar matter floating among the stars. Still later, with Jupiter high in the sky, a third group of astronomers would make infrared observations of that planet, searching for more details of its atmospheric composition.

Close by the CFHT rises the dome of the United Kingdom Infrared Telescope, or UKIRT, built and run by British astronomers. On this particular night, however, the telescope was under the guidance of two astronomers from the University of California at Los Angeles, Eric Becklin and Ben Zuckerman. A visit from an inquiring colleague pleased Becklin, a friendly, balding Viking. His partner, Zuckerman, is a tall, thin, rakish gentleman with a bandit's black mustache and hair trimmed to medium length. While a much sought-after viewing session is generally cause for professional excitement, astronomical observations do have an inherent boredom factor. If you plan things right, the telescope does its work and the supporting instruments do theirs. In accordance with a predetermined schedule, you feed into a computer the astronomical coordinates of each object that you seek to observe. The computer tells the telescope where to point, and keeps it pointed toward that object as the Earth turns. The telescope gathers the light and focuses it into a camera or into various other types of detectors that you have chosen to use. Additional computers record the data that the telescope sends to the instruments—data that you will not seek to interpret on the spot, but will later run through a larger computer at your home institution for detailed analysis. Becklin and Zuckerman were using the UKIRT to examine the aging stars that puff out rings of gas, misnamed "planetary nebulae" by bygone astronomers. They hoped to check on a theory that some of these stars—the ones that spew out gas preferentially in certain directions—tend to be binary stars, two stars orbiting one another in mutual gravitational embrace.

Leaving these scientists to their precisely planned evening, you could drive downhill to reach "submillimeter valley," some 400 vertical feet below the summit. The valley contains the large dishes used to catch *submillimeter radiation*—also known as long-wavelength infrared waves. One of these instruments, the United Kingdom's James Clerk Maxwell Telescope, was undergoing calibration tests on that night, but the other, Caltech's Submillimeter Observatory, was in operation, after a manner of speaking. Dan Jaffe from the University of Texas, accompanied by a graduate student, had hoped to observe submillimeter waves with wavelengths of 350 microns—nearly 20 times the wavelength of the radiation that Becklin and Zuckerman were observing. A micron equals one-millionth of a meter (or one one-thousandth of a millimeter). Thus a wavelength of 350 microns is about a third of a millimeter. Submillimeter observations are the most daunting challenge on the mountain, because water vapor blocks this radiation efficiently. On Mauna Kea, nearly three miles high, some of the driest nights do allow observations of radiation at the wavelengths that interest Jaffe. But on this night, even though the relative humidity was below 20 percent (unheard of at low altitudes), the air above the summit was allowing only 5 percent of the submillimeter radiation through, so accurate observations were not feasible.

The final stop on the visit would be NASA's Infrared Telescope Facility, where Dan Gezari and his colleagues from NASA's Goddard Space Flight Center were testing a new type of camera that they had designed and built for use in the *far infrared*. Such infrared radiation has wavelengths much longer than those of visible light. Far infrared represents one of the last astronomical frontiers: Only now has technology advanced to the point at which astronomers can hope to obtain reasonably sharp images of the objects that emit this type. Gezari has achieved new prominence by building a far-infrared camera better than anyone else's.

One of the obstacles to an efficient camera system is that at temperatures like those on Earth, *everything radiates infrared:* Your hands glow with this kind of invisible energy, your feet glow, the telescope glows, the walls glow. Hence the first order of business is to cool the immediate surroundings of the telescope in order to minimize the local glow from all directions. This gives the infrared detectors a chance to receive the infrared focused by the telescope, and thus to record faraway sources of infrared rather than the ones in the dome itself. The instruments reside within a tank, known as a dewar, containing supercold fluid and mounted at the focus of the telescope to maintain the infrared detectors at an exceedingly low temperature of -348 Fahrenheit. On the previous day, Gezari and his colleagues had filled the dewar with liquid nitrogen. That afternoon, they had filled the inner dewar (a smaller tank inside the main dewar) with liquid helium, at a temperature of -454 Fahrenheit—just 6 degrees above absolute zero, the coldest possible temperature. The helium would evaporate through the night, but while it lasted, their camera had a chance to work, and Gezari aimed to take the first true photographs ever of Saturn and other familiar objects at wavelengths of 20 microns. The astronomers were tired, drugged by altitude, but ready to work all through the night.

Like Gezari and his colleagues, the astronomers, technicians, and engineers who study the cosmos from Mauna Kea work under extreme conditions. They do it for love: love of discovery, love of modest fame, and the love of creating better instruments and using them to study the cosmos. In the Mauna Kea Observatory's first two decades of existence, the astronomers who use its facilities have already made notable contributions to science, including the discovery of the most distant galaxies known, and the most detailed observations of the center of our Milky Way galaxy. Mauna Kea's astronomers have made progress in visible-light, infrared, and submillimeter observations, in each case with arrays of specialized detectors that represent the finest systems humanity can now devise and construct. But perhaps the most exciting observational results from Mauna Kea during the past decade have dealt not with what astronomers can see in the cosmos, but what they *can't* see: the *dark matter.* To understand this advance, we must first understand the technological triumph at the heart of astronomers' improved observational results.

TONY TYSON AND THE CHARGE-COUPLED DEVICE

Things are not what they seem: The cosmos that we can *see* may be nothing like the "real" universe. This statement, which most astronomers now consider to be true, moves astronomy into a strange limbo in which most of the universe remains to be discovered. Through skilled detective work, relying on processes of deduction from the physical laws that we know, astronomers have reached a strange conclusion. *The bulk of all the material in the universe cannot be observed through measurement of any of the types of electromagnetic radiation that we've discussed thus far.* This unseen material, which amounts to 90 percent of all the matter (at a conservative estimate), or even to 99 percent of everything in the universe (according to more radical estimates), consists of an unknown form of matter, visible neither to our eyes nor to our radio, infrared, ultraviolet, x-ray, and gamma-ray detectors. Astronomers have deduced the existence of this "dark matter" by indirect means, but its nature is a complete mystery and will probably remain so for many years to come. For now, a great astronomical goal is at least to determine the amount and distribution of the so-called dark matter. One man with a plan to do so is J. Anthony Tyson (Figure 6).

Tyson, typical of the new breed of astronomers, draws his expertise as an astronomical observer from the world of advanced physics. On the one hand, Tyson has used telescopes around the world to study galaxies fainter than any ever seen before. On the other hand, the heart of Tyson's work—and the key to his success—consists not so much of his skill with telescopes as of his expertise at designing and building better *detectors,* that is, better equipment to record and analyze the light that telescopes collect and focus.

Using his skills in both observation and detector technology, Tyson has spent a decade studying the light from distant galaxies. The heart of his search concentrates not on these concentrations of stars but on how dark matter

Figure 6. J. Anthony Tyson of Bell Labs ranks among the world's leaders in the production of new charge-coupled devices (CCDs). (Photograph by Donald Goldsmith.)

between ourselves and distant objects can affect the light we perceive. Tyson has become a cosmic detective, a man who deduces enormous quantities of dark matter from a few clues hidden in the faint glow from galaxies near the edge of the visible universe.

Now just past his fiftieth birthday, a compact, handsome man who looks as though he could easily fit into an advertisement for Ivy League shirts, Tony Tyson displays an eagerness to learn typically associated with much younger men. He was born in Pasadena, California, the son of a man who worked his way from messenger boy to truck driver for an oil company, and the grandson of the editor of the *Los Angeles Star*. As a boy, Tyson developed rheumatic fever and lung disease, presumably from his exposure to the smog belt; his family then moved south to Carlsbad, two-thirds of the way from Los Angeles to San Diego. There Tyson attended the local military-academy high school. Later, intent on a career as an engineer, he departed for undergraduate studies at Stanford University. By his junior year in college, Tyson had discovered the joys of "pure science" and adopted physics as his career choice. By 1962, when he graduated from Stanford, he enrolled at the University of Wisconsin, seeking to study the physics of extremely low temperatures. During graduate school, however, he switched to the University of Chicago; after receiving his Ph.D., he spent a year in Chicago as a postdoctoral fellow and another in England.

In 1969, Tyson was a well-trained physicist in the expanding field of low-temperature physics. He began to work at the Bell Telephone Laboratories in New Jersey (now called simply the Bell Laboratories), a company that had won his heart by offering him the chance to work on any research he chose; he has remained with Bell Labs for more than two decades. Tyson spends most of his waking hours either in astronomical thought or in discussion with astronomers, physicists, engineers, and technicians. In 1981 he married a fellow astronomer, Pat Boeshaar, an expert on stars; their son Kristofer, now nine years old, has a lively interest in astronomy—perhaps from an instinct for self-preservation.

At the time that Tyson joined Bell Labs, he had become fascinated by the search for gravity waves. Albert Einstein's theories had predicted these tiny ripples in the fabric of space, but they have never been observed. To detect gravity waves, physicists have attempted to measure near-infinitesimal displacements in the positions of large masses, and the best way to do so involved cooling the masses as close to absolute zero as possible: Tyson's specialty. Tyson spent a decade on his quest for gravity waves; today others continue this quest, to which we shall return in chapter 13 of this book. But in 1984, judging that the effort could not pay off in the near or even the medium term, Bell Labs and Tyson decided to shut down their gravity-wave experiment. After ten years of unsuccessful attempts to find gravity waves that were presumably too weak to register on the detectors, Tyson "looked around for something with a measurable signal." He turned his attention to charge-coupled devices (CCDs).

To an observational astronomer, CCDs are the great new advance of the late twentieth century, the key to the technology that has revolutionized the way that astronomers work. To the consumer, CCDs are the unsung hero in most of the video cameras and auto-focus still cameras sold to the public. To a nonscientist CCDs simply offer a tremendous improvement over photography. But because of their enormous importance in the processes that astronomers use to gather and analyze light, CCDs deserve more than passing notice. Like television itself, they are far more often used than understood.

Like the transistor and the maser, CCDs were developed at Bell Labs. There, during the late 1960s, researchers found that certain types of silicon chips would respond to *light* by generating tiny electrical currents. Since Bell Labs scientists well knew how to collect and analyze such currents, they saw that these CCD chips offered an excellent way to record light as a series of electronic pulses. The scientists used simple computers to convert the light recorded by the chips into a stream of zeroes and ones. The process encodes the light input into combinations of these digits, and the digitized record of electronic pulses can then be used to produce an image. The charge-coupled devices in home video cameras do just that. A great advantage offered by CCDs lies in the ease with which a computer can manipulate digitized data. This advantage alone makes CCDs superior to photographic plates in recording the light from celestial objects for later analysis. Photographic plates can cover a much wider area of the sky, but to analyze them by computer requires long and complex programs that transform a photograph on paper or glass into the stream of data that a computer can handle.

The advantage offered by the digital data stream from CCDs might have seemed modest. However, CCDs owe their stunning success to a still greater advantage: Even though they produce grainier images, they record those images far more quickly than photographic plates do, and can record fainter objects than any plate can. The best plates record only 1 or 2 percent of the light that reaches them, while the other 98 or 99 percent effectively goes to waste. This is so because of every hundred photons of visible light that strike a photographic plate, only one or two will induce a chemical change in the emulsion that leaves an image on the plate. In contrast, CCDs can detect nearly every photon and thus nearly all the light that strikes them. An astronomer who replaces a photographic plate with a CCD system gains "eyes" that are 50 to 100 times more sensitive to incoming light!

And this is not all. Photographic plates record only visible light, and many of them record only certain colors of light. CCDs typically can detect not only visible light but other types of electromagnetic radiation as well—ultraviolet, infrared, and x rays. Furthermore, CCDs are inherently more stable than photographic plates, and their response to a particular amount of light is more predictable. Small wonder, then, that as CCDs became available during the late 1970s and early 1980s, astronomers rushed to adopt these new marvels for their telescopic systems, hoping to use CCDs to see objects too faint to be detected by conventional astronomical photography.

By now, two decades after CCDs first came into use, the great astronomical observatories have become almost completely digitized. The famed 200-inch telescope on Palomar Mountain recently sent its last photographic plates to the archive; from now on, only CCD images will emerge from its cameras. Despite the wider area covered by a photographic plate, CCD detectors obtain images so much more rapidly that their efficiency has totally swept the former technology from the field of astronomical endeavor.

But CCDs have a problem—a problem that Tony Tyson has helped to overcome. A CCD detector consists of thousands of individual "pixels" (short for "picture elements"), which collectively resemble the compound eye of an insect. And just as an insect can perceive more details if its mosaic eye contains more individual elements, so too can a CCD detector obtain a sharper view of the world if it can be made with more pixels.

To see the world with high precision requires enormous numbers of these pixels. Photographic plates provide just such clarity, because even a grainy photograph contains the equivalent of tens of millions of individual picture elements. A CCD detector that sees the cosmos as well as a photographic system would require a similar number of pixels—a goal that astronomers are only now approaching. The Hubble Space Telescope, launched in the spring of 1990 but built a decade earlier, contains a CCD system that once held the record for pixel number: 2.56 million.

Tyson's new CCD array, which has just finished its lab tests, does much better. Its four panels each number 2,048 × 2,048 pixels and therefore contain more than four million pixels. The four panels total more than 16 million pixels: six times the number of pixels in the CCD detector aboard the Hubble Space Telescope. With this new detector, Tyson hopes to continue his fantastic studies of regions of space that appear to be nearly devoid of stars but actually teem with faint galaxies!

FAR BEYOND THE MILKY WAY

Tyson's discovery of these distant collections of stars, since verified by other groups of astronomers, was made when he built a better CCD detector and trained the telescope on patches of "empty" sky.

Tony Tyson found that these "empty" regions contained faint blue galaxies in great numbers. These galaxies are too faint to have their distances determined effectively, but most of them are many billion light years away—so distant that we see them not as they are now, but as they were billions of years ago, when they produced the light that now arrives at our planet. The faint galaxies are blue in all probability because in their youth they produced enormous numbers of young, hot, blue stars. The hotter a star's surface, the bluer its light will be, in contrast to the reddish glow from a cool star or the yellow light from our mid-range sun.

In his search for the most distant galaxies, Tyson has now acquired an intelligent, helpful, hard-working younger colleague. Puragra Guhathakurta, also known as "Raja," was born in Calcutta in 1961, the youngest of three sons of a chemical engineer (Figure 8). Having demonstrated both interest and ability·in science during his high-school years, Raja studied physics at St. Xavier's College, a Jesuit-run institution with a fine reputation. He then entered a master's program at the University of Calcutta, but once he decided to pursue astronomical studies, Raja applied to U.S. institutions and went to Princeton in the fall of 1985. There he earned a reputation as one of the best students to reach the Princeton astronomy

The Order of the Universe

The visible universe consists of galaxies. A galaxy is a collection of millions or billions of stars. We live in the Milky Way galaxy, a giant (but hardly the largest) spiral galaxy. Our galaxy is so large that light, traveling at six trillion miles per year, takes more than 100,000 years to leap from rim to rim. The astronomy profession uses the *light year*—the distance that light travels in one year—as a basic unit of measure. One light year equals about six trillion miles—approximately two billion times the distance across the United States, or 25 million times the distance to the moon.

Using the speed of light as a measuring rod makes sense, so long as we remember that a light year measures distance, not time. It also helps us to realize that although all astronomical distances are enormous by Earthly standards, some are far more enormous than others (Figure 7). In light-travel units, the sun lies 8 "light minutes" away. Should the sun disappear in the blink of an eye, we'd have 8 minutes of grace before we found out. All the stars visible to the naked eye on a clear night are about a *million* times farther away from us than the sun is. These stellar distances range from 8 to 800 light years. And those objects all lie within our immediate surroundings in the Milky Way, whose center lies about 25,000 light years away (Color Plate 2).

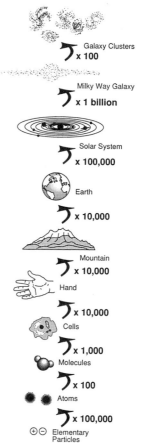

Galaxy Clusters
x 100

Milky Way Galaxy
x 1 billion

Solar System
x 100,000

Earth
x 10,000

Mountain
x 10,000

Hand
x 10,000

Cells
x 1,000

Molecules
x 100

Atoms
x 100,000

Elementary Particles

Figure 7. A rough comparison among the sizes of different types of objects spans a total range of a hundred trillion trillion, from the sizes of elementary particles to the sizes of galaxy clusters. (Drawing by Crystal Stevenson.)

department in many years. Tyson, a few miles down the road at Bell Labs, was looking for a Ph.D. student to work with him on his project; Raja was looking for an advisor to supervise his Ph.D. research. By the winter of 1987, they were collaborators, and by the fall of 1988, shortly after Raja married Sharmila Bhattacharya, a molecular biologist also from Calcutta, he made his first observing run with Tyson. They got along well and continued their work together. Raja got his degree. Fresh out of graduate school at Princeton, Raja has secured a three-year postdoctoral fellowship at Princeton's Institute for Advanced Study, about as successful a start as is possible in science. He plans eventually to return to India, which continues to maintain a serious research effort in astronomy.

Figure 8. Puragra ("Raja") Guhathakurta of the Institute for Advanced Study at Princeton, New Jersey, has collaborated extensively with Tony Tyson in attempts to detect the faintest observable galaxies. (Photograph by Randall Hagadorn.)

Working in the close collaboration that any good scientific team must draw upon, Tony Tyson and Raja Guhathakurta have found something truly remarkable. The light from the thousands of faint blue galaxies revealed by the CCD detector carries important clues about dark matter in the universe. These clues arise from a phenomenon first predicted accurately by Albert Einstein: Gravity bends light. Tyson and Guhathakurta have found evidence of this bending of light waves by gravity. They have used this evidence to deduce how much dark matter the universe contains.

In 1916, Einstein published his *general theory of relativity,* which included the amazing prediction (explored in more detail in chapter 13) that *gravity bends light.* Verification of this prediction in 1919 made Einstein famous and led to the acceptance of his theory among physicists and astronomers. Today the theory seems in better shape than ever before, as experiment after experiment has yielded results that are consistent, within experimental error limitations, with what Einstein's mathematics predicts.

In the widest realm of the universe, Einstein's theory predicts that any localized source of gravity, that is, any material not spread evenly through space, will bend light that passes by it. If, for example, a dark object happens to lie exactly between us and a source of light, the object's gravity will bend the light around it

The Milky Way contains about 300 billion stars. (Some astronomers will tell you 100 billion; others, 200 billion; and still others, 400 billion.) These stars come in a wide range of intrinsic brightnesses—the brightnesses the stars would appear to have if they all were the same distance away from Earth. When astronomers look for the faintest visible objects, they find that most of these are not stars but *galaxies*. In almost all directions these galaxies can be seen behind the screen of stars in our own galaxy (Color Plate 5).

on all sides, producing an *Einstein ring* of light. If the object lies nearly, but not exactly, between ourselves and the light source, the gravitational bending of light will produce a partial ring, a *gravitational arc* of light that reveals the presence of dark matter by its effect on light passing by from a greater distance. In some cases, different parts of the ring will appear as separate images (Color Plate 3).

Once thought to be impossible to detect, Einstein rings and gravitational arcs have now been found by several astronomers (Color Plate 4). Since greater masses produce a greater bending effect, the most easily visible Einstein rings and gravitational arcs apparently arise when light passes by enormous concentrations of mass within clusters of galaxies. These concentrations may be the "supermassive black holes," discussed in chapter 10, that astronomers love to speculate about.

Einstein rings and gravitational arcs offer a fine way to detect completely invisible matter. Tyson has seized on this possibility, and the observations that he and Guhathakurta have made at the Mauna Kea Observatory and at the Cerro Tololo International Observatory in Chile have yielded a new vision of the cosmos. When the astronomers look through a distant cluster of galaxies to the faint galaxies far behind, they invariably find gravitational arcs—the distorted images of remote galaxies.

Einstein's general theory of relativity allows the astronomers to calculate how much material must exist to bend light into a gravitational arc of a given size. In practice, Tyson and Guhathakurta use a computer to calculate the size of the arc that a given amount of matter lying between ourselves and the distant galaxies would produce. They compare the size of the arcs in their photographs with various arcs predicted by computer models until they find the amount of mass that, according to the computer, would create the kind of arc they have observed.

Because the effect that produces gravitational arcs does not depend on whether or not matter is visible, Tyson and Guhathakurta can use the arcs to measure the *total* amount of matter, visible or invisible, that lies between ourselves and the source of light. No object with mass can evade Tyson's net, because he finds matter not by the light it emits but by the *bending it produces* in the light from another object, in this case, the distant galaxies that sparkle by the hundreds on each of his CCD images.

And how much matter does Tyson find by this method? At least 10 times more than we see in galaxies! Tyson's results show that, on the average, every million cubic light years in the universe contains an amount of *visible* matter that about equals the amount of matter in the sun. But this volume contains at least *10* solar masses worth of dark, *invisible* matter. Since no one knows what form this invisible matter takes, astronomers have now reached the nearly fantastic conclusion that at least 90 percent of the universe consists of an unknown type of dark matter. Some theorists would even set the figure at 99 percent.

Tony Tyson continues to refine his observational techniques, to develop better detectors, and to engage in the amazing feat of measuring ever more accurately the amount of invisible matter in the universe. Today astronomers quite easily accept the notion that by far the bulk of the universe is invisible. If we want to understand how invisible matter in the universe came to be accepted as real, we must take a look at the efforts of a remarkable woman named Vera Rubin.

Figure 9. Vera Rubin of the Carnegie Institution of Washington's Department of Terrestrial Magnetism, an expert on the nature of galaxies, is shown here with her granddaughter Laura Young. (Photograph by Donald Goldsmith.)

2. The Dark Matter

ON A LEAFY hilltop in Washington, D.C., in a classic stone building, astronomers of the Carnegie Institution of Washington strive to enhance our understanding of galaxies. Chief among these scientists is Vera Rubin, the woman who first firmly established the existence of great amounts of dark matter in the Milky Way and in other spiral galaxies. It was Rubin's work that made astronomers like Tony Tyson take dark matter seriously. Just as Tyson is an expert on the dark matter in the farthest reaches of space, Rubin has long been the leading expert on dark matter in more familiar spiral galaxies, those that lie much closer to the Milky Way and are therefore susceptible to more careful scrutiny.

Rubin is a compact, gray-haired woman in her sixties with a quick smile that comes and goes in an instant. She might remind you of your grandmother—if you had a grandmother who felt that only by constant attention to work could you realize your full potential as a human being. Rubin is now a leader in the study of how stars move within galaxies. But she hardly reached this position overnight, and her astronomical career, like those of many other women, has been more tortuous than most scientists' paths to the top.

Born in Philadelphia, Rubin moved with her family some 10 years later to Washington, D.C., where she attended public high school before entering Vassar College. Rubin must have developed an early love for the cosmos, for she recalls that as a child, "I had a window facing north. That turned me into an astronomer." When she told her family that she wanted to study astronomy, her father, an electrical engineer, suggested something more practical, such as mathematics. But he helped her build a telescope and accompanied her to local meetings of amateur astronomers. At Calvin Coolidge High School, Rubin kept her astronomical desires a secret from her teachers. When she received a scholarship to Vassar, her physics instructor, not known for his ability to encourage young women, told her that "as long as you stay away from science, you should do O.K."

Vassar College was exclusively devoted in those days to the education of women. College proved to be an entirely positive experience for Rubin: The science and mathematics professors were all capable, quite able to encourage merit in their young students, and the astronomy instruction was particularly good. Upon graduation, Vera married Robert Rubin, who was a graduate student of physical chemistry at Cornell University. When Rubin enrolled in Cornell's physics department as a graduate student, she found that women students received no encouragement and were treated as interlopers. "Had I stayed at Cornell," she notes, "I would have been too intimidated to become an astronomer."

When Robert Rubin finished his graduate studies and obtained a job in Washington, D.C., Vera, now the possessor of a master's degree, moved with him back to the nation's capital and looked for a chance to continue her graduate studies. By then her first child had been born. "Nothing had taught me that a year after Cornell, my husband would be out doing science and I would be home changing diapers," she says. Before long, Rubin had enrolled in the Ph.D. program in astronomy at Georgetown University. Her husband's parents took care of the children while Robert Rubin drove Vera to night classes at Georgetown, and ate his dinner in the car while she studied.

By 1954, Vera and Robert Rubin had two children and two Ph.D. degrees. Eventually they raised four children—three sons and a daughter; two geologists, a mathematician, and an astronomer. The astronomer is their daughter, Judy Young, a professor at the University of Massachusetts. Mother-and-daughter astronomers will some day be common, but today Vera Rubin and Judy Young are the only ones that come to mind. Judy in turn has a six-year-old daughter, Laura, who finds astronomy intriguing. Vera Rubin had Laura in mind when she wrote a book entitled *My Grandmother Is an Astronomer,* in which the narrator explains to a young girl what an astronomer does (Figure 9).

Vera Rubin has spent nearly her entire career at the Carnegie Institution's Department of Terrestrial Magnetism, a place that fascinated her since she first visited it. The Carnegie Institution deserves a closer look. At first glance, it appears to be an anomaly in the modern world of big science: a small, privately funded organization (which does obtain federal research grants) endowed by a wealthy philanthropist. The operation may be small in comparison with those at large state universities or federal research laboratories, but it is nevertheless capable of producing results at the forefront of modern science.

The Carnegie Institution dates from 1902, when Andrew Carnegie founded it; two years later, the scientists there created its Department of Terrestrial Magnetism (DTM) to study the Earth's magnetic properties. In 1939, as part of the work that led to the development of the first atomic bombs, the DTM was the site of the first nuclear-fission experiment to be successfully performed in the United States. The DTM's seismologists and geologists have also played important roles in analyzing the interior of the Earth. But from any astronomer's viewpoint the most important research at the DTM in many decades has been astronomical, conducted by astronomers such as Kent Ford, François Schweizer, and Vera Rubin.

The astronomical aspect of the DTM's research efforts arose from the vision of Merle Tuve, a remarkable physicist who specialized in studies of the ionosphere—the layer of the Earth's atmosphere that teems with electrically charged particles. Tuve became the director of the DTM during the Second World War and decided that astronomy deserved research support. Rubin had written her Ph.D. thesis at Georgetown under the guidance of the renowned Russian physicist George Gamow. He drew Rubin's attention to the new program in astronomy at Carnegie's DTM. She liked the calm atmosphere and support for research at the institution, but as she tells it, it took her years to work up the courage to ask for a job. When she did, the DTM gave her one— and there she has been for nearly thirty years.

STARS WHEEL IN MAJESTIC COURSES

For the past two decades and more, Rubin has been an expert on galactic dynamics, the *motions* of the stars that form galaxies. Her work has dealt both with our own Milky Way galaxy and with the myriad galaxies that surround us. These galaxies share a fundamental resemblance: Each consists of millions or billions of stars held together by the stars' mutual gravitational attraction, the gravitational pull that each of the stars feels from all the other stars in the galaxy.

Spiral galaxies like our own Milky Way were formed from immense clouds of gas and dust. These clouds somehow acquired some rotation, though astronomers do not know how or why. As the clouds shrank under the effect of their own gravitation, they rotated more rapidly, like a figure skater who pulls in his arms to spin faster. The contraction and spin together produced a flattened, rotating disk that became a spiral galaxy. Within the disk, stars such as our sun were thus born from material already in motion (Color Plate 5).

Our sun, one of the Milky Way's 300 billion stars, has a nearly circular orbit around the galactic center, which lies about 25,000 light years away, in the direction of the constellation Sagittarius (Figure 11). Since the sun's gravity carries its planets along with it, the Earth accompanies the sun on its immense journey around the center of the Milky Way. Our solar system's orbit around the galaxy has a diameter almost two billion times larger than the diameter of the Earth's orbit around the sun. Yet the solar system is moving in this galactic orbit about eight times more rapidly than the Earth is moving around the sun. Our planet's orbit around the sun (at a speed of 20 miles per second) therefore amounts to only a small detail, a tiny correction to the fundamental motion of the entire solar system around the galactic center.

Vera Rubin has long studied the motions of stars in the Milky Way and in other galaxies. This by itself is an important effort, but the payoff comes at the next stage: Rubin uses her observations of stars' motions to *deduce the causes* of these motions. Ever since the end of the seventeenth century—the era of Isaac

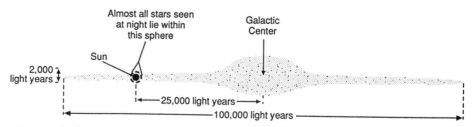

Figure 11. A schematic view of the Milky Way shows that our galaxy has a thin, disklike shape, and that the sun is located roughly half of the distance outward from the galaxy's center toward its diffuse outer boundary. (Drawing by Crystal Stevenson.)

Newton's Laws and the Milky Way

Astronomers and physicists have understood gravity—at least its effects—since Isaac Newton first expounded his *universal law of gravitation.* In the summer of 1666, Newton—while passing a few quiet months at his family home near Grantham, England, at a time when plague threatened to ravage his university at Cambridge—began to wonder whether a single force could be responsible for objects falling to Earth and for the moon's motion in orbit around the Earth. (The appealing story that an apple's fall started Newton along this train of thought, publicized by the famous French writer Voltaire, appeared in print only long after Newton's death and must be regarded as apocryphal.)

Working with insight that has never been exceeded since, Newton soon showed that by making one simple assumption—that all objects in the universe attract one another in accordance with a simple relationship—he could explain the fall of objects to the ground, the moon's orbit around the Earth, and the planets' motions around the sun. The relationship Newton conceived was this: Every object attracts every other object, with an amount of force that varies in proportion to the product of the two objects' masses, and in inverse proportion to the square of the distance between the centers of the objects.

Using his universal law of gravitation, Newton even anticipated the advent of artificial satellites of Earth: He showed that a projectile launched at sufficiently great speed, in a direction parallel to the Earth's surface, would not fall down to Earth but would fall *around and around* the Earth. So too the moon continuously falls around the Earth, and the planets fall around the sun. Each of these objects balances the sun's force of gravity with its own momentum, that is, with its innate tendency to keep moving in the same direction at the same speed. Take away the sun's force of gravity, and the planets would sail into space in whatever direction at whatever speed they happened to have. Take away a planet's momentum (perhaps with a giant hand that stops it in orbit), and it would head straight for the sun, drawn by the sun's gravitational force. But because *both* gravity and momentum are

Newton—astronomers have known that in nearly all cases celestial objects owe their motions to a single cause: the force of gravity. Gravity, in turn, arises from objects with mass. Rubin's effort to determine the cause of motions therefore amounts to an effort to calculate the amount and location of the mass that produces the motions that astronomers observe. Many astronomers besides Rubin have relied on the observations that she and other astronomers have made. Their results reinforce one another in a single conclusion: Most of the matter in the galaxy-strewn universe is invisible.

How does an astronomer manage to measure the motions of stars in our Milky Way and in other galaxies as well? The information lies in the details of the colors of starlight from galaxies (Color Plate 6). By passing starlight through a prism, or reflecting it from a grating ruled with finely spaced parallel lines, astronomers can separate light into its component colors with great precision. As explained in more detail in chapter 4, they can then measure changes in the color of starlight that arise from the Doppler effect, that is, from the motion of the source of light toward or away from an observer. Similarly, the frequency or "pitch" of sound waves—analogous to the color of light—changes when the source of sound moves toward or away from us. When astronomers detect starlight with colors different from those they expect from previous experience, they ask themselves whether these changes in color might not arise from motion toward or away from the Earth. If so, then the Doppler effect links the amount of the change to the speed of the motion.

Long experience has taught astronomers that starlight typically lacks certain colors, which have been blocked by various atomic elements present in the stars' outer layers. The colors are not removed at random; instead, astronomers can recognize patterns in the missing colors of starlight, as if some of the "notes"—perhaps all the B-flats—had been removed from an otherwise full mixture of sound. When a source of light lacks colors that are slightly different from the usual missing set, astronomers often see that the pattern looks familiar but that the "missing notes" have been transposed into a different key. It is as if instead of all the B-flats having been removed as usual, now all the F-sharps are missing. Such transposition is the sign of the Doppler effect, which changes all colors (all the "notes") in the same way. Therefore, when astronomers see such a "transposition" pattern in the colors of starlight, they usually conclude that the Doppler effect

at work, the planets "fall," not down but around, forever as they move in elliptical (but nearly circular) orbits.

Newton's vision of gravity and momentum replaced magical notions as the key explanation of the motions in the solar system. Two decades later, when Newton's friend Edmond Halley asked what the shape of a planet's orbit would be under the influence of the sun's gravity, Newton told him "an ellipse." "How do you know?" Halley asked. "Why, I have calculated it," replied Newton. Halley eventually persuaded Newton to commit his calculations to print and had the additional thrill of shepherding through the press (and paying for in part) one of the grandest, most influential books in history, Newton's *Principia Mathematica Philosophiae Naturalis* (mathematical principles of natural philosophy—that is, of science), which appeared in 1686.

Newton's calculations proved stunningly accurate and led to the nearly immediate acceptance of his theories of gravitation and dynamics (objects in motion). The triumph of Newton's view of the universe led to the philosophical view of a "clockwork universe," one in which all events proceed through the working of the laws of physics. Some thinkers proclaimed that a deity was needed only to set the works in original motion. For more than two centuries, Newton's vision deeply affected those who looked for explanations of the heavens. In this century, quantum mechanics and relativity theory have produced serious reworkings of Newton's ideas, so that no scientist now feels that all the events in the universe could, in theory or in practice, be explained solely by a few simple laws of nature. Nevertheless, the basic concept of a universe run by natural law has an appeal for many and, with certain modifications, can still fit within the principles of modern science.

Consider what happens when we apply the balance between gravity and momentum to the orbit of a star in a galaxy. Since large galaxies like our Milky Way contain hundreds of billions of stars, it might seem an impossible task for astronomers to calculate the total force that this multitude exerts on any one particular star. But here, too, the genius of Isaac Newton lends a hand. As part of his work in writing his

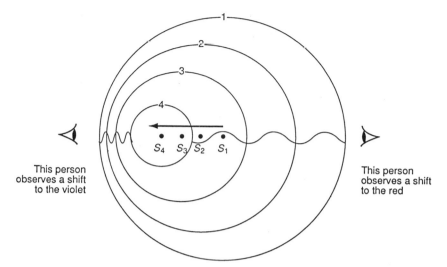

Figure 12. The Doppler effect describes the change in wavelength and frequency that will be observed when a source of waves ("*S*") approaches an observer, such as the one on the left in this diagram, or recedes from an observer, as on the right. As seen by an observer whom the source approaches, the crowding together of the waves shortens the wavelengths and lessens the frequencies. For the observer from whom the source recedes, the observed wavelengths increase, and the frequency (time interval between successive waves) decreases, in comparison with a situation of no relative motion. (Drawing by Crystal Stevenson.)

is at work. The greater the velocity of the star, the greater the change in color (or in the pitch of musical notes). Motion toward us raises the pitch of musical notes and makes starlight more violet; motion away from us lowers the pitch and makes light redder (Figure 12). By using what they know about the Doppler effect, astronomers such as Rubin can deduce whether stars in the outer regions of the Milky Way are moving toward us or away from us, and can also find their speeds of approach or recession with respect to the solar system as it too moves in space.

DEDUCING MASS FROM GRAVITY'S EFFECT ON MOTION

Rubin's greatest coup occurred when she used the technique of analyzing starlight colors to measure stellar motions in the outer parts of our own galaxy and in nearby spiral galaxies. Although astronomers had found some indication of what they now call dark

great book, Newton showed that when we attempt to calculate the gravitational force that a large group of objects (in this case, stars) exerts upon another object (the sun, for instance), we can obtain a tremendous simplification of the problem. This simplification is possible so long as we assume that the distribution of stars through the galaxy is comparatively even. Given this assumption, we can conveniently divide the stars into two groups: stars *closer* to the center of the galaxy than the sun, and stars *farther* from the center.

The first part of the simplification allowed by Newton's laws is as follows: We can show that the combined gravitational pull from all the stars *closer* to the center exactly equals the pull from a single imaginary object at the center of the galaxy. The mass of this hypothetical object must equal the total mass of all the stars closer to the center (Figure 10). For example, if the Milky Way contains 300 billion stars that lie closer to its center than the sun does, and if the average mass of each of these stars equals half the sun's mass, then the combined pull from the 300 billion stars equals the pull from a single object with a mass 150 billion times the mass of the sun, located at the center of the Milky Way.

The second part of Newton's simplification of the problem works even better: The combined gravitational forces from the stars *farther* from the center yield a *zero* net force! Some of those stars pull in a given direction, while others pull in the opposite direction, and so long as the stars are distributed rather evenly in space, the net gravitational effects will exactly cancel one another. Hence Newton's simplification

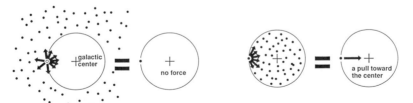

Figure 10. Newton's simplification has two parts: (a) The stars closer to the center of a galaxy than a star such as our sun have a combined gravitational force equal to the force from a single object at the center. This imaginary object has a mass equal to the sum of the masses of all those stars closer to the center than the sun. (b) The forces from stars farther from the center than the sun cancel one another, producing a zero net force. (Drawing by Crystal Stevenson.)

matter throughout the twentieth century, Rubin's work during the past two decades has made dark matter a reality in most astronomers' minds. Before Rubin's work, astronomers who counted the numbers of stars visible to their telescopes thought that they knew the distribution of stars in the Milky Way rather well. They had determined that most of the Milky Way's stars have distances either less than or comparable to the sun's distance from the center of the galaxy. If this were so, then Newton's laws of gravitation and dynamics lead to certain predictions about the speeds at which the stars at greater distances from the center orbit around the Milky Way.

The calculations begin with Newton's work, which showed that any star in the Milky Way effectively feels a gravitational pull only from stars *closer* to the galactic center. (See the explanation of Newton's simplification of the problem, page 37.) As discussed above, this pull equals the pull that would arise from a mass equal to that of all the stars that lie closer to the center than the sun, assuming that all these stars occupied the center itself. The few "outrider" stars, lying outside nearly all the other stars in the Milky Way, should therefore feel a gravitational pull that is easily calculable by imagining a hypothetical central mass equal to the mass of all the stars in the Milky Way closer to the galactic center.

Rubin's work depends on a second stage in the calculation. The outlying stars all respond to the same hypothetical mass—the mass of nearly all the stars in the galaxy, which lie closer to the center than the outlying stars do. But if this is so, then the outlying stars *farther* from the galactic center should move *more slowly* in orbit than the closer ones, just as the sun's planets move progressively more slowly at greater distances from the sun. This is because, as Newton correctly saw, the gravitational force that one object exerts on another decreases in proportion to the square of the distance between the two objects. With a lesser force acting upon them, the stars would move more slowly. Since nearly all the stars in the Milky Way had been accounted for in general terms, and since their numbers fall to near-insignificance in the outer portions of the Milky Way, astronomers did not doubt that the outlying stars, progressively more distant from the center of the Milky Way, would be found to be moving progressively more slowly in their orbits.

Rubin found otherwise. Her studies of starlight colors revealed the motions of stars in orbit in the Milky Way and in

amounts to the statement that stars closer to the center combine their forces to yield a net gravitational pull toward the center, while stars farther from the center pull in all different directions and therefore cancel each other's effects.

Newton's simplification has useful applications. Astronomers can see that although a giant spiral galaxy such as our Milky Way contains billions of stars, and therefore seems—indeed, *is*—far more complex than our solar system, the gravitational facts of life are nearly identical for the two systems. Any individual star in the Milky Way feels a gravitational force analogous to the force that the sun exerts on one of its planets. As explained above, the total force on an individual star in the Milky Way equals the force exerted by an object with a mass equal to the masses of all the stars closer to the center, with that aggregate mass placed at the center of the galaxy.

In the Milky Way, some 300 billion stars, with a total mass of 150 million times the sun's mass, lie closer to the galactic center than our sun and its planets. This mass, acting over an effective distance of about 25,000 light years, pulls on the solar system. If the solar system—the sun, planets, satellites, asteroids, and comets—were not moving in orbit *around* the center, we would fall straight in toward it, arriving a hundred million years from now. But because we do move (at about 150 miles per second) along a nearly circular path, the sun and its family of attendant worlds can spend billions of years calmly orbiting the center, taking 240 million years for each orbit—a time that astronomers sometimes call a "cosmic year." During the 4.6 billion years since the solar system formed, it has made nearly 20 such orbits, each of them covering some 150,000 light years of distance.

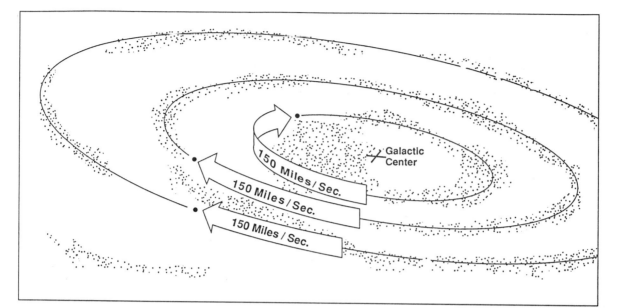

Figure 13. If most of the mass in the Milky Way resided in its stars, then astronomers would expect stars' orbital velocities to decrease for distances greater than the sun's distance from the galactic center. Instead, as Vera Rubin and other astronomers found, the velocities of stars far from the center, both in the Milky Way and in other spiral galaxies, do not decrease significantly below the velocity with which the sun orbits the center. (Drawing by Crystal Stevenson.)

other spiral galaxies. During the early 1970s, as she studied the details of these motions, she obtained a remarkable result. Instead of finding slower motions for the stars at greater distances from the center, Rubin showed that beyond the sun's distance, the speed with which stars move in orbit remains nearly constant: The much more distant stars move almost as rapidly as the merely distant stars (Figure 13). When Rubin turned her attention to other galaxies, such as the giant spiral in the constellation Andromeda (Color Plate 7), she found similar results. Rubin observed more than two dozen galaxies and found the same effect in each. The speed with which stars are moving in their orbits does decrease with increasing distance from the center, but only out to a distance from the center roughly equal to the sun's distance from the center of the Milky Way. Beyond that distance, the speed of stars in orbit ceases to decrease and instead remains constant (Color Plate 8).

Given Newton's laws of motion and gravity, Rubin's

findings provoked consternation in all practicing astronomers. Either she had made some sort of gross error or had studied some highly exceptional galaxies (including our own!), or (not easily accepted) her findings were both correct and generalizable. If most galaxies behave like the ones that Rubin has studied, then *most of the matter in galaxies resides in an unknown form and does not shine as stars do.*

This startling conclusion follows from a straightforward application of Newton's principles to the motions that Rubin observed. Rubin's discovery that outlying stars do *not* move progressively more slowly at greater distances from the center has only one likely explanation: The galaxy's matter does *not* all reside closer to the center than the outlying stars. Instead, *the amount of matter closer to the center must continue to increase as we go to greater distances from the center.* If this is so, stars progressively more distant from the center effectively feel the pull of larger amounts of mass, because we know from Newton's simplification that only the matter *closer* to the center than a particular star will exert a net gravitational force upon that star. The pulls on a star from matter farther from the center than that star will cancel one another. So long as we have not yet passed outward beyond all the matter in the galaxy, then as we go to greater distances the amount of matter closer to the center must increase.

Since astronomers cannot *see* significant amounts of matter in these outlying regions (the stars whose motions Rubin measured amount to only a tiny part of a galaxy's mass), they concluded that *the mass exists but does not shine.* All of our visible-light, ultraviolet, infrared, submillimeter, radio, x-ray, and gamma-ray observations have failed to reveal the bulk of our own and similar galaxies! Furthermore, astronomers can calculate how much mass a galaxy needs in its outlying regions to produce the observed motions, that is, to ensure that the progressively more distant stars do not move more slowly in orbit. Because the outer regions of a galaxy are much larger than its inner parts, this mass turns out to be enormous: The Milky Way must contain about 10 times more mass in *unknown* form than the amount we see shining in stars.

By analyzing the motions of outlying stars, Rubin's observations revealed enormous quantities of invisible matter in spiral galaxies such as our own Milky Way. Studies of the motions of galaxies in clusters, performed by other astronomers (and some by Rubin herself), showed that these *clusters* of galaxies (Figures 14

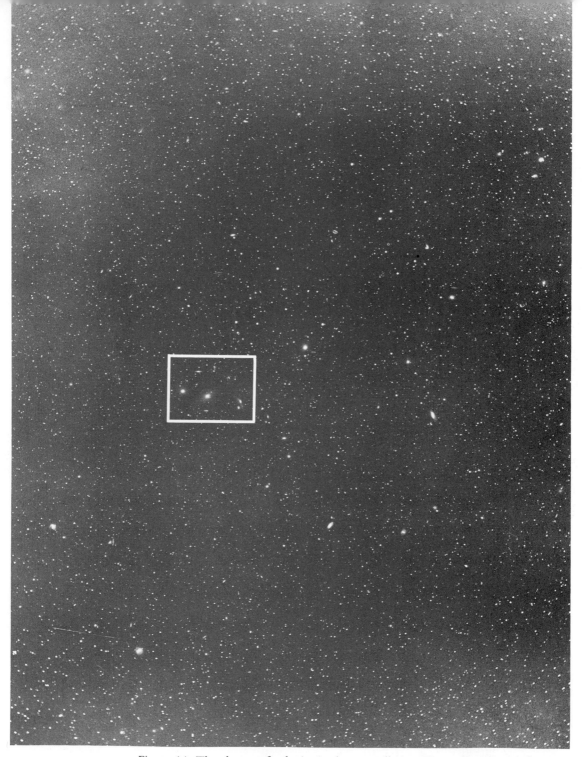

Figure 14. The cluster of galaxies in the constellation Virgo, 60 million light years from the Milky Way, contains several thousand member galaxies, some of them larger than our own. Although many of the points of light in this photograph are stars in our own galaxy, nearly every extended source of light is a galaxy in this cluster. The Local Group forms an outlying extension of the Virgo Cluster. (Yerkes Observatory photograph.)

Figure 15. This photograph shows the inner core of the Virgo Cluster, the region inside the box in Figure 14. (Photograph courtesy of the National Optical Astronomy Observatories.)

and 15) likewise contain tremendous amounts of invisible matter. Indeed, even before Rubin's work, astronomers had found that most large galaxy clusters appear to contain far more mass than can be explained by the stars that shine in their galaxies. But it took Rubin's detailed studies of the motions of stars within our own and other galaxies to convince astronomers that nearly every galaxy, and not just those in large galaxy clusters, has far more mass in invisible form than in stars.

In short, Rubin's work established the existence of a previously unconfirmed component of the cosmos, a component that is no small addition to what we know but (broadly speaking) the universe itself. Everything we see—all the stars, star clusters, star-forming regions, and gas clouds lit by newborn stars—apparently amounts to no more than 10 percent of the total mass of a large galaxy such as our own Milky Way. Hence Rubin's research implies that all the visible matter in the universe forms only a sort of light frosting on the cosmic cake, which consists basically of invisible matter.

Small wonder that the astronomical community was slow to take Rubin's findings seriously! It is not given to everyone to establish that 10 times more matter than previously suspected exists in galaxies, and by implication in the entire universe. Astronomers no doubt had an understandably conservative unwillingness to accept this fact, but their manner, as Rubin recalls it, was often far more abrasive than the situation seemed to merit.

What does the invisible matter consists of? What is its form and structure? Before we can confront this issue directly (and, to be honest, admit that we do not know), we must deal with the task of *naming* it. Astronomers at first referred to this invisible, unknown matter as the "missing mass," that is, the mass whose existence had been deduced but could not be seen. But the mass cannot be said to be "missing," since Vera Rubin and others had found it; its *nature* was all that was unknown. By the 1980s the term "missing mass" had been replaced by the now-current term "dark matter," which more accurately describes it. Today an astronomer who appraises the situation in the universe may happily tell you that most of the universe consists of "dark matter," as if naming the problem might resolve the whole issue.

WHAT IS THE DARK MATTER?

And what *is* this dark matter? We don't know. Astronomers can only tell you some things it is *not*. To begin with, the dark matter cannot consist of stars, or it would not be dark. It cannot consist of dust grains, or the amount of dust would be sufficiently large for us to detect the grains by their blockage of light from distant galaxies. Indeed, if current theories are correct, *the dark matter cannot consist of any form of matter ("ordinary matter") that we have yet observed!*

Astronomers now have well-worked-out theories that relate the behavior of the early universe to what we observe today, including the universe's rate of expansion, and the kinds of particles it contains. If the universe turned out to contain ten times more ordinary matter than those theories predicted, astronomers would have to abandon their incorrect ideas. The theories can survive only if the dark material consists almost entirely of "exotic matter"—a polite name for types of matter hypothesized to exist but entirely undetected by any experiment.

Exotic forms of matter may be purely hypothetical, but they have one thing going for them: the names given to such mental creations by particle physicists, men and women who spend their careers studying minute building blocks of nature that make up atoms. One of the most appealing particle types is the "axion," named by an enthusiastic theorist after a popular laundry detergent. Another is the "WIMP," an acronym for weakly interacting massive particle. Still others are the "photino" and "gravitino," whose suffixes attest to a certain order that particle physicists find in their families of particle types. This orderliness has led scientists to imagine a hypothetical "ino" particle that is associated with the known "w particle," thus creating the catchy name "wino." One of the best names applies to an exotic particle that technically is not a particle at all: the "cosmic string." This item is a sort of defect in the "fabric of spacetime." Cosmic strings are imagined to be tubes of great energy winding through the universe. They must either form closed loops or else have infinite length, so the hypothesis goes; in either case, every millimeter of a cosmic string would have a mass greater than Mount Everest's. Clearly, the discovery of even a single cosmic string would make pulses quicken throughout the world of science. Among other things, cosmic strings could be the source of gravitational "seeds" that might explain the formation of galaxies.

We do know of one type of particle that could perhaps be the solution to the mystery. The dark matter *might* consist of a certain subtype of the particle category called "neutrinos." Strange though neutrinos are, they have definitely been detected (and therefore fall outside the class of exotic particles), though hardly in the numbers they must have to provide the dark matter. However, for reasons much too complex for elaboration here, neutrinos currently appear to be a poor candidate for the dark matter, and are mentioned here in part to give neutrino-lovers their due.

Particle physicists have a respectable track record—not only for viable theories, but also for research that may impact upon our lives. We should not lightly ignore their work, and if they propose whole families of exotic particles, we might pause to consider whether one of these could turn out to include *most* of the cosmos.

For no matter how hard we may try, there is no escaping the fact that if we believe—and we do!—in Vera Rubin, Isaac Newton, the Doppler effect that measures velocities, and the conclusions that we draw from measurements of the amount of ordinary matter in the universe, then we cannot account for most of the mass in the universe with any types of particles that we know.

THE FUTURE OF THE UNIVERSE

Aside from its intrinsic interest, the dark matter has a significant role to play in the cosmos: It determines the ultimate fate of the universe. As described more fully in chapter 4, we know that the universe is expanding: All clusters of galaxies are moving away from all other galaxy clusters, everywhere. This implies that the clusters used to be closer together, and that the expansion started at a single moment in time—the "big bang"—approximately 15 billion years ago. Quite naturally, few of us who have learned that the universe is expanding can avoid the ultimate question: Where will it all end? Will the universe expand forever, or will it someday cease expanding and start to contract, perhaps toward another big bang and a sort of cosmic recycling?

The answer to this question, and the future of the universe, lie hidden within the dark matter. If the universe ever ceases to expand, this will occur because the combined gravitational effect of all the different pieces of matter finally overcomes the expansionist tendency. If the expansion never ceases, this will reflect the fact that too little matter exists for gravity ever to triumph over expansion. In order to determine the fate of the universe, we must measure the amount of matter contained within a representative volume. If that amount falls below a certain value, which astronomers can calculate quite accurately, expansion will rule forever. If the amount exceeds the critical value, expansion will cease—not soon, but after some tens of billions of years have elapsed. Then our descendants (at least in the sense of observers of the universe) will see a cosmos quite different in its overall behavior from what we have today, a cosmos in which the reign of contraction has begun, a cosmos headed not for the slow death of eternal expansion but for the renewing catastrophe of universal contraction and collision.

Does the universe contain sufficient dark matter to produce an eventual contraction? We don't know. Astronomers do know that if the dark matter amounts to "only" 10 times more matter than resides in stars and other visible forms of matter, then the universe will expand forever, with too little gravitational force among its components to ever pull itself together. To produce a universal contraction requires that the dark matter provide 100 times more matter than shines in the universe. The results obtained by Vera Rubin and by Tony Tyson do not rule out this possibility, but they make it unlikely.

Meanwhile, the incurious stars surround a wondering Earth. It is time to step back from the far reaches of the universe to take a look at the basic teachings of astronomy. From the author's viewpoint, among the best effects that this book could have would be to stimulate its readers to look at the points of light that sprinkle the night skies and to ask once again the age-old question: How can we tell which are which among the stars and planets? Even the barest answer to this question unites us with a simple fact: We are all astronomers.

Figure 16. When Halley's comet passed relatively close to the sun and Earth in 1986, it developed a long, complex tail made of gas and dust evaporated from the comet and pushed away from the sun by the solar wind. (Photograph by Dr. David Malin of the Anglo–Australian Observatory.)

3. We Are All Astronomers

WE ARE ALL astronomers. Or are we? The title of this chapter smacks of an attempt to slip astronomy into the reader's mind by insisting on its relevance to his or her daily life—the sort of thing that would-be friendly professors do to make their subjects "come alive." Who says that we are all astronomers? Who can prove it? Would it not be more accurate to say that one of the triumphs of modern civilization has been to reduce our dependence on astronomical knowledge to an awareness of daytime and nighttime? How then can we pretend that we are all astronomers?

The phrase "we are all astronomers" is not meant to imply that we all admire the heavens and study celestial objects. That activity remains, as it has throughout history, an occupation for a small minority, once called priests, now called scientists. "We are all astronomers" means only that everyone pays attention to astronomy—not to the astronomy that astronomers deal with, and still less to the "classical" astronomy that describes the seasons and the phases of the moon, but rather to "space."

This *is* new. Astronomy, oldest of the sciences, and often said to be the second-oldest profession, began when everyone examined the heavens to find important news about daily life. The cycles of night and dark, the lunar phases, the seasons, even the changing positions of the planets, all must have excited the imagination of the average citizen. But during the last three or four millennia, astronomy has become isolated from daily reality, no longer of general interest. This has gone on long enough for most people to "learn" to ignore astronomy. Even though modern methods of disseminating information have made astronomical knowledge accessible to all, few have cared to make use of it.

The space age has changed things. Astronomy deals with strange objects at immense distances from us, but "space" deals with human beings who bring those objects down to Earth. Thus "space" engages the most fundamental lever to the human imagination—placing the actor in the locale. Here the word "space" denotes what most members of the public think when they hear the word. To an astronomer, space is a familiar place—the universe, within which his or her objects of interest play out their lives. This is too cold and forbidding for most people, who use the word "space" to mean "the realm where astronauts work," or, in somewhat greater extension, "the place where NASA sends its rockets."

If you want to gain a proper understanding of space—an astronomer's view, a scientific perspective—you must start with the facts as we know them. Central among these facts is this: Space is enormous. Equally important, space is not simply enormous, but *even though all distances are immense, some distances are far more immense than others*. The stars in the Milky Way lie millions of times farther away than the planets, and the farthest galaxies are millions of times more distant than the stars! This makes space unimaginably vast. If all else fails, recall the words of the scientific cartoonist Sidney Harris:

> Space is big
> Space is dark
> It's hard to find
> A place to park.*

WHAT IS ASTRONOMY?

Astronomers have a saying: "To the general public, astronomy is just three things—the man in the moon, the rings of Saturn, and Halley's comet." And what makes the man in the moon, the rings of Saturn, and Halley's comet so appealing to the public? The moon is the most familiar object seen in the night sky, but only a tiny fraction of all citizens have ever seen the rings of Saturn or

---

*Copyright 1975 by Sidney Harris—*American Scientist* magazine.

Halley's comet. Something about those two objects exerts a fascination on the public, and that something cannot be the moon's sort of familiarity. What arouses public interest in Saturn's rings and Halley's comet may well be three elements that awaken deep and emotional ties to the cosmos, reminiscent of the days when everyone thought about the heavens: beauty, mystery, and distance.

Saturn's rings attract us because they look so marvelous (Color Plate 29). We can easily verify this statement, at least in part, by noting that when the rings did not look so good—in the days when telescopes much inferior to our present instruments showed the rings only indistinctly—the public gave them little attention. Only during the nineteenth century, as the complex patterns in Saturn's rings received worldwide publicity, did the public pay much attention to them, but from then on the rings became nearly *the* prime attraction of astronomy, so that no astronomical cartoon could be drawn without Saturn in the background. This tradition persists to the present day, though the rings are often imagined as a transparent sheet of material, rather than as a collection of solid particles orbiting the planet.

Halley's comet is another story. Like other comets, this one is a "dirty snowball" (to use the term that the astronomer Fred Whipple made famous) roughly 10 miles across, orbiting the sun along an elongated, elliptical trajectory. At the closer points of a comet's orbit to the sun, the solar heat vaporizes the outermost layers, and the particles expelled from the sun in the *solar wind* push the material outward. As a result, the otherwise invisible comet grows a fuzzy *coma* of gas and a long, gauzy *tail* that may extend for millions of miles (Figure 16).

Most comets known to astronomers fall into one of two categories. They are either *short-period comets,* whose orbits have been so affected by the gravitational force of Jupiter, the largest planet, that their orbital periods and orbit sizes roughly correspond to Jupiter's, or they are *long-period comets,* which typically take thousands of years, or even longer, to orbit the sun on trajectories much larger than those of any planet, but which are so elongated that their closest points to the sun bring them within the planetary system. Halley's comet provides the exception: With its orbital period of 76 years, it is the best-known among only a few examples of comets with intermediate periods.

Halley's comet owes its name to Edmond Halley, Isaac Newton's contemporary. Halley made important studies of the

Earth's magnetism, the motions of the planets, and the stars visible only from the Southern Hemisphere (he spent a year on the desolate island of St. Helena, in the South Atlantic Ocean, mapping the heavens invisible from England). He finally gained lasting fame from his studies of the comet that appeared in 1682. Referring to old records, and using his knowledge of orbits, Halley realized that this comet had visited the inner solar system at periodic intervals in the past. For example, the comet had appeared early in the year 1066, a harbinger of doom (as hindsight revealed, and as the Bayeux Tapestry shows to this day) to King Harold of England, whom William the Conqueror defeated later that year. (Had William lost the battle, the comet would have presaged *his* doom.) Halley worked out the comet's elongated orbit, which, he saw, takes it outward past all the planets then known (in fact, out to the orbit of Neptune) and then brings it back to the vicinity of Earth after about 76 years (slightly variable because of the influence that Jupiter and Saturn have on the comet's orbit). Halley predicted that the comet would return in 1759; when it did so, his triumphant vindication led astronomers to name it after the then deceased astronomer, who had become Britain's second Astronomer Royal in 1720 and had died in 1742.

In this century, Halley's comet has exerted a powerful emotional hold on the public, perhaps because its period roughly matches a human lifetime, so that most of us have but one chance (if that) to see it. Mark Twain, who was born in the year of Halley's comet's return to the inner solar system (1835), confidently predicted that he would die in the year of its following return and, perhaps slavishly, did so. That return (1910) saw a public aroused by the news that the Earth would actually pass through the tail of the comet—not a dangerous journey, since the gases in the tail are more rarefied than what we call a good vacuum on Earth, but an event that touched the well-known human impulse to view the unusual as dangerous. "Comet pills" enjoyed a brisk sale to those who feared the passage, and they worked to perfection.

In 1986, the second passage of Halley's comet in this century produced a great awakening of interest, once again tied to the fact that a rare, strange astronomical event was at hand. Sadly for those who make a living from public interest in astronomy, this reappearance of Halley's comet was unfavorable for viewing on Earth, because the comet's closest approach to the sun occurred when the Earth was on the other side of the sun. For this reason,

Halley's comet was not particularly bright, though it was still easily visible to the unaided eye. Unfortunately, the comet was far to the south of the celestial equator and so could be seen well only from the hemisphere where Halley had first made his reputation. For those who found themselves unable to travel to the south, Halley's comet in 1986 left a bad aftertaste, one that is barely relieved by the news that the comet's next return, in 2061, will bring it much closer to Earth, with a consequently far brighter appearance, and that the return after that, in 2137, will be one of the best in several millennia! Amateur astronomers of the twenty-first and twenty-second centuries will have much fonder memories of Halley's comet than today's crop; may they favor their astronomy popularizers in proportion.

THE COMMUNITY OF AMATEUR ASTRONOMERS

Astronomy differs from nearly every other branch of science in one aspect: A devoted group of amateurs seriously practice the discipline. These amateurs, who number several hundred thousand, have responded to the pull of the cosmos by devoting considerable amounts of time to studying the stars. They tend to divide into two groups, with some overlap: those who read about astronomy, and those who use small telescopes to study the heavens.

The telescope users have greater visibility and are more interesting to an outsider. Many of the telescope amateurs received their initial impetus from being given a small factory-made telescope, which they often found to be nearly worthless. Sadly enough, because telescopes are sold with an emphasis on their magnifying capabilities, the prospective purchasers often fail to recognize the importance of the telescope *mounting*. The mounting supports the telescope and allows it to be easily directed from one spot to another; in more advanced models, the mounting includes a *clock drive* to keep the telescope pointed at the same object as the Earth rotates and seems to carry the object across the sky. The finest optics are worthless if linked to a poor mounting.

Amateur astronomers who use telescopes quickly become intimately familiar with this aspect of observation. They either pay extra for a well-made telescope that includes both good optics and a good mounting, or they take the plunge and construct their own telescopes. The latter occupation ties the amateur directly to Galileo, Huygens, Newton, and all the other great astronomers who designed and built better telescopes, often discovering new physical or practical principles of optics along the way.

Today relatively few amateur astronomers build their own *refractors*—telescopes that use a primary lens to focus the light, thus producing an image that a secondary, smaller lens can magnify. To grind a lens well requires more than amateur skills, and in any case, a refractor typically requires a longer, hence less transportable telescope tube. Thus a refractor of a given diameter cannot be made so easily as the other basic type of telescope, the *reflector*. A reflector uses a mirror to collect and focus the light, and this mirror can be made by a patient, careful amateur who learns how to grind an initially flat mirror blank into a parabolic shape, using progressively finer grit to achieve near-perfection of the reflecting surface.

Making the mirror amounts, however, to only part of the job; constructing the mounting that will hold the telescope tube in a steady yet directable manner proves crucial. Many an amateur has ground a mirror and then despaired of building the rest of the telescope, but many others have not only completed the telescope but have also gone on to build others, bigger and better.

Such amateurs tend to make serious observations of the heavens, especially of *variable stars* and *occultations*. The American Association of Variable Star Observers includes hundreds of dedicated amateurs who attempt to record the fluctuating brightnesses of thousands of variable stars—a work that would overtax the professionals who follow these objects. Occultations occur when a celestial object passes in front of a star, as seen by an observer on Earth. The foreground object could be the moon, a planet, or an asteroid—one of a collection of objects ranging from the size of Wyoming to less than a mile across. Since each different location gives an observer a slightly different line of sight, careful observations of an occultation of a star by an asteroid, for example, can yield information about the size and shape of that object.

Thus a few hundred thousand amateur astronomers, some incredibly dedicated to their efforts, have helped a few thousand professional astronomers to understand the cosmos. In this way, the amateur community enriches the world of astronomy, and if each of us became an amateur astronomer, the world would doubtless be a better place. As things are, however, most of the United States—

and the rest of the world—remains relatively impervious to the joys of astronomy. Here amateur astronomers play another key role: They bring astronomy to the people. Many schoolchildren owe their first contact with astronomy to a dedicated amateur who took the trouble to participate in a school or museum program that attracted the students to look at the skies above.

JOHN DOBSON AND ASTRONOMY FOR THE PEOPLE

Of all the amateur astronomers who have contributed to the education of the public—solely for love in every case—none has done more, or in more oddball ways, than a one-time science student at the University of California at Berkeley, a former Vedantic monk born in China of impeccably Yankee lineage: John Dobson.

In reasonably normal circumstances—for example, having a beer in a quiet corner of a nearly empty bar—John Dobson resembles a gentleman uncle, one whose long grey hair has been properly combed back to let his intelligent face contribute its best to the conversation, and whose state of relative impecunity oppresses him not at all (Figure 17). But give Dobson an opportunity (and he doesn't ask for much) to show people heavenly objects, and he turns into a salesman whose urge to sell threatens at any minute to soar out of control. Dobson has been tagged in a variety of ways: chemist, monk, bum, hippie, educator, enthusiast. Thousands of amateur astronomers know his invention of the "Dobsonian" method for mounting telescopes to make them easily portable while sacrificing little in stability; thousands more of the public have met Dobson without knowing who was urging them to look through the large telescope set up on the street corner, or in a national park.

Dobson is now past 75, but his clear eyes and vigor would go well with a man of 60. He has had, to put it

Figure 17. John Dobson, a pioneer among amateur telescope makers. (Photograph by Sally Weare.)

mildly, an unusual life story. Dobson was born in September 1915 in Peking, which had become the capital of China only a few years before. At the time of the American Civil War, his mother's father had helped found Peking University; his father, who taught zoology there, married the university president's daughter. Dobson, one of four sons of this family, found himself by the accident of birth in the midst of turbulent times. The revolution that toppled the Manchu dynasty had produced the outward forms of democracy but gave rise to chaos that invited foreign intervention. In August 1915, the month before Dobson's birth, Japan presented its Twenty-One Demands, which in effect invited China to surrender its sovereignty. Three months later, the Chinese president, Yuan Shih-Kai, reacted to the Twenty-One Demands by declaring himself emperor of China. The declaration provoked an explosion of unrest that led to its repeal. When Yuan died early in 1916, his successor "could control nothing and the rout began," as Barbara Tuchman put it.

Peking felt the changing currents, and eventually educators who had lived for years in China saw that their time was up. Dobson's family left in 1927 for San Francisco, where John went to public high schools and then to the University of California. He had a keen interest in science and, in comparison to his fellow students, an unconventional view of the world. Dobson studied chemistry and, after his graduation from college as the Second World War began, embarked on a position at the university that would have made him part of the atom-bomb project, until an interview with the FBI made it clear that other fields should claim his attention instead. In 1944, he became a monk in the Vedanta Society of Northern California. Dobson stayed in San Francisco for 14 years and then moved to Sacramento for another 8 years as a monk. But in 1967, Dobson found himself ousted: for too much astronomy. The abbot had ordered that one of Dobson's handmade telescopes be thrown into the bay. When Dobson continued to absent himself at night, he was asked to leave the monastery and to pursue his astronomical interests on a fully freelance basis.

Dobson's interest in astronomy had grown naturally from the spiritual urges that led him into the monastery. His thoughts began with the fact we seem to have only one universe, and that if two descriptions conflict, either the conflict must be resolvable or at least one description must be wrong. As Dobson puts it, "I had realized that if the mystics and the physicists are right, then they must square somewhere, or someone is goofy." On further examination, "I found out that this is largely a matter of translation"—that the mystics and physicists were often saying the same thing. For example, Sanskrit texts describe five types of energy in the universe, those perceived primarily by the ear, the eye, the skin, the tongue, and the nose. Dobson identified these, in order, with gravity (since our inner ears allow us to maintain our balance), with light and other types of radiation, with kinetic energy (energy of motion), with electricity ("all chemists know that protons taste sour"), and with magnetism.

This sort of claim—that ancient texts speak scientific truths thought to be only recently discovered—drives scientists up the wall. The reasons for this reside in the value and belief system that scientists have developed (described more fully in chapter 9), but the crucial fact in considering the views of a man like Dobson is that scientists do not take seriously what a nonscientist has to tell them. Thirty years after Dobson first formed his views, best-selling books such as *The Tao of Physics* popularized the apparent affinity between Oriental religions and modern physics, intriguing many in the general public but annoying most physicists. To a physicist (or an astronomer), the fact that two sentences sound the same has no significance unless they proceed from the same set of assumptions about how to examine the universe. Physicists find nothing wrong with this attitude, because they know that the advance of science depends on a belief that the scientific world view makes sense. But they become depressed when the public considers that the world operates on entirely different rules. Dobson's cosmological views, which reflect the public's far more than those of university scientists, are unlikely ever to gain scientific approval, but he has learned to live with that fact. Besides, what draws him is not the theory of astronomy but the practice, and Dobson practices by showing people how to see the stars.

Dobson has never forgotten what originally fascinated him about astronomy: the view of the heavens that he saw through a telescope. "I thought, 'Everyone's gotta see this!'" he recalls. While still in the monastery, Dobson began to make telescopes. Once he was expelled for too much telescope-making, he found himself in his early fifties, a man without an abbot but with a plan: to make more telescopes. What distinguished Dobson's efforts from those of other amateur telescope makers was that he made *big* telescopes.

In the late 1960s, Dobson and a band of kindred souls created a free-floating organization called the San Francisco Sidewalk Astronomers, dedicated to the proposition that people will stop and look through a telescope, provided they can see something exciting. To carry out this program in a large city, whose lights and haze tend to spoil the view of the heavens, you need a large telescope, which is not so easy to produce. Making a large telescope *mirror* presents relatively little difficulty: You use the same techniques as you would for a small mirror, but more carefully and with more strength in the grinding. What gives trouble is the *mounting* for a large telescope.

While still in the monastery, Dobson had hit on a way to make a steady telescope mounting that allowed for easy disassembly and transport. The "Dobsonian mounting" does not use the traditional telescope configuration, in which the telescope tube rotates around the mounting's *equatorial axis,* a rod that is set parallel to the Earth's rotation axis. Dobson saw that for his purposes—giving the public a view of the sky—this approach was overkill. Dobson's telescopes have no equatorial axis and therefore cannot follow an object as the Earth's rotation carries it across the sky. Hence Dobson must reorient the telescope every few minutes, which he does with an ease based on years of experience.

During the 1960s, the Sidewalk Astronomers began to use Dobson's design to make a series of ever-larger reflecting telescopes: first one with a mirror 12 inches in diameter, then 16 inches, then 18, then 24. They took the 24-inch out to the public, who loved it. With a 24-inch telescope, you can see objects from downtown San Francisco that a 6-inch reflector (the standard tool of the serious amateur astronomer) can detect only if you take it to Yosemite National Park.

Dobson began to become famous within the community of amateur astronomers, especially when he exhibited his telescopes during the late 1970s at one of their largest gatherings, the annual telescope fair in Riverside, California. Not everyone liked him: Most serious amateur astronomers love technology and spend years improving their one-of-a-kind instruments, which bristle with highly machined parts and electronic aids to increase precision. Dobson has little use for this sort of technology and takes pride in the near-infinitesimal cost of his telescopes (not counting hours of labor), which results largely from the scavenged nature of their component parts. Besides, the telescopes often need rebuilding, subject as they are to long rides in aged vehicles, not to mention (as has often occurred for the 24-inch tube) being used to sleep in.

Not content with the cities, Dobson and his associates eventually took to the national parks, and today the Sidewalk

Astronomers oscillate between urban and park locales for their viewing. Similar groups, affiliated in spirit, have sprung up across the country and in Europe. Dobson has found that the best way to draw a crowd in a national park is to set up for daytime viewing, when people can see the telescope; that is, to show the public the sun that keeps us alive and the planets that orbit it (for planets shine brightly enough to be seen in the daytime through a telescope). He has learned—perhaps has more experience than anyone else—how best to overcome the lack of knowledge or the different mind-set of people, or at least adults, confronting something new, like our star and its planets. With amazing patience, Dobson invites the people to see the sun, hour after hour, shows the stars at night, and then drives on for another day's work. And as the people line up to look through the telescope, Dobson supplies them (but only if they ask; few people actively seek to be lectured) with basic information: The sun is so large that the moon's orbit around the Earth would fit comfortably inside. The Earth goes around the sun, not the other way around. Saturn is so distant that an automobile traveling 60 miles an hour would take 1,200 years to arrive. "I have to tell them things in ways that I hope that they can hang on to them," Dobson says. Let's give it a shot: Here are some basic facts about the solar system and the way that we came to know them.

THE SOLAR SYSTEM AND ITS EFFECTS

For most of the past two-and-a-half millennia, ever since learning began to be codified in books and disseminated to unknown readers, astronomy has dealt primarily with the sun and its planets, while the starry heavens remained little explored and still less understood. Good reasons existed for this. The planets—whose name means "wanderer" in Greek—stood out as bright objects that *moved,* changing their positions against the starry backdrop. In contrast, the stars maintained the same "fixed" positions with respect to each other, even as the entire "bowl of night" appeared to turn, so that the stars first rose and then set below the horizon.

The sun and moon attracted the most attention of all, simply because they are the brightest of all celestial objects in our skies. The sun lights the day and the moon (some of the time), the night—giving rise to the old joke that the moon is more valuable than the sun since the former shines only when no one needs it.

Cultures the world over built religions on worship of the sun and moon, lords of the life-giving Earth. As observers noted the changing positions of the sun, moon, and planets against the background of stars, they began to recognize patterns. They saw that a full moon recurs once every 29½ days (29.53 days to be more precise), and built their history-reckoning devices, now called calendars, around this renewed cycle of the lunar phases.

If you imagine (as many did) that all the stars lie at the same distance from us on a crystalline "celestial sphere," then you can trace the moon's path around this sphere once each month (or "moonth" as our Anglo-Saxon ancestors called it). If you can remember (and our ancestors were good at remembering) the patterns of the stars even when daytime prevents you from seeing them, you may realize that the sun also circles the celestial sphere, once each year, following the path among the stars that astronomers now call the *ecliptic*.

The ability to recognize the patterns of stars in the sky, together with the paths of the sun and moon among them, has become a feat beyond all but the most dedicated. Today anyone who wants to can easily find maps of the celestial sphere, clearly marked with the trajectories of the sun and moon around the sky. It is sobering to realize that many of our ancestors learned all this for themselves. More sobering still is the realization that the number of people on Earth who can point out the constellations around the celestial sphere, and trace out the paths of the sun and moon through some of those constellations, may total only a few hundred thousand worldwide—which would mean that only 1 person in 10,000 can do so!

Yet many hundreds of millions of people—a thousand times more!—know the *names* of the constellations through which the sun apparently passes; these are the twelve constellations of the zodiac, which mostly bear the names of animals, and therefore are collectively named after the Greek word for "life." The zodiac girdles the ecliptic on either side, marking a particular band around the celestial sphere. Since the zodiac is defined to embrace the sun's path among the stars, finding the sun in one or another of the zodiacal constellations was an act of homage rather than surprise. But the moon, too, always appears in the zodiac, and so do all the planets! Our ancestors had no good explanation for the fact that the sun, moon, and planets are always found within a small fraction of the entire sky, the portion included within the 12 constellations of the zodiac. They must have found this to be an amazing sign of the unknown ordering of the cosmos. In Mesopotamia, in Egypt, in China, and in Middle America, culture after culture identified the zodiac, although they subdivided it differently into constellations. The Chinese, for example, placed 28 star groups (rather than 12) around the zodiac. They did so because the moon takes 27⅓ days to circle the sky (it takes 29½ days to grow full again because the Earth is moving around the sun). Thus the moon could (roughly) occupy one such group on each successive day of its journey.

Early societies, lacking television and the cinema, took celestial events seriously. They saw the sky as an extension of the Earth; more precisely, they drew no distinction, as we do now, between the terrestrial and extraterrestrial realms. Quite naturally, therefore, they looked to events in the skies as an extension of events below and often searched the skies for portents of events on Earth. Because the zodiac contained all the "action"—all the changes in the otherwise immutable fabric of the heavens—cultural leaders interested in the well-being of their societies gave prominence to the zodiacal constellations, and to the wanderers within them. Soothsaying being the type of profession in which belief forms the essential ingredient, success was ensured once belief existed.

From such beliefs came astrology, the belief system that relates events on Earth to events in the heavens. The "logos" in astrology refers to divine law, as opposed to the "nomos" or human-made law that underlies the Greek word "astronomy." Astrology, born of the same wondering spirit as astronomy, sought to probe even deeper—to the hidden messages carried by astronomical objects. The desire deserves credence and support, but the results are flawed by the fact that astronomical objects do *not* influence human lives.

Of course the preceding sentence is wrong—but not when referring to astrological forecasts. Our lives are not simply influenced but indeed utterly *ruled* by astronomical objects. We depend on our sun for warmth and are held in a stable orbit that has allowed life to evolve by the sun's gravitational force upon us. The moon's much smaller gravitational force nevertheless plays the key role in raising ocean tides on Earth, because the tides depend on subtle *differences* in the amount of force, and these differences are greater in the force from the moon than from the sun. Stars that exploded billions of years ago, long before the sun and its planets began to form, provided all the chemical elements—other than hydrogen and helium—that are absolutely essential to our existence.

Given these facts (none of which were known more than a few hundred years ago), should we not be *more* inclined to believe in astrology, which was developed by ancients who lacked our knowledge? No one hears more often than an astronomer that if the moon can move the seas, surely it can affect something as small as a human! But to a scientist, the answer is a clear "no." The same advance in knowledge that has shown us *how* the universe affects us has utterly disproven the assumption that the motions of the sun, moon, or planets on the celestial sphere have any effect on individual lives. Precisely because we can calculate just how and why Mercury orbits the sun, we can determine that Mercury's position at any one time makes no difference to us. Furthermore, to assign a particular importance to the time of birth, as astrologers do, makes sense only if you elevate his moment to an incredibly significant position in a lifetime. The moon does affect the Earth by raising tides and exhibiting changing phases, but it does not affect different people differently, which is the fundamental assumption of modern astrology.

In its earliest known phases, astrology made far gentler assertions. Astrology began by predicting the fates and health not of individuals but of an entire society. Astrologers and astronomers (one and the same in those days) attempted to determine seasonal and weather patterns. They added to their efforts a search for clues to the future in the motions of the planets, the moon, and the sun. All early horoscopes dealt with the future of a kingdom or, as time went on, of the king as the exemplar of his people.

Modern astrology—astrology for the people—dates from ancient Rome. As Roman rule spread over nearly the entire world (in the Roman view of things), Rome changed from a republican form of government to an autocracy, ruled by a single Kaiser, Czar, or Caesar. Augustus, the first Emperor, as the Caesars came to be called, was an astrology enthusiast who put his *birth sign* (the zodiacal constellation that the sun occupied at the time of his birth) on his coins. The tenor of the times, coupled with the fact that Augustus had after all not been born an emperor, encouraged prominent Romans to have astrologers examine the zodiacal positions of the citizens themselves, rather than of the Roman empire. In addition, astrologers must have seen an avenue of increased employment and seized it. By the reign of Marcus Aurelius, nearly two centuries after Augustus's, "personal" astrology had spread throughout the Roman world. The triumph of Christianity did little or nothing to check its popularity, though authors such as Augustine railed at those who believed that the motions of the planets can determine our destiny—and indeed most Christian, Jewish, and Muslim theologians maintain that such a belief strikes at the heart of their religions.

But astrology was far too popular to yield to such arguments. The notion that the stars could speak to a person's individual existence had an emotional appeal far greater than anything that religion, let alone rational argument, could overcome. By the time of Augustine (early 5th century A.D.), astrology had a firm grip on the collective beliefs of what we now call Europe, North Africa, and the Middle East, while in China the "old" astrology—astrology for the ruler and his society—continued to dominate for another millennium. Throughout the European Middle Ages and the Renaissance, nearly every astronomer was also an astrologer, the more so as the latter role brought in the money.

As astronomers learned more about the cosmos, this situation gradually changed. At the watershed of belief systems we find Johannes Kepler, the man who first understood that the planets move in elliptical orbits around the sun (Figure 18). Kepler, born in 1571 (and therefore seven years younger than William Shakespeare), learned of the newfangled Copernican theory as a university student. His teacher, Michael Maestlin, described Copernicus's notion that the planets orbit the sun, though he did not himself believe it. But Kepler adopted the theory wholeheartedly, partly because of its pleasing simplicity but partly because of his spiritual feeling that the sun deserved better than to orbit the Earth, as it did in the Ptolemaic theory that ruled the academic roost. Kepler had a deep feeling that the planets, and still more the sun, emitted forces that drove the solar system. He saw nothing wrong with the notion that the planets can influence individual lives, but he did see that conventional astrology could not provide the answer to how (let alone why) such influences existed. Despite job titles such as Imperial Mathematician, Kepler was expected to cast—and did cast—many horoscopes. He was wise enough both to conceal his doubts about conventional astrology from his clients and to assess the future with advice that was judged correct. Kepler needed the money he earned from astrology, because his various jobs suffered from such handicaps as low pay, no pay (when he received only assurances but no cash), tyrannical bosses (Tycho Brahe, the great astronomer

Figure 18. Johannes Kepler (1571–1630) first discovered the correct shape of the planets' orbits around the sun. (Courtesy of the Mary Lea Shane Archives of Lick Observatory.)

of the age, refused to let Kepler—his assistant—look at his data), and witch hunting (he was dismissed from a job for having the wrong religion, and had to defend his mother against the charge of being an actual witch).

Kepler pushed on despite all obstacles. He successfully defended his mother against the charge of witchcraft; he found new jobs when turned out of previous ones; he succeeded to Tycho's job when Tycho drank too much at a banquet and suffered fatal damage by letting protocol interfere with the call of nature; and he found the rules that govern the motions of the planets around the sun. Since Kepler died nearly penniless, on a journey attempting to collect money from a publisher, his grave could be a shrine for authors' pilgrimages—had his bones not been scattered by the Thirty Years War that was ravaging Germany when he died.

In 1609 and again in 1619, Kepler published books that showed the mathematical underpinnings of the planets' motions— the "harmony of the worlds" that Kepler sought all his life. For nearly four centuries, astronomers and astronomy students have learned Kepler's *Three Laws of Planetary Motion:* The planets all move in elliptical orbits around the sun; the planets move more rapidly when closer to the sun, less rapidly when farther away, in accord with a particular mathematical formula; and the size of each planet's orbit is related to the length of time it takes to orbit the sun, in accord with another mathematical formula. (For those who love math, each planet's speed in orbit varies in inverse proportion to its distance from the sun, and the time to complete an orbit varies in proportion to the three-halves power of its average distance from the sun.)

With these three laws, Kepler brought a mathematical and (he would not have balked at the word) mystical beauty to the concept of the solar system that Copernicus had published in 1543. But Kepler had no explanation of why the planets should obey these laws, though he knew in his heart that there is a "force in the sun" that does the trick. Half a century after Kepler's death, in 1686, Isaac Newton (Figure 19) showed that all three of Kepler's laws, as well as the motion of the moon around the Earth, follow naturally from basic assumptions about the force of gravity and the way that objects respond to forces upon them. Newton thus advanced the view that the motions of objects in the solar system reflect the working of natural law that we can hope, eventually, to understand. This does not mean that Newton was no mystic, for his mysticism was as advanced as his physics, but he was mystical

Figure 19. Isaac Newton (1642–1727) discovered the law of universal gravitation and three basic laws of motion. (Courtesy of the University of Chicago.)

about the ultimate, metaphysical truths that underlie what we know as natural law.

Newton knew that his *universal law of gravitation* could explain the motions of the planets. But where did gravity come from? Newton could not say, and over two centuries passed before Albert Einstein conceived of gravity as a curvature of space-time (which does not answer the question completely for everyone). But as Newton's insights spread, medieval superstitions, including astrology, began to lose ground to the belief that life on Earth deals with conditions on Earth, and that human beings to a large extent can control their lives.

THE SCIENTIFIC WORLD VIEW

The essential aspect of the path traced by Kepler, Newton, Einstein, and their successors has been the belief that our knowledge of natural explanations for what we see in the universe will steadily increase (with occasional corrections). This increase in knowledge has—among scientists—steadily displaced earlier beliefs that have failed to correspond to what we find to be real. This does *not* mean that scientists lack religious beliefs or often find that their religious attitudes conflict with their scientific view of the universe. Indeed, scientists often express profound beliefs about the ultimate truths that may lie behind what we see, but they usually consider those beliefs as private and do not attempt to persuade others of their validity.

Astrology never vanished, of course, and in modern times has made a remarkable comeback in the Western world. This comeback draws on societal forces that cannot be easily manipulated, but it remains an intriguing fact that until 1930, few newspapers printed astrology columns and few people talked much about horoscopes. But then, searching for a way to distinguish its coverage from the rest, a London newspaper featured a horoscope in its story about the birth of Princess Margaret, Elizabeth's younger sister. This feature article touched a vein of interest, and before long, astrology had become a staple of the daily press. Public interest in astrology waned during the 1940s and 1950s, but the 1960s brought a resurgence of astrological appeal.

Although this interest may have peaked, it has barely diminished during the past decades. Indeed, many people love astrology. In this era, an exchange of introductory data, perhaps as part of the dating ritual, may involve a request for one's birth sign. (Some astronomers like to answer, "I'm an Orion"—or, when in a difficult mood, "I'm an Ophiuchus"—in the hopes of leading the discussion toward astronomy, but their listeners often take this as a refusal to enter into polite conversation.) To be sure, just as many scientists have belief systems in which science does not conflict with religion, most people keep in separate compartments beliefs that to a scientist seem to conflict directly. Most people would say, if pressed, that you can't *really* expect Mercury to influence human lives; but they would just as surely state that astrology must have *some* validity, because so many people believe in it, and astrology does often *seem* to predict the future correctly. The latter statement tends to infuriate scientists, but there is a worldly wisdom in not abandoning logically conflicting views so long as both make you happy and neither causes pain.

SCIENCE IS ORGANIZED SKEPTICISM

Science advances by using this golden rule: If you hope to advance knowledge, you must be skeptical in your view of the universe. Instead of adopting beliefs because they feel good, science makes progress through the continuous *doubting* of other scientists' results. (Human nature does not allow a system of continuous doubting of one's own efforts.) This approach—the backbone of all knowledge said to be "scientific"—reflects a crucial fact: Only by repeatedly doubting *everything* can you become at least partly sure of *anything*. Of course, scientists are human and therefore tend to fall for appealing theories. Furthermore, humans are not totally naive, so every human to some extent follows the scientists' rule of skepticism, a rule that allows experience to change beliefs, sometimes.

By making *skepticism* an organized, institutional goal, the scientific community has found a near-perfect way to use individual belief systems, odd though they may be, to advance the cause of scientific knowledge as a whole. Skepticism allows science to test its beliefs—the theories that organize observational facts—by harnessing the competitive spirit that lurks happily in all of us. A large fraction of scientific work indeed involves fruitful cooperation in making observations or elaborating hypotheses. But the bedrock aspect of science lies in the *ongoing competition among theories,* alternative explanations of a particular set of observations. To ensure that this competition performs its function of discriminating among theories, the structure of the world of science ensures that great merit will flow to the man or woman who *demonstrates the falsity* of a seemingly tenable theory. The more widely held that theory, the greater the reward that attaches to the one who brings its downfall.

The community of scientists in many ways resembles a cult of its own—the cult of what scientists call rationality. Seen from the outside, the most obvious aspects of the cult are (as usual) its own rules and its exclusiveness. Scientists don't earnestly listen (as scientists) to those who are not trained in science. This amounts to a rule of convenience. A nonscientist might have something important to say, but the probability is low (among other reasons, because the nonscientist probably does not follow the rule of skepticism and has not tested a theory in his or her mind by asking in advance what argues against it). Also, a working scientist has likely heard from enough nonscientists with theories to have lost any urge to chat, a nonscientific but human response.

Because few lovers love so well as a scientist with a theory, other scientists accept the fact that a scientist who brings forth a new theory may never abandon it, no matter what mountains of evidence may seem to contradict it. But in the long run, scientific theories must stand or fall not on the importance of their originators but on their success in the competition for the minds of other scientists. In the sociological context of science, a "correct" theory is one that commands such widespread approval among scientists as to be almost universally accepted.

Cosmology, the study of the universe as a whole, offers a fine example of the contrast between the scientific and the more general belief systems. Human societies the world over have found it comforting and proper to believe that the cosmos centers on the Earth. Today scientists, and some of the public, have replaced this belief (perhaps only in the more logical parts of their consciousness!) with a cosmological picture that makes our location in the universe merely an average and representative one. If you follow the crucial cosmological discoveries outlined in the next chapter, you can decide for yourself which picture makes the most sense—and provides the most comfort.

Figure 22. The Pleiades are an open star cluster about 50 million years old, still showing remnants of the gas that helped form the stars. (Lick Observatory photograph.)

4. Mapping the Universe

THE DISTANCE PROBLEM

WHEN YOU LOOK at the starry skies on a clear night, you see the entire universe as it is displayed to our eyes and our instruments: in only the two dimensions of the plane of the sky. Since ancient times, the map of the stars on the sky has become familiar to anyone who took the trouble to study and record the patterns of the constellations. During the second century A.D., the Greek astronomer Claudius Ptolemy, who lived and worked in Alexandria, the center of Greek science, made a star catalog that included several thousand stars, all those visible to the unaided eye from the latitude of the Nile Delta. This catalog remained unsurpassed for 14 centuries, until the Danish astronomer Tycho Brahe compiled a marginally better one during the late sixteenth century. Soon afterward, the invention of the telescope allowed astronomers to discover, and to record, thousands upon thousands of previously unknown stars, so that by the end of the nineteenth century, star catalogs with hundreds of thousands of entries existed, and only a lack of time and effort prevented the entries from growing into the millions.

But for nearly all these stars, and for the fuzzy objects called *nebulae,* a crucial dimension was lacking: the *distances.* On Earth, all human estimates of distance depend on a subconscious mental comparison between the *actual* size of an object—which we assume we know—and the size that the object *appears* to have, which astronomers call the object's *angular size.* Because we know the size of a human being, whenever we see a human figure, we immediately draw a conclusion (without realizing it) about the distance of the person from us, because we know that the farther the distance, the smaller the person appears to be, and the person's actual size provides the calibration that tells us how great the distance is.

But we lack all knowledge of the actual sizes of objects in the sky. Nowadays, as airplanes have become ever more abundant, this statement requires modification, but we can still easily mistake a small plane at a small distance from us for a large aircraft at a great distance from us. Since few people realize that any distance estimate relies on a knowledge of the object's actual size, an astronomer who deals with reports of unidentified flying objects continually encounters statements such as, "I saw an incredibly weird object in the sky, about 500 feet away." How did the observer know that the object was 500 feet away, and not 50 feet or 5 miles? The answer is that except for the vaguest of clues provided by lighting, the observer had no ability to judge the distance except by mentally assigning an actual size to the object. The larger the size of the object, the greater the distance would be judged to be.

So it was with celestial objects, except that most of the objects seen in the sky could not be assigned any definite size, since no one knew how large a mysterious thing called a "star" or a wandering "planet" might be. The two exceptions were the sun and the moon, which appear to cover a noticeable fraction of the sky, rather than appearing as pointlike sources, as the stars do. The sun and moon each appear to us with an angular size of half a degree—in a measuring system that descends to us from the ancient Babylonians, who divided a circle into 360 equal parts or "degrees." Thus the entire circle around the horizon, for example, spans 360 degrees, and it would require 720 suns, each half a degree in angular size, to stand shoulder to shoulder to fill out such a circle around the horizon.

The fact that the sun and moon each have an angular size of half a degree eloquently illustrates the problem of estimating astronomical distances. The most straightforward interpretation of this fact would assign the sun and moon the same distance—but that distance must remain unknown until the actual size of the object can be determined. An early Greek astronomer received opprobrium (to the point of execution as a heretic) for suggesting that the sun might be as large as the Peloponnesus, the southern half of Greece. During the third century B.C., the great astronomer Aristarchus—the first person known to have suggested that the sun is the center of the solar system—claimed, using geometrical insight, to have measured the relative distances of the sun and moon, and to have found that the sun has 19 times the moon's distance from Earth. Aristarchus's method is theoretically correct, but the practical difficulties in its execution introduced large errors: The sun in fact is 400 times the moon's distance from us. Since the sun and moon have the same *angular* size, the known ratio of distances means that the sun's actual size must be 400 times the moon's. This is so: The moon's diameter equals approximately 2,000 miles and the sun's, 800,000 miles.

Objects more distant than the sun and moon—most of the planets and all the stars—show angular sizes too small to be measured without a telescope. For nearly two millennia, astronomers remained ignorant of the distances to the planets and stars, and constructed a mental cosmos in which celestial objects formed part of transparent, crystalline spheres centered on the Earth, each sphere in marvelous rotation at a different speed and carrying a particular planet along with it. The farthest sphere carried the stars, all of which, in this cosmology, conveniently had identical distances from the center of the universe, our fair Earth.

This picture, like so much of our mental cosmology, was satisfying but incorrect. Far from having identical distances from us, the stars and other celestial objects that fill the night skies have immensely different distances. This fundamental truth only slowly dawned on astronomers.

First, over centuries, astronomers came to accept the fact that all stars beyond the sun have distances that mock any human scale: The closest among them lie 26 *trillion* miles away. Then astronomers had to proceed to establish that some objects in the night skies lie millions of times farther from us than the nearby stars do, despite the fact that the "nearby" stars are roughly a million times farther from us than our own star, the sun.

The first half of this process—the measurement of the distances to nearby stars—began in the mid-nineteenth century, when astronomers first succeeded in using triangulation to find stellar distances. The second half—the estimate of distances to much farther objects—got under way in the early 1920s and continues to undergo much-needed improvement even today. To understand how astronomers get a grip on the distances to galaxies that are millions or even billions of light years away, we must first deepen our intuitive understanding of how the distances of nearby stars are measured. Astronomers achieve this by using the same technique that our eyes and brains employ for terrestrial purposes: the parallax method.

Parallax is a Greek word that describes the apparent shift in position of a nearby object, in relation to more distance objects, when we change the angle from which we study the object. If you hold your finger at arm's length and close first one eye and then the other, you will see your finger undergo a *parallax shift* with respect to the background objects. Our brains continuously note and interpret such parallax shifts without conscious effort, and without requiring that we alternately close each eye, because each of us learned as an infant to employ both eyes in conjunction with the brain to make our grasp for objects more certain. The key point that we mastered, before we could think about it consciously, was that closer objects exhibit greater parallax shifts—that is, they appear to shift by greater amounts when viewed from two positions, the few inches that separate our two eyes.

What holds true in the nursery holds true in the universe: All astronomical objects shift their apparent positions when seen from two different points, and the closer objects show larger parallax shifts. For astronomical distances, the two human eyes provide far too short a "baseline" between two points to produce a useful parallax shift. We need a greater change of position, and we find it in the yearly motion of the Earth around the sun. Every year the Earth circles our star, so that in January, for example, it lies 93 million miles to one side of the sun, and in July an equal distance to the other side. This swing of 186 million miles in six months' time would provide large parallax shifts of the stars we observe, if the stars were not all so far from us (Figure 20). As things are, however, the closest stars to the sun have distances more than a quarter of a million times the Earth-sun distance, so that even the largest parallax shift, for the star Alpha Centauri, cannot be measured without excellent equipment.

In the mid-sixteenth century, Nicolaus Copernicus revived the long-discarded idea that the sun, not the Earth, forms the center of the solar system. Copernicus's critics scoffed that if his strange and heretical idea had validity, astronomers would have detected the shifts in stellar positions arising from the Earth's orbit around the sun. Copernicus had the correct answer: The stars are so distant that, in pretelescopic days, no parallax shifts could be measured— but it availed him little in the struggle for men's minds. (The fact that Copernicus cautiously delayed publication of his theory until the year that he died posed another, still more significant, barrier to personal vindication in his lifetime.)

Nearly three centuries elapsed between Copernicus's death in

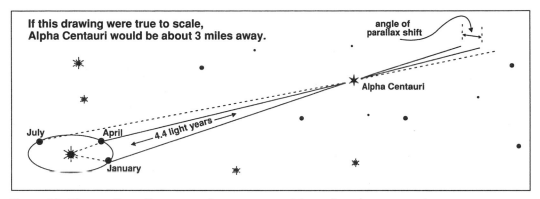

Figure 20. The parallax effect causes the apparent positions of nearby stars, such as Alpha Centauri, to shift back and forth against the background of much more distant stars as the Earth orbits the sun. By measuring the amount of the parallax shift, astronomers can determine the distances to nearby stars by trigonometry. (Drawing by Crystal Stevenson.)

the year 1543 and the first measurement of any star's parallax shift—a shift of only one-third of a "second of arc," about *one ten-thousandth* of a degree! (Each degree contains 60 minutes of arc, and each minute in turn contains 60 seconds of arc.) By the beginning of the twentieth century, astronomers had measured the parallax shifts of several hundred stars. In every case, the shift amounted to a small fraction of a second of arc and was determined only through painstaking measurements carried out over several years' time. Each measured parallax shift yields a stellar distance through triangulation. The Earth's yearly motion produces a triangle with the Earth-star distance as its two long legs and the span of the Earth's orbit as its short leg. By measuring the parallax shift astronomers can find the tiny angle between the two long legs. Since they know the length of the short leg, this angle lets them calculate the length of the long legs: the distance they seek.

Eventually, astronomers encountered—and still encounter—a practical limit to the size of the angle they can measure. Our atmosphere introduces a blurring effect in every stellar image, whether we record it through visual observation, through photography, or (as astronomers do now) through electronic sensors. This blurring sets a limit on the accuracy with which we can measure a star's position on the sky, and hence a limit on the accuracy with which we can determine any star's parallax shift.

The key to the parallax effect is that the amount of parallax shift *decreases* as the distance to a star *increases*. Therefore, if the amount of *error* in the parallax shift introduced by atmospheric blurring equals or exceeds the parallax shift itself, then we cannot hope to measure the shift in any meaningful way. This atmospherically induced limit prevents astronomers from measuring any angles smaller than about one-fiftieth of a second of arc. But even the closest stars have parallax shifts of less than one second of arc! In other words, our atmosphere prevents us from triangulating the distances to any stars that are more than 50 times farther from us than Alpha Centauri, the closest star to the sun.

This is merely a regret, not a tragedy. Fifty times the distance to Alpha Centauri takes us 220 light years outward from the solar system. Tens of thousands of stars lie within this distance, though some are so intrinsically faint that we can barely detect them. Nevertheless, many thousand stars have indeed been successfully measured for their parallax shifts, and it might seem overkill, or an astronomer's need for utter accuracy, to insist on more.

But from another perspective, the tens of thousands of stars with measurable and measured parallax shifts leave us hopelessly within our cosmic raindrop, unable to see the distance relationships in the forest around us. The stars within 220 light years of the sun encompass only 1 part in 10 million of the total number of stars in our Milky Way galaxy, which spans more than 100,000 light years! And the Milky Way is only one galaxy, albeit a large one, amidst billions of galaxies within the known universe. How trivially small a part must we then acknowledge our "measured" cosmos to be, if it includes less than one-millionth of our own galaxy. Yet that tiny fraction of all space within which astronomers can measure distances accurately provides the key to everything else that we know about the distribution of matter in the universe.

Consider, for example, the statements made above—that the solar neighborhood within 220 light years contains less than a millionth of the Milky Way, and that the Milky Way forms just one amidst billions of galaxies. On what authority do these statements rest? How, if we cannot measure their parallax shifts, can we begin to determine the distances to objects outside our sun's neighborhood and thus to obtain the overall picture of the universe we have just described? This question covers a great deal of mental depth, not to mention space in the universe. The answer to it has deep scientific meaning: We obtain our picture of the entire universe by starting with what we *do* know—the stellar distances we can measure—and applying to that body of knowledge the twin towers of scientific progress: deduction and extrapolation.

EDWIN HUBBLE AND THE UNIVERSE BEYOND THE MILKY WAY

Far beyond the Milky Way, visibly extending in all directions for billions of light years and—for all we know—continuing outward without limit, lies the realm of galaxies, "island universes" like our own. Well within living memory, astronomers discovered that we live in one galaxy among many. Today we know that visible matter in the universe has distributed itself into galaxies, each with millions or billions of stars, and that our home galaxy ranks merely as one of the larger of these galaxies. Former astronomers ended their textbooks with a brief overview of *nebulae*; today we know that this vague reference includes gas clouds within the Milky Way (still called nebulae) as well as far vaster objects that we now call galaxies, thousands of times more distant than the clouds of glowing gas. Once we lived in ignorance of the way that the universe has arranged itself; today we know (so we think!) much of the history of the cosmos, from the "big bang" that began the universe in a state of expansion to the details of collisions between galaxies.

If a single person can be called central to the story of how human beings came to understand that we live within a galaxy, and that myriad other galaxies surround us, that person is Edwin Powell Hubble (Figure 21). Hubble was born in Missouri in 1889; he attended the University of Chicago and then went as a Rhodes Scholar to Oxford University in England. He returned to the United States to become a lawyer but in fact never practiced law; instead, he returned to astronomy, his first academic love, and re-enrolled at the University of Chicago for graduate studies.

In 1917, shortly after Hubble had received his Ph.D. degree, the United States entered the First World War; this induced Hubble's enlistment in the army and led him to decline (temporarily) a job offer from the Mount Wilson Observatory in California. Hubble's service as an army officer apparently resonated deeply with his basic character. For the rest of his life he loved to be addressed as "major," and he maintained more of the military personality than civilian life generally requires. When Nicholas Mayall, Hubble's biographer for the National Academy of Sciences, and a lifelong friend and admirer, searched for endearing human

Figure 21. Edwin Hubble (1889–1953) made the distance determinations that allowed him to discover the expansion of the universe. (Photograph courtesy of The Huntington Library, San Marino, California.)

anecdotes about him, the best he could find was a story of how Hubble, challenged at a friendly dinner to display his alleged prowess at finding infractions of the rules during military inspections, promptly wiped a stove leg and an electrical cord to reveal dirt invisible to the untrained eye.

But a relaxed attitude has never been a prerequisite for great scientific achievement. (If it were, we might well still be using the Ptolemaic system of the cosmos.) Hubble had an innate feeling for what was significant and what was merely secondary in astronomical research; he had a good ability to use telescopes carefully (much rarer among astronomers than one might imagine); and he knew how to get things done. Finally, his timing was excellent: Hubble became a staff astronomer at the Mount Wilson Observatory, overlooking the Los Angeles basin, just at the time that the observatory was completing what was then the world's largest telescope, the 100-inch Hooker reflector (named after the wealthy donor who gave the Carnegie Institution the funds for the glass disk that became its mirror).

What most interested Hubble was the problem of finding the distances to *spiral nebulae*. The word *nebula* means "cloud" in Latin; in astronomy, a nebula is a diffuse-looking object, quite clearly not a star but of an unknown nature during the early years of this century. To astronomers, the truly great nebulae of the visible universe appear on the list compiled during the late eighteenth century by Charles Messier. Messier was a French amateur astronomer, a comet hunter who wanted to identify a list of objects that could *not* be potential new comets, his true interest. Today Messier's cometary discoveries barely rate a note in astronomical history, but the "Messier objects"—the list of noncometary nebulae—still play a key role in our knowledge of the universe.

With improved observations, astronomers later discovered that some of Messier's nebulae are star-forming regions in the Milky Way. These regions are giant clouds of gas and dust, lit from within by young, hot stars that are born in these stellar nurseries. Messier's list also includes star clusters, groups of stars born together. In most of these clusters, the gas left over from the process of star formation has evaporated (Figure 22, p. 68). But the

Plate 1. The Mauna Kea Observatory, located on the Big Island of Hawaii at an altitude of 13,700 feet, provides the world's best astronomical site, high above 90 percent of the water vapor and 40 percent of the mass in the Earth's atmosphere. This panorama shows (from left to right) the Canada-France-Hawaii Telescope, the University of Hawaii telescope, and the United Kingdom Infrared Telescope, with NASA's Infrared Telescope Facility in the center foreground.

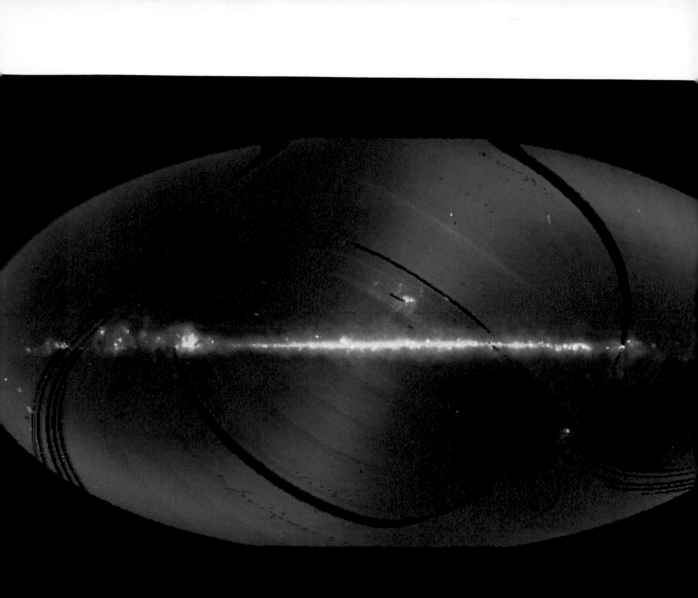

Plate 2. The Infrared Astronomy Satellite ("IRAS"), launched in 1983, made the first survey of the sky (missing a few unmapped swaths) in infrared radiation that cannot penetrate our atmosphere. The computer-generated colors signify different wavelengths of infrared.

...objects) also reveals
...blue galaxies has
...be seen in many

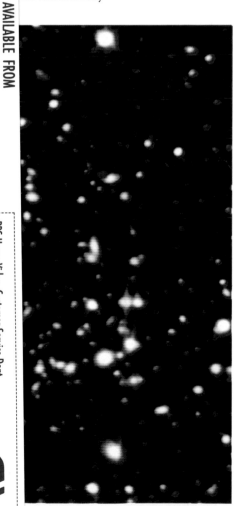

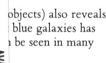

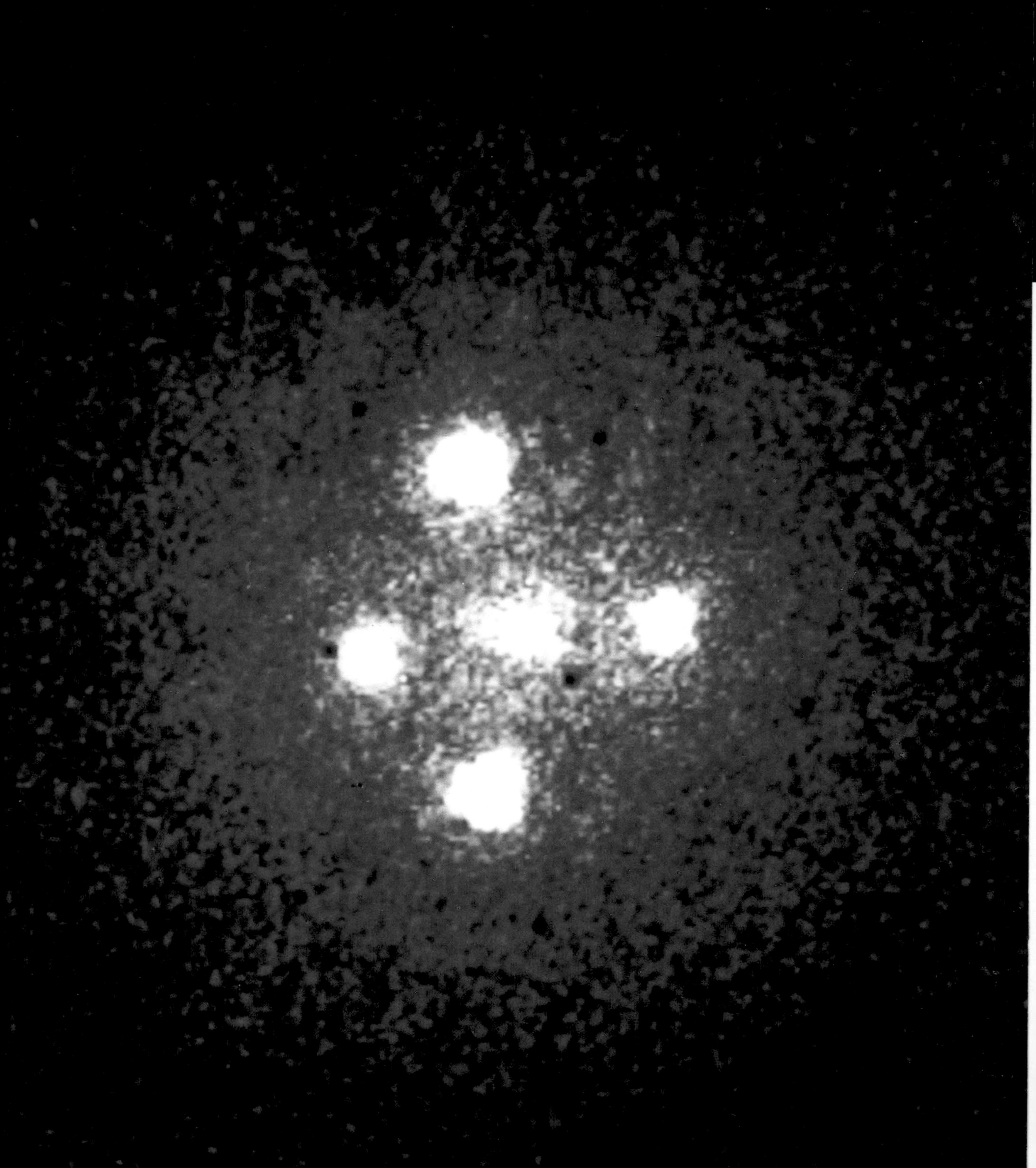

Plate 4. This Hubble Space Telescope photo shows a galaxy (center) surrounded by 4 images of a single quasar—a much more distant object that is 8 billion light years away from Earth. The quasar's light has been bent on its way to us by the galaxy's gravitational force.

Plate 5. An artist's rendition of a spiral galaxy such as our Milky Way emphasizes the color differences between the spiral arms, where young blue stars and reddish star-forming regions predominate, and the central bulge of the galaxy, with few young stars and a preponderance of yellowish, older stars.

Plate 6. If we could approach close to another spiral galaxy, we would begin to see the individual stars that orbit around the galactic center, which in this computer simulation contains a close-packed "bulge" of blue stars.

Plate 7. The great spiral galaxy in Andromeda, two million light years from the Milky Way, is the closest galaxy that resembles our own. Two elliptical satellite galaxies of the Andromeda spiral are visible above and below the large galaxy. The foreground stars all lie in the Milky Way at roughly one one-thousandth of the distance to Andromeda.

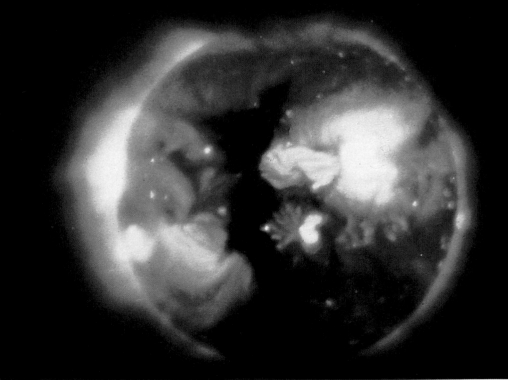

Plate 8. The spiral galaxy NGC 2997 shows well-defined spiral arms.

Plate 9. Seen in x-ray emission by the Einstein x-ray satellite, the sun's upper atmosphere glows brightly at temperatures of hundreds of thousands, or even millions, of degrees. Regions of less intense emission produce dark "coronal holes."

heart of Messier's list consists of the most prominent spiral nebulae. Spiral nebulae differed markedly in appearance from the gas clouds in the Milky Way, but their nature remained unknown because the distances to the spiral nebulae could not be determined.

Before Hubble's work, the distances of spiral nebulae, like those to all astronomical objects save the nearest stars, could not even be well estimated. But as telescopes improved during the nineteenth and early twentieth centuries, they revealed the complex structure of some of the most prominent spirals, such as the Andromeda Nebula, the Whirlpool Nebula, and the Sombrero Nebula. The improved observations made astronomers' lack of knowledge of the *distances* to these objects a subject of particular interest and intense controversy. Some astronomers had a view of the universe in which our system of stars—what we now call the Milky Way galaxy—embraced the entire visible cosmos, including the spiral nebulae. Others insisted that the spiral nebulae form counterparts to our own star system, galaxies in their own right, equal in majesty and importance to the galaxy in which we live.

During the early years of the 1920s, while Babe Ruth doubled the home-run record for a single season and Warren Harding's administration embarked on a new round of governmental mediocrity, astronomical debate over the nature of the spiral nebulae intensified. But by the time that President Harding had shuffled off this mortal coil at the Palace Hotel in San Francisco (August 2, 1923), Edwin Hubble had nearly resolved the problem of the distances to the spiral nebulae. Hubble relied on the power of deduction combined with key observations—and the fortunate existence of a type of star beloved by astronomers, the *Cepheid variable*.

CEPHEID VARIABLE STARS AS DISTANCE INDICATORS

Cepheid variable stars owe their name to Delta Cephei, the best-studied member of this class of stars. Most stars, like our sun, shine with an impressively constant brightness. But some stars, typically those in the late stages of life, *vary* their luminosities. They do so for subtly different reasons related to the stars' aging processes (and consequent diminishing supply of the "fuel" that makes stars shine). These different processes produce different *patterns* of change in the stars' light output. What most distinguishes Delta Cephei and its Cepheid cousins from other types of variable stars is that Cepheid variable stars change their brightnesses in a *cyclical* manner: The pattern of their variation repeats regularly and predictably.

Cepheid variable stars were discovered by, and became the bailiwick of, a remarkable woman named Henrietta Swan Leavitt, who worked on the staff of the Harvard College Observatory. Leavitt employed a group of sharp-eyed young women to help her in analyzing the photographic record of stellar brightness. These assistants painstakingly examined plate after plate of star fields—a visual history of the stellar cosmos during the early years of the century. (Today the Harvard plate collection remains one of the great treasures of astronomical record keeping.)

Comparing the plates to see whether any stars had changed their brightnesses, Leavitt's hard-working team of women obtained a precious result, a priceless tool for astronomers to use in their attempt to assign distances. For the class of Cepheid variable stars, Leavitt and her assistants found a relationship between the period of light variation (the time that a complete cycle of greater and lesser brightness took to occur) and the star's intrinsic average brightness or luminosity (the amount of energy that the star releases each second). Leavitt recognized that each Cepheid variable star with a given period of variation has a unique intrinsic brightness or luminosity. This meant that wherever a newfound Cepheid might be located, if that star took the same amount of time to pass through its regular cycle of brightness variation—4½ days, for example—then that star must have the same luminosity as any other Cepheid variable star whose period of variation also equals 4½ days. Leavitt also found that the longer the period, the greater the star's luminosity would be.

In human analogy, this was as if Leavitt had discovered that a person's wealth can be found by determining how often the person takes a vacation. Two Cepheid variables with *different* periods of light variation turned out to be stars with different amounts of energy output; two stars with the *same* period of variation had the same intrinsic brightness. After Leavitt's work, whenever astronomers have found two Cepheid variables with the same period of light variation, they could be almost certain that the two stars have the same energy output and the same luminosity.

Hubble knew the importance of Leavitt's work, and he went looking for Cepheid variable stars in the Andromeda Nebula, the spiral nebula with the largest angular size, and the one in which

Hubble thought he might most easily detect individual Cepheids. Using the Hooker telescope, Hubble took two- and three-hour exposures of Andromeda, night after night, during 1922 and 1923. (Today no astronomer receives so much time on a large telescope as Hubble did with the 100-inch; but then, few things work as they did in the old days.)

By the end of 1923, Hubble was sure that he had found Cepheid variables in the Andromeda Nebula and had measured their periods of light variation. He could then show that these Cepheids had the same periods as Cepheids known from Leavitt's work, and that the Andromeda Cepheids had an apparent brightness only about one ten-thousandth of those for the Cepheids catalogued by Leavitt. The apparent brightness of any object decreases in proportion to the *square* of its distance from the observer. Thus to make an object appear one ten-thousandth as bright, you must move it a hundred times farther away (since 100 squared equals 10,000). Hubble's Cepheids had to be a hundred times more distant than the ones Leavitt had found. Hubble thus placed the Andromeda Nebula at an astronomically immense distance—and Andromeda is the *closest* of all the spiral nebulae!

Hubble used a variety of indirect methods to determine the distances to the relatively nearby Cepheids studied by Leavitt. This allowed him to estimate that the hundred-times-more-distant Andromeda Nebula lies 900,000 light years from the solar system. (Astronomers' best estimates now assign more than twice this distance—about 2 million light years.) Hubble went on to find Cepheid variables in the two small elliptical galaxies that accompany the Andromeda Nebula, and in another nearby spiral, somewhat smaller than Andromeda, the galaxy M33 (number 33 on Messier's list) in the constellation Triangulum. These nebulae also lie too far away to be confined within the Milky Way, for no one then or now would suggest that the Milky Way's stars extend over a million light years or more. Thus the spiral nebulae gained recognition as galaxies in their own right. Today astronomers have replaced the outmoded term "spiral nebulae" with the modern term "spiral galaxies."

Hubble's method of using Cepheid variables to estimate galaxies' distances was a success for the few closest galaxies. Unfortunately for astronomers, even with today's largest telescopes, Cepheid variables can be seen as individual stars only in the few galaxies closest to the Milky Way. Hence the remainder of all other galaxies—the other few hundred billion galaxies that appear on photographic plates—cannot have their distances estimated by comparing individual Cepheid variable stars within the galaxies with Cepheids much closer to us. How, then, can we estimate distances to any other galaxies?

ESTIMATING THE DISTANCES TO GALAXIES

Hubble knew that the answer was simple, once a few assumptions were made. The closest galaxies by themselves provide the equivalent of the Cepheid variable stars. That is, as Hubble saw, *galaxies* could become the reference points with which astronomers could compare still more distant objects. To oversimplify astronomers' procedures, imagine that you observe two spiral galaxies that appear to have the same shape, general appearance, speeds of rotation, and mass. Astronomers then conclude that the two galaxies may be basically similar in size. But suppose that one of these spiral galaxies covers 10 times the width on the sky than the other; that is, the former has 10 times the angular size of the latter. Suppose also that the galaxy with the greater angular size has 100 times the apparent brightness of the other. Then, if we assume that the galaxies are much alike, the conclusion follows that the fainter galaxy must be 10 times more distant than the brighter one. An increase in distance reduces any object's angular size in direct proportion to the distance. That is why the galaxy 10 times farther away has $\frac{1}{10}$ the angular size of the closer galaxy. An increase in distance also reduces an object's apparent brightness, but in proportion to the *square* of the distance. (In algebraic terms, brightness~ $1/\text{distance}^2$.) That is why the closer galaxy appears not 10 but 100 times brighter than the more distant galaxy. These conclusions have appeared to be quite reasonable to astronomers ever since Edwin Hubble first established that galaxies lie beyond our own Milky Way.

Now if we know the distance to the first spiral—such as the Andromeda galaxy, 2 million light years away—we can then derive the distance to the second galaxy, which in this case would turn out to be 20 million light years. And if we then observe a third similarly shaped galaxy whose apparent brightness is only one one-hundredth that of the second galaxy, we can conclude—with some caution—that the third galaxy must be 200 million light years away.

By the mid-1930s, astronomers had thus derived a *pyramid of distances,* capped by Hubble's work, in which cosmic distances were derived by piling inference upon inference. The pyramid rests upon the distances to the closest stars (derived from their parallax shifts), proceeds to an estimate of the distances to the farther stars and the Cepheid variables in our Milky Way and nearby galaxies, and then uses these estimates to derive the distances to galaxies so far away that the light by which we now see them left before dinosaurs appeared on Earth.

The Pyramid of Distances

TYPICAL DISTANCE FROM OUR SOLAR SYSTEM (IN LIGHT YEARS)	MEASUREMENT METHOD
10–250	Parallax measurements of distance to closest stars
5,000 to 10 million	Cepheid-variable method used for more distant stars and nearby galaxies
20 million to 1 billion	Galaxy comparison used for measuring distances to more distant galaxies
1 to 10 billion	Measurement of redshift (p. 91) of galaxy yields estimate of its distance

To derive the greatest distances in the pyramid, Hubble used the method of comparing galaxies—one much more distant than the other—to estimate the distances to more and more distant galaxies. Working in conjunction with Milton Humason, a lovable, loyal man who had begun his career as a mule driver on the Mount Wilson supply road, Hubble became the world's leading expert on the distances to galaxies.

Of course, some error must inevitably appear at each step of the pyramid. No two galaxies are exactly identical, and even the assumption of close resemblance cannot be directly verified. Astronomers constantly search for some new analog of Cepheid variable stars, some "standard candle," a type of object of known luminosity that they can recognize at immense distances as identical, or nearly so, from galaxy to galaxy. Exploding stars, called supernovae, may yet furnish such a standard candle, despite the fact that different types of explosions preclude the easy conclusion that all supernovae reach the same maximum luminosity. For the time being, astronomers do the best they can with a margin of uncertainty and error. They know (but do not often stress to the general public) that when they say, for example, that the galaxy M 87 has a distance of 60 million light years, the actual distance almost certainly (they believe!) lies between 40 and 90 million light years. This is the price we pay for a glimpse across the ages of faraway galaxies: We see them well, but our knowledge of how long their light has traveled—of how distant they are— remains uncertain.

Nevertheless, the key fact about galaxies' distances is that in assigning a distance of 60 million light years to M 87, astronomers feel confident that the galaxy M 87 is *not* a mere 20 million light years away, nor so distant as 150 million light years. Our estimates may be imperfect, but within their error limits they are believed to be correct. Thanks to these estimates, we have come to understand the *ordering* of distances in the universe, even though we have an imprecise knowledge of the distances themselves. This was true even during the 1920s, as Edwin Hubble made the first good estimates of the distances to galaxies. We may call these estimates "good" despite the fact that subsequent generations of astronomers revised all Hubble's distance estimates upward by a factor of two or more. Indeed, Hubble's estimates were sufficiently good for him to make the single most significant astronomical discovery of the twentieth century: The universe is expanding.

THE DISCOVERY OF THE EXPANDING UNIVERSE

To reach his discovery of the expansion of the universe, Hubble had to combine his estimates of the *distances* to galaxies with measurements of the *motions* of those galaxies. Oddly enough, the motions—at least those toward or away from us—can be determined far more easily than the distances. Indeed, the motions of the brightest and closest agglomerations of stars had been determined well before Hubble unlocked the key to the galaxies' distance scale. Because the motion of a galaxy changes all the *colors* of the light emitted from it (as a result of the Doppler effect), astronomers could measure the change in color to derive how rapidly a galaxy is moving toward or away from us. The astronomers compared the colors of the light from galaxies with laboratory measurements of the colors of light produced by the types of atoms known to exist in the stars that compose the galaxies. Any differences in color presumably arose from the Doppler effect, and the amount of the difference revealed the galaxy's velocity toward or away from us.

During the first decade of the twentieth century, at the Lowell Observatory near Flagstaff, Arizona, Vesto Slipher measured galaxies' velocities toward or away from the Milky Way. He noted that velocities of recession predominated over velocities of approach but drew no conclusions about how the velocities are related to the galaxies' distances, for no such conclusion was possible without a knowledge of the relative distances of the galaxies on Slipher's list.

Hubble had the distances. In 1929, when he put his distance estimates together with the velocities found by Slipher and others, a remarkable fact leapt from the data: Except for the closest galaxies to the Milky Way (including the Andromeda galaxy), all galaxies are receding from us, and the *galaxies' speeds of recession increase in proportion to their distances from us* (Figure 23). This statement marks

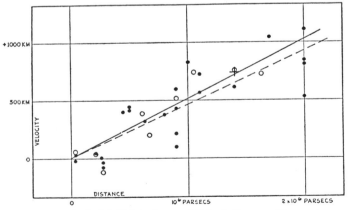

Figure 23. Edwin Hubble's first published diagram illustrating the expansion of the universe showed the direct relationship (indicated by the straight line) between the distances of galaxies from the Milky Way (horizontal axis) and their velocities of recession (vertical axis). The dots represent galaxies; the circles represent a statistical repositioning of groups of these galaxies. (Courtesy of the University of Chicago.)

the most significant astronomical discovery of the twentieth century. We ourselves are not expanding; nor is the solar system, the Milky Way galaxy, or even our local cluster of galaxies. But on the largest distance scales, clusters of galaxies are all receding from one another.

Hubble's discovery might be taken to mean that our Milky Way forms the center of the universe, since all galaxies appear to be receding from *us*. But astronomers—philosophically wary since Copernicus's time of assigning a special place to our planet, our sun, or our collection of stars—prefer a different assumption, which they call the *cosmological principle.*

According to the cosmological principle, *our view of the universe is representative;* that is, any observer, anywhere else, should see what we do: Galaxies are receding from the observer at speeds proportional to their distances from the observer. If we adopt the cosmological principle, then the cosmos must be expanding everywhere, since every observer sees a universe of receding galaxies. In other words, Hubble's observations plus the assumption that we have a representative view of the cosmos leads straight to a single conclusion: The entire universe is expanding.

If the universe is expanding, things must have been closer together in the past. Run the movie backward in your mind, and you reach a time, approximately 15 billion years ago, when everything occupied a single point. This moment, the "big bang," marks the limit of how far back into the past we can reasonably extrapolate from our observations and our assumptions about the universe. The universe might have existed before the big bang, but for now we don't know what it was doing then. We do know—based on our best understanding of the universe—that the big bang did not occur somewhere but rather *everywhere.* In other words, not only all the matter in the universe, but all the *space* as well, was packed together into the big bang. Since that primeval explosion, space has gone on expanding: New space has continuously come into being between the groups of matter that we call clusters of galaxies.

This continuous creation of new space avoids the apparent dilemma that arises when you tell someone about the big bang. "Where then," they invariably ask, "did the big bang occur?" If space simply "sat there," immutable and unchanging, this question would make sense. Astronomers would be forced to point to somewhere special in space—the locale of the big bang—that

Measuring Velocities Through the Doppler Effect

The Doppler effect, named after the Austrian physicist who first carefully described it, deals with the waves that spread out from a source. These waves may be ripples on the surface of a pond or sound waves from an ambulance that ripple through the air. Light waves also exhibit a regular, wavelike behavior, though unlike sound waves, they require no medium to "ripple in" and always travel at the same speed, the speed of light.

Sound waves, light waves, and all other types of wave motion are characterized by a frequency and a wavelength. The frequency measures the time interval between the passage of two successive wave crests, and the wavelength measures the distance between these crests. For sound waves, the frequency describes the pitch of the sound; for light waves, the frequency corresponds to the color of the light that we see.

The Doppler effect describes the change in the frequency of the waves that will occur if the source of the waves moves with respect to the observer (see figure 12, p. 36). If a car speeds toward you with its horn blaring, each successive sound wave starts at a position closer to you. As a result, each wave has a shorter distance to travel to your ear, and the time interval separating the wave crests becomes less than it would be if the car were stationary. A shorter interval between arriving wave crests means that the crests arrive more often, so the sound rises in pitch. When the car passes you and carries its horn to greater distances, the reverse effect occurs: The car's motion increases the distance that sound waves must travel, so the interval between wave crests increases and the pitch decreases.

The Doppler effect works just as well if the person hearing the waves, rather than the source of the waves, is in motion. Motion toward the source of the waves lessens the distance that each successive wave crest must travel to arrive, thus increasing the measured frequency and pitch. Motion away from the source of waves increases the time intervals and decreases the frequency of the sound waves perceived by the person in motion.

would violate their beloved *cosmological principle,* the rule of cosmic democracy that states that all places are basically equal. By imagining (if you can!) that all of space participated equally in the big bang, you achieve a head start toward the notion that no one point in space can claim to be *the* center of the expansion of the universe. Instead, all points in space have an equal claim to centrality, and all participated equally in the big bang.

This may seem difficult to grasp, but it works both mathematically and logically. In fact, the basic theory of the expanding universe had been derived by Albert Einstein and others even *before* Hubble discovered the universal expansion, but no one took the theory seriously until Hubble's observational support for it emerged. What seems still more unmanageable is the question of whether the universe is infinite or finite. No one, it turns out, lacks an intuitive feeling on this question, but intuition can be misleading when you deal with the entire universe.

If the universe is infinite, it extends forever in all directions. This may seem satisfying, but consider that in an infinite universe, every variant or any object or event that is possible *must* occur. No matter how small the probability—so long as it is not exactly zero—of a particular event's occurrence, the fact that the universe is infinitely large implies that the event will occur an infinite number of times! In an infinite universe, this book exists in every conceivable language, with every conceivable nuance, in every language of every planet—an infinite number of times in each variation—and so do its readers. This unbelievable result of the assumption of an infinite universe, which follows directly from the nature of infinity, emphasizes the difficulty of conceiving *either* a finite or an infinite universe.

In a finite universe, space curves back on itself, like the surface of the Earth, so that voyagers moving in a "straight line" eventually find themselves back at their starting point. This can be true even though space has nothing to "curve into"; that is, we cannot hope to step back into an added dimension, as we can to admire the curved surface of the Earth. A finite universe has nothing outside it. Mind-boggling though the curved space of a finite universe may be, astronomers consider it a serious possibility.

Meanwhile, in the mundane cosmos of a few billion light years that surrounds us, work goes on. One key aspect of the effort to know the universe consists of Margaret Geller's and John Huchra's extension of Hubble's work—the attempt to make ever-better maps of the realm of the galaxies.

Since the Doppler effect works equally well for a *source* in motion or an *observer* in motion, it is no surprise that a combination of motion by the source *and* the observer follows a simple rule: Only the total effect counts, and it matters not how much the source of the waves moves versus how much the observer of the waves moves. What does matter is the speed of relative motion. More rapid motion produces a greater change in the observed frequency than slower motion does. If a car approaches you at 80 miles per hour, sounding its horn, and then goes by at that speed, the change in pitch will be twice as large as it will be if the car passes at 40 miles per hour. The same will be true if you pass a stationary car at 40 or 80 miles per hour. In either case, if you can measure the amount by which the frequency of the sound waves has changed, you can determine the relative speed between yourself and the source of waves.

What works for sound waves works just as well for light waves: If a galaxy recedes from us (or we from it), the frequency of all the light waves from that galaxy will decrease by an amount that depends only on the velocity of recession. Light waves with different frequencies appear to us as different colors (see chapter 1). Red light has the lowest frequency of the types of light that our eyes can detect; violet light has the highest frequency, about twice that of red light; other colors have intermediate frequencies. Therefore, as explained below, astronomers must attempt to determine how much an object's color has *changed* from the color it would have if it were not in motion. Whenever they can do this, they can determine the object's motion with respect to us: whether it is approaching or receding, and how rapidly it is doing so. If, for example, astronomers observe a source that they know is emitting violet light but the source appears to us as a source of red light, they can calculate from the change in frequency that it must be receding from us at half the speed of light.

But how can astronomers measure the *change* in color? After all, they observe galaxies only as they are, not as they would be if they had no motion toward or away from us. Once again, astronomers are saved by the fact that they observe not one object but a host of objects, all roughly similar.

THE IMPORTANCE OF CAMBRIDGE

Some fifteen miles to the southwest of Boston rises the Charles River, one of the least prepossessing yet highly significant streams of life in the New World. The Charles flows first north and then eastward, passing at Weston beneath Interstate 95, formerly designated as Highway 128, where the electronics and computer industry first flourished. Three miles farther east, at Waltham, the river widens to a dozen yards across and continues in this modest dimension past the old industrial center of Watertown. Half a dozen miles farther downstream, on all but the coldest winter days (when the Charles freezes, though not to the point where skating becomes safe) the tourist will encounter men and women sculling up and down the river, strenuously or languidly as the mood takes them.

These oarspeople provide the first indication that the tourist has entered Cambridge, for centuries one of the intellectual cornerstones of the United States. At Cambridge, receiving the aqueous runoff from the suburbs of Newton and Brookline, the Charles becomes several times wider. In the western part of Cambridge the river bends sharply to the south, then curves to the east and finally to the northeast before flowing beneath the Tobin Bridge and into Boston Harbor, to mingle its fresh water with the much-polluted salt of the sea.

Within the first Cambridge bend of the Charles lies Harvard University. Founded in 1636, by far the oldest university in the United States, Harvard employed the first great North American professor of natural science, John Winthrop. Winthrop taught at Harvard for 40 years, numbering among his students John Adams, the first of the five Harvard alumni who became president of the United States. From a few rough buildings in the "Yard" (what would elsewhere be called the central campus), the university has continually expanded during its 355 years to embrace half a square mile of buildings dedicated to higher education in every form.

To the east of Harvard, past the great bend of the Charles River, two miles by sculling skiff or a mile and a half along Massachusetts Avenue, stands the other great educational institution of Cambridge, the Massachusetts Institute of Technology. MIT has a glowing reputation in science, mathematics, and engineering. Founded soon after the Civil War with a mission to train scientists

Galaxies consist of stars of different colors—red, yellow, blue, and intermediate colors as well. However, the *mixture* of stars of various colors in a galaxy tends to be about the same from galaxy to galaxy. This fact is especially true for galaxies of the same general appearance, such as spiral galaxies. Astronomers have learned this consistent distribution of star colors by studying nearby galaxies. In fact, they study not simply the general colors (red, orange, yellow, and so on) of the stars in a galaxy, but also the details of each color. They spread the light into the *spectrum* of all colors that the light contains, and study the details of this spectrum carefully (Figure 24, pp. 90–91). The spectrum of light from a star contains thousands (technically an infinite number) of individual frequencies. Careful analysis of the amount of light of each frequency or color will then reveal the star's temperature and the types of atoms in its surface layers.

For more than a century, astronomers have used instruments called *spectroscopes* to divide starlight into its component colors. Long experience has led astronomers who specialize in spectroscopy to know the amount of each individual color in the light from particular kinds of stars as well as a mother knows her children, indeed in many cases far better. These astronomers know not only that Betelgeuse is a red star and Rigel a blue one, but also the precise amount of each of the many thousands of colors that these and thousands of other stars emit. The astronomers who study stars in bulk can recognize the typical spectrum of the entire light output from a galaxy, which consists of the superposed contributions of billions of stars. A graduate student who seeks to become an expert in the spectrum of galaxies serves an apprenticeship of several years, in which he or she *begins* to grasp the details of these spectra as well as his or her mentor does—something like the young Mark Twain learning the waters and banks of the Mississippi. Eventually, the student will also become an expert on the light from galaxies, to the point where he or she, presented with a spectrum of the light from an object never before observed, can say almost instantly, "That's the light from a population of stars typical of a spiral galaxy." This instant appraisal relies on recognition of the pattern of relative brightness and darkness in the spec-

and engineers, MIT quickly ranked among the leading institutions in its domain.

Between Harvard and MIT stands the "other Cambridge," a city of a hundred thousand hard-working, Boston-accented citizens who look with barely concealed disdain on what they conceive to be the lazy, useless students and faculty who fill the streets with overpriced automobiles. A prototypical "town-gown" interaction (recalling by its name the long-vanished days when faculty members and students wore academic robes to class) places an academic in a supermarket's express check-out line holding 10 items for purchase while standing beneath a sign reading "6 items or less." "Which is it?" growls the check-out person, "Are you from MIT and can't read?—or from Harvard and can't count?"

The two great universities have dominated Cambridge for a century. They did so in the 1920s, when Harvard's Cecilia Payne realized that all stars contain basically the same elements, mainly hydrogen and helium, and during the Second World War, when scientists at MIT developed radar systems that proved crucial in both attack and defense. So it was in 1949, when two Harvard researchers, Harold Ewen and Edward Purcell (the latter one of the faculty Nobelists) made the first observations of cosmic radio waves from the hydrogen atoms that permeate the universe. And so it has been in recent years for studies of the universe at both ends of Massachusetts Avenue.

In 1847, using funds provided by citizens of Boston who prized their central role in the world of learning, Harvard built the world's largest telescope on the 60-foot eminence of Observatory Hill. Mounted on a pier of granite blocks that reach 25 feet below ground level, this beautiful refractor with a 15-inch lens fulfilled the dreams of John Quincy Adams, the American president who showed the greatest interest in astronomy. Adams had been influential in raising the money for the telescope and in encouraging

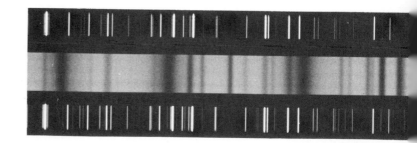

trum—the alternation of frequencies with greater or lesser amounts of light.

The Doppler effect changes the colors of light from receding or approaching sources. Happily, the effect changes *all* the frequencies of light from a particular star or galaxy by the same fractional amount. The Doppler effect therefore shifts the patterns in a spectrum—the distribution of bright and dark bands—without changing the pattern itself. If, for example, a galaxy is receding from us at 3 percent of the speed of light, all of the wavelengths of its spectrum will increase by 3 percent, but the complex alternation of bright and dark regions (see Figure 24) will remain unchanged. A skilled astronomer can easily recognize that the pattern is familar but that all the frequencies have been decreased by 3 percent from the frequencies that would be recorded if no motion existed. This *redshift* to longer wavelengths and lower frequencies (that is, toward the red end of the visible light spectrum) shows that the galaxy must have a relative motion of recession equal to 3 percent of the speed of light.

Figure 24. Astronomers spread the light from a star into the spectrum of all different colors, typically with laboratory reference lines on either side for easy measurement. Dark absorption lines appear at those wavelengths where particular types of atoms and molecules in the stars' outer layers have removed particular colors of light. (Lick Observatory photograph.)

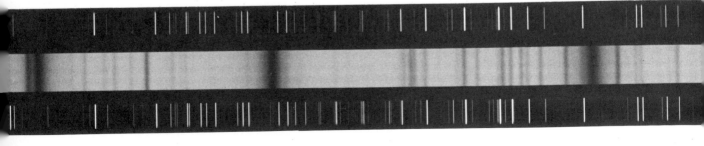

Harvard College to devote proper funds to its operation. One month after the telescope was inaugurated, the former president came with a crowd of notables that included the poet Henry Wadsworth Longfellow. As they looked at Saturn through the telescope, the observatory director noted that Adams was "very cheerful, and interested as ever in the prosperity of the Observatory." One year later, Saturn's eighth satellite was discovered with the Harvard telescope—an event that made European savants admit that the United States might eventually amount to something in astronomy.

By the turn of the century, when a Harvard telescope in Peru found Saturn's ninth satellite, the wooden building in Cambridge that housed the 15-inch refractor had acquired solid brick neighbors, as well as adjacent huts and domelets containing workshops and smaller astronomical instruments. The cluster of buildings expanded during the 1950s, and then, in a final outburst of construction, the Smithsonian Astrophysical Laboratory, persuaded to locate in Cambridge by key Harvard astronomers, built a modern building to provide offices and laboratories. During the 1970s, when the Harvard Observatory and Smithsonian were formally joined to become the Center for Astrophysics (CfA) one more building was added to the site.

There you will find the offices and computer laboratory of Margaret Geller, a leader among those who map the universe (Figure 25). Geller's first career plan was to become an actress, but she settled for the next best thing on her list—astronomer. She was born in Ithaca, New York, where her father was a postdoctoral fellow in Cornell University's chemistry department; his job with the Bell Laboratories took the family to Morristown, New Jersey, where Margaret and her younger sister grew up.

Geller finished high school in Los Angeles, where her family had moved during the early 1960s. She was an undergraduate at the University of California at Berkeley, where she spent the four turbulent years from 1966 to 1970. Geller did well in Berkeley but chose to go to Princeton for graduate school, where she enrolled as a physics student. Astronomy nonetheless held her interest: She decided to do a thesis with Jim Peebles, a physicist best known for his research into the early universe and for his analyses of the distribution of galaxies in space.

Working under Peebles's supervision, Geller attacked the latter problem, which eventually became her life's work. She saw that the field of mapping the universe was in effect not well organized. Surveys of various portions of the visible universe had been made and were being extended, but no coherent mapping program existed. Geller decided that this was worth further investigation.

In 1980, Harvard offered Geller an untenured position at the same time that Michigan asked her to join the tenured faculty. Conscious of its advantages, Geller decided to risk Harvard. There Geller has worked fruitfully in collaboration with an easygoing, much shyer astronomer about her age, John Huchra. Huchra, a balding, bearded man of middle stature, is an expert at obtaining and measuring the spectra of the light from galaxies. Enlisting the aid of Valerie DeLapperent, a French postdoctoral fellow, Geller and Huchra created a map of the galaxies around the Milky Way. This sounds simple but required years of effort—effort that, among other things, made Geller the second woman in 353 years to become a tenured professor of astronomy at Harvard.

Figure 25. Margaret Geller of the Harvard-Smithsonian Center for Astrophysics is one of the leaders in the effort to map the universe. (Photograph by Laurie Sieverts Snyder.)

Today Geller has just passed 40 and is a strong, verbal, and active woman, who recognizes that "I've had the opportunity to do what I wanted to do." When she speaks, her black hair bobs in time with the points that she makes, and the listener recognizes that there is nothing to doubt. Conscious that her success did not come easily and had to be achieved in the face of those who thought she would not succeed—"I've outwitted the people who discouraged me," she says—Geller hopes that her path may serve as a role model to women contemplating a career in science.

MODERN MAPS OF THE UNIVERSE

Just as Edwin Hubble worked during the 1920s on the problem of estimating the distances to galaxies, so too Margaret Geller and John Huchra worked through the 1980s on mapping the universe. This activity, though tied to astronomical activity since ancient times, completely depends for its reliability on Hubble's discovery of the expansion of the universe. Put plainly, Geller and Huchra have derived their map of the cosmos from a series of assumptions, of which the most important is that the universe is indeed expanding according to Hubble's Law. Science proceeds by building upon assumptions presumed to be reliable, and Geller and Huchra have used Hubble's Law as their bedrock assumption. In order to assess and appreciate their results, it is essential to understand the assumptions from which those results derive.

During the six decades since Hubble announced his discovery, all but a tiny minority of astronomers have accepted the proposition that the entire universe is expanding: All galaxies are moving apart from one another, at speeds proportional to their distances from one another. This is Hubble's Law plus the cosmological principle. But even the simple facts of Hubble's Law provide an immensely useful method to map the universe.

This method reverses the procedure that Hubble followed to make his discovery. *If* we accept that galaxies' speeds of recession are proportional to their distances, then we can derive the distances to various galaxies simply by measuring their recession velocities! This would never suffice to discover or to prove Hubble's Law, for it would involve purely circular reasoning. However, once Hubble's Law has been established—as almost all astronomers agree that it has been—then the law allows us to conclude that except for some uncertainty produced by galaxies' individual motions, every recession velocity observed for a galaxy corresponds to a particular distance for that galaxy. Astronomers can measure recession velocities far more easily than they can perform the difficult tasks involved in estimating galaxies' distances. A project to map the visible universe—or at least part of it—can therefore be accomplished in a mere few years, rather than the generations that would be needed if the distance of each observed galaxy were individually estimated. Such individual estimates require painstaking comparison of each galaxy, and the objects within it, with similar but closer objects whose distances are already known.

Suppose that you are ready to assume, along with Edwin Hubble and a host of later astronomers, that Hubble's Law is indeed correct, so that you accept the principle that every distant galaxy's recession velocity supplies that galaxy's distance. How then should you proceed to map the visible universe? Clearly, what you want to do is to observe galaxy after galaxy, recording both its position on the sky and its velocity of recession. The "position on the sky" supplies the two-dimensional map of galaxies, as if all the galaxies lay upon the mythical, crystalline celestial sphere of the ancients, and the recession velocity provides the crucial third dimension, the distances to the galaxies. Hence all you need do is obtain recession velocities of galaxy after galaxy, turn these velocities into distances with the help of Hubble's Law, and enter the galaxies' distances, along with the directions to the galaxies, in your high-powered computer. The computer can then draw a three-dimensional picture of the universe as you have mapped it, employing all the artifices of perspective and—if you choose—allowing you to sail through the three-dimensional map you have created to look at the universe around you from changing locations.

This is what Geller and Huchra have done. They were stimulated in their work by an early survey made by Robert Kirshner, Gus Oemler, Paul Schechter, and Stephen Shectman (collectively called KOSS), who mapped a cone-shaped region on the sky out to recession velocities of about 4,000 miles per second. The KOSS survey revealed that even within this highly limited segment of the visible universe, neither galaxies nor galaxy clusters are distributed randomly in space. Instead, definite patterns appeared in the distribution of galaxies. For example, the survey found a "great void"—a region millions of light years across that contains almost no galaxies. The "great void in Bootes" (the constellation Bootes marks the direction toward this empty region) naturally provoked astronomers to wonder how many similar, or even larger, voids might exist if larger maps were made.

And so Geller and Huchra set to work. They obtained the use of a "dedicated" telescope—a 60-inch reflector devoted to their research alone—at the Mount Hopkins Observatory, south of Tucson, Arizona. There, on every clear night, an assistant astronomer obtains the spectra of about a dozen galaxies. The most efficient way to do this is to map the sky in "slices," each slice defined by pointing the telescope to a particular height above the horizon and letting the Earth's rotation carry galaxies through the telescope's field of view. Geller and Huchra defined each slice as a strip 6 degrees "high" (in the north-south dimension) and nearly 180 degrees long, that is, extending nearly halfway around the sky. Since the slices are much "longer" than they are "high," the map of each slice can be compressed, with only a modest loss of accuracy, into a single pie-shaped view. Each single slice, starting with the first, has provided a great deal of intriguing information, but the best and most amazing mystery arises when the slices are "stacked" next to one another so that the true, three-dimensional map of the sky emerges.

The very first slice that Geller and Huchra plotted fully confirmed the void in Bootes and also revealed the existence, or at least the suggestion, of several similar voids (Figure 26). In this slice of astronomical reality, the most apparent feature to the novice is the distribution of galaxies that resembles a stick figure of a person (the "homunculus" is what Geller and Huchra call it) at the lower center. This concentration is in fact the Coma cluster of galaxies, well known to astronomers as the largest galaxy cluster within a few hundred million light years of the Milky Way. The concentration of galaxies seemingly aligned toward the observer— that is, toward our galaxy—is not a true concentration of galaxies in space. Instead, this alignment arises from the fact that within a giant cluster of galaxies such as the Coma Cluster, the galaxies are not moving at random but instead have most of their motion directed along a line between our galaxy and the cluster's center. Because these motions produce deviations from the simple rule of Hubble's Law, the distances derived from the galaxies' velocities of recession are not completely accurate for galaxies in clusters.

Bearing in mind that every object's distance estimate carries some error, we may proceed to admire the picture of the universe that Geller and Huchra have furnished to us. The map has grown to include just under 6,000 galaxies—all of those visible in the four slices out to distances of 500 million light years from the Milky Way (Figure 27). Even a cursory glance at these stacked slices reveals a monumental fact about the distribution of galaxies—a fact only dimly guessed at before this work. *Matter in the universe turns out to be distributed in giant sheets, far deeper and broader that they are thick, with large voids, containing nearly no visible galaxies, amidst the sheets.*

Look more carefully at the stacked maps, and you will see what Geller and Huchra dubbed in 1989 the "Great Wall," the concentration of galaxies that runs from the left center to the right center, crossing the "torso" of the "homunculus" that represents the giant Coma cluster of galaxies. The Great Wall of galaxies represents the largest ordering of matter now known in the universe, a structure bounded only by the size of the region that has been mapped. As currently known, the Great Wall extends through a "length" of about 500 million light years and a "height" (through the four slices) of some 200 million light years, but its thickness

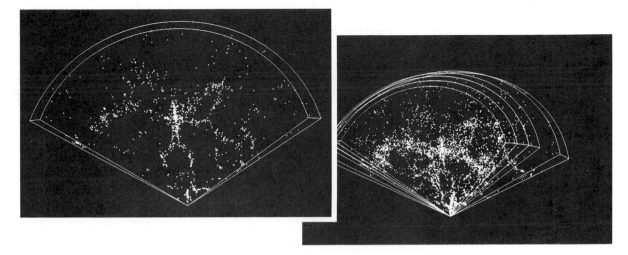

Figure 26, above left. The first slice of the sky mapped by Margaret Geller, John Huchra, and Valerie DeLapperent has its apex at the Milky Way and shows each galaxy within the slice as a dot. The map extends out to distances of about 500 million light years. What has been called the "homunculus" near the lower center of the map is the Coma Cluster of galaxies. This map revealed "structures" of galaxies that extend through space for tens of millions of light years. (Figure Copyright 1990, SAO. Courtesy of Margaret Geller/John Huchra and the Harvard-Smithsonian Center for Astrophysics.)

Figure 27, above right. Later maps made by Geller and Huchra included four separate slices, thus providing a broader view of the distribution of galaxies in space out to distances of about 500 million light years. This map reveals the "Great Wall" of galaxies that runs for 400 million light years across the center of the map. (Figure Copyright 1990, SAO. Courtesy of Margaret Geller/John Huchra and the Harvard-Smithsonian Center for Astrophysics.)

nowhere greatly exceeds 15 million light years. In other words, the largest structure in the universe has somehow acquired a compression in one dimension, compared to the other two, by a factor of more than 10. There is no good theory to explain this, and the mapping of larger regions may well reveal more to explain, since each progressively larger survey of the universe has revealed progressively larger structures.

Fascinating and mysterious though the Great Wall of galaxies may be, it represents only one example of the key revelation from the Geller-Huchra survey. As Geller and Huchra point out, in their map nearly every galaxy belongs to an extended structure, either a two-dimensional sheet or a one-dimensional filament, and these structures typically have long dimensions of hundreds of millions of light years. To a generation of astronomers who have sought to explain how galaxy clusters (typically 10–20 million light years across) ever formed, the discovery of structures dozens of times larger than galaxy clusters has proven difficult to absorb—but a flourishing industry now exists among theorists who try to explain how such enormous assemblages of matter could arise in a universe that is "only" 15 billion years old.

What is next in the quest to map the universe? Margaret Geller likes to point out that modern telescopes can observe galaxies much farther away than the 500-million-light-year limit of the survey she has led. In fact, since astronomers can (with great effort) obtain the spectra (that is, the color distribution) of the light from galaxies some 20 times more distant—out to 10 billion light years— the Geller-Huchra map includes *less than one part in ten thousand* of the visible universe (Figure 28)! In other words, with Geller's apt simile, using her map to describe the universe around us corresponds to making a map of Rhode Island and pronouncing it representative of the entire surface of the Earth.

What Geller wants is a larger telescope, preferably one located in the Southern Hemisphere, so that the map can both extend farther into space and include the portions of the sky that never rise above the deserts of Arizona. Of these two goals, the urge to look farther is primary. Geller and Huchra set the world of astronomy on its ear by making a map of the closest 500 million light years, and they have little doubt that something new and astounding will emerge once they ex-

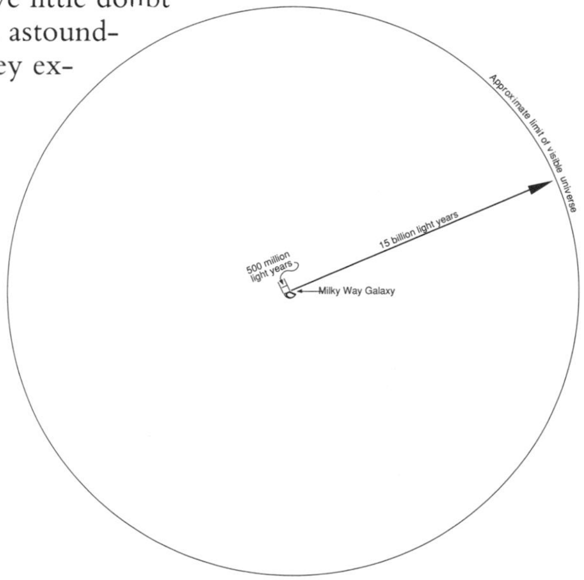

Figure 28. This drawing compares the four slices in the Geller-Huchra map with the limits of the observable universe to show how small a fraction of the universe has been mapped. The "limit of the visible universe" includes matter close enough to the Milky Way for its light to have reached us during the 15 billion years since the big bang. (Drawing by Crystal Stevenson.)

tend their survey out to two or three times this distance. Astronomers are famous (or notorious) among their scientific colleagues for claiming that something new will appear if only they receive more funds for more extended research, but this seems no more than a simple truism to those who have followed the saga of Margaret Geller.

The Geller-Huchra maps of the galaxies around us have had a great impact on those who try to explain how the universe came to be the way we see it now. But if you want to meet someone who has—in theory rather than with actual observations—truly stood the world of cosmology on its ear, you must visit the other end of Cambridge, where a man named Alan Guth keeps the universe in his head.

THE INFLATIONARY UNIVERSE

If you drive down Massachusetts Avenue through Cambridge and are fortunate to find a parking space just before the bridge over the Charles River, you can leave your car and ascend the wide steps of the main building of the Massachusetts Institute of Technology. After plunging into the hordes that crowd the building's transverse axis and penetrating to the rear of the building, you make your way up the stairs and turn eastward down a long corridor to find the spacious office, lined with books and scientific journals, of one of the great imaginers of the universe, Professor Alan Guth (Figure 29).

Guth is a true son of MIT, as advanced a professor as you might hope to meet, through whose brain run thoughts that even astrophysicists have difficulty following at the first (or even tenth) try. Born in New Jersey in 1946 and educated in its public schools, Guth discovered his love for science at an early age and entered MIT as an undergraduate in 1964. Eight years later, Guth emerged as an expert on the physics of elementary particles, the basic building blocks of matter, with bachelor of science and doctor of science degrees from MIT. He became a postdoctoral research fellow at Princeton University, Columbia University, Cornell University, and the Stanford Linear Accelerator Center (SLAC), a physics laboratory run by Stanford University in California. "I wasn't smart enough to know how to land a faculty job at a decent university," he says. In fact, the life of a postdoctoral fellow—job security aside—is a paradise for a research-oriented person. Freed from the administrative duties and internecine turf battles that plague faculty members, a "postdoc" does what he or she chooses, subject only to the "requirement" that the research produced during these years will most likely determine everything that follows in the postdoc's later career.

At Columbia, Guth found himself interested in cosmology as well as particle physics. At that time, in the late 1970s, particle physicists around the world focused on the problem of *grand unified theories* (GUTs) that would explain all of particle physics as manifestations of a single, "unified" force. Physicists classify the basic forces of nature into four varieties: strong, weak, gravitational, and electromagnetic. Strong and weak forces act only over submicroscopic distances and play a crucial role in the structure of atomic nuclei. Gravitational and electromagnetic forces act at all distances and hold together the largest assemblages of matter (by gravity) and systems of charged particles such as atoms (by electromagnetism). Today physicists believe that they can properly describe electromagnetic and weak forces as different aspects of a single "electroweak" force. They dream, as Einstein did for the latter part of his career, of a workable theory that would explain all types of forces as a single type seen in different guises.

Figure 29. Alan Guth of the Massachusetts Institute of Technology has played a crucial role in developing the new inflationary theory of the cosmos. (Photograph by Donald Goldsmith.)

The 1970s were a time of great creativity in the area of grand unified theories that would explain all forces as one. As these GUTs emerged from the minds of physicists, they had to be tested; otherwise no one could tell the wise from the not-so-wise. But the GUTs dealt with particles that meet and collide with unbelievable amounts of energy, amounts much greater than anything achievable in particle accelerators on Earth. The only testing ground imaginable would be the early universe—dubbed "the poor man's particle accelerator"—for only there, 15 billion years ago, could one expect to "find" particles colliding at the enormous energies that would test physicists' GUTs. Guth began to think about what GUTs seemed to say about the earliest moments of the universe.

In the fall of 1979, Guth went to SLAC, where the two-mile-long particle accelerator stretches westward from the Stanford campus, crosses the San Andreas Fault, passes beneath Interstate 280, and ends at the foothills of the San Francisco Peninsula. At SLAC, Guth ruminated on an apparent contradiction between theory and the real universe that the most appealing grand unified theories implied. A theorist named Dmitrios Kazanas had pointed out that these GUTs implied that the universe at its earliest moments would only have *appeared* empty. In fact, the universe would have been filled with something never seen on Earth: what physicists call the *false vacuum*. False vacuum is space that merely looks like nothing, while in fact it teems with invisible energy. The false vacuum would have eventually turned into what we think of as empty space, but as it did so, Kazanas had shown that within it hordes of particles should have come into being—particles embodying the energy formerly hidden in the false vacuum. However, the "model"—the mathematical equations that describe the universe—implied that an enormous number of particles called *magnetic monopoles* should exist in the universe today. But no magnetic monopoles have ever been detected in even our best accelerator experiments.

One evening in December 1979, Guth was bicycling homeward in the clear California air. A sudden insight struck him in a "Eureka" moment. Suppose, Guth saw, that during the first incredibly brief moments of the universe, the transition from false vacuum to real vacuum plus particles *had occurred far more slowly* than previously envisioned. Then, he saw, the theory might avoid the prediction of countless magnetic monopoles, which contradict what we observe. That is, the theory might describe the real universe, which apparently contains no such particles. Guth speedily applied himself to calculating the implications of a "slow" transition from false vacuum to true empty space. He soon found something amazing: With a slow transition, the early universe would expand, not as Edwin Hubble had found it, but at an enormously greater rate. Because the false vacuum in fact teems with energy, it tends to produce an explosion of space—everywhere!—with more power than anything imaginable on Earth, or for that matter, in the Milky Way. Drawing on an analogy from economics, Guth gave the name "inflation" to the enormously rapid expansion of all of space, which he calculated must have occurred only during the tiniest fraction of the first second after the big bang that began the universe. This rapid expansion turns out to have important consequences for the universe today, provided that the *inflationary theory* is correct.

Guth quickly recognized one key problem with the

inflationary theory. He could not see a mathematical way to make the "inflationary" phase of the universe merge smoothly into a later, only mildly expanding phase—the phase that we observe today. As interest in the inflationary universe grew, two other physicists solved the difficulty. Working independently, Andrei Linde in the Soviet Union and Paul Steinhardt at Pennsylvania State University found the mathematical equations to describe how a region of space undergoing inflation—that is, expanding at speeds much greater than the speed of light—could decelerate its expansion and gradually become the universe that we see today, the universe that obeys Hubble's Law.

According to the inflationary model, we live in a universe in which, at some random moment, a tiny region of false vacuum—space that looks empty but in fact teems with hidden energy—can begin to "inflate." The region will double in size, then double and double and double again, with hundreds of doublings in all! In this *inflationary model,* the speed of expansion of the universe far outstrips the speed of expansion in the standard big-bang model, the picture of the universe that had reigned supreme since Hubble discovered the expansion in 1929. In the early universe, the time for each doubling would be incredibly small, no more than ten to the minus thirty-third second—one billion trillion trillionth of a second! But each 10 doublings increase the size of the universe by a factor of a thousand, so 20 doublings would make the region's diameter a million times larger, and 100 doublings would increase its size by a million trillion trillion times! Since each doubling would have taken only the incredibly brief time quoted above, even a hundred doublings would require less than ten to the minus thirtieth second. In that tiny blink, what had been a submicroscopic region of space would have inflated into a region of space much larger than the bounds of the universe we can see today.

HOW CAN WE TEST THE INFLATIONARY THEORY?

Cosmologists now find the inflationary theory intriguing, and most believe that it has a fair to good chance of eventually proving correct. You can certainly find cosmologists who emphasize the fact that the inflationary model rests on unproven assumptions—that its GUTs are no better than yours. But everyone agrees that the inflationary model has one great virtue: By specifying what the average density of matter should be, the theory makes a testable prediction about the universe. The theory predicts that the density of matter should be about 100 times greater than the density of the matter that we can *see*. As discussed in earlier chapters, most of the universe turns out to consist of invisible *dark matter*. If we manage to measure its density, and if the dark matter amounts to a hundred times more than the visible matter, the inflationary theory's prediction will be verified. Within the next few decades, astronomers may be able to determine this density, and thus either to sink the theory or make it sail to glory.

Most people who hear about the inflationary universe, about a universe expanding far more rapdily than the speed of light during its first incredibly brief moments, react with incredulity, occasionally mixed with respect for the mind of Guth. But one aspect of the theory grabs nearly everyone. If Guth is right, then the universe inflated from what was originally a tiny region of false vacuum to become far larger than everything we can see today. Does this imply that the same thing must have happened, and could happen, over and over again? Has Guth produced a theory of multiple "universes," each of them incredibly large, but all of them embedded in some still much larger "metauniverse"?

Most cosmologists feel that he has. Guth, Linde, and the other particle physicists turned cosmologists who have produced the latest version of the inflationary model all happily admit that the theory implies that inflation-prone regions of false vacuum could easily be a repetitive phenomenon, not a one-shot occurrence.

Guth has moved on to different aspects of cosmology. He is now hard at work imagining the conditions that would produce an inflating region of false vacuum—as he puts it, how you might take 20 pounds of matter into your basement and make a universe.

If this ever does happen, it is fitting that it should happen in Cambridge, Massachusetts, where Margaret Geller maps the universe and Alan Guth thinks he sees how it was born.

Figure 30. The COBE satellite was launched in 1989 to study the cosmic background radiation, the oldest relic of the big bang. (NASA photograph.)

5. The Afterglow of Creation

FROM TIME TO time, either in casual conversation or in strenuous debate, astronomers must face the question, "How can you be sure that the big bang really happened?" Fortunately, unlike some questions of deep astronomical import, this question has a reasonably good answer, one that rests firmly on both theory and observation.

The strongest proof that a big bang actually did occur—and the best current way to investigate conditions soon after the big bang—consists of an electromagnetic whisper left over from the early years of the universe. This barely detectable clue to creation, a relic of eras when the universe was quite unlike what we see today, is called the *cosmic background radiation.*

In a triumph of the scientific method that astronomers love to celebrate (partially because it occurs so rarely), the existence of the cosmic background radiation was predicted on theoretical grounds nearly a decade before its actual detection. The men who made this prediction were George Gamow, a Russian-born physicist at the George Washington University in Washington, D.C., and his two collaborators, Ralph Alpher and Robert Herman. It is worth following the ideas that these cosmologists developed to see how the universe has changed through its 15-billion-year history.

The cosmic background radiation arose soon after the big bang, the moment some 15 billion years ago when all of matter— all of space too!—was compressed to a near-infinite density. Ever since that time, the universe as a whole has been changing, growing ever more rarefied, as pieces of matter have, on the largest scales of distance, steadily moved apart from one another. In contrast, on smaller distance scales, matter has actually clumped together to form individual objects such as galaxies, stars, and planets. Important though this clumping has been for beings such as ourselves, we must not let an essentially localized process obscure what has happened on the grand scale. On the average, the density of matter in the universe (the amount of material in every million cubic light years, for example) has steadily decreased.

In short, what was once a hot, dense, and homogenized universe has become, in the span of 15 billion years, a universe that is cool, rarefied, and lumpy. Individual stars may glow at temperatures of thousands of degrees, but most of the universe consists of nearly empty space at temperatures colder than most of us can easily imagine. In contrast, the universe in its early moments after the big bang resembled (to the extent that we can make any comparison at all) the center of a hydrogen bomb at the moment of its explosion—a seething, roiling mass of particles moving at enormous speeds, colliding with one another and transforming themselves into new types of particles far more rapidly than human thought could follow. The expansion of the universe changed this cosmos into a different sort of place. In the long sweep of this change—in the entire evolution of the universe—astronomers can point to the most signficant epoch in the span of cosmic history, and to an event that occurred throughout the universe at that time, the era when individual objects could begin to form. Calculations made by astronomy show that this time, about a million years after the big bang, also witnessed the release of the cosmic background radiation, the whisper of bygone eras that still brings us news of that long-vanished epoch.

THE MAN WHO SAW THROUGH TIME

George Gamow, born in Odessa in the Russian Empire, in 1904, stood out among the flow of émigré scientists who enriched U.S. culture with his wide-ranging knowledge, his ability as a cartoonist and a communicator of physics to the public, and his sense of humor (Figure 31). The latter trait rose to full flower among a good many of Gamow's generation, who found carefully concealed humor one of the few available tools to confront the difficulties of Stalinist Russia.

Gamow's parents were both teachers in Odessa, where in the late 1890s, Lev Bronstein, one of the father's best students,

circulated a petition seeking his teacher's dismissal;
later, under the new name of Leon Trotsky, Gamow's
father's pupil helped bring on a revolution. Gamow
grew through adolescence during the revolutionary
period and became a precocious student with an
interest in science. He was a thin, gangling youth
nearly six and a half feet tall, with blond hair, highly
noticeable ears, and a capacity for alcohol that amazed
even his fellow Russians. As a student at the
universities of Odessa and Leningrad, which had been
much changed by the revolution, Gamow studied
physics, but he had trouble finding a specialty that
would hold his interest.

Figure 31. George Gamow (1904–1968) was a Russian-born physicist who made important contributions to atomic physics and also predicted the existence of the cosmic microwave background. (Courtesy of the George Gamow collection of the Niels Bohr Library of the American Institute of Physics.)

Luck was on Gamow's side; in 1928 he was allowed
to spend a summer in Germany at the University of
Göttingen, then one of the world centers of theoretical
physics. There, browsing in the library, Gamow read
in a physics journal that the great physicist Ernest
Rutherford found phenomena related to radioactivity—
the spontaneous splitting apart of certain types of atomic
nuclei—extremely difficult to explain. Gamow read
Rutherford's explanation, derived from the traditional
theory called "classical mechanics," which was in the process of
being displaced by the new theory of tiny particles called *quantum
mechanics*. Gamow had learned the new theory; he quickly saw a
better—in fact, the correct—explanation of radioactivity as an
example of quantum mechanics, according to which certain types of
nuclei can split apart without having had any outside force applied
to them. In a few days he put the model for radioactive decay in
mathematically correct form and advanced the field of nuclear physics
a bit closer to an exact science. Gamow sent the paper to a leading
physics journal in Germany, which accepted it for publication.
From then on, Gamow was a name to reckon with in physics.

Upon his return to the Soviet Union, Gamow found himself
a hero. One newspaper wrote that "a son of the working class
[actually of the bourgeois class that Stalin would soon be
liquidating] has explained the tiniest piece of machinery in the
world." Gamow was allowed to travel abroad again, to visit
Rutherford himself in Cambridge, and to spend months at Niels
Bohr's physics institute in Denmark. But in 1931, back in the
Soviet Union once more, Gamow found a repressive climate, full
of suspicion and fear. Now, though he was a respected member of

the physics faculty at Leningrad University, he was denied official permission to attend meetings abroad.

Gamow and his wife decided to emigrate for good. Inventive as always, the couple conceived a plan to sail in a collapsible kayak across the Black Sea to Turkey, and they executed it well—except that an unforeseen storm blew them back to the north. Suddenly, and with (as usual) no explanation or advance notice, the Gamows were actually ordered to attend a scientific meeting in Brussels. They went—and never returned.

Safe in the United States, Gamow continued his research in nuclear physics and let his mind range over a wide variety of topics in science. During the mid-1930s, working in collaboration with Edward Teller, Gamow made an advance in describing nuclear interactions through what are now called the Gamow-Teller parameters. Later, indulging his irrepressible imagination, Gamow decided that calculations about the production of elements in the early universe that he had made in collaboration with his student Ralph Alpher were simply too important not to have Hans Bethe (Figure 40, p. 145) as a co-author. With Bethe on board, the results would forever be the Alpher-Bethe-Gamow theory. However, Bethe refused to sign on to the project, accurately noting that as he had nothing to do with its creation, academic rigor required his nonparticipation in the credit for the result. Undaunted, Gamow simply added Bethe's name to the paper without Bethe's approval, a rare instance of scientific credit being foisted on an unwilling "participant." To his colleagues, Gamow was—in addition to his talents as a theoretical physicist—a great practical joker, a stager of satiric skits, and an amateur magician. To the public, he was the author of easy-to-read books on science, explaining abstruse subjects such as relativity, quantum mechanics, and cosmology through the adventures of an imaginary character named Mr. C. G. H. Tompkins. Generations of students took long steps toward devoting themselves to science because of Gamow's books.

Well before the appearance of the eponymous Alpher-Bethe-Gamow paper in 1948, Gamow had become deeply interested in applying the results of nuclear physics—the science of the smallest known particles—to cosmology, the study of the universe on the largest scales of size. Since the big bang represented the mightiest explosion conceivable, a physicist with a nuclear bent might naturally ask: Which nuclear reactions predominated soon after the big bang? Which types of particles were most likely to have emerged from these reactions? In hindsight, these questions seem evident, but during the early 1950s only Gamow and his co-workers gave them much thought. Indeed the Alpher–Bethe–Gamow paper represents their best effort to see how the predictions of nuclear theory, as then understood, matched the actual universe we find around us. We can measure the relative amounts of the chemical elements on Earth, in the sun, and in other stars, and can compare the measured abundances with the predicted ones.

When Gamow, Alpher, and Herman carried out their research program, they found reasonably good agreement (with notable exceptions) between the observed and predicted abundances of the elements. Their research caused them to think long and hard about how the dense and violent early universe, which made new elements from old, eventually became the calmer, far more rarefied universe we see today. Their work led toward a key insight into the afterglow of creation: As the universe aged, a time must have come when the matter in the universe thinned out to the point that light and other forms of electromagnetic radiation could travel freely throughout the cosmos. From then on this cosmic background radiation has filled the universe with a ghostlike afterglow from the time of creation.

THE TIME OF DECOUPLING

How and why did a universe once opaque to light and other types of electromagnetic radiation suddenly become transparent? To answer this question, we must recognize what happened to radiation traveling through the early universe. In particular, we must think about *photons,* the constituents of the cosmic background radiation.

Photons are the massless particles that form light and all of the other types of electromagnetic radiation. We can think of a photon as a shimmering, vibrating entity that owes its existence solely to the energy that it carries as it moves. This energy is directly proportional to the photon's frequency. For visible light, the frequency specifies the *color*; for other forms of electromagnetic radiation, such as infrared and ultraviolet, the frequency simply specifies the type of radiation.

If you take away all of a photon's energy, the photon will simply vanish—not into some zero-energy, motionless limbo, but completely. And how does a photon lose all its energy? Typically by colliding with another type of particle and giving all its energy to that particle. Photons cannot lose only part of their energy in a collision but must lose all if they lose any. Hence in nearly all cases, when a photon encounters another particle, a hydrogen atom for example, one of two results must occur. Either the photon undergoes no interaction at all—emerging with the same energy it had before the encounter—or it gives *all* its energy to the particle that it hits, and disappears in this process.

In the dense, hot, photon-filled early universe, the second result, in which the photon disappears, occurred strikingly often. Throughout the early years of the universe, each photon would quickly strike a particle, typically a proton or an electron, and vanish. But the intensely hot gas continuously produced new photons, just as hot stars today produce photons because their heat energy makes new photons come into existence.

From the viewpoint of photons, the most signficant fact about the early universe was that, unlike the universe today, *the average time required for a photon to strike another particle and disappear was far less than the age of the universe.* In the early universe, all photons tended to undergo sudden, violent death by collision. Because the universe was hot, however, it continuously produced new photons, mostly of the types called gamma rays and x rays. If this situation had continued to the present day, we would now find the universe filled with a featureless swarm of high-energy photons, a universal photon sea, arriving from all directions in equal amounts.

But as the universe expanded, it cooled, just as the mist from a spray can cools upon exit simply because the escaping gas finds a larger volume to occupy. The cooling of the universe would have appeared to a hardy observer as a decrease in the average speed of the particles that filled the universe. This slowing down does not refer to the speeds of the photons, which have no mass and always travel at the speed of light, but to more familiar particles, such as protons and electrons, which do have mass and did slow down as the universe expanded.

The cooling of the universe allowed the protons to capture electrons into orbit around them by electromagnetic forces. The protons and electrons thus came to form hydrogen atoms, each made of one proton and one electron. For anyone in favor of forming atoms (such as all of us, who consist of atoms), this was a good thing. But for those who seek to find traces of the early universe, a more important effect of the universal expansion is this: *The expansion of the universe continuously robbed the photons of energy.*

How the Expanding Universe Robbed Photons of Energy

The decrease in photons' energy in the expanding universe can be understood as an intriguing aspect of the Doppler effect. As described in chapter 4, the Doppler effect explains why it is that when we observe the photons arriving from a receding source (such as a distant galaxy), we find that the photons have a smaller frequency and *less* energy than they would if no motion occurred. This is precisely what happened to *all* the photons produced in the early universe. Imagine yourself anywhere in the universe, and consider the photons arriving from all directions at random. Each of these photons was emitted at some time in the past; therefore, the photons arrive from parts of the universe—all of it!—that are receding from you. And this is so no matter what your location may be, for the cosmological principle implies that all parts of the universe observe all other parts to be receding.

We may recall that Hubble's Law, which describes the expanding universe, states that all distant objects in the universe are receding from us, and the speed of recession increases for points at greater distances. This means that if we observe a photon arriving from a greater distance, that photon must have spent more time on its journey and must therefore have originated in a point that is receding more rapidly. Thus longer stretches of time provide greater scope for the Doppler effect to do its work of reducing photon frequencies and energies, as seen by any observer, anywhere in the universe.

Suppose, then, that you were a newly formed hydrogen atom, made of a single electron in orbit around a proton. In the early years of the universe, your life would be brief, for the universe would be full of lethal, high-energy photons. Before long, one of these photons would smash into you, sending the electron and proton careening away in different directions, and leaving "you" without much claim to coherent existence, since you would no longer be a whole atom. Small consolation that the collision would also have annihilated the destructive photon! This scenario occurred countless times during the first million years after the big bang—an era when any atom that formed existed only temporarily.

All photons travel at the same *speed,* the speed of light, but they nonetheless have different *energies.* In visible light, the low-frequency, red-light photons have the least energy per photon, and the high-frequency, violet-light photons have the most. If a violet-light photon loses energy, it will become, for example, red light. Just this sort of thing happened as the universe expanded. The expansion of the universe caused every photon to lose energy, and this loss of energy produced a magic moment in the history of the universe, the *time of decoupling.* This moment marks the time when the photons that filled the universe no longer had sufficient energy to keep atoms from forming. Before then, any atom that formed would be quickly broken apart when a photon hit it; afterward, the photons were too weak to destroy atoms.

The time of decoupling occurred about a million years after the big bang. In truth, this was no single moment, but a phrase such as "the many millennia of decoupling" lacks firepower. Compared to the time that had already elapsed since the big bang, the time of decoupling *was* a mere moment. In that moment, the cosmos transformed itself from an opaque universe—one in which photons destroyed themselves by striking particles and therefore could not travel freely through the universe—into a transparent one, in which photons did move freely, because they no longer interacted with any other particles. With their energies lowered, the photons are said to have become "decoupled" from the rest of the universe, since they no longer could do anything to it—or have anything done to them.

The time of decoupling was significant not only for the photons but also for the protons and electrons in the universe: The protons captured electrons to form atoms. For the photons, an equally significant change arose: Photons could travel "forever" through the universe, since the average time for an interaction to occur began to exceed the age of the universe. This has remained true, with the result that most photons have had no interaction with matter since the time of decoupling. The time of decoupling marks the moment when nearly all the trillions upon trillions of photons that spread through the early universe found themselves in an unalterable state, unchanged by impacts with matter (which no longer occurred) and capable of carrying what amounts to the "fossil record" of their once-potent existence onward through billions of years. We call this record the cosmic background radiation.

One key change *did* occur: The expansion of the universe continued to reduce the energies of all the photons, just as it had

But the universal expansion brought a welcome relief: The Doppler effect steadily lowered the energy of each photon, at least as perceived by any atom, anywhere in the universe. Hence, eventually there came a time when, if you formed an atom, a photon might indeed collide with you, but—pity the photon!—it would have lacked sufficient energy to knock the electron out of its orbit around the proton. In such a case, the rules of atomic physics show that even if the photon heads straight for the atom, the photon will usually pass right by with no interaction whatsoever, something like a barfly with a bad opening line. Thus once the photons from the early moments of the universe no longer had sufficient energy to make a hydrogen's atom jump into a larger orbit, their days of interacting with the rest of the universe were over—except for rare instances such as those that occur in specialized detectors used by radio astronomers.

before decoupling. At the time of decoupling, most of the photons in the universe were ultraviolet photons, with energies slightly less than the minimum energy needed to destroy a hydrogen atom. During the ensuing 15 billion years, the ongoing expansion of the universe has decreased all the photons' energies by a factor of about *one thousand*. Because of this decline in energy, the photons that fill the universe today are a pale, low-energy version of what they were at the time of decoupling. During the 15 billion years following the time of decoupling, the photons that fill the universe have remained entirely unchanged by interactions with matter, but each of them has lost 99.9 percent of the energy it had at the time of decoupling—thanks to the continuing expansion of the universe.

IDEAL RADIATORS

The early universe emitted photons simply because it was hot, and all objects of temperatures above absolute zero emit photons. Once scientists recognized this fact, they reached an additional, highly significant conclusion. The spectrum of the photons in the cosmic

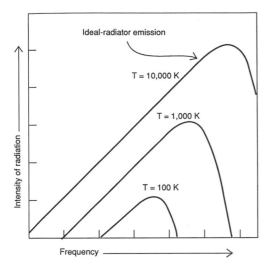

Figure 32. The spectrum of an ideal radiator shows a characteristic shape, in which the intensity of the emission peaks at a particular frequency, which depends on the temperature of the radiator. The intensity falls off sharply at frequencies greater than that of the peak emission. (Drawing by Crystal Stevenson.)

background radiation must have had a shape familiar to physicists, the shape of an *ideal radiator* (Figure 32).

The term "ideal radiator" (formerly called a "black body") refers to a mental construct of physicists, an idealized object that many familiar objects resemble but do not quite match. An ideal radiator absorbs *all* the radiation that impinges upon it. Furthermore, an ideal radiator reradiates into space, at every frequency, exactly as much energy each second as it absorbs. Familiar objects—people, houses, and trees, for example —do absorb and emit radiation simultaneously, as an ideal radiator does, but the absorption and emission in real objects are not perfectly matched. For example, a person's clothing absorbs some colors of visible light but emits infrared radiation and almost no visible light at all. (We see the person by the visible light that is reflected from his or her body, which is not the same thing as the actual emission of new photons.) At modest temperatures, such an ideal radiator would appear completely black, because it would emit and absorb only infrared radiation, but at higher temperatures an ideal radiator would glow like a star—and indeed, stars rather closely resemble ideal radiators.

THE SPECTRUM OF RADIATION FROM AN IDEAL RADIATOR

Because an ideal radiator emits and absorbs the same amount of radiation at all frequencies, it achieves a perfect equilibrium with its surroundings. Photons strike the ideal radiator and are absorbed, while at the same time the ideal radiator emits photons in exactly the same numbers and frequencies. For example, a black graphite brick provides a reasonable facsimile of an ideal radiator; almost all the photons—mostly infrared photons that we cannot see—striking the brick are absorbed, and the brick simultaneously emits photons. Almost all of the emitted photons are infrared because of the brick's low temperature.

During the last years of the nineteenth century and the early years of the twentieth, ideal radiators engaged the attention of physicists who sought to explain why *every ideal radiator emits radiation with a particular spectral shape.* Physicists knew this shape because an ideal radiator can be created rather easily (to a high degree of approximation) in a laboratory: You can attempt to make a perfectly absorbing object, perhaps a graphite brick, and let it stand quietly, so that it achieves equilibrium between the radiation it absorbs and the radiation it emits. Then you measure the amount of radiation emitted at each frequency. You will find that the object emits radiation whose spectrum—the amount of radiation emitted at each frequency—shows a slow rise to a peak at a particular frequency and then a precipitous falloff for radiation at higher frequencies. You will also find that the numerical value of the peak frequency depends only on the *temperature* of the ideal radiator, in a straightforward manner: An ideal radiator twice as hot as another will have its spectral peak at twice as high a frequency.

In the year 1900, the German physicist Max Planck showed that he could explain why the spectrum of an ideal radiator has the same shape for all ideal radiators, and why the peak in the spectrum depends only on the temperature—but only if he made a peculiar assumption. Planck assumed that *energy appears in the universe only in "quantized" form,* that is, only with numerical values that are multiples of a single basic unit, the "quantum" of energy. Physicists now call this quantum unit *Planck's constant* and easily accept the notion that energy can take only certain definite values, but Planck never quite believed in this principle, despite his success in explaining the spectrum of an ideal radiator. Planck's notion, which underlies the entire branch of physics called *quantum mechanics,* soon gained general acceptance. Physicists such as Albert Einstein, Niels Bohr, and Enrico Fermi demonstrated the wealth of phenomena in atomic and nuclear physics that could find a coherent explanation through the adoption of the *quantum postulate,* the idea that energy comes only in multiples of Planck's basic unit.

Once scientists seriously considered the radiation produced by the early universe, they saw that *the entire universe must have been an ideal radiator.* In the early universe, no type of electromagnetic radiation could travel far without hitting some particle, perhaps a proton or an electron, and being absorbed. But the particles, seething and frothing in constant motion, would promptly emit more radiation. Taken as a whole, the collection of particles would be a near-perfect ideal radiator, absorbing just as much energy each second as the particles were emitting, and at every frequency.

Hence radiation must have filled the universe, and this radiation must have had the spectrum of an ideal radiator. The radiation constitutes the cosmic background radiation, and the recognizable shape of the spectrum of the background radiation we measure today allows us to identify it as the relic of the early universe.

During the early stages of the expansion of the universe, the radiation that filled it kept interacting with the particles, continually being absorbed and re-emitted. Today, this radiation still has the spectral shape of an ideal-radiator spectrum. What has changed are the wavelengths of the radiation and the location of the *peak* in the spectrum. The Doppler effect in the expanding, cooling universe has continuously shifted the peak of the universe's ideal-radiator output to lower frequencies. Had an observer been present at a time anywhere from a few hours to a million years after the big bang, that observer would have been immersed in a bath of radiation, that is, among photons of all frequencies, but with a single frequency most strongly represented—the peak of the ideal-radiator spectrum.

And what happened after the time of decoupling, the time when the radiation stopped interacting with the matter (now mostly atoms)? Even though interactions had ceased, the radiation had nowhere to go. It continued to fill the universe, a pale spectre present everywhere. The only thing that must have happened to the radiation was a continuing decrease in the frequencies and an increase in the wavelengths of all the photons forming the radiation. These changes would have had the same fractional amount for every frequency and wavelength of the photons. The changes in frequency and wavelength arose from the Doppler effect caused by the expansion of the universe: Any observer detecting this "afterglow of the big bang," the radiation that fills the universe as a background to everything else we observe, must be detecting radiation from a source receding at high velocity—a distant part of the universe.

THE DISCOVERY OF THE BACKGROUND RADIATION

During the late 1940s, George Gamow and his colleagues Ralph Alpher and Robert Herman worked on the problem of the origin of the elements and pondered the early universe. Almost in passing (because their minds focused on the question of how the elements

were made), Alpher and Herman noted in a paper, published in
1948 in the British journal *Nature,* that the universe should be filled
with radiation, and that this radiation's spectrum would be that of
an ideal radiator with a temperature about 5 degrees Centigrade
above absolute zero.

Alpher, Gamow, and Herman thus saw that the universe
should contain an ancient cosmic relic, the residue of radiation left
over from the universe's first million years: photons of all
frequencies, with the spectral shape characteristic of an ideal
radiator. Their work was purely theoretical. For 15 years,
observational astronomers showed little interest in pursuing the
cosmic relic predicted by theory. Steven Weinberg, a Nobel
laureate in physics, has recalled that in those days all theories of the
early universe seemed so far removed from reality that no physicist
took any of them seriously—certainly not to the point of asking
what now seem brilliantly reasonable questions: Should we look for
the predicted relic of the early universe, the cosmic background
radiation produced 15 billion years ago? Wouldn't the existence of
this radiation help verify that the universe was indeed born in a hot
big bang, capable of filling the cosmos with a sea of photons,
characterized by the spectrum characteristic of an ideal radiator?
With these questions unasked, the cosmic background radiation,
the "afterglow of the big bang," went unlooked for—and
undetected.

The discovery of the cosmic background radiation occurred
in 1964, nearly two decades after Alpher, Gamow, and Herman had
hypothesized its existence. Sadly enough from the viewpoint of
theoreticians, this discovery occurred entirely without the scientists
involved knowing anything about the theoretical prediction that
had been made years before. Two radio astronomers at the Bell
Laboratories in New Jersey, Arno Penzias and Robert Wilson, set
out to test a new type of horn antenna constructed primarily to
detect radio echoes from satellites. Penzias and Wilson were puzzled
by the stray "noise" that their specialized antenna detected despite
their best efforts to eliminate all possible sources of extraneous
radiation. They consulted astronomers at Princeton University
who—influenced by their reexamination of the prediction made by
Alpher, Gamow, and Herman—were about to undertake an
experiment to look for the cosmic background radiation.

The Princeton professors immediately recognized that the
Bell Labs astronomers had gotten there first. Penzias and Wilson
had detected radiation in roughly the amount predicted by Gamow,

Alpher, and Herman. Furthermore, they found that *the radiation arrives in equal amounts from all directions.* This led to the hypothesis that the radiation must be a "cosmic background," for if the radiation came from "localized" sources—stars, the Milky Way, or even clusters of galaxies—it would arrive from different directions in different amounts.

Penzias and Wilson measured the radiation at several different wavelengths in the portion of the spectrum accessible to their telescope and detector, and they confirmed that, so far as they could tell, the radiation had the spectral shape predicted for an ideal radiator at a temperature just less than 3 degrees (Centigrade) above absolute zero. In this case, the ideal radiator that the scientists observed was the long-vanished early universe, and the temperature they measured for its radiation was not far different from the estimate made nearly two decades before by Alpher and Herman.

In 1978, Penzias and Wilson received the Nobel Prize in physics for their discovery, which brilliantly confirmed the theory of a universe that began expanding from a "big bang" and produced an afterglow of radiation that persists even today (Figure 33). Some maverick astronomers, of whom Fred Hoyle is the best known, have proposed alternative explanations for the diffuse radiation that arrives in equal amounts from all directions. Nevertheless, by far the majority of astronomers accept as its most reasonable explanation the hypothesis that the early, hot universe was permeated with radiation, and that this radiation, ever since the time of decoupling that allowed the radiation to travel freely, has continued to fill the cosmos, growing continuously cooler as the universe has gone on expanding.

Figure 33. Arno Penzias (right) and Robert Wilson (left) of Bell Labs are photographed in front of the radio antenna with which they first detected the cosmic background radiation. (Courtesy of Bell Laboratories.)

THE VEIL OF ATMOSPHERE

This sounds fine, and indeed is fine, so far as it goes. But as the initial excitement over the discovery faded, astronomers focused on the key problem that remained in observing the cosmic background radiation: the need for a *complete* view of the radiation that had been predicted long before its discovery. Measurements made by radio astronomers such as Penzias and Wilson revealed only a small part of the spectrum. The most significant spectral region—the frequencies and wavelengths where the radiation should reach a maximum amount—remained completely undetected and therefore unmeasured. This lack of key observational data arose from the action of a familiar culprit: the Earth's atmosphere.

As we saw in chapter 1, our atmosphere absorbs most types of electromagnetic radiation and permits only light waves and radio waves to penetrate to the Earth's surface. Penzias and Wilson detected and measured radio waves of relatively high frequencies (for radio waves), but they had no hope of detecting radiation with still higher frequencies—submillimeter waves and infrared radiation—because of atmospheric absorption. However, the theory of the early universe predicts that *most* of the cosmic background radiation has just these higher frequencies. If you hope to observe the bulk of the background radiation, you must therefore formulate a plan to observe from above the Earth's atmosphere. In the United States, the people who seek to do just that concentrate in a key location: Berkeley, California.

THE UNIVERSITY OF CALIFORNIA AND LICK OBSERVATORY

Three thousand miles to the west of Boston, far across the North American continent, once so distant from the East Coast that news took weeks to arrive from the newest of the United States, lies the fabulous land of California, a state of mind as well as of the Union.

The southern third of the state now contains the bulk of its population, along with the political clout, most of the millionaires, and the movie and television industry. Northern California nevertheless contains nearly 10 million people, more than half of them concentrated around the San Francisco Bay, the watery glory of the region, which opened California to settlement and commerce because of the calm anchorages it offered to ships that sailed in through its narrowing opening to the sea. This break in the coastal mountains, missed by Sir Francis Drake when he first sailed by in 1596, is the "Golden Gate." John C. Fremont, an adventurous explorer who awakened the world to the glories of the western half of the continent, bestowed this name, a happy prolepsis of the discovery that would bring a flood of fortune seekers around the world more than a decade later. Fremont became one of California's first two senators in 1850 and ran for president in 1856 as the Republican Party's first candidate, surprising his backers as well as the opposition by coming close to victory.

Most of the speculators and developers who came to California soon after Fremont did anticipated that the Bay Area would be dominated not by San Francisco, which occupies the northern tip of a promontory on the west side of San Francisco Bay, but instead by a site somewhere on the bay's east side, to which ships could easily sail to discharge their cargoes on what might be called the continental side of the water. Opinions varied as to the most favorable location; some looked to Oakland, directly across from San Francisco, while others favored the mouth of the San Joaquin River, near the town of Benicia (which briefly was California's capital). As a young army lieutenant, William T. Sherman, destined to become a San Francisco banker and then a Civil War hero, not only helped to survey the site for a city at the San Joaquin's mouth, modestly named "New York of the Pacific," but also cleared 500 dollars selling building lots to speculators more convinced than he of the town's future.

No one seemed much interested in land in Berkeley, just to the north of Oakland, where wood houses stood at several points along the creek that flows westward into the bay from the hills a mile east. But after the state legislature decided to create a state university along the lines of those in the East and Midwest, a committee was appointed to examine potential sites in the Bay Area. In April 1860, standing on what is now called "Founders' Rock," members of the committee chose a gently sloping site in Berkeley, directly opposite the Golden Gate, as the proper place for the University of California. Today the Berkeley campus, teeming with 32,000 students and a distinguished faculty, ranks as the largest (though tied with UCLA) of the nine campuses that make California's one of the finest of all state universities.

The university has astronomical research facilities far beyond the Berkeley campus. The oldest and still the most prominent of these is Lick Observatory, which was originally funded by James Lick. Lick arrived in San Francisco just before the Gold Rush and soon made a fortune in real estate that far outstripped Sherman's. He died a bachelor, a miser, and an atheist in an era when nonbelief was rarely admitted in polite society. During his later years, while living in the Lick House—a large hotel that he owned—Lick became interested in leaving a monument to himself and his parents: perhaps statues of all three large enough to be seen miles out at sea, or the world's largest pyramid, to be sited in downtown San Francisco. Wiser heads brought Lick to consider science for his memorial, and he thought of building the world's largest telescope in downtown San Francisco. But after further discussion, Lick decided to build the first year-round mountaintop observatory, on the summit of Mount Hamilton, 20 miles east of San Jose. There, more than 4,000 feet above sea level, the atmosphere was remarkably still; and once Santa Clara County had built what was called the "windingest road in the world," mules began to haul the equipment for the world's largest telescope, a refractor with a 36-inch lens, as fine as any that could be made even today.

Lick died in 1876, but before doing so, he had arranged to bequeath the money for the telescope and seemed to adopt the scientists' suggestion (hardly one that would naturally arise nowadays) that, in view of all that he had done, his body should eventually rest within its foundation. By 1887, with the telescope and the observatory nearing completion, the time for Lick's reburial had arrived. George Davidson, the pioneer California scientist who had done the most to persuade Lick to his benefaction, recalled that Lick had been dead set against cremation, insisting that "I intend to rot like a gentleman." Before being set into its vault within the telescope pier, Lick's coffin was opened for a final look, and Davidson reported that "it was evident that [Lick's] wish had been fulfilled."

Lick's resting place soon became the chief astronomical observatory in the United States (to be equaled, and eventually surpassed, by the Mount Wilson Observatory some 30 years later). A 36-inch reflecting telescope soon joined the 36-inch refractor (still the world's second largest telescope that uses a lens rather than a mirror). Despite antagonism between the incompetent first observatory director, Edward S. Holden, and his highly competent staff (one of whom would eventually refer to Holden as "our former colleague and fake"), significant results soon began to emerge on Mount Hamilton. Jupiter's fifth moon was discovered with the giant refractor in 1892, the first satellite of Jupiter to be found since Galileo saw the first four in the year 1610. Eventually Lick astronomers discovered Jupiter's sixth, seventh, eighth, ninth, and tenth satellites. They also pioneered the science of astronomical spectroscopy—the study of the composition of cosmic objects through analysis of the colors of light that they emit or absorb. Lick Observatory astronomers applied spectroscopy to the analysis of stars, with great success in showing what stars are made of. And at Lick, Heber Curtis made key observations of spiral galaxies— which would later prove that these objects lie far beyond our own Milky Way—while other astronomers determined the composition of gaseous nebulae such as the great cloud in Orion.

Today Lick Observatory remains a key player in the world of astronomy. Its largest telescope is the 120-inch reflector, built during the 1950s. But in contrast to its first half-century, when the observatory amounted to an extension of the Berkeley campus, the telescopes now serve astronomers associated with the university campuses in Berkeley, Los Angeles, San Diego, Santa Barbara, Irvine, and, most notably, Santa Cruz, which now has the responsibility for maintaining the observatory.

Today physicists as well as astronomers practice astronomy. During the last 20 years a steady influx of physicists into the field of astronomy has occurred, the result of physicists' (correct) perception that astronomy offers a host of intriguing problems waiting for their expertise. A typical university now does astronomical research in both its astronomy and physics departments. This is particularly true on the Berkeley campus.

The Berkeley physics department alone has had seven Nobelists on the faculty, of whom the most influential today is University Professor Charles Townes, the co-discoverer of the maser and laser. In the mid-1960s, at the height of his career, Townes left MIT for Berkeley and switched from physics to astrophysics. At Berkeley he attracted a group of students and fellow researchers who have played key roles in opening previously unobservable regions of the electromagnetic spectrum, most notably the infrared, submillimeter, and microwave (short-wavelength radio) domains, to astronomical observation. Townes also helped to attract Paul Richards, who more than anyone else has stood at the center of efforts to observe the cosmic microwave background from above the atmosphere.

PAUL RICHARDS AND THE QUEST TO RISE ABOVE THE ATMOSPHERE

Richards is a man notable not only for his own achievements but also (like Townes) for his "school" of former students, and their former students. Twenty years younger than Townes, Richards is now halfway through his fifties (Figure 34). He has a strikingly handsome face, framed with marvelous, nearly white hair, and with eyes that radiate a calm and can-do belief in himself.

Richards was born in Ithaca in 1934, where his father had finished his graduate studies in physics and was attempting to find the right job for his talents. This was not an easy task, for Richards's father wanted to apply his knowledge of physics to *agriculture* at a time when funds for agricultural research were near zero. Eventually, however, the right job came along at the Department of Agriculture's research station near Riverside, California. There his father studied how to grow better crops and wrote (among other things) *Soil Physics,* a textbook well-known to agriculture students.

Paul Richards grew up in Riverside and in Pasadena, close to Caltech, where his father had contacts with the physicists there (who referred to him behind his back as "that damn agronomist"). During World War II, Richards's father made use of his graduate physics training as head of a group that developed rocket launch systems. Richards's mother has said that Paul "had Ohm's Law [the fundamental principle of electricity] for dinner." In 1952, Richards was admitted to Harvard; and in 1960, three years after graduating from that college, he received his Ph.D. in physics from Berkeley, with a thesis on superconductivity.

Figure 34. Paul Richards, professor of physics at the University of California at Berkeley, is a pioneer in making observations of the cosmic background radiation from high altitudes. (Photograph by Sally Weare.)

Richards spent a postdoctoral year at Cambridge University in England and some time at Bell Labs in New Jersey, where Townes had been encouraged to develop the maser a few years earlier. In the mid-1960s, one of Richards's Berkeley professors recruited him for the Berkeley physics faculty. At that time Richards specialized in using infrared measurements to investigate the properties of solid objects. In the summer of 1969, when the university awarded him a coveted "Miller Fellowship" to spend time on pure research, he got interested in the attempts to measure the cosmic background radiation, the afterglow of the big bang that began the universe.

Richards was not the first astrophysicist to attempt to observe the cosmic background from above the atmosphere, but he has been the most persistent, and the most influential. In 1972, Richards was intrigued by the first balloon-borne experiments to measure the background radiation, which were conducted by an MIT team of scientists led by Rainer Weiss, one of the most innovative experimenters in physics today (see chapter 13). The balloon's results, rather crude by today's standards, seemed to match the predictions for an ideal radiator's spectrum, but they primarily led to additional, more sophisticated experiments.

During the 1970s, Paul Richards, in collaboration with another Berkeley professor, David Woody, and a student of Richards's, John Mather, launched a series of balloon-borne detectors. These experiments revealed for the first time that the spectrum of the cosmic background radiation does have a peak at almost the same frequency in the far infrared that theory had predicted. But the experiments also showed that the observed spectrum did not quite match the predicted spectrum—a result that was eventually shown to arise from difficulties with the balloon-borne detectors. Richards comments that "it can sometimes take as long as 10 years to pin down and understand the limitations of one's data in such experiments. . . . That is the most difficult aspect of [cosmic] background astronomy." This remark wryly sums up the difficulty of doing observational science on the cutting edge: Almost by definition, you are performing an experiment that is likely to go wrong, for if the experiment were easy, it would already have been performed. This point was emphasized by the results of the next key experiment, launched by Richards and his young colleague Andrew Lange.

Lange looks like an all-American boy, born in Illinois in 1957 and raised in Connecticut, the son of an architect and a schoolteacher (Figure 35). Like nearly every astronomer, he developed an interest in science early in life, and while still in high school he read many books about relativity and cosmology, including George Gamow's popularizations. In 1976, while Richards was struggling with his first balloon experiments, Lange entered Princeton University. As a freshman, he took a physics

Figure 35. Andrew Lange of the Physics Department at the University of California, Berkeley, has collaborated for many years with Paul Richards to measure the cosmic background radiation. (Photograph by Sally Weare.)

course from Dave Wilkinson, one of the professors most interested in the cosmic background (and who had just missed discovering it before Penzias and Wilson did). Impressed by Wilkinson, Lange began to hang out with the group studying the cosmic background radiation. When he decided to go to Berkeley for his graduate studies, Wilkinson suggested that he look up Paul Richards to discuss research projects. Lange did so and found his career.

Richards initially tried to steer Lange into observing the background in microwaves, some of which do pass through the atmosphere, but Lange, sensing that the action lay in rising above the atmosphere, managed to become part of the balloon project. The balloons (which never yielded much useful data during Lange's two years with the project) were launched from Palestine, Texas, chosen for its isolation. There, in 1982, Lange was passing the time waiting for proper launch conditions when Richards paid a visit on his way back to Berkeley from Munich and told Lange of a rewarding afternoon that he had spent in a beer garden with Satio Hayakawa—an afternoon that would redirect eight years of Lange's efforts.

Hayakawa was one of Japan's best-known astrophysicists, a professor (later rector) at Nagoya University. He knew Richards's work well and admired his efforts to develop detectors capable of measuring radiation whose frequencies lie close to those near the peak of the spectrum of the cosmic background. Hayakawa suggested a Japanese-American collaboration to launch a rocket above the atmosphere: The Japanese would build the rocket and the equipment to house the detector, which would be provided by the

Berkeley group. Lange made it clear that he wanted to work on this project, and after its approval by both universities, he started work in the spring of 1983 to design and build a detector to measure the afterglow of the big bang.

The key to any such detector, as in many areas of astronomy, would be to keep it *cold*. The attempt to measure a tiny amount of radiation—especially radiation arriving equally from all directions—could succeed only if stray, interfering sources of radiation could be kept to an absolute minimum. The closest and most obvious source would be the detector and the rocket. By observing only after the rocket motors have been left behind and by cooling the detector as close as possible to absolute zero by surrounding it with liquid helium, this interference would be reduced, though not eliminated.

Working with impressive speed, Lange and Richards had a detector ready to "fly," as rocket scientists still say, by the fall of 1985. Prepared for three minutes of observation, the Japanese rocket took off from the southern tip of Japan and worked perfectly, but the instrument cover never opened. Undaunted, the scientists returned to their drawing boards and produced an improved detector. The Japanese produced another rocket, and in 1987, the year that Lange received his Ph.D. from Berkeley, the rocket flew and the detector recorded data. Once the data were analyzed, Lange was invited to join the Berkeley faculty as an assistant professor, and theorists the world over speculated about the startling results from a three-minute flight 200 miles high.

THE GRAPH THAT LAUNCHED A HUNDRED PAPERS

In the spring of 1987, borne by the Japanese rocket from its launch pad on Kyushu, the southernmost island of Japan, the instrument package finally soared into space. Its sensitive detector had a few minutes to observe at six different frequencies before the rocket plunged into the sea. When Lange and his collaborators released their results, they provoked a firestorm of interest among cosmologists: The observations revealed a cosmic background that did not conform to the spectrum of an ideal radiator.

More precisely, the observations at *two* of the six frequencies did not conform (Figure 36). But these two discordant points,

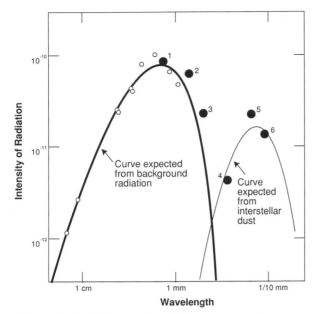

Figure 36. In 1987, a rocket flight measured the spectrum of the cosmic background radiation at six different points (indicated by numbers). Two of these six points—numbers two and three—differed from the spectrum produced by an ideal radiator (solid line). The difference may appear small but amounts to the measurement of a great deal more energy in the cosmic background radiation than conventional theory could explain. (Courtesy of Professor Paul Richards; drawing by Crystal Stevenson.)

whose frequencies lay just beyond the peak of the ideal-radiator spectrum, were the crucial ones: They could show for the first time whether the radiation beyond the peak did or did not follow the spectrum of an ideal radiator. It did not. Points 2 and 3 lay significantly above the ideal-radiator spectrum. The discrepancy may seem small on a graph, but to an expert, the deviation implied that the early universe had somehow created far more energy than the standard big-bang theory could explain. Even with the disclaimers issued by the Berkeley-Nagoya team concerning the difficulty of making these measurements, the rocket results brought a wave of excitement to cosmology. Since the two discrepant frequencies lie in the low-frequency part of the infrared region, the observations made at points 2 and 3 were called the *infrared excess*—more infrared radiation than could be explained by a cosmic background with an ideal-radiator spectrum. Cosmologists who calculated the amount of additional energy represented by the infrared excess, under the assumption that the excess represents a universal phenomenon, found this amount to be enormous, several times greater than all the energy in the previously assumed background radiation. If the Berkeley-Nagoya observations were correct, they had revealed what might be *most* of the energy in the universe!

Responding to news of the infrared excess, cosmological theorists quickly produced a host of papers that attempted to explain the excess radiation. These papers covered a cosmic range. Some theorists speculated about an entire new class of objects, some sort of superstars or primeval galaxies, that had somehow appeared in the early universe and exploded. In the excitement of the infrared excess, one thing stood out clearly: If its existence could be confirmed, theorists would be strained to their limits to explain it.

The key word here is "confirmed." No observation can command respect from scientists unless a repeated experiment yields the same result. For example, if the annals of humanity recorded a single tornado, scientists would doubt whether that tornado had indeed been real. The same holds true for Bigfoot and the Loch Ness monster: They remain unconfirmed to scientists until repeated, reliable, sightings have been reported; until then, with only anecdotal, usually unverified reports, scientists remain skeptical.

Hence from the moment that their 1987 rocket flight returned usable data, Lange, Richards, and their co-workers strove to launch another rocket experiment that would obtain further, independent observations to check points 2 and 3 from the 1987 flight—two data points that had produced a hundred scientific papers. Working as rapidly as they could, the Berkeley-Nagoya collaborators prepared a new detector. By using new techniques and a special kind of helium, this detector could be cooled not merely to one degree above absolute zero, but to one-tenth of a degree—the low-temperature record for experiments flown in space. By the summer of 1989, the scientists had their instrument package ready for launch to secure three additional minutes of observation that would either verify their first results or at least allow the announcement to come from their own lips that the earlier data had been mistaken.

Launching a rocket, even one that will simply rise and fall

without placing anything into orbit, takes an immense effort. It also requires some luck with the weather, and in the case of launches from the Kagoshima Science Center, some coordination with one of the key Japanese fishing fleets. To prevent unwanted mishaps, the fleet must avoid the area where the rocket will descend, but this means a loss of several days of fishing. Hence the launch in summer 1989 was poised on an edge of tension: If weather delayed it too long, it would be postponed indefinitely to let the fleet resume its work through the fishing season.

After several days of delay and intense concern, the Japanese rocket rose through its planned trajectory on the morning of July 11, 1989. The rocket-borne instrument package recorded data as planned, but when the scientists retrieved the data, they experienced a horrid anticlimax. The data lay buried beneath "interference"— the overlain effect of radio noise arising within their instruments— tantalizingly close to being recoverable through sophisticated computer analysis. Excruciatingly, although this analysis proceeded through the fall of 1989 and into early 1990, Lange and his co-workers never did obtain usable results from the 1989 rocket flight. And then events overtook the Nagoya-Berkeley experiments in a way that was both painful and joyful.

THE COBE SATELLITE: CRUCIAL MEASUREMENTS OF THE BACKGROUND

In November 1989, four months after the rocket flight in Japan, NASA launched its Cosmic Background Explorer satellite (COBE) from California into Earth orbit. COBE was created by teams of scientists and engineers, built at the Goddard Space Flight Center in Maryland, and redesigned and rebuilt after the Challenger accident made a shuttle launch impossible. The satellite was the product of fifteen years of labor by hundreds of people, many of whom had moved on to new positions, or retirement, before COBE was finally launched.

Of all those involved in the COBE project, none bore more of the responsibility, or more of the agony and ecstasy, than John Mather, the chief project scientist—another prize pupil of Paul Richards's (Figure 37). Born in New Jersey in 1946, the son of a professor of animal husbandry, Mather showed an early interest in science, particularly in astronomy: He devoured books on telescope making and soon showed a mastery of the experimental side of science.

Attending the University of California, Mather met two key physics professors, Charles Townes and Paul Richards. Richards drew Mather into a project to observe the cosmic background radiation from California's White Mountain, little known but more than 14,000 feet high. Some of the radiation incapable of reaching sea level penetrated to the summit of White Mountain, and there, despite the hardships brought on by altitude, one could hope to make significant observations.

Mather's results from White Mountain helped to refute the deviation from an ideal-radiator spectrum that Richards and his colleague David Woody had reported after an early flight of a balloon-borne detector. With the limits of White Mountain evident, Mather joined the effort to make further balloon-borne observations. Though the balloon's playload did not function properly on the flight that was meant to provide observational data for his Ph.D. thesis, Mather received his degree all the same. In science, negative results have their own worth, and Mather's White Mountain observations, combined with his efforts to gather data from the balloon flights, were sufficient.

From Berkeley, Mather went to a postdoctoral appointment at the Goddard Institute for Space Studies in New York (named after the United States' first pioneer of spaceflight, Robert Goddard), where he sought to leave behind observations of the

Figure 37. John Mather of the Goddard Space Flight Center led the COBE science team that first measured the spectrum of the cosmic background radiation from a satellite orbiting above the Earth's atmosphere. (Photograph by Donald Goldsmith.)

cosmic background radiation for other areas of radio astronomy. One day, however, the astronomer Pat Thaddeus drew Mather's attention to an "Announcement of Opportunity" sent out by NASA to potentially interested scientists, describing a potential satellite to observe the cosmic background. Thaddeus and Mather, along with Rainer Weiss of MIT, Dave Wilkinson of Princeton, and several other scientists, submitted a proposal for what became the COBE satellite.

By June 1976, Mather was in Greenbelt, Maryland, at NASA's Goddard Space Flight Center. Six years later, the COBE satellite received official approval, and by the beginning of 1986, the satellite was almost complete. Then, just when all seemed ready for an early launch on the Space Shuttle, on January 28, 1986, the *Challenger* exploded.

In the explosion's aftermath, it became clear that when Space Shuttle flights resumed, none of them would be made from Vandenberg Air Force Base in California. Only from Vandenberg could COBE achieve an orbit around the Earth's north and south poles, which was essential for accurate observation. Thus the COBE scientists had to redesign their satellite for launch by a Delta rocket, one of the last that NASA had at its disposal. "Redesign" meant stripping more than half the weight from the satellite, without sacrificing its ability to make accurate observations! But within two years the scientists and engineers on the COBE team had a re-formed satellite, two-and-a-half tons lighter than the original version. The reengineered COBE soared into space on November 18, 1989, deployed its sunshield and oriented itself in its polar orbit. Soon it began to return streams of data to Earth for analysis. These data set the record straight on the background radiation and deepened the mystery of how galaxies ever began to form in the universe.

What are these data, and what do they tell us about the early universe? COBE carries three detectors to reveal new facts about the cosmos. The first of these is Mather's chief instrument, the Far-Infrared Astronomical Spectrometer (FIRAS). FIRAS has a single goal: the accurate measurement of the spectrum of the cosmic background radiation, not at only a few frequencies, like those measured in the rocket flights, but at nearly a hundred different frequencies that include the peak in the ideal-radiator spectrum. In short, FIRAS aims to resolve once and for all the question of whether the background radiation does or does not match the spectrum of an ideal radiator.

The second of COBE's instruments is the Diffuse Infrared Background Explorer (DIRBE), which detects objects that radiate primarily in the far-infrared region of the spectrum. Such objects would most likely be far-distant galaxies, so distant that their radiation is highly redshifted by the universal expansion, and so old that they would not be much like galaxies today but instead should be full of warm dust in gas clouds that later formed stars.

The third COBE instrument is the Diffuse Microwave Radiometer (DMR), which maps the entire sky at three different microwave frequencies unobservable from the Earth's surface, seeking to find deviations from smoothness in the background radiation. Such deviations would have supreme importance to cosmologists, because they could and should be relics of the "seeds" that formed galaxies.

All theories of galaxy formation predict that as galaxies began to form—as matter collected into localized agglomerations— the act of clumping must have left an imprint on the background radiation passing through the clumps. This imprint would appear as slight differences in the amount of radiation produced in regions where matter was crowded together at densities somewhat higher or lower than average. Although the deviations from smoothness would be small, they are predictable in amount and should be detectable. If they are not, theorists would be at a loss to explain the formation of galaxies: They rely on the existence of the "seeds" of galaxies at the time of decoupling to explain how galaxies ever condensed.

Once COBE began to send data back to the Goddard Space Flight Center, the COBE scientists had to deal with a dilemma that they had anticipated and resolved. Spurred by the tension over whether or not the rocket data were correct, the scientists confronted the temptation to pass even their first data from COBE to colleagues around the world, all of whom were eager to learn whether or not the infrared excess existed, and what COBE had to say about the formation of galaxies. But the COBE scientists had no desire to apologize later for conclusions hastily drawn on the basis of insufficient data. They told the world not to expect much for many months and modified this dampening of enthusiasm only as they found that their instruments were performing magnificently. Then Mather and his colleagues decided to release their first results at the meeting of the American astronomical Society, the prime organization of North American Astronomers.

Held in Washington, D.C., early in January 1990, this meeting was the largest that the society had ever held: Nearly 2,000 of its 5,500 members appeared, not least because they had heard that the first COBE results would be announced.

And there John Mather gave his astronomical colleagues a thrill that far surpassed what they had felt when Vice President Quayle had addressed the meeting a few days earlier, stressing that "America is back in space" and urging forward the day when astronauts would plant the U.S. flag on Mars. The fact is that many space scientists are hostile to manned space flight. They believe that good scientific data can be more easily obtained with unmanned spacecraft at far less cost and with no risk to human life. (The vice president's reception was well summarized by the headline in the *Washington Post,* which read "Scientists a Tough Audience for Quayle.") Mather, a tall, long-jawed man with a patient, schoolteacher look, reached the high point of his talk on the FIRAS results with the first spectrum of the cosmic background radiation obtained by a satellite. As Mather laid the spectrum on the viewgraph that projected it to his audience, the astronomers broke into applause. The spectrum, made of 80 individual observations at 80 different frequencies, matched the ideal-radiator shape to perfection (Figure 38). The infrared excess had vanished with the applause that had swept through the hall.

Lange and Richards were downcast but not defeated. "We built a pretty good experiment," Lange said later, "but there are limits to what you can do." Of course, says Lange, "speaking selfishly, it would have been nice to see [that we were wrong] before COBE." The fact remains that science at the edge of technological capability can easily be wrong. Even today it is not obvious what subtle problem produced the two data points from the 1987 rocket flight that so baffled cosmologists. Lange and Richards made neither the first nor the last difficult experiment that ultimately proved incorrect; what counts is that they did what they could; they knew the difficulties well; and they approached their results with objectivity and skepticism.

COBE's success soon made the spectrum of the cosmic background radiation into old news. So far as COBE is concerned, attention now focuses on the Differential Microwave Radiometer—the instrument that may reveal the seeds of galaxy formation more than 10 billion years old. COBE has verified an effect already known to astronomers, the result of our own galaxy's motion

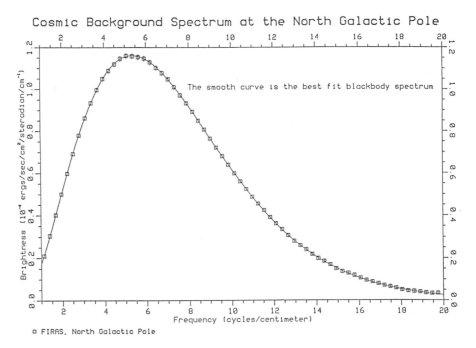

Figure 38. In 1989 and 1990, the COBE satellite measured the spectrum of the cosmic background radiation at many different wavelengths (boxes). COBE found a perfect fit to the spectrum of an ideal radiator (solid line). Because this drawing is made to a different scale than Figure 36, the shapes of the ideal-radiator curves in the two figures appear different. (Courtesy of NASA/John Mather.)

relative to the background. This motion produces a Doppler shift that arises solely because we have a motion of our own, with a speed of some 400 miles per second—an intriguing but not startling discovery, first made from the summit of White Mountain, then checked by instruments on high-flying U-2 aircraft, and now studied still better with COBE.

COBE's big news is that once the analysis removes the effect of our own particular motion, the background radiation still appears as smooth as can be measured. Where are the relics of the clumps that began galaxies? Scientists are puzzled but not baffled—not yet, at any rate. They know that COBE's ability to discriminate fine angles is limited, and that more sensitive instruments are scheduled to be flown on balloons during the coming year. These balloon-borne detectors, flown from Fort Sumner, New Mexico, or Palestine, Texas, are the bailiwick of still more of Paul Richards's present and former students, most notably Phil Lubin at the University of California at Santa Barbara.

Cosmologists will grow truly worried only if COBE's full year of operation through 1990 and the coming balloon flights in 1991 should fail to reveal any signs of deviation from smoothness in the background radiation. Sooner or later, the failure to find signs of galaxy formation in the early universe would cause cosmologists to discard their current models of how galaxies formed. Although it costs nothing (in dollars) to discard a theory, both the theorists and the observers would far prefer that COBE or the balloon-borne detectors reveal the traces of galaxies in their earliest stages. For without observations to match our theories, where would we be? Still here, no doubt, with our galaxy's existence contradicting what the theorists tell us. But we would lack the happy feeling that we know where we came from, not merely in the broad outlines of the big bang but in the smaller strokes that formed galaxies and the stars within them.

Figure 44. Soon after the first atomic bomb exploded on July 16, 1945, J. Robert Oppenheimer (left) stood with Brigadier General Leslie Groves (right) at the Trinity test site near Alamogordo, New Mexico. (Courtesy of the Los Alamos National Laboratory.)

6. Why Stars Shine

EVERY ASTRONOMICAL OBJECT that shines in the skies—the sun, the moon, the planets, and the stars—glows with starlight. This starlight may be either the object's own or the "pale fire" (to use the Shakespearean phrase that Vladimir Nabokov took for the title of a novel) that it snatches from stars and then reflects into space. If stars did not shine, the skies would be dark, but we would not be here to notice. As it is, starlight warms the Earth, bathes the moon, illuminates the planetary wanderers, and sprinkles the night with a thousand points of light.

Ancient Greek philosophers speculated that the sun must be a giant ball of fire, but the problem of what makes stars *shine* could not be well attacked by science until the late nineteenth century. By then, thermodynamics (the branch of physics that relates heat to other forms of energy) had established what many scientists consider the most fundamental scientific law: the *first law of thermodynamics*. They express it with elegant mathematics, but its message is simple: There is no free lunch. The first law states that within a closed system—one that is isolated from external influence—the total amount of energy (the system's total capacity to do work) remains constant. You can only *transform* energy from one form to another, but you cannot make more energy.

To a scientist, the technical term "energy" measures the capacity to "do work," that is, to move things around. This capacity may be actual, like that in a semitrailer rolling down the highway, or potential, like that stored in the diesel fuel for the semitrailer. The first law of thermodynamics, like all "laws" of science, summarizes part of what scientists believe to be an accurate description about the cosmos. The first law implies that if the Earth could be sealed off from the rest of the universe, our planet would become a closed system, and the total amount of energy on Earth could change only its form but never its amount.

At least in theory, the first law, like other laws of science, might someday prove invalid. For now, however, the fact that many observations support the first law, and that no phenomena contradict it, give it a hallowed place among scientific conclusions. Thus when an inventor states that he or she has violated the first law by devising a "perpetual-motion machine"—a device that *does* produce more energy in a closed system and thus provides a "free lunch" to its purchases—most scientists will not stop to give a response. The inventor just might be right but is far more likely to be mistaken or to be a charlatan. Since life is short and the observational support for the first law is enormous, inventors of perpetual-motion machines now face an uphill battle for recognition and acceptance, which they could easily win just as soon as their machines do indeed provide unlimited new energy.

Stars also obey the first law of thermodynamics. In order to understand them, we must find the source of their enormous energy—that is, we must find the form that the energy takes before it is transformed into starlight. Furthermore, we must find a mechanism that transforms one form of energy into another and does so for millions or even billions of years. The "millions" were already suspected before this century began: The great British physicist Lord Kelvin (born William Thomson) had produced an estimate of 20 million years for the age of the Earth. Although this estimate was based on the assumption—now seen as incorrect—that the Earth was born incandescent and has been cooling ever since, Kelvin's estimate made a great impression on his peers. Since the sun could hardly be younger than the Earth, if Kelvin were right, then the sun must have been shining for at least 20 million years. But calculations familiar to a coal-burning society showed that even if the sun were made entirely of the best coal, it could have lasted only a few million years at its present luminosity—that is, its present energy output—before burning itself out. To any believer in the first law of thermodynamics, our sun, and by implication all stars, must draw upon a source of energy more efficient and productive than the best that Victorian England could provide. What could that source be?

During the decades that spanned the end of the nineteenth

century and the beginning of the twentieth, astronomers and physicists pushed aside the problem of energy generation in stars so far as was mentally convenient. Unanswered questions are stimulating, but not to contemplate all day long, every day. When the editors of the *Encyclopaedia Britannica* compiled their famous eleventh edition, in the years just before the First World War, they sought articles from the greatest thinkers and writers of the English-speaking world—Edmund Gosse, Algernon Charles Swinburne, Peter Chalmers Mitchell, and a host of others. For their article on "Stars" they turned to Cambridge University's Arthur Stanley Eddington, who produced a masterly outline of stellar brightnesses, distances, variability, clustering, and observed motions.

On the subject of how stars *shine*, however, Eddington could say only that "the stars are known to be continually losing enormous quantities of energy by radiating their heat into space. Ordinary solid or liquid masses would cool very rapidly from this cause and would soon cease to shine. . . . Conflicting opinions are held as to the various steps in the process of [stellar] evolution."

In short, Eddington had to finesse the basic question of stellar energy generation. But the answer had already been provided in a scientific paper written by Albert Einstein in 1905, as Eddington realized within a few years. Indeed, Eddington played such a key role in determining what goes on inside stars that his name still trips from the lips of astronomers who study stellar interiors. Asked to list the scientists most significant in the quest to determine what happens within stars to release their energy, many astronomers would list three: Albert Einstein, Arthur S. Eddington, and Hans Bethe.

THE TRANSFORMATION OF ENERGY OF MASS

Albert Einstein's name appears on this list not for his research on stars but for a still better reason: Einstein saw how *any* object that shines with light could work.

During the first years of this century, Einstein worked as a patent examiner in Bern, the Swiss capital. His training as a physicist had produced no job offers, largely because of the anti-

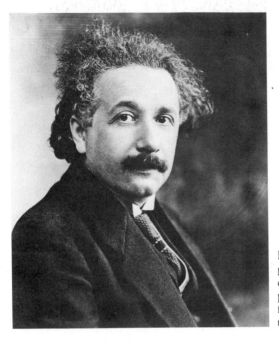

Figure 39. Albert Einstein (1879–1955), the greatest physicist of the twentieth century, did his most important work during the period of 1904–1916, before reaching his fortieth birthday. (Yerkes Observatory photograph.)

Semitism then prevalent in academic and other circles. In his job as a patent examiner, Einstein found the time to work on his true love, theoretical physics, while functioning well in the Swiss bureaucracy (Figure 39).

In 1905 Einstein had a year to end all years among theoretical physicists, the sort of achievement that allowed Babe Ruth to answer, when asked why he was being paid more than the President of the United States, that "I had a better year than Hoover." Einstein published four papers in the *Annalen der Physik,* the chief journal of the world of physics (then centered in Germany). One of these papers concerned the *Brownian motion,* which had been his thesis topic. This term refers to the continuous jiggling of small particles suspended in a fluid, which we now know (thanks to Einstein) arises from the ceaseless motion of the atoms and molecules within that fluid. A second paper dealt with the *photoelectric effect,* the ejection of electrons from a metal surface struck by high-intensity light. This work helped to establish the branch of physics called quantum mechanics and was specifically cited by the Nobel Prize committee in its award of the prize to Einstein in 1922—partly because the theory of relativity was then sufficiently controversial that the committee preferred not to mention it. Einstein's third paper introduced the *theory of relativity,* which set the world of physics on its ear by denying the existence of an absolute frame of reference in which to measure motion. And Einstein's fourth paper, briefest of all, showed that the theory of relativity predicts that *matter can be converted into energy and energy into matter*. The two quantities are related by Einstein's most famous formula: E equals m c squared.

$E = mc^2$ describes how much energy, E, lies locked within an amount of mass, m. You simply square the speed of light, c, and multiply that amount by whatever mass you have. Thus Einstein's equation predicts that greater amounts of mass contain greater amounts of energy. This energy remains completely hidden from view, locked in a previously unrecognized form called *energy of mass,* until and unless some process transforms the energy of mass into the more familiar energy possessed by objects in motion, called *kinetic energy.* This transformation must make matter actually disappear, thus reducing the total amount of matter in the object that transforms energy of mass into kinetic energy. The transformation of energy of mass into another form of energy implies that the original energy of mass, which exists simply because the mass exists, has become another form of energy—at the price of winking the mass out of being.

Quite naturally, the originality of Einstein's suggestions lcd the world of physics to show some hesitation in accepting his insights. But once physicists came to accept Einstein's theory of relativity, they saw that $E = mc^2$ provides the most likely way to make stars work. Since c, the speed of light, is an enormous number (186,000 miles per second in the English system of units), even a tiny mass (m) can potentially yield an enormous amount of kinetic energy, *if* you have a way to convert it into that form of energy. $E = mc^2$ offered physicists a way—the only known way—to explain the creation of the enormous amounts of kinetic energy that stars require to shine for billions of years.

Though no one knew just *how* stars employ Einstein's equation, astronomers soon concluded that *stars must convert matter into energy*. Every minute, the sun emits a certain amount of energy, which is enormous by human standards but only slightly above average as stars go. If you specify an amount of energy (E), then $E = mc^2$ tells you how much inert energy of mass must transform itself into kinetic energy. For the kinetic energy released in a minute by the sun, that amount equals the mass of a small mountain—one of the Berkshire Mountains, for example. If you could find a process that would magically transform the energy of mass of one of the Berkshire Mountains into kinetic energy each minute, then after five million years you would have consumed the Earth, whose mass would then have been reduced to zero.

Thus, if you had only the mass of the Earth, you could never make the sun shine for four and a half *billion* years, as geological records tell us it has shone. But the sun has 333,000 times more mass than the Earth. If the sun turns the mass of a mountain into energy every second (and it does), it can last for billions of years without consuming itself.

These numbers made sense to astronomers long before they discovered the details of how stars turn mass into energy. During the 1910s and 1920s, Arthur Stanley Eddington made calculation after calculation, all of them fundamentally correct, about the internal constitution of stars. Relying on what physicists then knew about what a star's own gravitational force would cause to happen within the star's interior, Eddington calculated the temperature, density, pressure, and rates of energy generation and transport at different points within a star. Eddington's calculations rested on the assumption that *some* process at the centers of stars turns mass into energy using Einstein's E = mc²—an assumption later explored in great detail by Hans Bethe and his colleagues.

Eddington also saw that whatever energy source exists must operate primarily at the *center* of a star, or else the star's center would collapse under the weight of its overlying layers. The star's center could avoid collapse only by releasing a continuous flood of energy. Hence Eddington quite rightly assumed that a star's energy source must lie at its center, hidden from prying eyes by hundreds of thousands of miles of overlying layers of gas.

In 1926, when Eddington published his seminal book *The Internal Constitution of the Stars,* he ruled out sources of energy other than "subatomic" (now called *nuclear*) energy on the grounds that other sources could not provide the energy needed for the full life of a star, or could not arise at the center of a star. But Eddington could not be sure of the *type* of nuclear process that makes stars shine. All of these processes, discovered only during the previous few decades, remained imperfectly understood. Do stars achieve their transformation of energy of mass into kinetic energy through radioactive decay? Radioactive decay occurs when a nucleus, the center of an atom, is "unstable" and turns into two or more lighter nuclei. As this happens, some of the mass of the nucleus turns into energy. Or do stars shine through particle-antiparticle annihilation? This would be the result of particles meeting their mirror-image antiparticles, with the result that the particles and antiparticles turn themselves entirely into energy, leaving no mass at all. Or was the answer *nuclear fusion,* the melding of two individual nuclei to make a heavier nucleus?

Casting his expert eye over the possibilities, Eddington leaned toward the third possibility, noting that "the only definitely known example of liberation of energy in the [fusion] of nuclei is in the formation of helium from hydrogen." These words, more a recitation of fact than a hypothesis, pointed presciently to what we know today: Stars indeed work by fusing together hydrogen nuclei, called protons, to make helium nuclei, a process that transforms energy of mass into energy of motion. Eddington's dispassionate statement foreshadowed the discovery of how stars generate energy—and three decades later, how to make a hydrogen bomb.

The 1920s, the decade that saw Eddington's best work, were a time of tremendous ferment in physics and astronomy. Stimulated by recent discoveries in physics, including radioactivity, the principles of atomic structure, and the photoelectric effect, a generation of physicists such as the world had never seen before— Niels Bohr, Arnold Sommerfeld, Erwin Schrödinger, Paul Dirac, Enrico Fermi, Werner Heisenberg, Wolfgang Pauli, and a host of others—created the world of quantum mechanics, a new vision of the physical universe (briefly discussed in Chapter 5). In the quantum world, which describes the behavior of tiny constituents of matter such as electrons and atomic nuclei, nothing has quite the certainty that it did in the older world of "classical mechanics." According to the "uncertainty principle," elucidated by Werner Heisenberg as one of the pillars of the theory of quantum mechanics, we can never be absolutely certain of the exact location of any particle, or of the exact velocity of that particle. This uncertainty arises not because scientists lack the tools for precise measurement, but because the universe fundamentally refuses to allow perfect certainty.

Philosophically, this conclusion of uncertainty proved a difficult pill to swallow. Albert Einstein, who had done as much as anyone to bring on the quantum revolution, looked upon the theoretical edifice that his slightly younger colleagues had created and pronounced it a workable model, but not the "real" description of the cosmos. To his dying day, Einstein remained unhappy with quantum mechanics.

The younger generation of physicists, educated after the demise of absolute certainty, understood Einstein's philosophical problem but did not share it. The quantum world fit nicely with the outside world of the 1920s, a world in which old certainties had vanished, to be replaced by a new certainty that uncertainty must exist. Nowhere did the world view of physicists better match the changed larger environment than in Germany, the center of the world of physics after the First World War just as before. Sommerfeld, Heisenberg, and Einstein were German; Pauli and Schrödinger were Austrians who worked for long periods of time in Germany; Bohr, Fermi, and Dirac made frequent visits to Germany from Denmark, Italy, and England.

Around this constellation of stars, located primarily in Berlin, Munich, and the small university town of Göttingen, revolved a host of lesser lights, some of whom eventually came to dominate the world of physics, studying and collaborating with the leaders of physics. From Hungary came Edward Teller and John von Neumann; from the Soviet Union, the irrepressible cartoonist (and physicist) George Gamow; from the United States, a pale, philosophical youth from a well-to-do family in New York, J. Robert Oppenheimer; and from the fringes of Germany itself, a tall, strapping physicist, two years younger than Oppenheimer, Hans Bethe.

HANS BETHE AND THE SECRETS OF STARLIGHT

Bethe was born in Strasbourg, then part of the German empire though now part of France; he grew up in Kiel (near the Danish border) and in Frankfurt. Bethe's father came from a Prussian family of Protestant heritage, while his mother was Jewish. Affinities of interest seemed far more meaningful than those of religious background: Bethe's father was a physiologist who taught at Strasbourg University, and his mother's father was a professor of medicine there.

In high school, Bethe shone at his studies, not simply as many hardworking, bright German youths did, but far beyond ordinary expectations. After graduating from Frankfurt's Goethe Gymnasium, Bethe entered the Universities of Frankfurt and Stuttgart, where he displayed such ability that his instructors persuaded him to transfer to the University of Munich.

In Munich, Arnold Sommerfeld, an early pioneer of

quantum mechanics and other new branches of physics, presided over perhaps the most brilliant collection of physicists ever seen in a decade at a single department. Pauli and Heisenberg were Sommerfeld's students; Linus Pauling, Edward Condon, and Isidor Rabi came from the United States to study there; Edward Teller spent a year with Sommerfeld. Bethe joined Sommerfeld's group in 1926, the year that Eddington published his masterwork on the internal constitution of the stars. Bethe soon showed an impressive ability to use the newly developed quantum mechanics to calculate details of the structure of atoms—in particular, of the ways in which the electrons in an atom move in orbit around the atomic nucleus, which consists of protons and electrons. Quantum mechanics had shown that the "classical" concept of an orbit could not

Figure 40. Hans Bethe, professor of physics at Cornell University, discovered the carbon cycle of energy production within stars in 1938. (Photograph by Laurie Sieverts Snyder.)

hold: Since the electrons had no definitive position, the best that could be said was that a particular electron was more likely to move in certain "probability clouds" than in others. Bethe and others used this concept to great advantage, unlocking mystery after mystery, especially about the structure of the simpler atoms, those with only one electron (hydrogen) or two electrons (helium).

If the structure of *atoms* yielded relatively easily to the sharp minds in Germany, the structure of *nuclei* did not. The nuclei that form the hearts of every atom are far smaller, and their constituent particles are far more tightly bound together, than the atoms themselves. If we analogize the atom to our solar system, as physicists often do, then the electrons resemble the planets in orbit around the "sun," the atomic nucleus. Hydrogen atoms, everyone then knew, each have the simplest possible nucleus: a single proton. Helium nuclei each contain two protons and two neutrons. Carbon nuclei have six protons and six neutrons, and each type of element contains a different number of protons in the nuclei of its atoms.

But what holds these nuclei together? Why do some nuclei spontaneously "decay" in a process that yields other, smaller nuclei? Can larger nuclei be made by crashing smaller nuclei into one another? These and a host of questions begged for answers. Bethe and other theoretical physicists responded by combining new data from particle accelerators with the quantum theory. The accelerators, the brainchild of Ernest Lawrence at the University of California at Berkeley, allowed physicists to make atomic nuclei collide at high velocities, sometimes changing into, or producing, new types of particles. By studying the results of these acclerator-made collisions, physicists learned more about the ways that nuclei are put together (something like gaining knowledge of high-speed automobiles by studying the wreckage at a race track).

Throughout the 1920s and 1930s, Bethe and his colleagues grew ever more knowledgeable about atomic nuclei and their interactions, until the secrets of the stars were revealed. World history did not unfold so smoothly as the preceding sentence might suggest. Bethe finished his studies in 1930 and obtained a fellowship from the Rockefeller Foundation that enabled him to spend two years as a visiting scholar at the Cavendish Laboratory in Cambridge, England, and in Rome, where he worked with Enrico Fermi. Then, trained by the best physicists and having demonstrated a powerful mind of his own, Hans Bethe returned to Germany in November 1932 to join the physics faculty at the University of Tübingen, where Johannes Kepler had studied astronomy three and a half centuries before.

Bethe's timing was inauspicious. In December 1932, Albert Einstein left Germany for a visit to Princeton, inwardly convinced he would never return. On January 30 of the new year, Adolf Hitler became chancellor of the German republic. Within two months, the Reichstag fire gave the Nazis the excuse to eliminate all left-wing and Communist parties; by 1935, the infamous Nuremburg Laws forbade the employment of anyone defined as Jewish from teaching at a German university.

Thousands of men and women who, like Hans Bethe (with a Jewish and non-Jewish parent), had not considered themselves Jewish, found their opinions on the matter of no consequence. While on vacation, Bethe received a letter from one of his students that mentioned his dismissal from the faculty. This prompted him to write to his former mentor, Professor Hans Geiger, who confirmed that under the "changed circumstances" it would be necessary to dispense with Bethe's further services. Bethe's career as a German scientist was over.

Of course, by "dispensing with" thousands of scholars of Jewish ancestry, the Nazis unwittingly performed a great service to those they dismissed, who by and large thus acquired the time—

and the insight—to leave Germany. And the Nazis deprived themselves, and sent to their future enemies, many of the best minds in Germany. Bethe, Teller, Einstein, and Pauli left, along with a host of others, including Leo Szilard, Eugene Wigner, and John von Neumann. Those fortunate enough to have achieved a reputation found jobs abroad with relative ease; many of those helped many others in difficulty. From Germany, and later from Austria, Czechoslovakia, and other countries that the Nazis occupied, a flow of émigrés reached the United States, Britain, Australia, South Africa, and Canada—a flow that shifted the center of world physics westward and led science in the United States to impressive new feats.

Bethe went first to England, to the Universities of Manchester and Bristol, before he accepted an offer to join the physics faculty at Cornell University, in Ithaca, New York, in 1935. And there, with significant time off, Hans Bethe has remained. Fifty-six years after beginning what many would call his second career, Bethe continues to do important physics research (Figure 40). When he attends a physics or astronomy conference, perhaps to debate the processes that cause some stars to explode, his fellow physicists provide an accolade that a Nobel prizewinner well past 80 can appreciate: They treat him like anyone else. Although Bethe has made significant contributions in many branches of atomic and nuclear physics, he remains best known for research he performed only a few years after reaching Cornell: the discovery of the way that stars work.

In March 1938, two weeks after Adolf Hitler finally achieved the *Anschluss* that annexed his native Austria to Nazi Germany, Hans Bethe boarded a train to take him southward from Ithaca to Washington, D.C., to attend a meeting of physicists. At the age of 31, Bethe had demonstrated extraordinary prowess as a theoretical physicist. As the frontiers of atomic physics had moved inward, toward the nuclei at the centers of atoms, Bethe had steeped himself in nuclear mysteries. During the three years since he had arrived at Cornell, Bethe had written three long review articles on the physics of atomic nuclei, collectively known to physicists as "Bethe's bible."

Bethe's bible drew on the existing experimental data to confront a host of theoretical questions. What holds together the nuclear hearts of atoms? What sort of structure do they have? Why are certain types of nuclei—for instance, helium nuclei with two protons and two neutrons each—far more favored by nature to exist, and hence far more abundant, than other types? (For example, nature simply does not allow nuclei with five "nucleons" [protons or neutrons] to exist. We find *no* nuclei with three protons and two neutrons, or with two protons and three neutrons.) What happens when nuclei strike one another? Will they fuse together? If so, what circumstances promote this fusion, and which hinder it? Why do radioactive nuclei undergo fission and fall into pieces? Which processes are more likely to produce kinetic energy from energy of mass—those of fusion or those of fission?

Investigations of these and other questions were proceeding apace in the United States and England—and in Germany, where the emigration of a significant number of leading physicists had hampered but by no means ended physics research. At the Washington meeting, the physicists who specialized in "atomic research" (the phrase "nuclear research" had yet to become common currency among scientists) gave their papers and exchanged their insights on a host of topics (Figure 41). And there

Figure 41. The March 1938 meeting of atomic physicists at the Carnegie Institution of Washington, at the Department of Terrestrial Magnetism, stimulated Hans Bethe to work out the mechanism by which stars release energy through nuclear fusion. Bethe is the coatless man in the left center of the middle row. George Gamow is the tall man at the left rear, and Edward Teller is standing to Bethe's immediate left. (Courtesy of the Carnegie Institution of Washington.)

Bethe was confronted by a question he had considered only fleetingly: What makes stars shine?

This question was on the minds of two of Bethe's émigré acquaintances, George Gamow and Edward Teller, who had become members of the physics faculty of George Washington University in the nation's capital. Like all physicists who gave much thought to energy generation in stars, Gamow and Teller felt sure that stars shine by converting energy of mass into kinetic energy. They also knew that at the high temperature within stars, particles collide so violently that no atoms exist. Instead, the collisions strip all the electrons loose from the nuclei, leaving an intermixture of nuclei and electrons. Gamow and Teller had recently become intrigued by the problem of determining just which types of nuclei, and which reactions among nuclei, produce energy within stars. Knowing that Bethe understood atomic nuclei as well as anyone, they confronted him with this question and challenged him to solve it.

No one doubted that Bethe was equal to the challenge: His expertise was matched only by his bulldog tenacity to find a solution, and there were physicists at the meeting who speculated, only half in jest, that Bethe would have an answer by the time that his train returned him to Ithaca. Back at Cornell, Bethe plunged into an investigation of which nuclear fusion reactions are most likely to occur at temperatures of 20 or 30 million degrees, which Eddington and others had calculated must characterize the centers of stars. Within a few weeks—by the time of the "May crisis" that marked the start of the Nazi attempt to annex first part and then all of Czechoslovakia—Bethe had his answer: the *carbon cycle* of nuclear reactions that release energy in stars.

WHAT STARS ARE MADE OF

Bethe's carbon cycle, the fruit of his search for the secrets of the stars, drew on his knowledge not only of the reactions that occur among nuclei but also of the *abundances* of different types of nuclei in the stars. Previous generations of astronomers had determined these abundances—the amounts of each nuclear type—with increasing accuracy. Their determinations relied on observations of the detailed colors of starlight. Some astronomers observed light from the surfaces of stars with spectrographs, instruments capable of revealing the different types of atoms within them by recording the specific colors that the atoms remove from the starlight as it escapes into space. Other astronomers analyzed the spectra showing the details of how much light of each particular color emerged, in order to determine what these spectra revealed about the star as a whole.

During the 1920s, Cecilia Payne, one of the greatest astronomers of the first half of this century, first applied the new theory of atoms, and of the spectral lines they produce, to reach a momentous conclusion about the elemental composition of the universe. Payne learned the new theory at Cambridge University in England and then crossed the Atlantic to enroll as a graduate student in astronomy at Harvard University in 1923. There, two years later, she produced what a distinguished astronomer called "undoubtedly the most brilliant Ph.D. thesis ever written in astronomy." In this thesis, Payne showed that the great differences observed among stellar spectra arise primarily from differences in the *temperatures* of the stars' outer layers, and that the *abundances* of the atomic elements are in fact remarkably constant from star to star. Her thesis concluded that *stars consist primarily of the two lightest elements, hydrogen and helium.* This conclusion took years to gain acceptance because on Earth, helium is a rare gas, and hydrogen, though part of water, forms only a tiny fraction of the solid planet on which we live. Payne herself inserted a sort of disclaimer into her brilliant work, doubting that hydrogen and helium really dominate the visible universe—as indeed they do. But today, the work of Payne and her successors allows astronomers to treat the ratio of the amount of one element with respect to another as a "cosmic" value, relatively constant throughout the universe. Payne remained at Harvard, where she was successively a National Research Fellow, a Harvard Observatory Astronomer, and then (for nearly 20 years) the Phillips Astronomer. Thirty years after she wrote her epochal thesis, by then Cecilia Payne-Gaposchkin, she was invited to join the Harvard faculty—the first woman member of that august group.

In 1938, while seeking the answer to stellar energy generation, Bethe knew the rough contours of Payne's work of the previous decade. He knew that astronomers had found that the most abundant elements in stars are hydrogen and helium, followed by carbon, nitrogen, and oxygen. The great abundance of these elements naturally brought them forward as the most likely candidates for energy-generating reactions among nuclei. Since none of the common forms of these five elements are subject to radioactive decay, Bethe knew that he could rule out nuclear fission, the splitting of atomic nuclei. Instead, nuclear *fusion*—the melding of nuclei—must provide the solution. If so, the nuclear fusion must produce new nuclei, formed from the old, that have slightly *less* mass than the original nuclei contained. This loss of mass represents a decrease in the energy of mass and a corresponding increase in kinetic energy (energy of motion). But which type of nuclear-fusion reaction would make the stars shine?

Bethe was particularly interested in the intrinsically brighter stars, which shine with more energy than fainter ones do. His approach was straightforward: He knew that hydrogen is extremely abundant in stars and therefore looked for reactions in which hydrogen nuclei—protons—fuse with other types of nuclei. As Bethe later recalled, "I went through the periodic table [of the elements] step by step and looked at the various nuclei that could react with protons. Nothing seemed to work, and I was almost ready to give up. But when I tried carbon, it worked. So, you see, this was a discovery by persistence, not by brains."

Bethe had found a series of nuclear reactions called the *carbon cycle*. This process has six steps whose overall effect is to fuse four protons (hydrogen nuclei) into one helium nucleus (Figure 42). *Each of the six steps in the cycle turns energy of mass into kinetic energy*, in accordance with Einstein's formula $E = mc^2$. The release of this new kinetic energy makes the particles at the star's center dance in ever-greater frenzy, and through collisions the particles communicate their additional kinetic energy to other particles that lie farther out from the center. Through such collisions, the energy released through nuclear fusion at the star's center diffuses outward, warming the entire star; and the star's surface layers, heated to tens of thousands of degrees, radiate energy into space. The

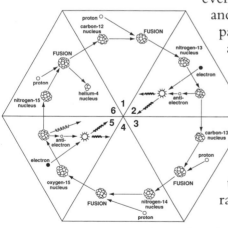

Figure 42. The carbon cycle involves six separate nuclear reactions, which cumulatively have the effect of fusing four protons into a nucleus of helium-4. Each of these six reactions either fuses a proton with a heavier nucleus (steps 1, 3, 4, and 6) or involves the decay of a nucleus (steps 2 and 5) into a lighter nucleus, an anti-electron, and a neutrino. (Drawing by Crystal Stevenson.)

How to Convert Matter into Energy

The carbon cycle that Hans Bethe invoked to explain stellar energy generation includes six separate interactions among atomic nuclei. All of these reactions occur within the seething caldrons at the centers of stars, where atomic nuclei collide at enormous speeds nearly countless times each second. This carbon cycle uses a carbon nucleus as a site where hydrogen nuclei (protons) fuse to produce helium nuclei. Each passage through the six steps of the cycle turns four protons—nuclei of hydrogen—into one nucleus of helium.

The first step of the carbon cycle fuses a proton with a carbon nucleus to produce a rare, radioactive type of nitrogen nucleus. After a few minutes, this nitrogen nucleus *decays*—splits apart into a carbon nucleus plus an antielectron, the *antiparticle* of an electron. (The antielectron soon meets an electron, and the two particles annihilate one another; however, the small mass of the electron and antielectron prevents this process from releasing much energy.)

Since the decay of the nitrogen nucleus produces a carbon nucleus, it might seem that so far nothing has happened. But the type of carbon nucleus that appears when the nitrogen nucleus decays has a small but subtle difference from the carbon nucleus that underwent the original fusion: It has an additional neutron. Most carbon nuclei have six protons and six neutrons; this one has six protons and *seven* neutrons. This difference proves crucial in the star's deep interior, once another proton collides at high speed and fuses with the new type of carbon nucleus. Bethe saw that the nitrogen nucleus that arises from this latest fusion belongs to the normal, garden-variety type of nitrogen, which does not undergo radioactive decay. Thus the second fusion of a proton with a carbon nucleus produces a nitrogen nucleus that remains in existence. When another fast-moving proton—the third to appear in the carbon cycle—fuses with this nitrogen nucleus, the fusion reaction in the stellar interior produces a nucleus of oxygen. This newly made nucleus does not represent the common form of the element. Instead, this type of oxygen has one fewer neutron than most oxygen nuclei. Such a nucleus will decay radioactively in about a minute to yield two new par-

dance of the nuclei, most intense at the star's center, turns hydrogen into helium and energy of mass into kinetic energy. This makes the stars shine; all else is detail.

By the late spring of 1939, when Bethe completed his work on the carbon cycle, the world was headed for war. In July, when it was clear to all who cared to look that Hitler would soon attack Poland or another of Germany's neighbors, several of Albert Einstein's fellow émigré scientists visited him a number of times at his summer cottage on Long Island. Among then were Edward Teller and Eugene Wigner, another brilliant Hungarian-born physicist, but the prime mover was yet another physicist from Hungary, Leo Szilard, the most political of these scientists. The purpose of these visits to Einstein was to persuade him to write a letter to President Roosevelt, urging him to increase experimental work into the release of energy through nuclear fission—that is, through the splitting apart of atomic nuclei.

In August, Einstein wrote a letter to the president, pointing out that "it may become possible to set up nuclear chain reactions in a large mass of uranium, by which vast amounts of power . . . would be generated." The letter also pointed out that Germany had ended the sale of uranium ore from the mines in Czechoslovakia, and that the son of a prominent Nazi official was engaged in research on uranium fission. This letter has become famous among scientists as marking a key time when scientists became involved in the political process. Einstein, a pacifist during the First World War, later called this letter "the greatest mistake" of his life.

Einstein and his fellow scientists probably exaggerated their influence. Roosevelt received the letter, hand-carried by the economist Alexander Sachs, and took it seriously, remarking, "Alex, what you are after is to see that the Nazis don't blow us up." However, despite the fact that Roosevelt created a committee to investigate the possibilities of nuclear fission (which invited Einstein to join and received a polite refusal), essentially no expansion of research into nuclear fission occurred for more than two years.

Finally, by the fall of 1942—almost a year after the Japanese attack on Pearl Harbor on December 7, 1941—Brigadier General Leslie Groves, the army's head of the atomic bomb project, had chosen J. Robert Oppenheimer, probably the outstanding atomic physicist born in the U.S., to direct the laboratory that would manufacture the atomic bomb. Oppenheimer, though a New

ticles: a nitrogen nucleus with one more neutron than most nitrogen nuclei, and an antielectron, the antiparticle of an electron.

Finally, however, a proton (the fourth in the cycle) fuses with the nitrogen nucleus and produces a nucleus of helium and a nucleus of carbon. Furthermore, the type of carbon nucleus produced in this last step of the cycle is the common type of carbon—the same type that participated in the first step. The carbon nucleus thus turns out to act as a *catalyst*—a site upon which reactions can occur but which reappears in the same form when the reactions are over (Figure 42). The net result of the six steps of the carbon cycle are these: Four protons fuse to produce a single nucleus of helium, plus two antielectrons (each arising from radioactive decay of nitrogen and oxygen) and more obscure particles called neutrinos (which also arise when radioactive nuclei decay). The kinetic energy released in these reactions takes the form of *additional* kinetic energy carried by the new particles that the fusion process creates.

Later research into nuclear fusion showed that only the more massive, more luminous stars produce most of their kinetic energy through the six steps of the carbon cycle. The less massive, less exciting stars—our own sun included—do most of their nuclear fusion through another series of nuclear reactions, called the *proton-proton cycle*. This series of reactions begins with the fusion of two protons. Like the carbon cycle, the proton-proton cycle turns four protons into a helium nucleus, transforming some energy of mass into kinetic energy. The fact that the proton-proton cycle does not use a carbon nucleus as a catalyst makes it even simpler than the carbon cycle; furthermore, the cycle involves only three steps, rather than the six of the carbon cycle.

The proton-proton cycle begins when two protons fuse to produce a deuteron (a nucleus of *deuterium*), a rare type of hydrogen nucleus that includes a neutron along with the proton. In addition to the deuterium nucleus, the proton-proton fusion produces an antielectron (also known as a positron) and a neutrino (Figure 43). The antielectron soon annihilates with an electron to release a bit more energy from mass, but the neutrino (like all neutrinos) passes through matter with al-

Yorker by birth, knew the plateaus of northern New Mexico from the time when a bout of dysentery, contracted just before he was supposed to enter Harvard, had led him to take a pack trip there as part of his convalescence. With Groves's approval, Oppenheimer chose a mesa near Los Alamos as the site of the bomb laboratory and proceeded to recruit the men and women who would design and build the bomb. The man Oppenheimer wanted most to lead the work on the *theory* of how to make an atomic bomb was Hans Bethe.

Oppenheimer arranged to meet Bethe in December 1942 in Cambridge, Massachusetts, and attempted to persuade him and his wife (Bethe had married the daughter of one of his German professors in 1939) to join his team. Hans and Rose Bethe listened long and hard to Oppenheimer's description of life on the mesa at Los Alamos. Oppenheimer naturally stressed the value to the war effort and the positive aspects of the community that would be born; less was said about the security aspects, which the scientists would find galling in the extreme. By March, Bethe agreed to join the effort; by April 1943, working in buildings hastily erected by Groves's corps of army engineers, Bethe and his fellow scientists, whose average age was less than 30, were deep in discussions of how to make a bomb from radioactive uranium nuclei.

Through the remainder of 1943, and all through 1944, working under Bethe's guidance and with Oppenheimer's constant support and encouragement, the theorists produced two different designs for atomic bombs. Mammoth factories, rising from bare earth in Hanford, Washington, and Oak Ridge, Tennessee, produced the material to undergo a *chain reaction* that would release a violent flood of energy. By the early summer of 1945, both types of bomb neared readiness. After the first nuclear explosion lit the sky over the test area near Alamogordo, New Mexico, in July 1945 (Figure 44, p. 136), the United States dropped the "Fat Man" and "Little Boy" bombs over Hiroshima and Nagasaki in August. The world changed forever—and still more so a few years later, when first the United States, then the Soviet Union, and then Great Britain, France, and China developed the *hydrogen bomb*. Far more powerful than atomic bombs, hydrogen bombs work on the same principles as the stars: They fuse hydrogen nuclei into helium, releasing enormous amounts of kinetic energy in the process.

In 1945, Hans Bethe had resumed his professorship at Cornell. Despite Edward Teller's continual entreaties, he declined to join the Los Alamos Laboratory, though he has often consulted

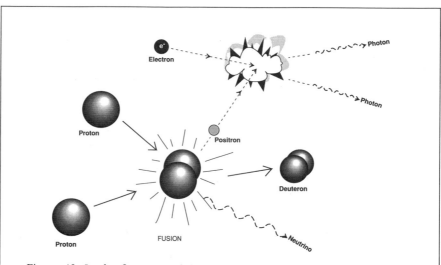

Figure 43. In the first step of the proton–proton cycle, two protons fuse to form a deuteron, a neutrino, and a positron (also called an antielectron). The positron soon meets an electron, and those two particles annihilate, producing two photons. (Drawing by Crystal Stevenson.)

most no interaction and escapes directly from the star's center.

In the second step of the proton-proton cycle, a proton fuses with the newly made deuterium nucleus to produce a nucleus of *helium-three* (a rare type of helium) with two protons and one neutron per nucleus. Again more energy emerges, both in the form of gamma rays and as extra kinetic energy in the helium nucleus.

The third and final part of the proton-proton cycle involves the fusion of two nuclei of helium-three. The fusion of the two helium-three nuclei produces two protons plus a nucleus of helium-four, the common variety of helium, with two protons and two neutrons in the nucleus. Like all such nuclear-fusion reactions, this turns some energy of mass into kinetic energy.

If you count carefully, you will see that the proton-proton cycle, like the carbon cycle, turns four protons into a nucleus of helium and releases kinetic energy from energy of mass, because the mass contained in the particles emerging from the fusion reactions is less than the total mass of the particles entering the reactions. Basically this is all you need to know about nuclear fusion within stars to lead a long and happy life.

there. Bethe regards his work on nuclear weapons as a necessary and important diversion, but still a diversion, from his main goal in life: to understand the nature of the physical universe. And indeed, during the 46 post-war years, Bethe's chief interests have focused on the same topics as his 20 years of pre-war research: How are atomic nuclei constructed, and how do they interact? How do these facts help to explain what goes on in stars? The fantastic progress in these fields has inspired Bethe and a host of other astrophysicists to seek further details about nature, in continuing their attempts to understand all that they can about the stars.

The foremost among these details, so far as stars are concerned, is the fact that *only the most luminous stars employ the carbon cycle as their primary means to turn mass into energy*. This important distinction among stars leads to a question that is fundamental to astronomy: Why do stars differ in their colors, their lifetimes, and their rates of energy output?

WHAT MAKES ONE STAR DIFFERENT FROM ANOTHER?

Astronomers who spend their lives analyzing and cataloging the different types of stars draw on a long tradition, one that goes back to the days of Claudius Ptolemy and beyond. However, only when astronomers gained the capacity to estimate the *distances* to stars could they begin to determine the stars' *luminosities*—that is, the amount of energy that stars emit each second. This knowledge began to accumulate during the last years of the nineteenth century; by the early years of the twentieth century, astronomers saw that stars come in a bewildering variety of luminosities. Related to the luminosities, in ways that could only be guessed, were the *colors* of stars. Some stars emit a million times more energy per second than others; some stars are red, others are yellow, others blue.

A great leap in our understanding of stars came when astronomers realized that the fundamental property that distinguishes one star from another is one that we cannot easily observe: the star's *mass*. The mass measures the amount of matter that the star acquired when it formed. The more massive spheres of gas are (forgive the comparison) the "rock stars" of the skies: They lead more luminous, more exciting, but far shorter lives than their less massive cousins, which pass their long lives in comparatively quiet circumstances.

Why does a star's greater mass produce a brief but glorious incandescence for the star? Gravity is the culprit, gravity whose force increases in a more massive star, because the greater mass means that every part of the star feels a greater attraction from all the other stellar pieces. Squeezed more tightly by the greater force of gravity, the particles in the star move more rapidly. Since the temperature of a group of particles simply measures the particle's average speed, this means that the temperature within the star increases.

Even a small rise in temperature within a star can produce a tremendous increase in the rate of nuclear fusion. Enormous temperatures are required for nuclear fusion to occur (Color Plate 9). Despite the fact that a typical star's central temperature hovers near 20 million degrees, most of the nuclei there are moving too slowly for nuclear fusion. Since all nuclei, such as protons, helium nuclei, and carbon nuclei, have positive electric charges, they repel one another, as charges of the same sign invariably do. The strength of this repulsion increases as the nuclei approach one another. Only a tiny fraction of the nuclei—perhaps one in a thousand—have speeds large enough for the nuclei to come sufficiently close, even in a head-on collision, for fusion to occur. Because the particles capable of fusion represent only this tiny fraction of the total, even a modest increase in the temperature can double or triple the number of nuclei that are moving rapidly enough for fusion to occur when they collide. A 10-percent increase in the temperature can double the rate of nuclear fusion—and thus double the rate at which the star produces kinetic energy from energy of mass!

The masses of stars span only a rather modest range, from the most massive stars, with about a hundred times the sun's mass, to the least massive, with about one-tenth the mass of the sun. In comparison, stars' luminosities—the rates at which they release energy—vary from one million times the sun's luminosity down to about one hundred-thousandth of this luminosity. Thus the total range of stellar masses spans "only" a factor of a thousand, whereas the span of stellar luminosities varies by a factor of nearly *one trillion*. The much greater range of luminosities testifies to the difference that mass makes: A rather minor change in the temperature at the star's center, where fusion occurs, can produce a huge change in the star's energy output and luminosity.

This insight into the connection between a star's mass and the rate at which it transforms matter into kinetic energy became ever clearer during the years just after the Second World War. During his years at Los Alamos, Bethe, like most scientists in that period, had devoted little thought to the stars. He discussed many topics with Oppenheimer, but never stellar structure or stellar evolution. Yet just before the war, Oppenheimer had written fascinating scientific speculation about the death of stars. Only when Bethe returned to Cornell in 1945 did stellar interiors engage him directly.

Freed from the need to engage in hectic war-related research, many nuclear physicists turned their attention to the stars. The same sorts of calculations that had shaped the atomic bomb, and that were being used to produce the hydrogen bomb, could uncover the details of stellar energy generation. To this day, the Los Alamos National Laboratory contains a significant group of researchers involved in understanding how stars live and die. During the 1950s, when astronomers truly came to understand the centers of stars, the primary research center for this activity was Princeton University, where Henry Norris Russell had become the leading astronomer in the United States. Russell's successor as director of Princeton Observatory, Lyman Spitzer, was keenly interested in the birth and death of stars, but the key player in piercing to the hearts of stars by calculation was Martin Schwarzschild, a German-born professor, educated at Göttingen, the son of the physicist Karl Schwarzschild, one of Einstein's contemporaries. Hans Bethe had discovered a key cycle of nuclear fusion reactions in stars; Martin Schwarzschild and his colleagues planned to calculate the details of what happens in the fiery stellar furnaces.

Working together and in friendly competition with several dozen other astronomers, Schwarzschild combined what nuclear physicists knew about nuclear-fusion reactions with detailed calculations of the temperature, pressure, and density within a star. By the mid-1950s, these astronomers had determined which reactions occur in which stars, and at what rates. Their success was complete: We now know in exquisite detail how ordinary stars produce kinetic energy and how that energy diffuses outward through the stars. Indeed, the completeness of the astronomers' solution has made "stellar interiors" rather a backwater of astronomical research, but we should not let the frontier nature of other fields obscure the triumph made by the pioneers of nuclear fusion in stars.

Schwarzschild and his co-workers found that Bethe's carbon

cycle has a tremendous sensitivity to temperature. The carbon cycle produces only insignificant amounts of kinetic energy from energy of mass so long as the temperature stays at or below a balmy 25 million degrees Fahrenheit. But whenever the temperature rises above this amount, the carbon cycle dominates the scene.

Hence the more massive stars, which have the higher central temperatures, release their energy through the carbon cycle. In less massive stars, energy generation proceeds through the proton-proton cycle; although this process is also sensitive to temperature, it does not fall off so rapidly with lower temperatures as the carbon cycle does. For a star with the sun's mass, the central temperature rises to "only" 20 million degrees, and the proton-proton cycle dominates. The crossover point occurs for stars with about one and a half times the sun's mass, in which about half the energy arises from the carbon cycle and half from the proton-proton cycle.

The struggle to understand what goes on inside stars has engaged the efforts of many astronomers since the pioneering insights gained by Eddington and Bethe. Among those who have used the tools of mathematical physics to probe stellar interiors, one of the most engaging is a genial, gray-haired, hard-working man in his late sixties, the astronomer Benjamin Peery (Figure 45). Peery's father had the now-vanished occupation of railway mail clerk, and moved each time a different railroad employed him. As a result, Peery spent his boyhood in several small towns in southeastern Minnesota, in each of which his family was the sole "colored" representative. Because one of his childhood delights was to build and to fly model airplanes, he announced himself as a student of aeronautical engineering when he entered the University of Minnesota in 1940. But at the university Peery discovered the joys of pure physics, and changed his major to that field. Then, as a senior, he began to wonder more deeply about the stars that sparkled so brilliantly in the skies above the Twin Cities. "I thought it was absurd—shameful—not to know what made them shine," he recalls. He resolved to pursue graduate studies in astrophysics, and enrolled to that end at the University of Michigan.

Throughout the 1950s and 1960s, first as a graduate student and then as a member of the

Figure 45. Professor Benjamin Peery of Howard University, an expert on stellar atmospheres, has devoted much of his career to training the next generations of scientists. (Photograph courtesy of Professor Peery.)

astronomy faculty at Indiana University, Peery joined in the efforts
that laid bare the secrets of stellar interiors. Not only at Cornell and
Princeton, where Bethe and Schwarzschild worked, but at dozens
of universities in this country and abroad, astronomers solved
complex questions concerning the way that stars generate energy in
their centers, and how the interiors of stars respond to changes that
arise as the supply of protons for nuclear fusion becomes depleted.
Peery concentrated on what happens within stars that belong to
"close binary star systems," in which two stars are close enough for
one star's evolution to affect its companion star.

In the case of two stars in close proximity, the stars can
actually merge their outer layers, so the pair resembles a giant,
swollen dumbbell. If the stars are separated by somewhat greater
distances, this merger does not occur, but material from one star
can be drawn to the other by gravity. This effect becomes more
important if one of the stars becomes a "red giant," a star that
swells its outer layers prodigiously as it ages. The red giant's
outermost gases will be drawn toward the other star, still in the
prime of life, by gravitational forces. However, the material will
not fall straight onto the star. Instead, because the two stars are
moving in orbit around their common center of mass, the matter
will spiral inward, forming an "accretion disk" around the star.
The gravitational force from the star that provided this matter will
then affect the shape and behavior of both the accretion disk and
the object at its center. The interplay of activity among the two
stars and the accretion disk may explain various intriguing
phenomena. These include variable stars in which one star (or its
accretion disk) eclipses the light from the other star, and the sudden
appearance of novae ("new stars" in Latin) in systems where matter
from the accretion disk gradually accumulates on the surface of the
star that it surrounds, until a thermonuclear explosion occurs that
briefly lights the skies.

Peery enjoyed a successful career as an investigator of what
goes on inside stars that belong to binary systems. But after two
happy decades in Indiana, he decided on a new approach to
astronomy. Well into his fifties, he chose to move from an
outstanding state university, where research receives wide attention
and support, to a less well-endowed institution, where hard work
at teaching consumes nearly all of his working hours. Peery noted
that although the American Astronomical Society has more than
five thousand members, these include fewer than a dozen African
Americans. He believed that he could do something to redress the

balance, and to convince minority students that science in general, and astronomy in particular, offer not just passing fascination but excellent career opportunities as well. Besides, the institution seeking Peery for its faculty was Howard University, for more than a century the best-known educational establishment with a primarily black student body.

Howard University had been founded by the United States Government in 1867, largely at the urging of Oliver Otis Howard. Howard was a highly motivated professional soldier who had served as a general in the Civil War and had lost an arm in that cause; his sole recorded joke was the suggestion to a fellow general in a complementary situation that they could save money by purchasing their gloves together. During the war, Howard became intensely interested in the fate of negroes freed by the Emancipation Proclamation and the Thirteenth Amendment, and that interest grew even stronger once the war ended in 1865. Since the United States Congress largely exhausted its interest in Howard University by passing the act to create it, the university's students, faculty, and alumni have had the primary responsibility of doing whatever they could to maintain Howard as a viable institution of higher learning. Asked several times to help Howard in its educational mission, Peery finally could not resist. "I decided to stop saying no, and to seek my fortune," he remarks laconically. After a heartfelt leave-taking at Indiana, he moved to the nation's capital. And there during the past decade, beneath frequently cloudy skies that obscure the stars, Peery has taught with verve and skill. His students, like students everywhere, often have initial doubts about the "usefulness" of astronomy, but under Peery's guidance prove remarkably quick to discover its delights.

The world of astronomical research has proceeded apace. Today, thanks to the efforts of Bethe, Schwarzschild, Peery, and dozens of other researchers, astronomers can read the insides of stars—at least of stars in their prime of life—like an open book. They now know that stars such as Sirius or Vega, with about twice the sun's mass, still have interiors dominated by the carbon cycle. Sirius, the brightest star in the night sky, has a mass 2.3 times, but a luminosity *23* times the sun's. Sirius owes its brightness in *our* skies to its relative proximity to the solar system: It is our eighth-closest stellar neighbor. Procyon, the heart of the Little Dog (as Sirius marks the heart of the Big Dog), is more sunlike: It has one and three-quarter times the sun's mass. In Procyon's interior, the proton-proton cycle plays a significant but minority part in the dance of nuclear fusion, which is still dominated by the carbon cycle. At any lower temperatures, the proton-proton cycle will outperform the carbon cycle at transforming energy of mass into kinetic energy.

In the sun the situation is reversed: The proton-proton cycle dominates, and the carbon cycle furnishes only a few percent of the energy released per second. For stars of still lower mass, the carbon cycle becomes completely unimportant. The star 61 Cygni, another of the sun's close neighbors, has a mass only 60 percent of the sun's. This modest difference in mass reduces the luminosity of 61 Cygni, in comparison to the sun's, by a factor of 10. Thus astronomers—not to mention the general public—rate 61 Cygni as quite an ordinary star despite its proximity to us (though it was the first star whose distance was measured by the parallax effect).

As Elizabethan England produced far more John Bulls than William Shakespeares, so too the universe contains far more 61 Cygnis than Procyons and Siriuses, that is, far more low-mass than high-mass stars. The bulk of the stars in the Milky Way, and in any other galaxy, contain less than half the sun's mass and shine with less than five percent of the sun's luminosity. We *notice* the Siriuses far more because we respond more readily to greater amounts of light. But the sun in fact represents a star that is above average in mass and luminosity. For every Sirius, the Milky Way contains fifteen suns and fifty 61 Cygnis.

When we order stars from those with the largest masses to those with the smallest, we therefore also order stars from the rarest (high-mass and blue stars) to the most common (low-mass and red stars). Life for stars at the top of the heap in mass and energy output is lonely, radiant, and brief. As stars transform energy of mass into kinetic energy through nuclear fusion, the high-mass stars "burn" their nuclear "fuel" at enormous rates in comparison to the low-mass stars. Toward the bottom, stars live their lives far more modestly, and the low-mass stars can live, though not forever, far longer than the present age of the universe.

We must save for the next two chapters the stories of what happens to stars when life goes sour—when the nuclear fuel bill can no longer be paid. First, having gained a good working knowledge of stars in midlife, we should take a look at a younger generation of astronomers who work on a hot topic: how stars are born.

Figure 50. The globular star cluster Omega Centauri contains nearly a million stars, all born at almost the same time. (Photograph courtesy of National Optical Astronomy Observatories.)

7. Stars from Birth to Old Age

LEO BLITZ, A rugged-looking man in his mid-forties, has black hair showing signs of gray, a nose just slightly askew, and a wide smile. Blitz, whose family took flight from the ruins of Europe, specializes in studying the birth of stars. The story of his family's passage from Poland to Maryland includes an intriguing bureaucratic wrinkle: Leo Blitz owes five months to the government of the United States but will never have to pay.

This situation arose in the following manner: Blitz's father, born in Poland but raised in Vienna, served during World War II in the Soviet army; in the spring of 1945, as the German army collapsed, he was part of the Russian garrison in Krakow. Blitz's mother, born and raised in Poland, had managed to survive the Nazi extermination camp at Auschwitz, a few dozen kilometers away. Father and mother met in Krakow; their search for the mother's brother, who had been rumored to be in Germany, led the couple to Munich, where the brother was indeed living; and there Leo Blitz was born early in 1946.

But when Blitz's parents, like many other displaced persons during the immediate postwar years, sought to emigrate to the United States, they confronted a set of bureaucratic rules that favored a situation in which their son would have been born in 1945 in Poland. So Leo acquired a new origin: date of birth, 21 October 1945; place of birth, Krakow, Poland. For social-security purposes, Blitz's 65th birthday will occur in the year 2010, and he will have a free five-month ride in comparison to his biological clock—an intriguing compensation for the hardship of his early years.

By the spring of 1949 the Blitzes were in New Jersey, where

Leo's father began a grocery business that achieved sufficient success for the parents to fulfill the American dream of a college education for their children. In 1962, Leo entered Cornell University; although he had wanted to become an astronomer since the first grade, he studied physics on the grounds that it could provide a better career. After receiving his bachelor of science degree, Blitz worked for six years as a nuclear engineer involved in safety aspects of nuclear-power plants. "Then I got religion," he says. "I missed the pure science." Fearful that it might be too late to start over, Blitz enrolled in a graduate astrophysics course at Columbia University; when he did well in it, he left nuclear engineering and began graduate research in astronomy with a summer job under the supervision of Patrick Thaddeus, an unconventional, inspirational radio astronomer.

Continuing research under Thaddeus's guidance, Blitz made radio observations of clouds of interstellar gas that are about to form stars, or have recently formed them. Two decades later, he still happily pursues these observations, which he has always believed to lie at a cutting edge of astronomy. After three years as a postdoctoral fellow in Berkeley, Blitz joined the astronomy faculty at the University of Maryland, where he now ranks among its valued professors—prepared to teach as best he can and also eager to devote great effort to astronomical research.

Good professorial research requires a good assistant. Astronomy and other sciences have long used the apprenticeship system, in which a maturing scientist first puts in a few years as a barely paid graduate student and then, armed with a Ph.D., spends a few more years as an underpaid postdoctoral fellow. The beauty of the postdoctoral years (usually perceived only in hindsight) rests in the fact that research constitutes the only job requirement. Ahead, for many astronomers, lie years as a professor, involving frequent, nearly interminable committee meetings; disputes with often intolerable colleagues seeking more and better office space, office supplies, and teaching assistants; and meetings with undergraduates whose interest in astronomy appears to consist solely of the need for a good grade—or at least a passing one—that will satisfy a science-course requirement for graduation. Combine these negative aspects with the fact that no one's mind grows sharper with age, and many a successful middle-aged professor will admit that life seems not to be growing in its charms.

But science, the desire to find new facts about the universe, remains as alluring as ever. The secret of success is to find sharp young graduate students and "postdocs" to supervise and encourage. Here maturity does count on the professorial side: Graduate students and postdocs never lose sight of their need to engage in research that will help them into a real job. They therefore seek out the professors most likely to help bring about this happy result. A true symbiosis often arises: The professor can help a good student or postdoc to secure a job—or a respectable postdoctoral appointment—but only if good research emerges from their joint effort. Good results increase the professor's reputation and thus his or her ability to secure research grants, laboratory and office space, and just plain respect, more or less in proportion. Hence every professor keeps a lookout for students and postdocs of apparent merit; the good professors know not only how to identify ability but also how to encourage it.

Blitz made an inspired choice when he offered a postdoctoral fellowship to Eugene DeGeus (Figure 46). DeGeus (the G has the same sound as the first G in Vincent Van Gogh) was born in Holland, in the famous university town of Leiden, some 14 years after Blitz was born a few hundred miles across the European plain to the east. Like Blitz, DeGeus studied physics in college; when he completed his undergraduate studies at Leiden University, he switched to astronomy, which had interested him but never completely engaged his imagination—until he fell in with the astronomers. Leiden University enjoys a tremendous reputation in the world of astronomy, dating back at least to the time when Jan Oort, the outstanding Dutch astronomer of this century, joined its faculty during the late 1920s. Oort's research has ranged over a

Figure 46. Leo Blitz (right) and Eugene DeGeus (left) are two experts in studying star-forming regions with radio waves. (Photograph by Donald Goldsmith.)

wide variety of subjects, from the formation of the solar system to the ways that stars explode. He did pioneering work in radio astronomy even during World War II, when the Nazis occupied Holland for nearly five years: For a brief time, the Gestapo held Oort as a hostage. Thanks to Oort's inspiration, the Dutch have been leaders in radio astronomy for the past five decades, during which Oort has been first the director and then the director emeritus of the Leiden Observatory. The world has only a few non-English-speaking countries to which scientists will migrate from the U.S., but in astronomy, Holland is one, and DeGeus's thesis advisor at Leiden was W. Butler Burton, a Virginia-born astronomer who has taught at Leiden for more than a decade.

Like Blitz, Burton is a radio astronomer, and he led DeGeus into research on a region where stars have recently formed—the Scorpio-Centaurus association. From northern latitudes, the constellation Scorpio, with its red heart, Antares, and its hooklike tail, dominates the southern skies in summer. If you travel farther toward the south, you can see the constellation below Scorpio, Centaurus the Centaur, which never rises for latitudes north of 30 degrees. Nearly all the stars in Scorpio and Centaurus are young and were apparently formed at roughly the same time, a few tens of millions of years ago. Still more interesting to those who study star formation, parts of the Scorpio-Centaurus association are still forming stars. DeGeus received his Ph.D. in 1988 with a study that produced detailed maps of the radio emission from this star-forming region. He then wrote to several institutions seeking a postdoctoral fellowship and went to the University of Maryland for the eminently practical reason that they offered him one. There he and Blitz have engaged in fruitful collaboration, making observations of star-forming regions.

STAR-FORMING REGIONS

During the past century, astronomers have developed a fairly detailed conceptual model of a star-forming region—a model that Blitz and DeGeus have helped to refine (Color Plate 10). Once astronomers found that interstellar realms are not empty, they realized that vast, diffuse clouds of gas and dust could provide stellar nurseries. Within these interstellar clouds, stars are typically born in groups that include anywhere from a few thousand to many million new stars. To imagine such a stellar nursery, picture an interstellar cloud about a hundred light years across—25 times the distance from the sun to its closest neighbors (Color Plates 11 and 12). Astronomers still do not know just how such clouds form, but they have indeed formed, and within them, stars can also form. Inside such a cloud, the density (the amount of matter per cubic centimeter) rises several thousand times above the average density in interstellar space. Yet the "cloud" would qualify as a near-total vacuum on Earth—one that would require expensive facilities to maintain at a high-class laboratory.

In the Milky Way, the space between the stars has a density that averages one atom per cubic centimeter. Suppose that in your eagerness to understand interstellar space, you decided to spread out the atoms in the air that fills your bedroom until you have reduced the density to only one atom per cubic centimeter. You would require a lot of real estate: The room's atoms must occupy a volume considerably larger than the Earth! Hence a gas cloud with a thousand atoms per cubic centimeter, dense though it may be by interstellar standards, hardly represents a region crowded with atoms. Even though such a cloud may be hundreds of light years across, light could easily penetrate through the cloud without being blocked (*absorbed,* as astronomers say)—so long as the cloud contained only *gas.* The rub is that the cloud also contains *dust*, and the dust blocks the view (Color Plate 13).

Interstellar dust grains are agglomerations of thousands or millions of individual atoms, held together by the mutual attraction arising from the interplay of the atoms' electrons. Many dust particles consist either of carbon atoms (like the graphite in a "lead" pencil) or of "ices"—molecules of water, methane, or ammonia, frozen in clumps. The dust particles permeate interstellar space, because some process, as yet not well understood, encourages atoms to collect by the millions into tiny specks, not even one one-thousandth of an inch across, but far larger than any individual atom.

Dust grains are apparently made in the outer layers of aging stars and then gently blown into interstellar space. Since dust grains are enormous in comparison to atoms, they can do something no atom can: They can absorb light of *all* colors. An atom, with a diameter of only about one hundred-millionth of an inch, can affect only specific frequencies (that is, certain colors) of visible light. Only certain frequencies or

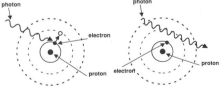

Figure 47. When a photon encounters an atom, it can make one of the atom's electrons jump into a larger orbit, but only if the photon carries exactly the right amount of energy to make such a jump occur. Otherwise, the photon will pass right by the atom with no interaction whatsoever. (Drawing by Crystal Stevenson.)

colors carry just the right amount of energy to make an atom's electron jump into a larger orbit. Other colors of light will pass by the atom completely unaffected (Figure 47).

With dust, no such color details arise. Dust particles simply absorb light—all of it. However, they absorb blue light more efficiently than red light, so that in some cases, astronomers can look through a modest dust cloud by studying only the red light from stars behind, while the stars' blue light is completely absorbed. But for all but the most modest dust-rich clouds, *no* light comes through at all. To look into such clouds you need a different type of radiation, a type that can pass through and escape from even dusty regions.

PROBING STAR-FORMING REGIONS WITH RADIO WAVES

If you want to uncover the mysteries of star formation, you need a way to observe stars *before* they have fully formed. Your best bet is to use radio waves (Figure 48). This is precisely what Leo Blitz and Eugene DeGeus do when they observe star-forming regions with the giant radio antennas at the University of California's Hat Creek Observatory. Radio waves are produced by gas and dust about to form stars. But radio waves can penetrate interstellar clouds without being absorbed by the dusty material that shrouds star-forming regions. Radio waves' penetrating powers arise from the fact that their wavelengths (the distance between successive wave crests) exceeds the size of most interstellar dust particles. As a result, radio waves can pass by dust particles and barely notice their

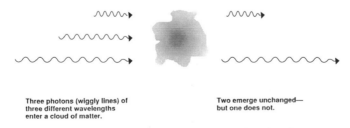

Three photons (wiggly lines) of three different wavelengths enter a cloud of matter.

Two emerge unchanged—but one does not.

Figure 48. Interstellar clouds typically absorb only photons with certain wavelengths and let others, such as radio waves, travel freely through the clouds. (Drawing by Crystal Stevenson.)

presence, as an ocean wave will roll unaffected past an obstacle smaller than its wavelength.

Radio waves have two great virtues in the quest to examine star-forming regions. Not only do they penetrate dusty regions, but in addition star-forming regions *emit* large amounts of radio waves, even though no stars may yet have formed. A star-forming region represents part of the Milky Way (or some other galaxy) that has grown denser than average and within which individual clumps are condensing, or will soon condense. The matter within the region contains a mixture of atoms typical of the Milky Way: hydrogen, helium, oxygen, nitrogen, carbon, and neon are its most abundant elements. The stars also contain these elements, as do the giant planets around the sun and almost all the objects in the universe save some exceptional, dense rocky planets such as the Earth.

Any gaseous mixture rich in carbon and oxygen atoms will form large numbers of *carbon monoxide* molecules, in which carbon and oxygen atoms join together. On Earth, carbon monoxide is a colorless, odorless gas produced by combustion in gasoline engines, dangerous to those who foolishly attempt to use an automobile's exhaust for heat. In the universe, however, carbon monoxide is one of the most abundant types of molecules, difficult to break apart once oxygen and carbon atoms have joined to form it. To radio astronomers—especially those who study star-forming regions— carbon monoxide is a friendly molecule, the guidepost to the structure and motions of the region.

This is so because carbon monoxide molecules, even in the cold of interstellar space, emit radio waves of a particular frequency and wavelength. This emission arises from subtle changes in the motions of the carbon and oxygen nuclei within the molecule; because the changes are subtle, they involve only tiny amounts of energy and produce radio waves, which have low energies, rather than higher-energy light waves. Because the carbon and oxygen atoms must fit together in specific patterns, any changes within the carbon-monoxide molecules produce radio waves of specific frequencies. Radio astronomers have learned to recognize these frequencies, indeed to search them out with specialized detectors like those at the Hat Creek Observatory in Northern California or at Caltech's Owens Valley Radio Observatory. And because the frequencies are specific, astronomers can recognize modest changes in those frequencies produced by the Doppler effect, changes that arise from the motion of the radio-emitting gas either toward or away from the Earth.

Armed with this knowledge and experience, radio astronomers such as Blitz and DeGeus can make a *radio map* of a star-forming region. The map consists of *contour lines* that plot the intensity of the emission from a given region. These contour lines provide a two-dimensional picture in which the third dimension, along the line of sight, can only be guessed at. But when the astronomers add the information gained from the Doppler-shift measurements, they can begin to piece together a three-dimensional view of the star-forming region.

BIPOLAR OUTFLOWS: THE SIGNATURE OF STAR FORMATION

In recent years, radio astronomers have made a key observational discovery: *bipolar outflow*—localized volumes within a star-forming region where a contracting gas cloud is squirting out material in two opposite directions. Theorists interpret these observed bipolar outflows as relatively late stages in the process of star formation. Radio observations indicate that most contracting gas clouds acquire some rotation as they begin to condense. Just why this occurs remains a mystery, but the rotation keeps the gas cloud from contracting by equal amounts in all directions. Theoretical research by many astronomers has shown clearly that once a star-forming region develops subclumps, then the gravity within these clumps— the pull of each part of the clump for every other part—will make the clumps contract. If the clump has some overall rotation, even at a low rate of spin, the process of contraction will increase the rate of rotation, much as a figure skater contracts to increase the rate of spin. As a result, when the cloud shrinks in response to its own gravity, it contracts more easily in the direction along its spin axis, and therefore assumes a flattened, pancakelike shape. Once the contraction along the spin axis is nearly complete, some material begins to squirt outward along the spin axis, though the cloud can retain most of its original mass. Hence the observations of bipolar outflow now reveal—so most astronomers think!—localized clumps within a star-forming region where matter has contracted to the point that some material is being forced outward. Bipolar outflows thus provide observational evidence, though not direct proof, that stars are about to be born.

If the astronomers are right, it won't be long—a few

hundred thousand years at most—before stars formed from the clumps with observed bipolar outflows actually begin to shine. This will occur when the density and temperature at the center of such a clump rise to the point that nuclear fusion, the melding together of atomic nuclei, can begin. The *protostar* (star in formation) then, by definition, becomes a star.

Once nuclear fusion begins, the star will emit enough energy to heat the material around it to hundreds or thousands of degrees. This heat will evaporate the gas within which the star formed. Radiation pressure—the intense light from the newborn stars—will push surrounding dust particles outward, clearing the cocoon within which the star first saw the light. Within star-forming regions, astronomers can now identify newborn stars, no more than a few hundred thousand years old, still surrounded by relatively dense layers of gas (Color Plate 15). The closest star-forming region, the Orion Nebula, provides a fine example (Color Plate 14). Within the Orion Nebula, a cluster of young, hot, luminous stars, called the Trapezium, shines brightly despite the gas that envelops them. After a few million years, with more stars born within the Trapezium, the heat from the new stars will have evaporated this gauzy veil almost completely, as has happened to the gas that once enveloped the star cluster called the Pleiades. Between the ages of the Trapezium and the Pleiades lie about a hundred million years— just a couple of days if the Milky Way's history spanned a year. But the Trapezium stars, in this analogy, are only a few minutes old!

The Orion Nebula, home of the Trapezium cluster, provides another important insight into star formation: The newborn star cluster contains less than one one-thousandth of the total amount of matter in the star-forming region! The cluster-in-progress may include matter that totals a few thousand times the mass of the sun, but the entire region has *many million* solar masses. Radio and infrared observations revealed this fact, for most of the region contains no stars or conceals any newborn stars within dense cocoons of surrounding dusty gas. The Orion Nebula therefore reminds us once again that an overemphasis on visible light, the type of electromagnetic radiation that our eyes detect, may deceive us. We need radio astronomers and their observations of *invisible* radiation in order to understand important parts of the galaxy in which we live.

The Orion Nebula glows with the light from some of the youngest stars in the Milky Way. On a clear winter's night, when you look to the east you can see the constellation of Orion the Hunter, easily identified by the three bright stars that form the hunter's belt, with one bright shoulder, the star Betelgeuse, to the north, and one bright foot, Rigel, to the south (Figure 49). Between the belt and Rigel are three dimmer stars that represent Orions' sword, but the middle "star," as you can see with binoculars, is in fact no star at all; it is the Orion Nebula, nearly 1,500 light years away, shining with the radiance of a new generation of stars. If you could see the entire star-forming region, it would cover all of Orion between the belt and the foot—as if the hunter had acquired a dark tumor half his size.

THE TWO TYPES OF STAR CLUSTERS

Later generations of humans—may they come to pass—will see the Trapezium stars when they are no longer embedded in their gaseous nebula, as they are today. Instead, the Trapezium will become a young, easily visible star cluster. The Trapezium will be an *open cluster*, one of the two basic types of star clusters, containing a few thousand stars. Other open clusters include the Hyades, the Pleiades (Figure 22, p. 68), and the "Double Cluster" in Perseus, so named because the loose aggregation of stars has a double center. Of these clusters, the closest to us, just 160 light years away, is the Hyades, which form the horns of Taurus, the Bull, just to the west of Orion. Because the Hyades stars are several hundred million years old, all the remaining gas within which the stars formed has escaped into interstellar space, leaving behind simply an open cluster of stars.

Globular clusters are the second basic type of star cluster (Figure 50, p. 164). Each globular cluster consists of a hundred thousand to a *million* stars, far more densely packed than the stars in an open cluster. Both types of star cluster typically have diameters of several dozen, perhaps a hundred, light years. However, the density of stars within a globular cluster rises about a thousand times above the density in the open cluster. If we lived within a globular cluster, the closest stars to the sun would seem brighter than the full moon! Astronomy might then lie closer to our hearts but would be more difficult in practice, thanks to the far greater interference from the sun's closest neighbors.

Figure 49. The Orion Nebula is the middle "star" in the sword of the constellation Orion. This sword lies between the three stars of Orion's belt (top) and the bright stars Rigel (lower right) and Saiph (lower left), which represent Orion's feet. The Horsehead Nebula is visible just below the left-hand star in the belt. At the lower center, the photograph has captured the trail of a "shooting star" or meteor, a pin-sized object burning up through friction in the Earth's atmosphere. (Yerkes Observatory photograph.)

MYSTERIES OF STAR FORMATION

Did the sun form as part of a star cluster? Where then are the sun's brothers and sisters? Astronomers have found that star clusters represent the exception, not the rule, as long as we use the word "cluster" to designate a group of stars that remains together for hundreds of millions, if not billions, of years. Most stars are born as part of a looser group called an *association*, such as the Scorpio-Centaurus association that Eugene DeGeus studied for his Ph.D. The stars in an association are all born together, but within a few million years they drift apart because of their random individual motions. This must have been true of the sun, some five billion years ago, and the stars born with the sun must still orbit the center of the Milky Way, unidentified to us as our birth cousins.

One key question about star-formation still intrigues and puzzles astronomers: Why do stars ever begin to form? We have no good explanation of how clouds of interstellar gas condense in the first place, or of how clumps within these clouds grow sufficiently dense that the clumps' own gravity will make stars form from them.

But it would hardly be proper to solve all problems of star formation in a single generation. Someday astronomers will find better ways to study interstellar matter floating among the stars and to guess at how it develops clouds, and clumps within those clouds, which eventually yield new stars. Someday Eugene DeGeus will need a good postdoctoral fellow, and someday he or she will need one too. Astronomer trains astronomer; fellowship breeds fellowship; and research continues on the question of where stars come from.

WHEN STARS GO BAD

Nothing lasts forever. The first law of thermodynamics keeps cosmic bank accounts in order. This law states that you can only *transform* energy from one form to another; you can never make energy out of nothing. Hence if you want to produce the energy that makes stars shine, you must have a way to do so. If this method consists of turning energy of mass (Einstein's $E = mc^2$) into kinetic energy as stars do, you face a serious problem when you exhaust your supply of mass that will yield kinetic energy through nuclear fusion. If you are a star, you may not admit it, but you have been cooking your own goose and must pay the piper. (Or is it the other way around, as Sid Caesar liked to ask?) In short, stars begin life with limited supplies of nuclear "fuel," the hydrogen nuclei (protons) that they meld together to make helium nuclei and thus to transform energy of mass into kinetic energy. Each star must eventually consume its fuel, whereupon it can no longer continue life as a true star.

As we discussed in the previous chapter, all stars shine for most of their lives by fusing protons (hydrogen nuclei) at the stars' centers, where the temperature and density of matter rise highest. Whether this fusion proceeds through the three steps of the proton-proton cycle or the six steps of the carbon cycle, the net result is the same: Four protons (hydrogen nuclei) produce a single nucleus of helium-four, plus two antielectrons, two neutrinos, and—last but most important—new kinetic energy in the form of more rapid motion of the particles. The kinetic energy diffuses outward through countless collisions. As it does so, the newly made energy plays two key roles: It heats the entire star and thus makes it shine, and still more important, the energy produced in the star's center keeps the entire star from collapsing as it diffuses outward through enormous numbers of collisions, like the energy released by a street brawl at the center of a crowd.

A star's life may be seen as one long battle against its own gravity. Stars owe their existence to gravity: They formed because their mass drew itself together through gravitational forces. These forces increased as the protostar (star in formation) contracted, because each part of the protostar drew closer to all the other parts. As we have discussed, the protostar's contraction increased the density of matter—the amount of mass per cubic centimeter—within it. This increase in density made the temperature rise. If no such thing as nuclear fusion occurred in the universe, the contraction might have continued indefinitely, as the protostar grew ever denser and hotter, shrinking to an ever-smaller size.

When nuclear fusion begins in a protostar, the fusion has the intriguing effect of avoiding further heating of the protostar and of halting its contraction. Because nuclear fusion turns energy of mass into kinetic energy, fusion gives the protostar a way to avoid eternal contraction. *Nuclear fusion provides the protostar—now a star—with a continuous flow of new kinetic energy that pushes outward and resists the star's tendency to contract under its own gravity.* Ever since nuclear fusion began in the star's interior, there has been a titanic battleground between two opposing forces: the star's tendency to contract because of gravitational forces and its tendency to explode from the violent release of energy by nuclear fusion.

During most of a star's life, this battleground has no victor. Instead, the star leads a finely balanced existence, in equipoise between two mighty forces. Take away nuclear fusion, and the star would collapse in an instant. Remove gravity, and the star would explode almost as rapidly. Keep both gravity and fusion, as the universe has done, and the star can maintain a nearly constant size and rate of energy release for billions of years.

But eventually any star begins to run out of protons—the basic fuel for fusion—in its central regions. The star then embarks upon a complex course of events, all of which represent a struggle to maintain some sort of balance between gravity and fusion. In the long run, this struggle cannot succeed, but the long run lies in the distant future, and the star—though of course not consciously fighting to stay alive—does remarkably well at staving off its eventual demise.

If a star were a steam locomotive, then when it began to exhaust the protons at its center, it would simply shovel in more proton "fuel" from the regions that surround the core. In an actual star, however, material tends to remain stationary, held in place by material above and below—that is, by the gravitational forces within the star. Hence, as the star's center becomes almost entirely helium nuclei, with no protons left, *nuclear fusion moves outward*, enveloping regions surrounding the central core, which has ceased to fuse protons into helium nuclei.

During the years when nuclear fusion occurred in the core, the temperature within the surrounding regions was insufficient for nuclear fusion. But as the star's core and the material surrounding it shrink, the temperature of the regions around the core rises—because gas squeezed into a smaller volume grows hotter—and eventually becomes so hot that fusion can proceed. The shrinkage occurs because the core itself no longer releases much new energy to oppose its own gravitational force. The nuclear fusion region therefore embraces a progressively larger region around the core, producing a "shell" where nuclear fusion goes on, and leaving within the shell a "core" in which almost all the nuclei are helium.

By fusing protons (hydrogen nuclei) in a shell around its helium core, the star achieves "quasi-equilibrium," a state in which the energy released by the continuing nuclear fusion opposes the star's tendency to contract under its own gravity. But *within* the core, gravity is winning, for the core no longer produces energy by nuclear fusion. Only the high temperature of the helium nuclei in the core, caused by the compression of the core into a smaller volume, prevents collapse to a much smaller size.

As more material joins the core, as shell after shell around it likewise become almost pure helium, the problem grows worse: The core has more mass and a greater tendency to contract, because its own gravitational force has grown larger. The core can therefore support itself only by achieving a still higher temperature, so that the particles in the core will move still more rapidly to avoid collapse. The increase in temperature arises from the continuing contraction of the core, which squeezes the nuclei into a smaller space, producing a higher temperature. As the core grows smaller, denser, and hotter, so too do the regions surrounding the core. The temperature of the nuclear-fusing regions therefore increases.

This increase in temperature means that the star actually fuses a dwindling supply of protons more rapidly than before. Natural forces impel the star to burn an ever-smaller store of fuel ever more rapidly. The star behaves something like an overwrought motorist on a dark night with a dwindling fuel supply, who, desperate to reach the next gas station, pushes the accelerator pedal toward the floorboard, consuming the last gallon of gas more rapidly than the first ten.

Just as the misguided motorist may pass a few minutes speeding at ever-increasing velocities, an aging star can spend its final proton-fusing years in luminous glory. The increased rate of nuclear fusion produces more energy each second, and this energy continues to diffuse to the surface, making the star shine more brightly than before. Furthermore, the outward passage of larger amounts of energy pushes against the star's outer layers and expands them. Thus the entire star grows larger as it becomes more luminous.

RED GIANTS: SWOLLEN STARS WITH CONTRACTED CORES

Since the expansion cools the gas within an aging star, a strange dance toward death arises: *As the core grows hotter and denser, the star's outer layers grow cooler and more rarefied, and the star becomes a red giant.* A red-giant star consists of a bloated envelope of gas—typically reddish in color because it is rather cool—that surrounds and conceals the star's ever-contracting core and the nuclear-fusing layers around the core. Red giants are aged stars, their main-sequence lives over, still temporarily glorious but headed for extinction.

In about 5 billion years, the sun will begin to become a red giant. At that time, some 10 billion years after fusion first began in the sun, nuclear fusion will continue to occur in a shell surrounding the sun's helium-rich core. As described above, the aging sun will actually produce more energy per second than it does now. And as the energy fights its way to the surface, the increased flow of energy will distend the sun's outer layers. At a time 100 million years or so after its core becomes pure helium, the sun's surface will reach halfway to the Earth. Then the sun's outer regions, as diffuse as what we call a vacuum on Earth, will span 100 million miles. The total energy radiated by the sun each second will increase a hundredfold, burning away much of the Earth's atmosphere and raising the Earth's temperature by several hundred degrees. Here lies the true "energy crisis" that no politician will confront: What can you do with a sun out of control?

(Doubtless the first thing to do is for our species to survive—in some form—for five billion years. If we can do this, all else may seem easy. Perhaps we can arrange to move the Earth progressively farther from the sun, into a larger orbit that lengthens the cycle of summer and winter but leaves our planet's average temperature unchanged.)

The sun's red-giant phase lies five billion years in the future, but many stars have already become red giants. Typically, a star shines as a red giant for about one-tenth the total time that it spent fusing protons in its core. During the star's red-giant phase, the core's increased energy output continuously expands the star's outer layers (even as the core goes on shrinking), until the heat released from the core pushes the outer layers completely away.

THE PLANETARY NEBULA THAT ENDS THE RED GIANT

The expansion of the star's outer layers gradually lays bare the much hotter, inner regions: the helium core, surrounded by the proton-fusing shell of material, which in turn is surrounded by layers of unfused material. This arrangement of matter produces one of the finest sights in the sky, called a *planetary nebula* (Color Plate 16).

A planetary nebula has nothing to do with planets. (However, seen through a small telescope, such a nebula may appear to resemble a planet.) In a planetary nebula, the puffed-out sphere of gas is lit from within by the star's hot core. Indeed, this core comprises the functioning "star." The core is so hot that most of its energy now emerges as ultraviolet radiation, not as visible light. This is so because hotter objects produce more violet light than red; at a sufficiently high temperature, an object will glow mostly in the ultraviolet and only a little in visible light.

The spheres of gas surrounding the star—its former outer layers—trap some of the ultraviolet radiation, which strikes atoms and knocks some of their electrons loose from the atomic nuclei. As the electrons recombine with the nuclei, they jump into orbits closer to the centers of the atoms and emit visible light. A visible-light photograph of a planetary nebula therefore shows a bright nebula surrounding a dim star. But if we had "ultraviolet eyes," we could see that in ultraviolet, the nebula shines far more dimly than the star. As it is, we see mostly the effects that the star's ultraviolet radiation produce in visible light on the layers previously expelled into space.

The planetary-nebula phase lasts only a brief time in astronomical terms—perhaps a hundred thousand to a million years. Each view of a planetary nebula in the Milky Way therefore represents a snapshot we are lucky enough to obtain now; a few million years hence, astronomers must find other former red giants, by then planetary nebulae, to illustrate books such as this.

At the center of events, the core of the star might continue to contract and grow ever hotter and denser, were it not for a new phenomenon—the start of helium fusion—investigated by Hans Bethe's longtime collaborator Ed Salpeter.

HELIUM FUSION IN AGED STARS

We have seen that stars eventually fuse protons in a shell of matter surrounding a contracting helium core. The next stages on the road to stellar death seemed complex and mysterious, until Ed Salpeter made a key discovery. Edwin Ernest Salpeter was born in Vienna in 1924. By the time he entered his teenage years, the Nazis were at the gates and the Salpeter family wisely emigrated to Australia. Ed Salpeter graduated from the University of Sydney and went to England for graduate study. As a specialist in the physics of nuclei, he naturally gravitated toward Ithaca, New York, where Hans Bethe and his fellow professors had made Cornell a leader in nuclear research. He joined the Cornell faculty in 1949 and now, forty-two years later, with a brilliant career that ranges among much of astrophysics as well as nuclear physics, Salpeter occasionally thinks about retirement—some day (Figure 51).

To astronomers, Salpeter is best known for his attempts over the past three decades to understand how stars form, but some of

Figure 51. Professor Edwin Salpeter of Cornell University has made important contributions to the study of star formation and late stellar evolution. (Photograph by Laurie Sieverts Snyder.)

his earliest work in astrophysics dealt with a crucial question about stellar aging: How do stars ever begin to fuse *helium* nuclei?

Each helium nucleus produced by the fusion of protons contains four *nucleons* (a nucleon is either a proton or a neutron). The fusion of two such nuclei produces a nucleus with *eight* nucleons. But research with particle accelerators revealed that *no nucleus with eight nucleons can be stable*. Instead, any such nucleus will decay in a tiny fraction of a second, and the decay in effect reverses the fusion. An attempt to find a way for nature to fuse helium nuclei therefore seemed akin to shoveling fleas across a barnyard. Into this stable stepped Ed Salpeter and other physicists turned astrophysicists. They discovered how nature fuses helium: not by twos but effectively by threes.

Suppose, the physicists said, you fused two helium nuclei to form a nucleus of beryllium-8, and then, in the trillionth of a second before that nucleus decayed, you managed to bring in another helium nucleus for fusion. The second fusion—with the third helium nucleus—would produce a nucleus containing *twelve* nucleons, and such nuclei, called carbon-12, rank among nature's most stable.

And so it goes in stars, but only when the temperature and density are enormous. You need a high temperature to make helium nuclei fuse together, and you need a high density for the second helium fusion to occur before the beryllium nucleus decays. By 1952, Ed Salpeter had worked out the basics of this process.

Salpeter thus showed how stars can "burn" their helium. In effect, the star discovers that the "ashes" of its chief nuclear fusion—hydrogen burning—are themselves good fuel. All the star needs to do is raise its temperature to about *100 million* degrees! Amazingly, the star can do so simply by letting gravity work: Gravity makes the star contract and grow hotter until the helium in the core, which remains inert at low temperatures, begins to fuse.

The helium fuel does indeed "burn," but not so well as hydrogen. Helium-to-carbon fusion yields only about 10 percent as much energy as hydrogen-to-helium fusion; that is, only about 10 percent as much energy of mass turns into kinetic energy in each fusion reaction. The additional energy supply that a star gains from "discovering" helium fusion therefore lasts for only an astronomically brief time. A star like the sun may spend 10 billion years as a prime-of-life star, and then another billion as a red giant, fusing its remaining protons, which occupy a shell surrounding its core of nearly pure helium. Then helium fusion can suddenly begin, as the star undergoes what theoretical astrophysicists call the *helium flash*, an event much calculated but not yet observed. The helium flash, which marks the start of helium fusion, temporarily brightens the star and loosens its central regions a bit, but the star soon settles down to its task of fusing helium nuclei into carbon. For a billion years more the star can perform this function, a sort of reprise of its 10 billion years of hydrogen (proton) fusion. Once nearly all the helium nuclei have fused into carbon nuclei, the star seems poised on the brink of further exciting possibilities. But a strange development then ensues: The star settles down to die.

THE EXCLUSION PRINCIPLE AND THE DEATH OF STARS

Stars made mainly of carbon nuclei undergo no further nuclear fusion but instead fade away quietly as *white dwarfs*. A white dwarf finds its support against gravity from a sort of invisible hand called the *exclusion principle*, a cornerstone of quantum mechanics, first conceived by Wolfgang Pauli in 1925 and first applied to calculations of stellar structure during the 1930s by the great Indian-born astrophysicist Subrahmanyan Chandrasekhar.

Chandrasekhar, who won the Nobel Prize for his investigations into the depths of aged stars, studied with the great British astronomer Arthur Eddington at Cambridge but found his professorship at the University of Chicago. There he spun the elegant mathematics that showed what happens when the matter in a star's interior reaches a density a million times the density of water. This occurs only as the star completes the fusion of its helium nuclei into carbon nuclei. In addition to the nuclei that participate in nuclear fusion, the star still contains—just as stars do now—a multitude of electrons, the tiny particles that orbit atomic nuclei.

Electrons are bystanders in nuclear fusion, nonparticipants in the mechanism that makes stars shine. However, Chandrasekhar demonstrated by elegant mathematical analysis that the operation of the exclusion principle prevents the electrons from squeezing into any smaller volume, and thus to any higher density, beyond a certain critical value. If the electrons can't be packed any tighter, neither can the nuclei: The negatively charged electrons exert attractive forces on the positively charged nuclei and keep them from moving far. Thus the entire star—electrons and carbon nuclei—will contract no further, gravity or no gravity, because the exclusion principle says it may not.

This exclusion principle may seem a deus ex machina, a device to avoid imagining the further contraction of stars, but physicists believe in it absolutely, and for the best of reasons: Quantum mechanics, which includes the exclusion principle as one of its fundamental attributes, has been a knockout success in explaining the structure of atoms and nuclei. Sooner than give up the exclusion principle, most physicists would sacrifice any political belief they may hold—but no one asks these days.

Furthermore, astronomers have observed hosts of white-dwarf stars, all of which Chandrasekhar's calculations can explain—a good thing, for the astronomers were baffled before the truth emerged. White-dwarf stars have surface temperatures much like those of the sun or Sirius, but their luminosities, that is, energy outflows per second, are no more than one ten-thousandth the luminosity of ordinary stars with the same surface temperature.

Every object not at a temperature of absolute zero (the lowest temperature theoretically achievable) radiates energy into space, just as a star athlete does. And every astronomer knows that if two objects have the same temperature, the energy that they radiate per second will be directly proportional to the objects' surface areas. Thus even before white dwarfs were named, astronomers knew that they must each have one ten-thousandth of the surface area of a star like the sun, simply because they have (roughly) the same temperature as the sun but produce only one ten-thousandth of the sun's energy outflow each second as they radiate into space. But a star with one ten-thousandth of the sun's surface area must have one one-hundredth (the square root of one ten-thousandth) of the sun's radius. Hence a white dwarf must be a star no larger than the Earth, with a surface glowing at 10,000 degrees. Some white dwarfs, such as the companions to Sirius, belong to double-star systems and move in orbit with relatively ordinary stars. This motion allowed astronomers to measure the masses of some white dwarfs. Because these masses roughly equaled the mass of the sun, pre-Chandrasekhar astronomers faced a conundrum: How could the mass of a *star* be packed into the size of the *Earth* yet radiate with only one ten-thousandth the luminosity of an ordinary star?

Chandrasekhar provided an explanation of the observational facts based on mathematical theory. He showed that objects with a million times the density of water can exist and indeed *persist*. White dwarfs can support themselves indefinitely against their own gravity through the invisible hand of the exclusion principle. The price paid for this support includes the end of all nuclear fusion, for when electrons and nuclei cannot be squeezed any more tightly, any nuclei are likewise prevented from moving rapidly enough to fuse upon collision.

In brief, Subrahmanyan Chandrasekhar showed that each white dwarf is the dying ember of a star, the once-violent center that fused hydrogen into helium and then helium into carbon

Figure 52. The bright star Sirius A has a faint white-dwarf companion, Sirius B (at left), which is almost lost in the glare from its bright neighbor. The spikes around Sirius A arise in the telescope's optical system. (Lick Observatory photograph.)

nuclei. This ember now quietly does nothing but radiate away its stored supplies of energy into space, supported against its own collapse by the exclusion principle. Every white dwarf thus steadily though slowly cools and grows dimmer, taking billions of years to fade into invisibility (Figure 52).

Since nearly every star has become or will become a white dwarf, they exist by the billions throughout the Milky Way. To be honest, astronomers have found white dwarfs only by the thousands, but since white dwarfs are intrinsically faint, we know that we have found only those closest to us and thus can extrapolate with confidence to derive an enormous total for the number of white dwarfs.

Their fate will be ours. At a time six or seven billion years in the future, the sun—more precisely, the sun's inner regions—

will become a white dwarf. The sun's loss of its outer layers as a red giant will change the planets' orbits somewhat, but the Earth will move in orbit around the white-dwarf sun much as it does now. Space in the outer solar system, previously in demand to escape the heat of the sun's red-giant and planetary-nebula phases, will then sell at bargain prices: The reduced ouput from the now-faded sun will be unable to warm even the planet Mercury to room temperature. Although astronomers know that the public is sufficiently gullible to purchase desert lots for development, none has had the gall (or is it the initiative?) to sell shares in future building sites within a million miles of the white-dwarf sun. Indeed, most of us can contemplate with equanimity the difficulties to be created by the sun's red-giant and white-dwarf developments, dealing with these as we do with many problems: by leaving them to the next generation. Before we do that, we ought to look at what happens to the rare stars that cannot become white dwarfs but instead blow themselves up.

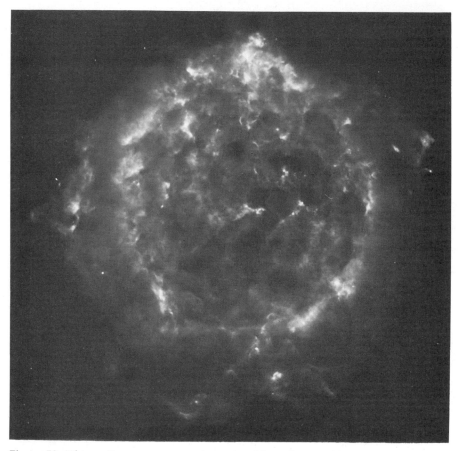

Figure 53. This radio map, processed to resemble a photograph, records the radio emission from Cassiopeia A, the expanding remnant of a star whose explosion apparently appeared in our skies during the late seventeenth century but went nearly unrecorded. (Courtesy of the National Radio Astronomy Observatory.)

8. The Stellar Explosions that Made Us

MOST STARS FADE quietly as they age, as our sun will itself fade into white-dwarf obscurity in about five billion years. But a small minority of stars explode at the ends of their lives, seeding the universe with nuclei made in their interiors. These exploding stars deserve respect, because in elemental terms, they made the Earth, the oceans, the atmosphere, and the creatures that live there. In fact, wherever life exists in the universe, life owes its origin to *supernovae*: exploding stars whose death helped bring forth life elsewhere.

THE EXPLODING STAR OF 1987

About 160,000 years ago, a star exploded in the irregular galaxy called the Large Magellanic Cloud, a satellite of our own Milky Way galaxy (Color Plate 17). Because the Large Magellanic Cloud lies about 160,000 light years from the solar system, the light from the exploding star arrived on Earth only a few years ago, to blaze forth as a supernova on the night of February 23, 1987 (Color Plates 18 and 19). And because the Large Magellanic Cloud lies in a direction on the sky that never rises for most Northern Hemisphere observers, this exploding star, called Supernova 1987A, could never be seen with the giant telescopes in California and Arizona. Instead, observers rushed to the Southern Hemisphere, where they had the finest opportunities to study a relatively nearby supernova. The astronomers used the three great observatories in Chile and the optical and radio observatories in Australia, where the flourishing astronomical community seized this heaven-sent opportunity and followed the slow decline of the exploding star through the past four years.

Among the foremost astronomers in Australia is Richard Manchester, an expert on what supernova explosions leave behind: *pulsars,* sources of radio emission that intensifies at regular intervals. Manchester has been the discoverer or co-discoverer of close to half of the five hundred pulsars found during the past 25 years. Born and educated in New Zealand, he has worked at the Australian National Radio Astronomy Observatory for many years, using as his chief observational tool the giant radio dish at Parkes, 150 miles west of Sydney, and its associated receivers and amplifiers. In 1965, Manchester received his doctorate in radio astronomy just as the first pulsar was discovered, and promptly adopted pulsar observations as his specialty. When he heard that a supernova had appeared in the Large Magellanic Cloud, he resolved to see whether he and his colleagues couldn't find its pulsar—if the supernova produced one. Four years later, with no pulsar found, Manchester continues to search, even though the chance of a pulsar revealing itself within the supernova remnant seems slim.

Manchester's search for the pulsar forms just one of the multiple lines of attack upon the supernova and its remnant. At the Siding Spring Observatory, Australia's finest telescope site, another Australian astronomer named Mike Dopita has been following the changes in the material that the star ejected into space. Like Dick Manchester, Dopita has a home base (in his case, the capital city of Canberra) far from the mountaintop observatory that offers excellent telescopic views of the sky—on those few nights when Dopita has access to the telescope.

The unexpected appearance of the supernova in Australian skies promoted Dopita's claims to telescope time. Capitalizing upon the opportunity, he has made some five dozen trips by light plane from Canberra 350 miles northward, to Coonabarabran, the town at the edge of the "great Australian dry" whose airport lies closest to the observatory. (Australian astronomers who have spent too long in this small hamlet, with a main street approximately five blocks long, refer to it as "Coonabloodybarabran.") From the airport, a half-hour ride takes Dopita—or any other astronomer— to the observatory through the Warrumbungle Mountains National Park, past what foreigners call "exotic" animals (kangaroos and echidnas, for example) but which Australians see mostly as potential road hazards. Every observatory vehicle mounts sturdy "roo bars" to diminish the effect of a collision with a kangaroo, and a highway encounter with the spiny echidna can prove as fatal to ordinary tires as to the echidna itself.

To appreciate what drives astronomers such as Manchester and Dopita to winkle out the secrets of exploding stars, it is important to understand what distinguishes the stars that *explode* as they die from all other stars, which simply fade away as white dwarfs. Every star as it ages becomes a red giant: bloated and rouged on the outside; hot, dense, and continuously contracting at its center. In nearly all stars, the red giant's outer layers eventually evaporate to reveal the core as an inert white dwarf. Inside such a white dwarf, whose enormous density of matter might seem to make the core ready to collapse, the exclusion principle (discussed in the previous chapter) exerts its calming influence within the star. The exclusion principle holds the nuclei in place and provides support against gravitational collapse. From then on, the star neither expands nor contracts. It produces no new energy at all but instead slowly radiates away its store of energy, the heat accumulated during its glory days.

Ninety-nine point nine percent of all stars have become, or will become, white dwarfs. Only one-tenth of a percent—possibly even fewer—of all stars escape white-dwarfdom and explode. What makes the difference that distinguishes this small minority of stars?

The key determining factor is the *mass* of the star, that is, the amount of matter that it accumulated as it formed. Only those stars with the *largest* masses become supernovae; all the rest fade away quietly as white dwarfs. The mass of a star proves critically important because a star with a larger mass will squeeze its core *more strongly* through the force of its own gravity. As a result of this extra squeezing, the star's central temperature rises more easily: The star can reach a given temperature without packing its matter quite so tightly. This difference is subtle—but it allows some stars to explode.

In any star, the exclusion principle waits in the wings, ready to play a crucial role. If the density of matter rises to a certain critical value, the exclusion principle prevents any further nuclear fusion. Mathematical models of stellar interiors have shown that in most stars, the density will rise to the critical value, about a million times the density of water, as soon as the star has fused all of its helium nuclei into carbon nuclei. But in the stars that are destined to explode, the density in the core does not rise to the critical value by the time the helium-to-carbon fusion is complete. Such stars therefore cannot rely on the support offered by the exclusion principle. They cannot quietly fade away as white dwarfs. These stars remain in thrall to the basic rule of stellar structure: Release sufficient energy through nuclear fusion or collapse.

So nuclear fusion continues in the center of a high-mass star. A high-mass star goes on to fuse carbon nuclei with the remaining helium nuclei to form oxygen; it fuses oxygen nuclei with helium to form neon; it fuses carbon with carbon to form silicon; and it eventually fuses silicon with silicon to form nickel, cobalt, and iron. Each of these fusion reactions releases some kinetic energy from mass and therefore offers the star some support against collapse. But the star is scraping the bottom of its nuclear barrel: The fusion reactions provide progressively *less* energy per reaction.

In order to avoid collapse, the star must obtain the same amount of energy each second (or even more as its core continues to shrink) from progressively less efficient types of nuclear fusion. The star therefore fuses its newly made nuclei more and more *rapidly*, consuming its ever-poorer fuel at an ever-increasing rate. The fusion of carbon takes millions of years, but the fusion of silicon requires only thousands of years. The next step in fusion requires merely a few years, and the final stages of fusion, during which nuclei fuse to make iron, require only a few weeks. (Those who enjoy anthropomorphizing stars may compare the star to a convict on death row, postponing the inevitable final moment with a last meal, a last sermon, and finally, a last cigarette.)

But the end arrives. Once the star has fused most of the nuclei at its center into iron nuclei, it has no further means of releasing kinetic energy through nuclear fusion. To fuse iron nuclei into still heavier nuclei would require the *addition* of kinetic energy, rather than the release of it.

This reversal marks iron as a special member of the list of elements. The fusion of nuclei that are lighter than iron releases energy from mass, but the fusion of iron or heavier nuclei *adds* to the mass of the resultant nuclei and *takes* kinetic energy from the supply. Hence a star with mostly iron nuclei at its center, unable to find a source of additional energy, gives up the ghost and collapses, a victim of its own gravity. (The collapse, as we shall see, involves a maneuver whereby nature finds a way to sneak around the exclusion principle.)

NEUTRON STARS: COLLAPSED CORES OF MASSIVE STARS

In most cases, the star's collapse produces one of the great beasts of the cosmos: a *neutron star*. As its name so vividly implies, a neutron star consists almost entirely of neutrons, one of the two types of particles (protons are the other) that form atomic nuclei. A star made mostly of neutrons has properties that are extraordinary by human standards, though relatively common in the universe.

As particles, neutrons exhibit a fascinating behavior. Neutrons cannot exist for long as isolated particles. Left by itself, a neutron will, in about half an hour, decay (fall apart) into a proton, an electron, and an antineutrino. Hence space contains almost no neutrons sailing freely by themselves. However, as part of an atomic nucleus, a neutron can persist indefinitely. If you assemble enormous numbers of neutrons, you can form what amounts to a single giant atomic nucleus. The neutrons in this giant nucleus, like those in a smaller nucleus, remain neutrons. (To be precise, some of the neutrons decay into protons and electrons, but the star almost immediately squeezes protons and electrons back together to form new, replacement neutrons.)

The theory of neutron stars began in earnest in Berkeley, California, under the guidance of J. Robert Oppenheimer, the man who led the Manhattan Project to fruition. In 1939, as World War II approached in Europe, Oppenheimer and a physics graduate student, George Volkoff, published a paper in the *Physical Review* entitled "On Massive Neutron Stars," which calculated what would happen to a group of neutrons compressed to enormous densities. Kip Thorne, one of the leading astrophysicists of our era, has called this paper "one of the great astrophysics articles of our time." Oppenheimer and Volkoff knew that the Soviet physicist Lev Landau had speculated, in a general way, that a sufficiently massive star might end its life by squeezing all its matter into neutrons. To scientists, speculation is fine but never decisive. Drawing on their knowledge of recent advances in nuclear physics, Oppenheimer and Volkoff made the first real calculations of the structure of a neutron star, and they were the first to predict (imperfectly, because their data on atomic nuclei were incorrect) how massive a star would have to be to become a neutron star.

As often occurs in science, Oppenheimer and Volkoff reached an inexact conclusion, but one with important consequences. Using the existing data concerning the behavior of nuclei (now known to have been in error), the two physicists calculated that no neutron star can exist with a mass greater than about 70 percent of the sun's mass. Since they knew that low-mass stars would never reach such a condensed state, they naturally, but wrongly, concluded that what they called "neutron cores" were "unlikely . . . to play any great part in stellar evolution." Wrong though this conclusion may have been, the work by Oppenheimer and Volkoff had two key effects: It stimulated Oppenheimer to think about *black holes*, the alternative end state for high-mass stars, and it established neutron cores (that is, neutron stars) as objects worthy of theoretical interest.

In hindsight, part of the difficulty in allowing even theoretical existence to neutron stars lay in the fantastic nature of these beasts. A neutron star is an object only 10 miles across, with a mass roughly equal to the sun's, but it is made entirely of neutrons. Imagine the mass of a star in a space the size of Manhattan; squeezed to this density, the Sears Tower could fit comfortably into the volume of a pea! The density of matter in a neutron star makes the density in a white dwarf look like a vacuum: At 100 trillion grams per cubic centimeter, the neutron-star density is a *hundred million times greater* than the density in a white dwarf.

How does a collapsing stellar core turn itself into neutrons? Lacking our modern data on nuclear fusion, Oppenheimer and Volkoff could not answer this question. Today we have the data to furnish most of the scenario. As the core collapses, violent collisions among the nuclei strip them all apart into individual protons and neutrons. The protons then fuse with electrons to produce neutrons and neutrinos.

Our earlier statement that electrons do not participate in nuclear fusion is true until the density rises to nearly 100 trillion grams per cubic centimeter. At this point, the usual rule no longer holds, and electrons *do* fuse with protons. (The fusion arises from what physicists call "weak" forces, reflecting the fact that they play a secondary role in nuclear fusion.) Because protons finally fuse with electrons to form neutrons, the entire collapsing core—nuclei and electrons—transforms itself into a single nucleus made of neutrons: a neutron star.

What, then, prevents a neutron star from collapsing still further? After all, its own gravitational force rises immensely, since the entire mass of a star now lies within a 10-mile diameter. Oppenheimer and Volkoff saw an answer in the exclusion principle, familiar to them as a basic part of the theory of quantum mechanics, which Oppenheimer had helped to create. Just as the exclusion principle acts on the electrons in a white dwarf, so too it affects the neutrons in a neutron star. The exclusion principle prevents any further contraction of the core and makes it a sort of nuclear crystal, with each neutron almost locked into place. But for the exclusion principle to become important for neutrons, the density of matter must reach an enormously higher value than is the case for electrons. Electrons in a white-dwarf star sit quietly at a density merely a *million* times the density of water, but the density in a neutron star must rise to *100 trillion* times the density of water in order for the exclusion principle to lend the star support against collapse.

In a few short pages, Oppenheimer and Volkoff gave birth to neutron stars—on paper. For nearly three decades neutron stars remained the plaything of astrophysical theorists, and few observationally oriented astronomers took them entirely seriously. This all changed in 1968 with the discovery of *pulsars,* which turn out to be rapidly rotating neutron stars. We shall have a bit more to say about pulsars, but must first ask: How can the *collapse* of a star's core produce an *explosion?* How can a star take matter falling inward and turn it around at high speed to create an explosion?

The neutron star must be part of the answer, for astronomers are convinced that the collapse of a massive star usually produces a neutron star. The most promising theories involve the hypothesized "bounce" of a new-formed neutron star: As the neutron star forms in the collapse, the inrush of matter actually squeezes the star a bit tighter than the exclusion principle will allow over the long haul. The squeezed core "bounces" like a firm rubber ball compressed by the hand of a powerful child. The sudden expansion of the neutron star creates a wave that moves outward, propelling the material it encounters into space.

The preceding sentences may sound good (to those who like such ideas), but problems remain. The core exerts so much gravitational force that instead of accelerating outward, the outer layers must eventually fall backward toward the core, unless something else reaccelerates them. In other words, *two* explosive mechanisms are required: The first loosens the star's outer layers. The second, operating on the material that would otherwise be pulled back onto the core by the core's gravity, blasts these layers outward for good.

Stirling Colgate, one of the leading supernova theorists, believes that the key to supernova explosions lies in the *neutrinos* that the collapse of the core produces in great abundance when protons fuse with electrons.

Neutrinos have either no mass or a negligible amount of mass, but they do possess kinetic energy (energy of motion). They can transfer this energy to another particle whenever they interact with it. In the realm of normal matter, such as that found in the Earth or in stars, neutrinos almost never interact with other particles (and therefore never transfer their energy). A newly collapsed star, however, hardly consists of matter with a familiar density and behavior. Instead, the matter immediately around the stellar core grows so dense that even though most of the neutrinos escape, some of them actually interact with the matter there. The neutrinos deposit their energy in the matter, heating it to billion-degree temperatures. This heating starts a shock wave that sweeps the matter outward. Here, Colgate says, we may have the secret of supernovae: Not only does the collapse form a neutron star, but the neutrinos generated in the collapse also produce a blast wave that blows the outer layers into space at enormous velocities. The result is a supernova, a star that shares its outer layers with the cosmos.

One supernova by itself has little effect—unless it happens to occur among one of the million or so closest stars, in which case its high-energy particles and radiation might wipe out all life on Earth, save for a few denizens of the deep. But taken all in all, the millions upon millions of supernova that explode during a galaxy's lifetime have a profound effect upon the complexity of matter in the galaxy (Color Plate 20). Although red-giant stars do part of the work as their outer layers evaporate, supernovae provide the key means by which most of the various types of the nuclei of all elements are spread through space (Color Plate 21).

MULCHING THE UNIVERSE WITH STAR-MADE ELEMENTS

Human beings and other forms of life consist primarily of five elements: hydrogen, carbon, nitrogen, oxygen, and phosphorus. The early universe made hydrogen—but of hydrogen alone only wraiths are made. Supernovae produced four of life's five chief elements, carbon, nitrogen, oxygen, and phosphorus, fusing them from smaller, less complex types of nuclei. Somehow, about four billion years ago, assemblages of these four elements and hydrogen produced the first primitive forms of life on Earth. From then to now, all life on Earth has consisted largely of star-made, star-flung nuclei that percolated through the Milky Way galaxy long before the sun and Earth formed. In short, stars that died have "mulched" the cosmos with their ashes, and the Earth and life upon it arose from these ashes.

But supernovae do even more. Thanks to the enormous energy of motion in an exploding star, the explosion for a brief time produces additional nuclear fusion that makes still heavier nuclei from the carbon, oxygen, and iron. Recall that the fusion of iron nuclei marks the end of nuclear fusion inside a massive star: Once the core has become mostly iron, it collapses. If supernovae produced only the elements up to and including iron, the universe would contain only those elements with less complex nuclei than iron, plus iron itself. Most of the elements more complex than iron (that is, with more protons and neutrons in each nucleus than iron has) have been created in the brief fury of a supernova explosion, although a few such elements come from aging stars, which produce a few heavy nuclei as a sort of side effect of their basic nuclear fusion.

This helps explain a fundamental fact of "economic" life on Earth: Heavy nuclei (those more massive and complex than iron) are scarce, while lighter nuclei are abundant. When you prospect for different elements on Earth, you are looking for nuclei that were made long before the solar system formed and were incorporated in the Earth four and a half billion years ago. If you look for rocks made of silicon, oxygen, aluminum, or iron, you can find them easily in your backyard; but if you seek silver, gold, mercury, uranium, or even lead, you face a long, hard sifting process. The latter, more complex elements are there, but they are not at all abundant. Each ton of seawater contains about a dollar's worth of gold, but it would cost more than a dollar per ton to extract this worldwide supply.

The same holds true for the universe, which basically consists of the two elements that emerged from the big bang—hydrogen and helium—plus the elements provided by supernova explosions. Four and a half billion years ago, the Earth and the sun's other planets formed from an interstellar gas cloud, whose composition reflected the explosion of countless supernovae during the previous billions of years. These explosions had enriched the interstellar gas, once nearly pure hydrogen and helium, to the point that one percent of its mass consisted of elements heavier than these two. Almost all of this one percent consisted of just seven elements: oxygen, silicon, carbon, nitrogen, aluminum, neon, and iron. Once the sun began to shine, the Earth-in-formation lost almost all its hydrogen, helium, nitrogen, and neon. We therefore find ourselves today on a planet made almost entirely of oxygen, silicon, carbon, aluminum, and iron. A tiny admixture consists of elements heavier than iron, elements that we prize both for their rarity and for their intriguing chemical properties.

SUPERNOVAE AS THE KEY TO LIFE

Supernovae did still more: They shaped our evolution as well as furnishing the stuff from which we are made. This statement looks beyond the fact that supernovae produced nearly all of the nuclei save hydrogen and helium; it recognizes that *supernovae may be the driving force behind evolution itself.* Evolution proceeds through mutations, random changes in organisms that may affect an organism's chances at survival and reproductive success. Because most mutations are "failures"—that is, the mutated organisms prove unsuccessful in the competition to produce offspring that survive—the term "mutant" carries a whiff of opprobrium in popular culture. But the mutations that are successful—those that increase the number of an organism's offspring—are likely to sweep the field, provided that the mutation can be inherited by succeeding generations. Enough successful mutations produce a new species— one that need show no shame at the word "mutant." Although most new species become extinct after geologically brief periods of time, the interplay of species, driven by mutations, has produced all the evolutionary diversity of life we find on Earth.

And what drives mutations? The most widely accepted theory holds that mutations arise from *cosmic rays,* which, despite their name, are not radiation but particles such as electrons, protons, and helium nuclei, traveling at nearly the speed of light and impacting the Earth randomly from all directions. Such a high-energy particle may, upon striking the genetic material in the cell of an offspring, induce a mutation in the succeeding generation. And what produces cosmic rays? Supernovae are the most likely source. Blown outward at enormous velocities, some of them close to the speed of light, the outermost layers of exploding stars probably provide the bath of cosmic-ray particles that fills the Milky Way.

Thus stellar explosions both make the heavy elements and drive the process that has assembled some of these elements into complex creatures. The eye that reads this sentence, the paper on which it rests, the brain that interprets it, the evolution that brought it into being, and the planet that carries life onward—all came from the fiery furnaces of the stars. Study of the universe reveals varied and profound ways in which we are linked to the cosmos, but none so deep and direct as our debt to supernovae.

THE GREAT SUPERNOVA OF 1987

In a large galaxy such as our Milky Way, a supernova appears about twice a century. Since a supernova's luminosity exceeds that of an ordinary star by many millionfold, a supernova anywhere in the Milky Way will shine for a few months' time more brightly than any star in the sky. Small wonder, then, that many cultures would note a Milky Way supernova as an exciting new star and would trace its decline in brightness as a possible portent of events on Earth.

The annals of supernova history, which are mostly Chinese records for the period before the European Renaissance, reveal that likely supernovae have appeared at about half the rate at which we now observe supernovae in galaxies similar to our own. The lack of recorded supernovae probably arises from the fact that many supernovae, bright though they are, passed unnoticed by astronomers and historians. Some of these supernovae may have exploded in regions of the Milky Way that are heavily obscured by interstellar dust. If the obscuration reduced the supernova's apparent brightness to that of an ordinary star, an easygoing observer of the stars in the heavens might have missed the temporary newcomer.

Such an oversight may well have occurred as recently as 300 years ago, in the time of Isaac Newton, for we have strong evidence that a supernova appeared then but passed almost completely unrecorded. The evidence consists of the remnant of the supernova—gases expanding away from the point of explosion in the star Cassiopeia A—whose motion can be traced backward in time to yield the approximate time of explosion, late in the seventeenth century. John Flamsteed, the British Astronomer

Royal, was the only person who left a record of what may have been the supernova, and this in a time when astronomy flourished. This suggests that the supernova's light must have been strongly obscured by interstellar dust, and indeed the supernova's remnant lies along a line of sight that includes abundant absorbing dust (Figure 53, p. 188).

The "missed" seventeenth-century supernova, cloaked by dust, may have grown as bright as a relatively dim star visible to the unaided eye. In contrast, consider the startling effect of the supernova seen in the year 1572, which appeared one evening, soon became the brightest star in the sky, and retained that distinction for many weeks, gradually fading away as the year went on. The supernova made such an impact on a young Dane named Tycho Brahe, one of the first persons to record the appearance of the supernova, that he decided to become an astronomer.

The supernova of 1572 played a role in moving people's minds closer to an acceptance of the newfangled Copernican cosmos. By placing the sun at the center of the solar system, Copernicus had dethroned the Earth as the hub of the universe. The Copernican world view was at odds with the traditional belief in an unchanging, Earth-centered cosmos, in which the perfect heavenly bodies moved forever in stately orbits around our world. Hence the supernova of 1572, by shattering the myth of the unchanging heavens, played a role in persuading European thinkers that the entire cosmos, not simply the mundane and sublunary sphere, could change, and change rapidly.

In 1604, just a generation after Tycho Brahe, another supernova appeared in the Milky Way. With the exception of the possible supernova of Newton's time, the supernova of 1604 represents the last supernova seen in our galaxy. This seems an oddly long interval if, on the average, supernovae explode in the Milky Way every 50 years or so, but random events often produce such results. The timing of supernovae in the heavens seen from Earth depends, of course, not only on the date of the supernova's explosion but also on the distance from the supernova to the solar system. Since the average supernova in the Milky Way explodes at a distance of about 30,000 light years, we see a supernova as it was at the time when humanity first settled into agriculture. Astronomers who specialize in supernovae feel some frustration at the realization that (according to all their theories) *the Milky Way contains many hundred supernovae that have already exploded but whose light has not yet reached us!*

Happily the cosmos has its own way of redressing these

balances. While we are still waiting to find the first supernova in the Milky Way in nearly four centuries, we can revel in one of the great astronomical events of the past decade: the appearance of a supernova in the closest galaxy to our own.

Supernova 1987A (its astronomical name) exploded about 160,000 years ago in the Large Magellanic Cloud. This galaxy is one of the two satellite galaxies, both irregular in form, that were first seen (or at least first carefully noted) by Europeans during the world-girdling expedition begun by Ferdinand Magellan in the year 1519. Each of the Magellanic Clouds contains an amount of matter equal to only a few percent of the mass of the Milky Way; nevertheless, they are quite formidable galaxies.

The Magellanic Clouds contain huge star-forming regions and an abundance of relatively young stars. Some of these are high-mass objects that proceed rapidly through their evolutionary phases. The stars fuse heavier and heavier nuclei until they become nearly pure iron and collapse to produce supernova explosions. One such collapse gave birth to Supernova 1987A, an object of immediate attention among astronomers, beginning with those at the Las Campanas Observatory in Chile, where the supernova was discovered on February 23, 1987, and then the world over.

What distinguished observations of Supernova 1987A from those of exploding stars close to the Milky Way in previous centuries was the chance to make entirely new types of observations. For the first time, a relatively nearby stellar explosion occurred when a battery of astronomical instruments already hovered in orbit above the Earth's atmosphere. With these orbiting observatories, astronomers could study the supernova in types of radiation that in the past had eluded detection, because they cannot penetrate the atmosphere surrounding our planet.

Chief among these satellite-borne observatories were the International Ultraviolet Explorer (IUE) satellite and the Solar Maximum Mission (SMM) satellite, both of which had been constructed and launched by the United States, as well as the Mir and Ginga satellites sent into space by the Soviet Union and Japan. None of these satellites had been specifically designed to observe a relatively close supernova (since no such supernova had appeared during more than three centuries). However, all of them had observational capabilities never before available, and all made significant new observations.

Under the guidance of U.S. astronomers, the IUE satellite observed the radiation from the supernova that lay in the ultraviolet region of the electromagnetic spectrum. This satellite recorded, as was never before possible, the story of how the supernova rose and fell in brightness, called the supernova's *light curve*. A supernova releases much of its energy in ultraviolet radiation, invisible to the human eye. Thus the IUE observations added greatly to our knowledge of how supernovae radiate energy during the days and weeks after they explode.

In contrast to the IUE, the SMM satellite observed gamma rays, the type of electromagnetic radiation that has the highest energies, greatest frequencies, and shortest wavelengths. However, the SMM first detected gamma rays from the supernova in August 1987, six months after the explosion was first seen on Earth. This delay occurred because the dense, expanding shells of material in the explosion trapped all the gamma rays, blocking their escape. Only after the matter that was blasted outward had expanded for six months could the gamma rays escape, threading their way through gaps in the expanding shells of material. Likewise, the Mir and Ginga satellites, which observed x rays from the supernova, saw nothing until June of 1987. Until then, the x rays were trapped within the supernova's expanding gas. Once they escaped and this could be detected, these high-energy photons provided key insights into the theory of how a supernova explosion produces *light*.

And what makes the light from a supernova? In the years before Supernova 1987A appeared, supernova theorists had generated elaborate mathematical models of the way that an exploding star would shine. They had calculated that a massive star first collapses its core to make a neutron star and almost immediately explodes its outer layers to produce a supernova. This explosion fuses less complex nuclei together to make more complex, heavier nuclei. The calculations predicted that among the most abundant types of nuclei produced in this way would be nuclei of the element cobalt.

Furthermore, these cobalt nuclei would be a special type of cobalt, an *isotope* of cobalt called cobalt-56 that is unstable and subject to radioactive decay. In this decay, each cobalt nucleus falls apart, producing a nucleus of nickel and a gamma ray. Such gamma rays, trapped within the expanding shell of material ejected by the supernova, provide the power that produces the light from a supernova. They do so by heating the expanding shells of gas, which then emit visible light and ultraviolet radiation.

Thus supernova theorists saw that as a result of the nuclear fusion in the supernova explosion, most of the electromagnetic radiation within the shell would consist of high-energy gamma rays. Indeed these gamma rays would be mostly of one particular type—those emitted by the decay of the cobalt nuclei produced by the supernova. Cobalt is element number 28; its nuclei are slightly heavier and more complex than those of iron, element number 26. Before it explodes, a star makes only the first 26 elements, which include iron but not cobalt. Hence cobalt-56 arises in supernova explosions, but not otherwise.

Quite a complex little story that the theorists had cooked up! The key to its verification lay in a simple prediction. Experiments had shown that nuclei of cobalt-56 decay spontaneously into nickel nuclei plus gamma rays. These decays occur randomly but at a known rate. That is, during each 77-day period after the explosion, the number of cobalt-56 nuclei would decrease by 50 percent. Since the supernova's light arises from the gamma-ray heating of the gas, the supernova's brightness would also decrease by half every 77 days. Confident in their calculations, theorists had predicted that if a supernova were to explode sufficiently close to Earth for astronomers to observe its decreasing brightness over many months, the supernova's brightness should decline by 50 percent in every 77-day interval past the peak of the explosion.

And so it proved to be. A plot of Supernova 1987A's light curve shows the 77-day falloff beautifully (Figure 54). Theoreticians were heartened. Proven right in their predictions of the supernova's brightness, they might yet be correct in their computer models of conditions within the exploding material.

What will happen to the supernova as its ejected material travels farther and farther from the star, eventually to merge with the rest of the interstellar medium? This question intrigues Mike

Figure 54. The light curve of Supernova 1987A records the supernova's changing brightness as observed on Earth (using a specialized "magnitude" scale in which five units correspond to a factor of 100 in brightness). The long period of straight-line decline corresponds to a decrease in brightness by a factor of one-half every 77 days. (Courtesy of Robert Kirshner; drawing by Crystal Stevenson.)

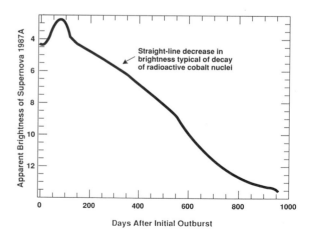

Dopita, whose approach to the supernova follows familiar astronomical lines: He makes spectroscopic observations of the supernova, spreading its light into its various colors. This reveals which chemical elements, in what amounts, and at what temperatures, exist within the material ejected by the explosion. All of this information—and more!—lies hidden within the light from the supernova. Each type of element absorbs different colors of light, and the effectiveness of the absorption depends on the temperature of the atoms. Once Dopita or another astronomer spreads the light into its component colors, the oxygen, silicon, magnesium, neon, manganese, iron, and three dozen other elements reveal themselves in the details of just which colors have been absorbed and which colors appear with more intensity than average. By gathering this information on many different nights since the explosion first appeared in southern skies, Dopita and other astronomers hope to learn how the material processed within an exploding star begins to merge with the surrounding interstellar medium, eventually to help form new generations of stars.

NEUTRINO ASTRONOMY COMES OF AGE

Even before the theoreticians could prove what happens in the gas a supernova blasts outward into space, other scientists—some hardly astronomers at all—had still greater cause to celebrate the exploding star. For the first time, physicists detected *neutrinos* from a supernova, the first neutrinos ever observed from *any* cosmic object save the sun. Because neutrinos are amazingly elusive particles, exceedingly difficult to capture in a detector, until 1987 scientists' best efforts had allowed them to detect only neutrinos from the sun, which is by far the closest cosmic source of neutrinos. The neutrinos detected from Supernova 1987A marked the birth of "neutrino astronomy" for objects outside the solar system—in fact, for an object about *10 billion times* more distant than the sun!

Was this detection made from an advanced satellite orbiting above the atmosphere? Not in the least: To make neutrino observations, you need to burrow at least half a mile into the Earth. Neutrinos interact so rarely with other forms of matter that most neutrinos striking the Earth will pass straight through it, emerging unchanged on the other side to continue their journey. To detect even a single neutrino among billions and billions, you need a giant

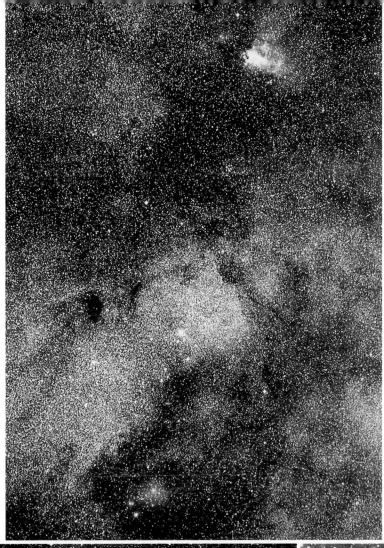

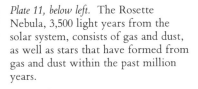

Plate 10. When we look along the plane of our Milky Way galaxy, a host of stars, gas clouds, and absorbing dust grains block our view.

Plate 11, below left. The Rosette Nebula, 3,500 light years from the solar system, consists of gas and dust, as well as stars that have formed from gas and dust within the past million years.

Plate 12, below. An enlarged view of the Rosette Nebula shows the nearly empty cavity at the center, where the radiation from hot, young stars has expelled the remnants of the star-forming gas.

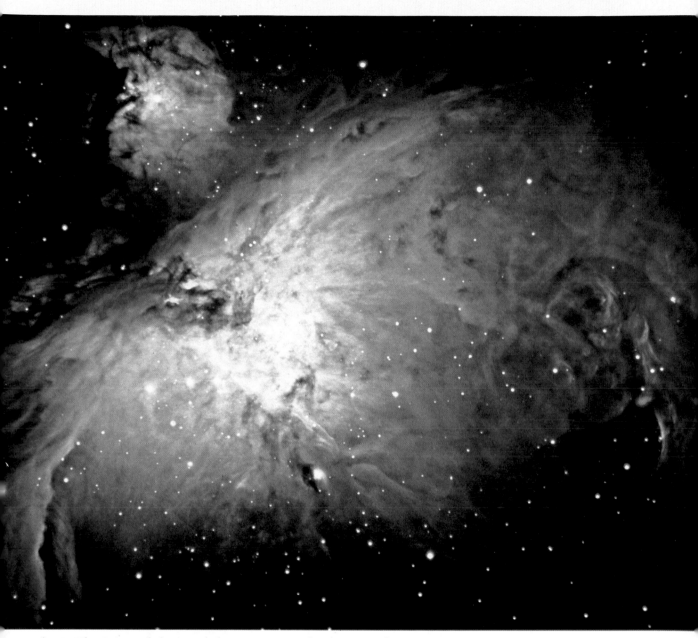

Plate 14. The Orion Nebula, 1,500 light years away, is the closest star-forming region. Stars less than a million years old shine brightly within the matter that formed them.

Plate 13. A thousand light years from Earth, in the direction of the constellation Orion, the Horsehead Nebula consists of a protuberance of matter laden with dust grains, which block the light from the star-forming region behind the nebula.

Plate 15. The Trifid Nebula in the constellation Sagittarius, 3,000 light years away, contains lanes of dust that block the light from young stars that are illuminating the gaseous cocoon from which they recently formed.

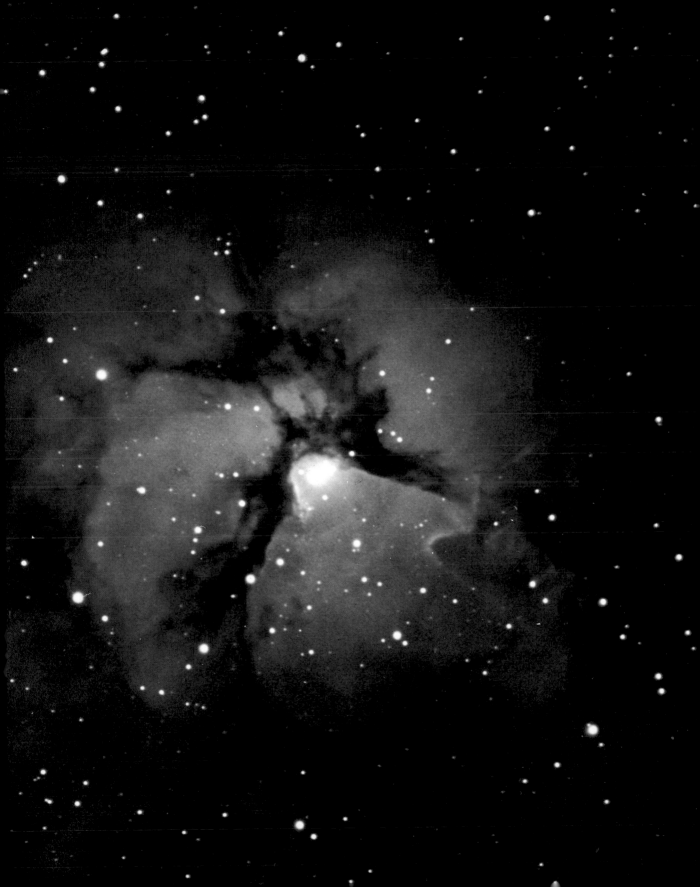

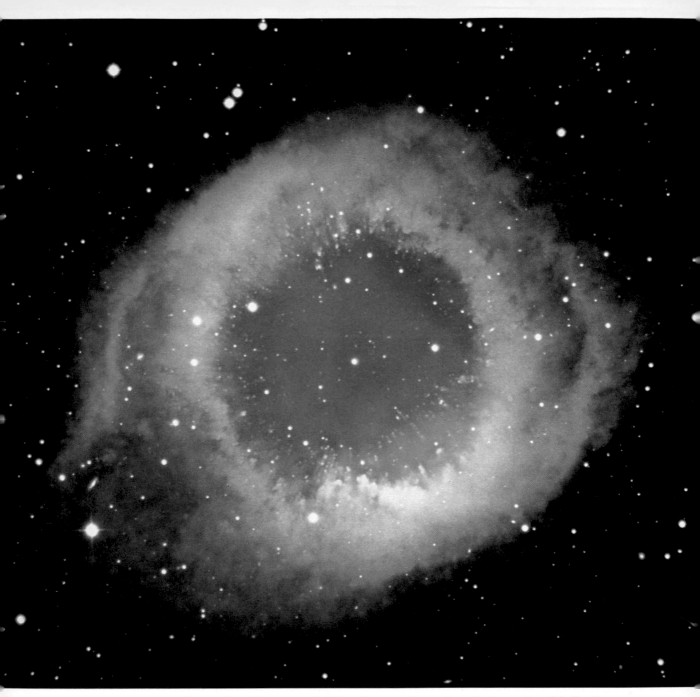

Plate 16. This "planetary nebula" in the constellation Aquarius is a series of shells of gas expelled by the aging star at the center, which emits immense amounts of ultraviolet radiation that causes the gaseous shells to glow in different colors.

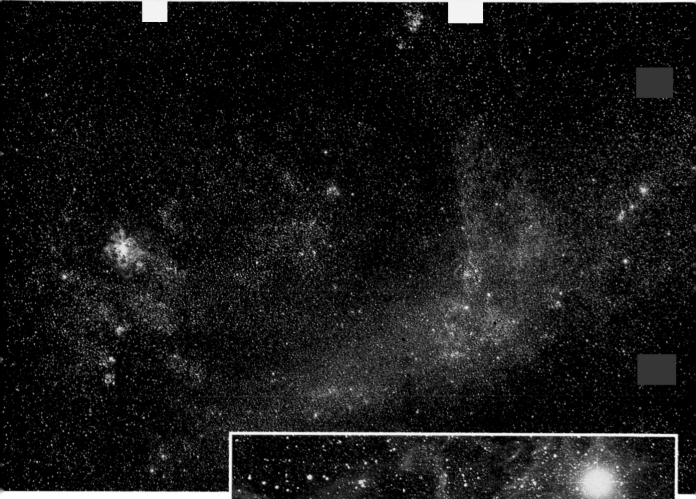

Plate 17, above. The Large
Magellanic Cloud,
visible only from
southern latitudes, lies at
the distance of 160,000
light years. Its most
prominent feature, the
Tarantula Nebula (left
center), is an immense
star-forming region.

Plates 18 and 19. On February 23, 1987, a supernova
(bright star at upper right) appeared in the Large
Magellanic Cloud, the closest galaxy to the Milky Way.
The inset photograph with the arrow shows the same
region of sky before the explosion.

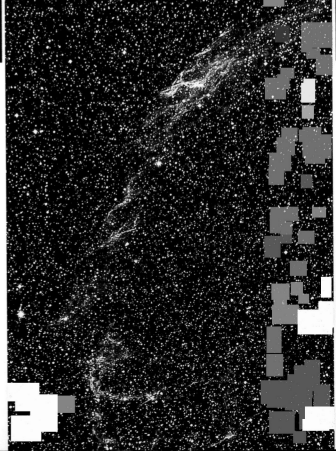

Plate 20, above. In the constellation Taurus, the Crab Nebula consists of material ejected by a supernova explosion, first seen on Earth in the year 1054 A.D.

Plate 21, right. The Veil Nebula in Cygnus contains material expelled into interstellar space by a supernova that exploded tens of thousands of years ago.

tank of fluid (water, cheap and abundant, will do fine) and specialized recorders that register the odd event, the one time in many billions that a neutrino *does* interact with an atomic nucleus. This tank is placed deep underground to filter out the effects from other, less penetrating particles that could otherwise mimic the effects of a neutrino impact and thereby confuse the detector scheme.

Just as you could not have sold NASA a satellite on the chance of observing a supernova, no scientist would have agreed to invest in building a neutrino detector for possible supernovae—prior to 1987. As luck would have it, however, *four* neutrino detectors were in operation on February 23 of that year, in (or under) Ohio, in Japan, in the Caucasus mountains of the Soviet Union, and in the Mont Blanc tunnel that connects France and Italy. All four detectors lay in the province not of astronomy but of physics: They were designed and built not so much to detect neutrinos (though they could do that well) but to look for a theoretically predicted event, the occasional decay of a proton.

This hypothetical proton decay underlay a key set of theories of modern physics, the *grand unified theories*. As discussed in chapter 4, these theories deal with attempts to describe all types of forces in the universe as aspects of a single force. The grand unified theories predict, as a sort of side effect, that the universe contains no particles that last forever. Intrigued by the chance to test this theory, physicists had persuaded their governments to construct elaborate equipment that could reveal the decay of protons (hydrogen nuclei), if such decay occurred. Two of the detectors, those in Japan and the United States, used giant tanks of highly purified water. The other two detectors used a mixture of rare elements more sensitive to proton decays—and to neutrinos from outer space—so that they required only a few tons, rather than the hundreds of tons of water used in Japan and Ohio, to achieve a comparable sensitivity.

Three of the four detectors—those in Japan, Ohio, and the Soviet Union—detected neutrinos from the supernova outburst. The fourth detector, under the Mont Blanc, gave a confusing result best interpreted (so neutrino leaders tell us) as no detection of the supernova. But three out of four proved sufficient to mark the arrival of neutrinos that had passed through the Earth and *outward* through the detector. (The supernova never rose above the horizon in midnorthern latitudes, but since neutrinos easily penetrate "solid" Earth, they could pass "upward" through our planet before reaching the detector.)

The neutrinos from the supernova were automatically recorded by computer but passed unnoticed by humans until the following day. In hindsight, these neutrinos proved to be the *first* particles from the explosion to reach the Earth. Because the matter ejected in the explosion blocked electromagnetic radiation—visible light, x rays, and gamma rays—from escaping for at least a few hours, while the neutrinos passed directly outward from the star's collapsing core, the neutrinos had a head start on the light from the supernova. After traveling through intergalactic space for 160,000 years, a small fraction of the supernova's neutrinos went through our planet on February 23, 1987.

Fittingly enough, none of the neutrino detectors (as we may now call them) has yet recorded a single proton decay. The version of the grand unified theories that predicts such decays therefore faces possible rejection by physicists, but the theory that predicts neutrinos from supernovae looks good. That theory, we may recall, involves the squeezing together of protons and electrons during the collapse of a star's core. This compression makes neutrons and neutrinos. The neutrons stay behind to make the neutron star, but the neutrinos move outward at the speed of light.

So the story all fits together, once you have a neutrino detector. About a million neutrinos from the supernova passed through each of us on February 23, 1987, treating alike those indoors and outside, climbing at high altitudes or laboring deep underground in coal mines. Because neutrinos interact so little with "ordinary" matter, most of us looked like empty space to the neutrinos. One in a million of us, however, *did* have a neutrino interact with one of our atomic nuclei, but lacking expensive, sensitive equipment, we failed to notice anything. Luckily we had funded scientific projects that serendipitously found these messengers from collapsing stellar cores for astronomers. Neutrino astronomers—a small but growing group—plan to be loaded for bear when the next nearby supernova is seen, perhaps a few centuries from now.

DID SUPERNOVA 1987A PRODUCE A PULSAR?

Meanwhile, the big news from Supernova 1987A concerns the possibility of detecting its *pulsar*. Pulsars, known to astronomers since 1968, are sources of radio emission (sometimes of visible light as well) that flash repeatedly with an amazingly constant interval between flashes. The fact that some pulsars appear within the remnants of exploded stars clinches observationally what theorists had predicted: Each pulsar arises from a rapidly rotating neutron star, born in the stellar collapse that produced a supernova.

This collapse magnifies two key properties of the newborn neutron star: its rate of rotation and the strength of its magnetic field. The rotation rate increases dramatically simply because the star's core shrinks to a much smaller size as it becomes a neutron star. Nature has a basic rule that describes rotating objects: Any object's total amount of rotation, called its *angular momentum,* remains the same so long as no net force acts upon the object. The angular momentum varies in proportion to the object's rate of rotation times the square of its size. Hence, in order for this angular momentum to remain unchanged, *if the object decreases in size, it must spin more rapidly.* For example, if a star shrinks in size by a factor of five, it must rotate 25 times more rapidly. Ice skaters and gymnasts know this rule well: To spin more rapidly, they contract their bodies, and to slow their rate of spin, they extend themselves to maximum size.

Nearly all stars have some rotation. Our sun, for example, rotates about once each month, as shown by the march of sunspots across its surface from day to day. Speaking hypothetically, if the sun's core collapsed, it would spin far more rapidly, simply because the matter in the core would occupy a smaller region. If the collapse shrank the core by a factor of 1,000, its spin rate would increase *one million* times. Just this sort of thing occurs when supernovae spawn neutron stars, which are born spinning many times per second.

Collapsing stars also increase the strength of any magnetic field they may have, a result that is analogous to the increase in their rotation rates. Stars such as our sun have relatively weak magnetic fields, which affect the motions of charged particles streaming outward but otherwise have little effect on the cosmos. In a collapsing star, however, the magnetic field follows a law of nature similar to that for the rotation of objects. This law implies that the strength of the magnetic field (like the rate of rotation for an object of constant mass) increases in proportion to the *square* of the decrease in size. The collapse of the stellar core by a factor of 1,000 in size—from a few thousand miles across to just a few miles in diameter—therefore raises the strength of the magnetic feld in the core one millionfold.

During the 1960s, astronomers who sought to explain

pulsars saw that the increases in both the rotation rate and the magnetic field strength make a newborn neutron star a giant, fast-spinning magnet. Any charged particles close to the surface of the magnet will be accelerated by the field into rapid motion. This motion in turn causes the particles to produce streams of electromagnetic radiation. If the neutron star contains regions of especially intense magnetic field, these regions will emit particularly large amounts of radiation. Theorists hypothesize that a neutron star has such regions near its magnetic poles, corresponding to the two ends of a bar magnet. If an imaginary line linking the magnetic poles does not coincide with the star's spin axis, then as the star rotates, the two oppositely directed beams of intense radiation arising near the magnetic poles will sweep over various parts of the sky. An observer who happens to be located in the path of one of the beams will see a strong pulse of radiation (Figure 55). The interval between successive pulsations of strong radio emission measures the star's rotation rate even though we cannot *see* the neutron star at all. Instead, we detect the pulsar that the neutron star produces. By now, astronomers have found several thousand pulsars in the Milky Way and several dozen in other galaxies.

With the passage of time, the very act of emitting radiation take energy from the rotating neutron star. As a result, the neutron star gradually slows its rotation rate as it ages. In the simplest model of pulsars, the rotation rate steadily declines from the moment that the pulsar appears. (In more complex models, external events and internal "starquakes" also have an effect on the rate of rotation.) Hence astronomers expect that if they find a pulsar in Supernova 1987A, it should rank among the *fastest* pulsars yet found. The announcement in January 1989 that just such a pulsar

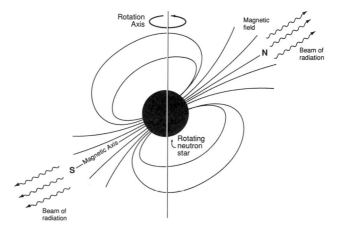

Figure 55. A pulsar arises from a rotating, highly magnetic neutron star, which accelerates charged particles in the star's vicinity to nearly the speed of light. The rotating neutron star produces beams of intense radiation along the line joining its magnetic poles. If the star is oriented so that these beams sweep by us, we shall observe a "pulse" of intense radiation each time the star rotates. (Drawing by Crystal Stevenson.)

had been discovered in the direction of Supernova 1987A electrified the astronomical community; the term proved unfortunately apt when the astronomers who had made the apparent detection announced a year and a half afterward that they had been misled by electrical interference in their television camera. Once again, research at the frontiers of astronomy had proven hazardous to a reputation for perfection, which must be sacrificed if advances are to occur.

It is quite possible that Supernova 1987A left a pulsar behind, but one whose beams of radiation do not point in our direction. In that case, astronomers still hope to find *indirect* evidence that the pulsar exists. At Australia's Siding Spring Observatory, a team of astronomers led by David Allen has been making infrared observations of the region surrounding the supernova. A pulsar there would inevitably inject energy into this region as its beams of radiation sweep through it. Astronomers expect that the material surrounding the supernova explosion would be relatively warm, and observers such as Allen are looking for temperatures even higher than theory predicts—temperatures arising from extra heating that would be the mark of a pulsar. The additional heating from the pulsar would arise even if the pulsar's beams turned out not to pass by our direction, so that the supernova would never show *us* a pulsar. Allen has found some intriguing and unexpected aspects of the supernova; for example, he has detected hydrogen gas spewn out by the explosion, relatively unaffected by the stellar violence, which no one had predicted would exist.

So far Allen and his colleagues have yet to turn up anything like convincing evidence that the supernova remnant contains a pulsar. Likewise, Mike Dopita has yet to find anything in Supernova 1987A that is completely different from what other supernovae have revealed. But their energy and enthusiasm are hardly diminished. If astronomers grew excited only when they made a new discovery, most of them would live in a continuous state of low arousal. We may yet learn that a pulsar has been found in the supernova, or that completely unexpected elements exist there. But whatever the verdict on what we have learned—or failed to learn—from the great supernova of 1987, one fact remains clear. Taken in the context of our Local Group of galaxies, the supernova in the Large Magellanic Cloud was *the* explosion of the century—a nearby example of the multitude of similar explosions, each of which occurred more than 5 billion years ago, that produced the elements for life on Earth.

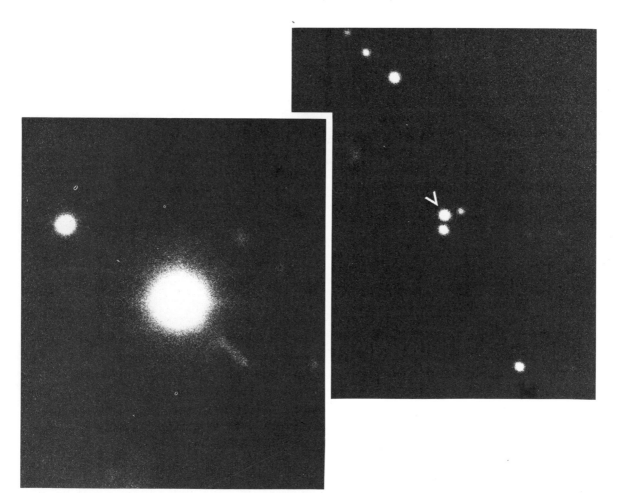

Figure 56. Photographs of quasars such as 3C 273 (left) and 3C 147 (right) reveal them as looking exactly like stars, with some exceptions, such as the "jet" of material apparently emerging from the quasar at left. (Hale Observatories photographs.)

9. Quasars and Peculiar Galaxies

IN PASADENA, CALIFORNIA, in the northeastern portion of the Los Angeles basin, lies a rectangular plot of land that includes less than one-fifth a square mile of area—and one of the greatest concentrations of scientific brainpower in the world. This is the California Institute of Technology, a university with only a hundred professors and a thousand undergraduate students, but one that has a dozen Nobel Prize winners on its faculty and another dozen among its alumni.

This elite center of learning, now world renowned and rich in endowment, began life with a different name, just a century ago, in 1892, the same year as the University of Chicago and Stanford University. The Throop Polytechnic Institute was founded by the educational reformer Amos Throop, who lived in Pasadena and saw a need for colleges that would train young men in modern science and technology. In 1903, the trustees of Throop Polytechnic renamed their institution the Throop College of Technology; in 1920, with a second building added to the original Throop Hall, they changed the name again, to the California Institute of Technology. In that same year, the small band of scientists who taught at Throop embarked on a working relationship with the Mount Wilson Observatory, an association that soon gave them an important role in astronomical research.

In 1904, George Ellery Hale, the greatest astronomical promoter of this century, concluded his search for the finest site in the United States for a solar telescope. Hale left the University of Chicago, where he had helped to found the Yerkes Observatory, to become the director of the solar observatory at Mount Wilson, just north of Pasadena. The observatory was funded by the Carnegie

Institution of Washington, D.C., which had been incorporated by an act of Congress in that year "to encourage, in the broadest and most liberal manner, investigation, research, and discovery, and the application of knowledge to the improvement of mankind." As the result of Hale's persuasive powers over Andrew Carnegie, astronomy ranked highest among the beneficiaries of the foundation that Carnegie had endowed.

Before long, with the solar telescope in operation, Hale had arranged for the world's largest telescope, the 60-inch reflector, to be built on Mount Wilson with Carnegie funds. Completed in 1908, the 60-inch produced far better images of star clusters, nebulae, and galaxies than any previous telescope. Ten years later, as the First World War drew to a close, the giant 100-inch Hooker telescope was constructed on Mount Wilson; this was the telescope that Edwin Hubble used to determine the extragalactic distance scale and to discover the expansion of the universe.

During the 1920s, the California Institute of Technology (Caltech) prospered mightily under the leadership of Robert Millikan, a brilliant physicist who won a Nobel Prize for his measurement of the fundamental unit of electric charge. Millikan had been successfully wooed from the University of Chicago by the promise of far greater funds and research opportunities in the burgeoning southland of California. By the time that Millikan retired as Caltech's president in 1950, the university had become a world leader in most branches of physics and chemistry. Since then, its reputation and strength have increased apace, and many of the most notable discoveries and personalities in the annals of astronomy have had a Caltech connection.

Working with the Carnegie Institution of Washington, Caltech has built three of the world's great astronomical observatories. First came the Mount Wilson Observatory, and then, a long generation later, the Palomar Mountain Observatory, 80 miles southeast of Los Angeles, where the 200-inch telescope (now officially named the Hale Telescope) was assembled in 1948 after its mirror had been ground and polished on the Caltech campus. Finally, during the 1970s, Caltech built the Las Campanas Observatory in Chile to observe the southern skies.

All colleges and universities attempt to secure the quiet efforts of important citizens to promote their projects, but Caltech has been more successful in its neighborhood than any similar institution. And in no area of research has Caltech been more successful than in astronomy. In his autobiography, Millikan recounted that in 1928, when the millionaire Henry Robinson, one of the most influential of Caltech's trustees, learned that Caltech might be unable to build the 200-inch telescope without an endowment of $2 million to fund the telescope's continuing operation, he promptly changed his will to leave his entire estate to fund the telescope. As Millikan noted with general approval, "Mr. Robinson lost heavily in the Depression and his estate was not as large as he expected it to be, but the whole of it is now in the 200-inch telescope project." With such assistance, Caltech weathered the Depression, built the mighty Hale Telescope, and entered the post-World War II era as a leader in all aspects of astronomical research.

THE ASTRONOMERS WHO FOUND QUASARS

In a large corner office of the Robinson Astrophysics Laboratory, a genial, balding gentleman of middle size, who is just past 80 but looks a decade younger, has seen nearly 50 years come and go at Caltech (Figure 57). Jesse Greenstein was born in New York City in 1909; when he was 8, his grandfather gave him a beautiful brass telescope, and he was hooked. Greenstein devoured popular books on astronomy (a flourishing business even then) and created a laboratory in the basement of his home. There he used a spectroscope to separate light into its various colors, seeking to identify different atomic elements from the variously colored sparks that they made when he heated them. By age 16, Greenstein was a student at Harvard, where he met Naomi Kitay, to whom he has been married since 1934; their son George is now a mature, successful astronomer at Amherst College.

Figure 57. Jesse Greenstein of the California Institute of Technology is an expert on the spectra of the light from stars and quasars. (Courtesy of the California Institute of Technology.)

Greenstein's graduation in 1929 was followed shortly by the collapse on Wall Street and the Great Depression, which modified his plan to study astronomy at Oxford. Instead, Greenstein entered his family's real-estate enterprise in New York, where he worked for four years; during that time he met the great physicist Isidor Rabi, who encouraged him to continue his studies. When Greenstein visited his alma mater, the director of the Harvard Observatory, Harlow Shapley, told him that science had advanced too rapidly for him to hope to catch up!—a remark that seems fatuous in hindsight. Nevertheless, Greenstein began his graduate studies at Harvard in 1934 and received his Ph.D. in 1937. After several years at the Yerkes Observatory and wartime service involving specialized optical instruments, Greenstein went to Caltech in 1948 to join both the astronomy faculty and the staff of the Mount Wilson and Palomar Observatories.

At that time, Caltech's astronomers were part of the physics department. When the Graduate School of Astrophysics was created, Greenstein became its first chairman. His astronomical career has centered on the study of celestial objects through spectroscopy—spreading the objects' light into different colors, each color providing clues to what the objects are made of. But Greenstein's astronomical research has ranged remarkably far and wide, from pioneering efforts in radio astronomy during the 1950s, through studies of red-giant stars and white dwarfs, to theories of what interstellar dust particles are made of and what tends to align them in the spaces among the stars. Now, as a Caltech professor emeritus, the recipient of more honors than can be easily listed, Greenstein continues to maintain a lively interest in all areas of astronomy. This is particularly true in the area of Greenstein's most famous work—the discovery of quasars—which arose from a long-term collaboration with his friend and colleague Maarten Schmidt.

Maarten Schmidt was born in Groningen in northern Holland in 1930; he was intrigued by astronomy as a teenager and studied at Leiden University with Jan Oort,

Figure 58. Maarten Schmidt, a professor of astronomy at Caltech and a staff member of the Carnegie Observatories, discovered quasars in collaboration with Jesse Greenstein. (Photograph by Donald Goldsmith.)

the greatest Dutch astronomer of the twentieth century (which is saying a great deal). Eager to use the world's greatest telescopes, Schmidt came to this country in 1954 to join the staff of the Mount Wilson and Palomar Observatories (Figure 58). There he met Greenstein, 14 years his senior, and soon formed a friendship that would last a lifetime. Tall, lithe, and handsome, towering a head above Greenstein, Schmidt formed half of a team that in 1964 set the world of astronomy agog with the discovery of quasars.

QUASARS

Quasars, an acronym formed from the original name "quasi-stellar radio sources," are the most distant, most luminous objects known to exist in the universe. On photographs taken in visible light, quasars look just like stars, that is, like bright points of light with no greater extent than that provided by the scattering of light in our atmosphere (Figure 56, p. 210). But unlike stars, quasars also emit great amounts of *radio waves*.

Greenstein was one of the pioneers of radio astronomy, which began in earnest soon after World War II. The first order of business was to make a survey of the "radio sky"—a map to show the radio-emitting sources around the heavens. As radio astronomers made their first all-sky radio maps, they found radio emission from some familiar objects, such as the Crab Nebula supernova remnant, and from objects they had never noted before, such as what seemed to be two distant, colliding galaxies in the constellation Cygnus. The radio astronomers sought to classify radio sources into overall types and did so with some success. But during the early 1960s, they found a number of radio sources that looked like stars on their photographic survey plates. The astronomers named them quasi-stellar ("like a star") radio sources and often puzzled over their true nature during the relaxed lunches at the Athenaeum, one of the rewards of service on the Caltech faculty.

No one knew how stars, or objects that looked like stars in visible light, could be powerful sources of radio waves. At one point, Greenstein presented a theory that quasars must be collapsed supernova remnants whose light arose from the decay of huge numbers of radioactive nuclei within them—a theory that he was quick to withdraw before its publication, once the true nature of quasars became evident. Astronomers did know that certain types of "peculiar galaxies"—galaxies notable for their unusual, perturbed shapes—emit large amounts of energy. For example, Seyfert galaxies, named after the man who first cataloged them, resemble spiral galaxies but have remarkably intense central regions or nuclei (see p. 225). Seyfert-galaxy nuclei produce energy on a scale many thousand times greater than the center of an ordinary spiral galaxy such as our Milky Way. However, the quasi-stellar sources of radio emission showed no sign of a galaxy but instead were obstinately stellar and pointlike.

No one knew better than Greenstein and Schmidt that the key to any celestial object's true nature is its *spectrum,* the description of how much light the object emits at different colors, that is, at different frequencies and wavelengths. Because each chemical element affects light in a different way, study of the spectrum is the royal road to determining the composition of even incredibly distant objects. Spectral observations had unlocked the mystery of the chemical composition of stars and galaxies. Furthermore (as discussed in chapter 4), spectral observations of galaxies had revealed the expansion of the universe. Relying on this marvelous tool, Greenstein and Schmidt set out to unravel the spectra of the enigmatic quasars.

Quasars' spectra were like no spectra seen before. Stars have spectra that are dominated by *absorption lines,* sharp drops in the amount of light at certain frequencies or colors. The light from galaxies, which are basically collections of stars, likewise shows a spectral distribution characterized by absorption lines. Astronomers knew that the absorption lines seen in stellar spectra arise in the outer layers of stars when particular types of atoms, ions, and molecules there absorb particular frequencies of the light emitted by the star. The precise frequencies that are blocked depend on the structure of the atoms, of the ions (atoms missing one or more electrons), or of the molecules (groups of two or more atoms) that exist near the star's surface. During the 40 years prior to the discovery of quasars, astronomers had learned how to read a spectrum comprised of absorption lines as if they were reading a book. They could identify the type and calculate the amount of nearly every species of atom, ion, or molecule present in the outer layers of stars thousands or millions of light years away.

In contrast to the familiar spectra of stars and galaxies, the quasars' visible-light spectra showed only faint absorption lines. The spectra were dominated by prominent *emission lines—extra* amounts of light emitted at certain definite frequencies and wavelengths. Astronomers knew that in certain laboratory situations, some types of atoms and ions can emit particularly large amounts of light at certain frequencies, thus producing one or more emission lines. But they also knew that such situations almost never arise in stars. This gave them another reason, in addition to the radio emission from quasars, to conclude that quasars must be something other than stars.

What puzzled astronomers most of all was the fact that the measured *frequencies* of the emission lines in quasars' spectra lay nowhere near those produced by the types of atoms and ions with which they were familiar. In other words, quasars were peculiar twice over: Not only did they show emission lines in their spectra, but the lines also had colors (that is, frequencies) at which emission lines had never been seen before. The resolution of the mystery of the emission-line frequencies brought quasars to the forefront of astronomers' attention. The answer turned out to be that *quasars are receding from us at enormous velocities.*

At that time, three decades ago, the most distant galaxy known to astronomers had a *redshift* of about one-tenth; that is, the spectra showed a shift to wavelengths about 10 percent longer and to frequencies about 10 percent less than the values observed in the laboratory. These redshifts were presumed to arise from the Doppler effect that is caused by the expansion of the universe. The Doppler effect increases all the wavelengths, and lowers all the frequencies, of a source of light moving away from an observer. Since red light has the longest wavelengths of all the colors of visible light, astronomers call a shift to longer wavelengths a "redshift." When they observed that a distant galaxy's redshift had increased all the wavelengths in that galaxy's spectrum by 10 percent, they used their knowledge of the Doppler shift to conclude that this galaxy must be receding from the Milky Way at one-tenth the speed of light.

A galaxy receding at fully one-tenth the speed of light must be immensely distant, since Hubble's Law for the expanding universe says that greater recession velocities correspond to greater distances. Not surprisingly, such a distant galaxy appears to astronomers only as a faint smudge of light in their best telescopes.

But most easily visible quasars were startlingly bright to astronomers, much brighter than the faint, far-distant galaxies with the largest known redshifts. At first, quasars' relatively large apparent brightnesses made it difficult for astronomers even to consider the possibility that quasars might have redshifts greater than the 10 percent measured for the most distant galaxies. Enormous redshifts would imply correspondingly enormous distances, and at these distances, no galaxy could appear as bright as the quasars do. But one night in February 1963, trying to make sense of the spectrum of a quasar called 3C 273, Maarten Schmidt began to play in his mind with its spectrum—the graph that showed the frequencies at which the quasar emitted especially large amounts of light. Thinking of the ratios of the wavelengths of these emission lines, Schmidt allowed himself to envision a spectrum shifted by much larger amounts than anyone had previously considered. Suddenly he saw that with a large redshift, the pattern of emission lines in the quasar's spectrum would match a pattern familiar to him from his knowledge of immensely hot stars! In fact, the quasar's emission lines are produced by abundant elements such as hydrogen, oxygen, and magnesium, but all shifted toward the red end of the spectrum by nearly 16 percent.

When Maarten Schmidt asked Jesse Greenstein what he thought of a spectrum for 3C 273 with a redshift of 16 percent, Greenstein suddenly saw the flaw in a scientific paper he had written but not yet published. In this paper, he analyzed the spectrum of another quasar, 3C 48. (The "3C" stands for the Third Catalogue of Radio Sources compiled at Cambridge University in England.) Greenstein had considered but rejected the possibility that 3C 48 had a huge redshift. Now, as Greenstein later said, "the psychological logjam was broken." Freed by Schmidt's pronouncement of a 16-percent redshift for 3C 273, Greenstein reached for the spectrum of 3C 48 once again. Everything fit: 3C 48 also revealed a familiar pattern in its emission lines, shifted to the red not by 16 but by *37* percent!

In one night, Greenstein and Schmidt had pushed back the boundaries of the universe by more than a factor of three, increasing the volume of known space thirtyfold! Since Hubble's Law for the expanding universe matches greater redshifts with great distances, a redshift of 37 percent implies a distance to the quasar three and a half times greater than that of the most distant galaxies then known. Schmidt and Greenstein immediately recognized that they had made a discovery startling in its implications. Their two quasars were the most distant objects in the universe, some 3 billion and 7 billion light years away! But at these enormous distances, the quasars must be emitting simply fantastic amounts of energy. For although they are too dim to be seen without a good-sized telescope, 3C 273 and 3C 48 shine far more brightly than the faintest galaxies we can see. Yet they have distances much greater than the faintest, most distant, of the ordinary galaxies then known—galaxies that contain hundreds of billions of individual stars.

CURIOUSER AND CURIOUSER

Greenstein and Schmidt had discovered not merely the most *distant* but by far the most *energy-prolific* objects in the cosmos. The astronomers quickly calculated that 3C 273 and 3C 48 each radiate hundreds of times more energy per second than the most energetic galaxies. This was amazing, but something still more stupendous about quasars quickly became apparent. Tremendously energetic as they are, *quasars have sizes far smaller than the smallest galaxies!*

Astronomers, including Greenstein and Schmidt, soon discovered the small sizes of quasars through a sort of cosmic trick (described above) that depends on the fact that quasars vary their light output. The more rapid the light variation, the smaller the limitation we can place on the quasars' sizes. Soon after Greenstein and Schmidt announced their discovery, astronomers began to search through their photographic archives, hunting for years-old images of pointlike quasars (which, of course, had been thought to be merely stars). When the astronomers obtained detailed spectra of the light from these "stars," already known to be sources of radio emission, the spectra revealed tremendous redshifts: They too were quasars. The archival photographs showed that 3C 273 had changed in brightness by 20 percent over a time scale of decades, implying a size for this object less than one one-thousandth of the diameter of the Milky Way.

Soon afterward, as more quasars were identified, astronomers who observed them found some quasars that varied in brightness within a few weeks and even a few days! These spectacular discoveries of quasars' light variation implied a result

A Clever Way to Determine Objects' Sizes

When astronomers observe nearby objects such as the sun or moon, they can easily determine the diameter of the object once they know its distance. Triangulation provides the answer: Imagine a triangle with its sharp apex at the observer, whose two long legs are the object's distance. The triangle's short side is the object's diameter. You can then measure the object's *angular diameter,* the fraction of a complete circle that the object appears to span on the sky. The more distant the object, the smaller the fraction will be. Trigonometry shows, for example, that an object covering a degree (1/360 of a complete circle) must have a diameter 1/57 of the distance to the object. If the object covers only half a degree, the diameter must be 1/114 of the distance to the object. Both the sun and moon have angular diameters of half a degree; both have diameters equal to 1/114 of their distances from us.

But this triangulation method does not work for objects so small and distant as the quasars, because they appear to us only as points of light, and we cannot measure the diameter that the objects appear to span on the sky. In the case of some quasars, astronomers have used another method, quite distinct and immensely clever, to determine quasars' diameters. This method requires no knowledge of the objects' distances. It hinges on one key observation—that some quasars vary in brightness as we observe them—and on one key belief—that nothing moves more rapidly than light.

Because light has a finite speed, when we look at a transparent, or nearly transparent, object, the light from the object's far side arrives a bit later than light emitted at the same time from the object's near side. Consider, for example, an object with a diameter of one light-day (the distance that light travels in a day). If this object grows brighter all over *instantaneously,* we shall *not* observe an instantaneous change in the object's brightness. Instead, we shall see first the brightness increase from the object's near side, then the brightness increase from the middle, and finally the brightness increase from the object's far side. The entire brightening process, as

so startling as to give astronomers pause: Whatever process may be producing the quasars' enormous energy outflows must occur within a region only a few times larger than our solar system! But the solar system has a diameter *about one hundred-millionth* the diameter of the Milky Way galaxy. Hence the rapidly varying quasars produce a hundred times the energy output of the Milky Way within a volume that would occupy less than one billion-billionth of our galaxy— a feat comparable to finding a rock that can outshine the sun.

Within a year after the original discovery by Schmidt and Greenstein, a dozen quasars were known; a year later, the total neared a hundred; today, less than 30 years after the first quasar was named, the list reaches into the thousands. Most of these quasars show a basic resemblance to the first two, but their spectra show still *larger* redshifts. Applying Hubble's Law, quasars' enormous redshifts imply distances of many billion light years. But at such fantastic distances, the quasars must have simply enormous luminosities—energy output per second—for us to be able to see them at all.

And there is even more to the amazing energy output from quasars. Once astronomers began to make observations of quasars in *infrared* radiation, they found that many quasars emit much more energy in infrared than they do in radio waves or visible light. In visible light, 3C 273 has a luminosity about a thousand times greater than the Milky Way's. But in infrared, 3C 273 produces 20 times more energy each second than it does in visible radiation! Compared to the infrared, this quasar's output in visible light—and in radio waves, the tip-off to its original discovery—barely registers at all.

What could be the origin of such immense floods of energy? As we shall see, astronomical theorists have risen to the challenge implicit in this question. They have constructed a hypothetical model in which *gravity* provides the ultimate source of quasars' energy. Before we sail into this maelstrom in the next chapter, we might pause to note the latest news from the quasar front: the quest for the most distant object in the universe.

we observe it, will last a full day—the time that it takes light to cross the object's diameter (Figure 59).

We can turn this analysis around and conclude that if we see an object grow brighter in a single day, then no matter what process increased the brightness, and no matter how rapidly it occurred, the region in which the brightness increased can be no more than one light-day across. Notice that we have assumed the object to be transparent, or nearly so. This means that our method determines the diameter of the region with the object producing the light that we *see*—that is, the light that reaches us without being blocked from our view. (More light may be emitted but absorbed within the object; we do not detect this light and cannot use our analysis to estimate the size of the region producing it.) The method therefore establishes a *minimum* size for the object—the size of the region that emits the light that we see. If the brightness increases in one hour, this region can span no more than one light-hour, a distance less than the diameter of Jupiter's orbit around the sun. Since some quasars have been observed to increase or decrease in brightness significantly within a single hour, astronomers have concluded, with reluctance and amazement, that in these quasars at least, a large portion (if not all) of the energy must be radiating from a region no larger than the inner regions of the solar system!

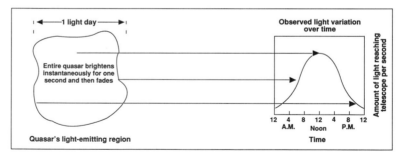

Figure 59. If the light-producing region of a quasar measures one light-day across, then even if this region grows instantaneously brighter, an observer on Earth will see the brightness increase spread out over one day of time, because light from the front of the quasar reaches us sooner than light from the back. (Drawing by Crystal Stevenson.)

THE SEARCH FOR THE MOST DISTANT QUASARS

For nearly three decades, ever since the first quasars were discovered, astonomers have outdone one another by finding ever more distant quasars. Since all estimates of quasar distances rely on Hubble's Law, the hunt for the most distant quasars corresponds to a search for the quasars with the greatest redshifts in their spectra.

In this hunt, many astronomers have succeeded, but only briefly. Today, as astronomers push their detector systems to find objects of lower and lower apparent brightness, they have reached the point where any pointlike object they detect is likely to be a quasar. The redshifts of these quasars, however, can stagger the imagination of the unwary.

Redshifts that are only a small fraction of the speed of light directly measure the recession velocity as a fraction of the speed of light. But this direct proportionality breaks down for redshifts that equal a large fraction of the original wavelengths. When astronomers speak of an object whose "redshift equals one," they are describing a spectrum in which all the wavelengths have been *increased* by an amount equal to the original wavelength. Thus all the observed wavelengths are now *double* the original wavelengths. Einstein's theory of relativity shows that such an object has a recession velocity equal to 60 percent of the speed of light. According to Hubble's Law, which must also be modified by the theory of relativity for speeds that approach the speed of light, such an object must have a distance of 9 billion light years, so that we see it not as it is but as it was 9 billion years ago, when the universe had less than half of its present age (estimated at 15 billion years).

Do the most distant quasars have redshifts of one? Far from it: That paltry mark was reached and passed during the 1960s. Today the most distant known quasar has a redshift of 4.73! Its spectrum shows features whose observed wavelengths are 5.73 times their original values. (The redshift of 4.73 measures the *increase* is the wavelength, which, when added to an original value of 1.00 times the original wavelength, gives a total of 5.73.) This quasar is receding from us at 94 percent of the speed of light, and its distance from us equals 13.5 billion light years—90 percent of the distance from us at which the cosmic background radiation that we now observe was produced. When we observe this quasar, we are looking back through 90 percent of the time since the big bang, to a time when the universe had one-tenth of its present age and galaxies had barely begun to form.

If *galaxies* had barely begun to form, what about *quasars?* This question, pregnant with implication, takes us into another chapter: the attempt to explain the mysterious power of quasars. For this you need a special tool from the domain of radio astronomy, the field that first revealed quasars to us. You need the power of interferometry.

An example of a Seyfert galaxy. (Hale Observatories photograph.)

Figure 60. The Very Large Array (VLA) of radio telescopes, whose antennas move along three railroad tracks. Each track extends 13 miles into the desert of New Mexico. The array is photographed here with the antennas relatively close together. (Courtesy of the Very Large Array.)

10. The Beast in the Middle

ON THE HIGH plains of New Mexico, not far from where two forlorn Civil War armies fought the desert and each other in the summer of 1862, 27 radio dishes, each of them 80 feet across, spread in a Y-shaped array with three legs, each 13 miles long (Figure 60). These 27 antennas, erected in central New Mexico for its environment of radio quiet and stable atmospheric conditions, collectively form the Very Large Array (VLA), a prosaic name for one of the greatest instruments humans have built to observe the cosmos.

The VLA was built during the late 1970s near Socorro, New Mexico, as the finest fruit of an astronomers' committee to survey what astronomy needed most. At the top of the committee's list was a recommendation that an array of radio telescopes be built, linked together by computer so that they could function effectively as pieces of a single enormous telescope. Funded by the National Science Foundation, the VLA construction was completed on schedule and on budget. For the past dozen years, the VLA has been a crucial research tool for astronomers who attempt to probe the universe with ever finer resolving power.

During the last decade, with progressively greater abilities as more antennas have come on line, the VLA has fulfilled its mission of allowing astronomers throughout the world to apply for observing time and, if successful, to obtain radio maps of a fineness far beyond anything previously available. The VLA can map the radio emission from a cosmic object with a sharpness equal to that obtainable with any visible-light telescope. It can do this despite the fact that an astronomer mapping an object through its radio emission faces a tremendous handicap in comparison with one who obtains an image in visible light. The clarity with which we can see an object depends on the *wavelength* of the radiation used to observe it: the longer the wavelength, the coarser the grain of the image that we obtain. The radio waves used by the VLA in making its observations have wavelengths nearly *one million times longer* than those of visible light, yet the VLA obtains sharper images than even the Palomar Mountain Telescope. How can it do this?

THE MAGIC OF INTERFEROMETRY

The secret to the sharpness of the Very Large Array's images lies in the great size of the array of radio dishes, plus the fact that modern techniques allow the astronomers to use the VLA as an *interferometer,* a device that can process into a single image the signals received by all 27 dishes. The VLA's computer receives all the data from all the dishes and uses the slight differences in the view seen by each dish, in comparison to the others, to make a map that is just as sharp as the map that would emerge from a single dish as large as the VLA array.

BLACK HOLES: THE ENGINES FOR POWERFUL RADIO SOURCES

Since its first observations in 1978, the VLA has delighted astronomers with its radio maps of cosmic objects, which have revealed detail never before seen, and only dimly suspected, in many different types of radio sources (Color Plate 22). During the 40 years since radio astronomy began in earnest, the most intriguing sources of radio waves fall into what astronomers now believe forms a single category: the radio emission from whatever surrounds *supermassive black holes.*

   We have mentioned black holes before, in chapter 8, as the alternative to neutron stars for the possible endpoints of the massive stars that collapse to begin supernova explosions. Black holes are objects that exert such enormous gravitational force on their immediate surroundings that nothing, not even light, can escape. In radio sources we may have the same basic type of object, but on a phenomenally larger scale. The supermassive black holes hypothesized to provide

The Principle of Interferometry

Combinations of radio telescopes such as the VLA are called *interferometers* because they rely on the principle of *interferometry* for their power to produce sharp, crisp images. Both words refer to a fundamental property of all wave motion, which applies to all types of electromagnetic radiation such as light and radio: Two waves can either "cohere" or "interfere" with one another. Coherent waves tend to *add* their effects, but interfering waves tend to *cancel* one another.

Consider, for example, two ocean waves—perhaps tsunamis (tidal waves) raised by underwater earthquakes—that are traveling in nearly the same direction and happen to encounter each other. If, at the time that the waves meet, the positions of their crests and troughs match, the combined wave will have higher wave crests, and deeper wave troughs, than either wave did alone. But if the waves collide with one wave's crest meeting the other's trough, the combined wave will be smaller than either. The cancellation—that is, the "interference" of the two waves—might be so complete that almost no visible wave would survive.

Now consider two radio waves, both from the same distant object, that reach two neighboring radio dishes, each of which detects the radio waves and sends its data to a central computer (Figure 61). If the source is directly overhead, then both radio dishes will detect wave crests at the same time, because the distance from the object to each dish will be identical. But if the source is observed at a small angle from overhead, one dish will detect a wave crest slightly before the other one does, because the distances from the radio source to each of the two dishes will differ slightly. Thus the waves will interfere with one another, at least in part.

The computer that combines the signals from the two dishes can sense this interference, because it can tell the difference between a signal with no interference (when the wave crests arrive simultaneously) and one with some interference. The computer measures the *amount* of the interference and uses this measurement to determine the *difference* in the distances that the two waves have traveled to reach the two radio dishes. This difference can be measured to a fraction of a

the explanation of certain radio sources must contain *billions and billions* of times the mass of the sun. Here we find ourselves finally face to face with something commensurate with a theorist's capacity to wonder, as F. Scott Fitzgerald remarked in a different context. Let us have a look at the sort of radio-emitting object that might be a black hole with billions of times the mass of our star, and dream, as astronomers do, of how we might investigate such an object in still more detail.

Begin, as theorists do, with a basic idea: Black holes *can* exist—according to Einstein's theory of relativity—and therefore are *likely* to exist—according to what seems to be a natural principle, that "whatever is not absolutely forbidden is certain to happen, somewhere, sometime." And theorists *need* black holes most of all to explain the objects for which we have the least explanation.

QUASARS AND SUPERMASSIVE BLACK HOLES

Quasars produce more energy each second than the most luminous galaxy, and this energy often flows outward from regions of space not much larger than the solar system. No theory based on the way that stars work can explain a quasar's energy output: Any star remotely large enough to shine with a quasar's luminosity would destroy itself through the tremendous outrush of its own radiation. Thus, as quasars became firmly established as "real" objects during the late 1960s and 1970s, theoreticians strove to imagine new types of objects, capable of producing floods of energy equal to those seen from quasars. Their best find, first taken as purely speculative but now rather well accepted by the astronomical community, was the supermassive black hole.

All black holes, whether theoretical or real, share a basic property. They each pack so much mass into so small a region that gravity prevents everything, including light, from escaping. This statement holds true for anything that comes within a certain distance from the center of the black hole. This critical distance, called the *Schwarzschild radius*, equals two miles times the ratio of the mass of the object to the mass of the sun. Once anything comes closer to the center than the critical distance, it will never emerge again; outside, it has at least a fighting chance.

A black hole with a mass equal to the sun's has a critical radius of two miles. Shrink this much mass into a region two miles or less in radius, and you have a black hole, and nothing can escape

wavelength. In this way the interferometer system can determine the difference in distance from the source to each of two radio antennas with a precision of *better than one centimeter* for a source trillions of miles away! The interferometer uses this precision to make a crisp map of the details in the source. Any change in the location of the details on the source—any deviation from the map the interferometer is making—would cause a measurable change in the distance differences that the interferometer measures.

And this is not all. The next step is to let the Earth's rotation make the source appear in a slightly different position on the sky. As the source assumes a new apparent position, the amount of interference recorded in the computer changes, because the waves from the source now reach the dishes from a slightly different angle. The amount of interference depends on the angle at which the radio telescope views the source. Hence accurate measurements of the changing interference allows *aperture synthesis*—the construction of a still more accurate map of the source of the radio waves.

Although the principle of interferometry will work with only two dishes, it yields still better images, in even less time, if a system of more than two dishes exists. The VLA was judged op timum (in terms of results per dollar invested) with nine radio dishes on each of its three 13-mile-long arms. Because the VLA observes at several different radio wavelengths and makes different kinds of detailed measurements, its dishes can be moved along rail road tracks to different positions, each of them best for a certain type of observation.

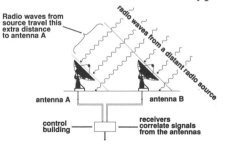

Figure 61. An interferometer uses two or more antennas and notes the difference in arrival times of the incoming waves at the different antennas. From accurate measurements of these differences, a computer can pinpoint the location of specific sources of radio emission, and then draw a detailed map of the radio source. (Drawing by Crystal Stevenson.)

from within two miles of its center. Think bigger (note how easy this sort of thinking is) and try an object with an amount of matter equal to a billion solar masses. If you shrink this object into a region no more than two billion miles in radius—the size of Saturn's orbit—nothing can escape, and you will have a black hole. No one says that the black hole must be this large, but once you have packed the mass into this radius, anything within 2 billion miles of the center will never emerge. And your billion-solar-mass black hole, made without missing a beat in the depths of your supple mind, will do nothing but sit there—until you imagine what happens to the matter around it.

ACCRETION DISKS AROUND BLACK HOLES

Since the fundamental property of a black hole arises from its enormous gravitational force, when one asks what happens to the material around a black hole, the natural reply is, "It falls right in." On occasion, you will even hear the misstatement "It is sucked right in," but this must be fought as error. To be more precise, the material around a black hole typically does *not* fall right in but instead orbits in ever-tightening spirals, closer and closer, faster and faster, before it comes within the black hole's Schwarzschild radius and disappears forever. The reason for this lies in the fact that most black holes—so astronomers believe—are *rotating*. The rotation of whatever formed them is magnified by the contraction process that produces the black hole. The black hole's rotation affects matter nearby, pulled inward by the gravitational force from the black hole. Because of the rotation, matter falling toward the black hole tends to swirl *around* the black hole in an ever-tightening spiral trajectory as it moves ever closer to the black hole's center.

As a result, every black hole (or at least every rotating black hole) into which matter falls must be surrounded by an *accretion disk*—a thin, circular sheet of matter perpendicular to the black hole's axis of rotation. Matter in the accretion disk moves most languidly at the disk's outer edges, and most rapidly near its center—the black hole itself. Attracted by the black hole's gravitation, matter joins the accretion disk and can reside there for years, slowly spiraling closer and closer until it falls completely into the black hole (Figure 62).

An accretion disk is the secret by which *infall* of matter into a black hole produces an *outflow* of energy from the black hole's neighborhood. The outflow arises because as the matter moves in ever-tighter spirals, the individual particles within the accretion disk collide. The collisions turn kinetic energy into heat, and the particles then radiate energy into space simply because they are hot. Calculations made by accretion-disk experts (in the age of specialization, we now have such scientists), such as Caltech's Roger Blandford, show that for an extremely massive black hole, the inner portions of an accretion disk—those just outside the critical radius that marks the entry into the pit of no return—can reach temperatures of hundreds of thousands, even millions of degrees.

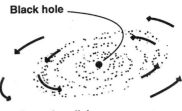

Figure 62. A supermassive black hole should be surrounded by an accretion disk, made of matter orbiting the black hole in ever-tightening spirals. Such an accretion disk could grow extremely hot and would be capable of emitting large amounts of energy. (Drawing by Crystal Stevenson.)

The existence and properties of an accretion disk complicate what intuition tells us about black holes: that black holes simply attract, which they do. Intuition tends to ignore the fact that the attracted matter, spiraling inward, can heat itself to enormous temperatures through collisions and can therefore shine brightly on its way toward oblivion. Theoretically minded astronomers, however, have been quick to discern the "uses" of an accretion disk. Today they expect that nearly every "compact object," such as a black hole or a neutron star (the condensed former core of a collapsed star) should have an accretion disk of matter spiraling around it. Theorists use accretion disks to explain most of the sources of x rays observed in the Milky Way and in nearby galaxies: Matter swirling toward a star-mass neutron star or black hole has heated to nearly a million degrees or more and therefore glows in the x-ray portion of the electromagnetic spectrum.

THE BEAST IN THE MIDDLE

But the greatest success of accretion disks—as a theory—comes with quasars. Many theorists now favor a *unified theory* that describes both quasars and galaxies with "active" (highly energetic) nuclei. In the unified theory, the heart of each object and the secret of its success is a supermassive black hole, the size of the solar system but with the mass of a small galaxy (as if the United States were squeezed into Yankee Stadium). Surrounding these supermassive black holes are accretion disks many times larger (but still far smaller than the distance from the sun to the closest stars). These disks are warm at their outsides, much hotter farther in, and incredibly hot toward their centers.

In this model of quasars and related objects, the accretion disks contain hundreds of thousands of solar masses of material at any time. It is this matter, spiraling inward toward the black hole and heated by collisions among the individual particles, that produces the tremendous outpouring of energy from a quasar. The beast in the middle—the supermassive black hole and the accretion disk around it—thus produces all the energy that we record billions of light years away, billions of years later.

Such an accretion disk, even one a hundred times the size of the solar system, could never be seen in a distant galaxy with our best telescopes as anything but a point of light. If we hope to verify or disprove the theory that quasars owe their enormous flows of energy to an accretion disk, we must find ways to test the hypothesis other than by using even our most advanced optical telescopes.

In their attempts to refine the accretion-disk model of quasars, the theorists have added another wrinkle: the jets of matter that escape from the accretion disk. Their calculations show that although most of the matter in the disk will eventually fall into the black hole, some of it—well before it moves inside the black hole's outer limit—will not. Instead, some matter will be squirted outward like matter ejected from a tube of toothpaste squeezed by a great hand. The ejection of matter will occur in two opposite directions, which are perpendicular to the accretion disk and lie along the rotation axis of the accretion disk. The jets allow for an additional possibility: In some cases, we might observe a quasar almost exactly *along* one of the outflowing jets. The effect would resemble a cosmic firehose aimed directly at us instead of being seen from the side.

This "down-the-firehose" orientation might explain an intriguing class of objects: *blazars,* which are quasars of particularly high luminosity, whose spectra show almost none of the emission lines that helped to identify quasars in the first place. Recall that emission lines are particular colors (that is, frequencies and wavelengths) at which an object emits especially great amounts of radiation. The explanation for their absence in blazars would run as follows: If our line of sight has us looking straight down the firehose of a jet, we would see a tremendously bright object, as we do when a powerful light shines straight into our eyes. In such a case, the Doppler effect (which changes the frequency from a source of radiation in motion) would "smear out" the emission lines, because the matter within the jet moves at widely varying speeds. Then even though the matter in the jet produces large amounts of radiation that would appear at a particular frequency if the matter were motionless, we on Earth would see the single frequency "smeared" over a wide range of frequencies, because the differences in velocities at which matter moved along the jet would be tremendous.

ACCRETION DISKS THROUGHOUT THE UNIVERSE

On a somewhat more modest scale, the accretion-disk model could also explain what astronomers call *active galactic nuclei,* galaxies with remarkably luminous central regions (Color Plates 23 and 24). In these galaxies, supermassive black holes with, say, not a billion but a hundred million solar masses would have correspondingly smaller (though still impressive) accretion disks, capable of producing luminosities of a few percent, or a few tenths of a percent, of a typical quasar's energy output.

Astronomers think they have found an example of such a "modest" supermassive black hole in the giant elliptical galaxy M 87, the brightest galaxy in the Virgo cluster of galaxies, 60 million light years away. Careful observations of how the motions of stars close to the galactic center have been affected by nearby masses indicate that a large amount of mass—close to a hundred million solar masses—apparently concentrates within the central one-tenth of one percent of the galaxy. This might be an incredibly rich star cluster, but it *might* be a supermassive black hole. Furthermore, short-exposure photographs reveal something odd at the center of M 87: A jet of material, rich in knotty detail, is emerging (Figure 63). This jet is thousands of times larger and much less powerful than the jets we described in connection with the accretion disk, but it testifies to the violent release of energy near the heart of M 87.

On the most modest scale of all, the center of the Milky

Figure 63. A photograph of the giant elliptical galaxy M 87 (left) taken with a short exposure (right) reveals that at the galaxy's core, a jet of matter extends outward in a straight line, broken into "knots." This jet probably consists of matter being ejected from the heart of the galaxy. (Lick Observatory photographs.)

Way—like that of many other spiral galaxies—may itself contain a black hole, perhaps one with a million times the mass of the sun. Chary of superlatives as they are, astronomers hesitate to denominate a million-solar-mass black hole as "supermassive," so they simply call it a "large" black hole. In recent years, some astronomers have interpreted radio and infrared observations of the galactic center as indicating the presence of a mass of approximately one million solar masses concentrated within a few light years of the galactic center. If this concentration exists, few doubt that a black hole provides the most likely form for the matter to take, for theoretical astonomers have no way to keep a million-solar-mass object from becoming a black hole once it occupies only a few cubic light years of volume. But other astronomers question the detailed interpretation of the observations, claiming that so large a concentration of matter does not necessarily exist at the galactic center. The next decade should reveal the truth about the black hole at the center of the Milky Way. Whether or not this black hole exists, the accretion-disk model creates the greatest excitement (and rightly so) on the largest scales, those that could explain quasars and galaxies with active centers.

Notice that in order for the accretion-disk model of quasars to work, we must have not only a supermassive black hole but also material to keep adding to the accretion disk. In other words, so long as we "feed" the black hole, we get a quasar, but when we stop feeding it, we soon (astronomically speaking) have only a bare black hole. This could help explain why we see thousands of quasars today at enormous distances—typically billions of light years away—but no quasars close to the Milky Way, even in cosmic terms. Looking outward in space always implies looking backward in time, so we see objects billions of light years away as they *were* billions of years ago. The best explanation for the lack of quasars at lesser distances would be that the supermassive black holes within quasars formed early, ate whatever they could, and eventually—having consumed everything in their vicinities—continued to exist but were bereft of the accretion disks that make quasars shine.

Thus the best theory we have for quasars states, in a nutshell, that they depend on supermassive black holes plus material to feed the accretion disks that make quasars shine. To an observational astronomer, this statement represents another far-out triumph of theoretical astronomers: The theorists have dreamed of an object (the accretion disk) too small to be observed directly but capable of the most astounding feats. Are the observers right to be skeptical? How can we test the accretion-disk theory directly, to see whether it merits our belief?

THE SEARCH FOR THE ACCRETION DISK

The best test would be to look for the accretion disk with a telescope capable of observing it. Find the accretion disk, and the observers take the theorists to dinner; fail to find it, and we reverse the process. Only one difficulty stands beween someone and a free dinner—the lack of a telescope. Here we see a need for cleverness in observation.

Radio astronomers who specialize in the use of interferometers know that the most basic descriptive fact about the Very Large Array, or any other system that links radio dishes together, is its *baseline*—the distance between the most widely spaced radio dishes. The longer the baseline, the finer the detail that the system of radio telescopes can observe. Since the VLA in New Mexico cannot hope to observe the accretion disk in a quasar or a galaxy with an active nucleus, then the solution appears to be simple: Lengthen the baseline! With a baseline 10 times longer than the VLA's 20 miles, you can make maps with a sharpness 10 times better than that produced with the VLA. Increase the baseline 300 times, and the sharpness increases by a factor of 300. Three hundred times 20 miles equals 6000 miles—three-quarters the diameter of the Earth! We are talking about making an interferometer nearly as large as the Earth, precisely the goal that a team of Caltech radio astronomers set out to accomplish.

This team works in Very Long Baseline Interferometry (VLBI). "Interferometry" describes the technique of using two or more radio dishes to obtain a far sharper image than a single dish can provide, and "Very Long" means "more than a few dozen miles." VLBI astronomers, a breed not more than two decades old, continually construct systems of radio telescopes as large as the Earth. They do so not by building new radio dishes distributed over the seven continents, but rather through the use of existing radio dishes to make simultaneous observations of an object.

Even with VLBI—even by making an interferometer with a diameter equal to the Earth's—we cannot hope to observe an accretion disk at a quasar's distance. We cannot even come close to doing so. But if we look at galaxies much closer to us than quasars are, we *can* hope to see at least the immediate surroundings of an accretion disk within the active nucleus of a galaxy. The Caltech group's efforts focused on a galaxy called NGC 1275, an elliptical galaxy 220 million light years away in the direction of the constellation Perseus (Figure 63).

NGC 1275 appears as the 1275th galaxy in the *New General Catalogue of Galaxies* (NGC), compiled a century ago by J. L. E. Dreyer, who knew that this data base would be useful for decades thereafter. Half a century after the creation of the NGC (as

Figure 64. The galaxy NGC 1275, one of the class called Seyfert galaxies, has a particularly energetic center that is characteristic of its class. This relatively long exposure has somewhat smeared out the intense light from the center. (National Optical Astronomy Observatories.)

astronomers call it), radio astronomers found that NGC 1275 emits large amounts of radio waves, which make it the most intense radio source in Perseus. The "3C" catalog of radio sources, third in a series compiled by radio astronomers at Cambridge University, contains such prominent quasars as 3C 48 and 3C 273, and lists NGC 1275 as 3C 84. During the 1970s, a decade after the 3C catalog was complete, x-ray astronomers who sent their instruments above the atmosphere found that NGC 1275 also produces x rays in great abundance. At about the same time, new techniques in astronomical photography revealed that at the center of the galaxy lies a small nucleus, intensely bright in visible light.

Furthermore, high-resolution radio observations made with the VLA showed that the central regions of NGC 1275 produce a jet of material, reminiscent of the jet in M 87. All in all, NGC 1275 well represents a galaxy with an active nucleus. We see this galaxy as it was 220 million years ago—a short while in the 15-billion-year history of the universe, and just yesterday in comparison to the billions of years we look back into the past when we observe quasars. Could NGC 1275 be a former quasar, whose supermassive black hole receives less "food" than it did billions of years ago? The best way to find out would be to search for a black hole in the center of NGC 1275 by using the much higher resolution obtainable with VLBI.

TONY READHEAD AND VLBI ASTRONOMY

This was a matter for Tony Readhead's VLBI group at Caltech. Readhead, born in South Africa and a Cambridge Ph.D., has now spent more than a third of his nearly 50 years in the United States (Figure 65). Like most other astronomers, he was drawn into the field at an early age through reading about it. "It was an easy conversion," he says. "Reading the first book was enough." While still in high school, Readhead worked as a night assistant at the Radcliffe Observatory, the largest in the country, and was encouraged by the chief astronomer there, Andrew David Thackeray. An engaging man—the grandson of the poet William Makepeace Thackeray—the older astronomer gave Readhead two sound pieces of advice: Study math and physics at Cambridge and Caltech.

Readhead took this advice. He first studied physics and math at Witwatersrand University and then journeyed to Cambridge in 1966 to enroll for graduate studies at the Cavendish Laboratory. Like other astronomy students at that time, Readhead was fascinated by the discoveries of quasars, the cosmic microwave background, and pulsars—all of which had been made during the last three years of Readhead's college career. He decided to become a radio astronomer. In fact, by the time that he finished his undergraduate studies, Readhead already knew that he wanted to work on the details of the radio emission from compact radio sources such as quasars, which in fact he has done for more than two decades.

At the Cavendish, Readhead had two excellent professors to guide him, Anthony Hewish and Martin Ryle, who shared the Nobel Prize in 1974 for the discovery of pulsars and the development of VLBI, respectively. Readhead proved an excellent researcher—good enough to receive a five-year fellowship, following his Ph.D., that allowed him to travel where he liked. He visited Caltech for 15 months in 1974 and 1975, intrigued by the possibilities of VLBI, and worked with Marshall Cohen, the leader of the interferometry group there. At just this time, Alan Rogers at MIT published a paper showing how to use interferometry in a clever way called *phase closure*. Phase closure, a technique for correlating the data from the different antennas, is too complex to be explained here, but it allows astronomers to use VLBI techniques to produce superior images of radio-emitting objects. Readhead and his colleague Peter Wilkinson began to use this method, which "turned out to be more powerful than we had any right to expect."

Back in Cambridge, Readhead discussed the phase-closure method with his former professor Martin Ryle. Ryle was skeptical that the method could yield actual radio maps of an object. He suggested a series of "blind tests," in which Readhead would be given radio data from an unidentified source and challenged to use the new technique to make a detailed map of the source. At Caltech, Marshall Cohen gave Readhead and Wilkinson test after test, manufacturing data as if arriving from a collection of radio antennas. For every source, the two young astronomers produced an accurate map, thus convincing Cohen and Ryle that the new technique would work.

Figure 65. Tony Readhead, a radio astronomer at Caltech, is a leader in the field of very long baseline interferometry. (Photograph courtesy of the California Institute of Technology.)

By 1977, Readhead was a senior research fellow at Caltech; then he became a senior research associate, and then professor of radio astronomy and, for several years, director of Caltech's radio observatory. Through the last 15 years Readhead has helped to develop better and better ideas for improving radio maps and has seen these ideas assisted by improvements in the technological methods of making the observations. One key improvement has arisen from simply observing at shorter radio wavelengths. Though technologically difficult, this method is valuable because the sharpness of the image increases directly as the wavelength decreases, since you are observing the same object with a finer mesh, as if you substituted your fingers for your fist in examining an elephant. Another key improvement hinges on the development of faster and better computers to process the flood of data from the telescopes that observe around the world in a VLBI experiment.

Readhead was also a pioneer in developing unified theories of active galaxies—theories that hope to explain quasars, Seyfert galaxies, and galaxies with active nuclei as three different aspects of the same phenomenon. In 1989, he was focusing on the galaxy NGC 1275 in collaboration with a postdoc from Italy named

Tiziana Venturi. Venturi, entirely Sicilian in appearance, is a short, dark-haired, wide-eyed woman, who was born, raised, and educated in Bologna, the home of the oldest university in Europe (Figure 66). Venturi discovered at an early age that she was "crazy at numbers"; in high school, astronomy proved so fascinating that she "fell in love." Drawn by the future of Italian radio astronomy, Venturi chose that specialty. By 1988, as she received her doctoral degree, she began to learn about VLBI observations; by January 1989, she was a postdoctoral fellow with Tony Readhead's group at Caltech. And there Readhead suddenly realized that what was needed to peer into the heart of NGC 1275 was a VLBI observation of this galaxy, using a new technique—*multi-frequency VLBI*—that had been developed by a young Englishman named John Conway.

Figure 66. Tiziana Venturi, a post-doctoral fellow at Caltech, participated in the September 1989 VLBI experiment. (Photograph by Donald Goldsmith.)

Conway was born in Liverpool, England, in 1960; he talks like Paul McCartney and arguably resembles McCartney two decades ago (Figure 67). Conway graduated from Cambridge University in physics and then worked at the Jodrell Bank Radio Observatory in central England before returning to graduate studies at Cambridge. In 1988, armed with a Ph.D. that had been gained by his new method of making VLBI observations at several different radio frequencies, Conway obtained a postdoctoral fellowship at Caltech. There he joined the VLBI group led by Tony Readhead. Just as Marshall Cohen had given Readhead and Wilkinson the freedom to develop the new observational techniques that are standard today, Readhead arranged for Conway to become the "principal investigator" of the VLBI team that would attempt to peer into the heart of NGC 1275.

By using Conway's plan of observing at three slightly different frequencies, the VLBI astronomers hoped to achieve far more detail in their observations than a map made at any single frequency could reveal. Because each frequency maps the source in waves of slightly different length, each map would show detail at a slightly different spacing—as if you took a photograph in three different colors, and each color revealed different types of detail.

Combining all three colors in a single photograph would then provide more detail than any one of the three individual pictures.

In theory, using three frequencies rather than one simply requires more computer tape to record the data and more computer time to analyze it. In practice, however, every time that a radio telescope observes at a different frequency, its operators must retune its receivers, as if they were tuning a giant radio dial in a highly complex manner. On occasion, observing at a new frequency requires the physical replacement of one detector, mounted at the focus of the radio dish, with another. Since Conway had 11 sites to worry about, at any one of which some astronomer could make an error, he had an excuse for sleeplessness.

By September 1989, the VLBI group led by John Conway had enlisted the cooperation of 11 different radio observatories in California, New Mexico (the location of the Very Large Array), Massachusetts, West Virginia, England, Sweden, West Germany, and Italy. They had chosen the wavelengths of observations to be as short as possible in order to increase the sharpness of their images to the maximum. Then, with all systems ready to observe at the same time, observers at each of the 11 sites pointed their radio telescopes for three days toward NGC 1275 and recorded their signals.

Figure 67. John Conway, the principal investigator of the VLBI experiment in September 1989, carried an impressive responsibility for an astronomer not yet 30 years old. (Photograph by Donald Goldsmith.)

Conway, conscious that the role of principal investigator rarely devolves on an astronomer under 35—let alone on one who is 28 and looks 19—is not one to take responsibility lightly. He did not rest easily during the three days of the VLBI observing run. Ordinarily Conway could draw comfort from the fact that each of the 11 observing sites had a competent observer to supervise the still more competent technical staff. But this was not an "ordinary" VLBI observation: For the first time, the astronomers would attempt to observe a faraway radio source at three different frequencies, rather than at a single frequency.

Brought back to Caltech for processing in a master computer, the signals—so the astronomers hoped—would reveal details of NGC 1275 on an unprecedentedly fine scale. Astronomers measure such resolving power in *seconds of arc,* fractions of a circle around the horizon. The moon and sun each span 1800 seconds of arc, and the best optical telescopes can—on the clearest of nights—see detail on scales of a few tenths of a second of arc. The VLBI astronomers hoped to achieve a resolving power *better than one one-thousandth of a second of arc.* To a conventional (visible-light) astronomer, this sharpness seems astounding. Even when the atmosphere has its most transparent quality, at the times of most perfect "seeing," the finest optical telescopes can see with a sharpness no better than one-tenth of a second of arc—vision a hundred times coarser than that of the VLBI observations!

As the data analysis progressed, Conway noted triumphs and failures. The observations from Noto in Sicily, for reasons still unexplained, produced no usable data. At Owens Valley, the system worked, but imperfectly. However, all the other observing sites performed brilliantly—in particular, the one near Bonn, where the world's largest steerable radio telescope points to the sky. These observations did not, and could not, decide unambiguously whether or not a supermassive black hole lies at the center of the galaxy. As the map emerged, it revealed that the heart of NGC 1275 shows a complex structure with a central point of strongest radio emission (Figure 68). This structure's complexity indicates that astronomers are finally probing near the region that produces the bulk of the energy. Only far *outside* the energy-producing region would anything as orderly as a straight jet be visible.

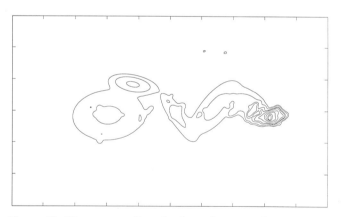

Figure 68. The contour lines in the radio map of NGC 1275 produced by the VLBI observations in 1989 show that the region of the most intense radio emission (right center) has remained almost unchanged during the past five years. To radio astronomers, this suggests the existence of an accretion disk surrounding a supermassive black hole. To the south (left in this map) of this suspected black hole, "blobs" of radio emission detach themselves at intervals and move away from the intense source at speeds up to half the speed of light. The map spans about 20 light years at the very center of NGC 1275. (Courtesy of Tony Readhead, John Conway, and the California Institute of Technology.)

Radio astronomers are conservative scientists, loath to leap to conclusions that may later prove erroneous. Readhead, Conway, and their colleagues emphasize that the *indications* of a black hole surrounded by an accretion disk is hardly conclusive proof. They seek ways to make even more detailed maps of sources such as NGC 1275, and eventually to probe deeply enough into its center to determine what lurks at the center of this closest quasarlike galaxy. For now, astronomers take pride in what they have accomplished with their metaphorical "telescope as large as the Earth." Most astronomers feel that continuing progress in optical and radio astronomy has led to a coherent picture of energetic objects such as quasars: objects whose hearts of darkness may well be supermassive black holes.

But science has—and needs—its doubters. It is worth our while to step back for a moment and consider how sure we ought to be of the sweeping conclusions we make about the universe at large—for example, that the entire universe is expanding according to Hubble's Law. As discussed in chapter 3, only by reviewing scientific conclusions from a skeptical viewpoint can one claim to follow a scientific method. The nature of quasars provides a fine opportunity to see how confident we may be in our knowledge of the expanding universe—and of the physical laws that describe distant galaxies.

THE CASE OF HALTON ARP

All of extragalactic astronomy rests on a basic premise: The redshifts we measure for galaxies beyond the Local Group primarily arise from the Doppler effect, which reflects the galaxies' motions away from us as part of the expansion of the universe. But a maverick astronomer named Halton Arp, currently on the scientific staff at the Max Planck Institute for Physics and Astrophysics near Munich, Germany, has questioned this fundamental hypothesis of extragalactic astronomy. Born in 1924, Arp is a distant cousin of the renowned French painter Jean Arp. A tall, slim, strikingly handsome man in his mid-sixties, Arp was a fencing champion in his younger days, and it would still be inadvisable to provoke him into a duel with the épée (Figure 69).

As a graduate student at Caltech, Arp specialized in observations of distant galaxies. By 1953, when he received his Ph.D., the

Figure 69. Halton Arp, now at the Max Planck Institute for Physics and Radiophysics near Munich, West Germany, has urged controversial theories of quasars on his fellow astronomers for the past 25 years. (Photograph by Earl Fisher.)

small world of astronomers (much smaller then than now) knew him as "Chip" Arp, a man of much promise, who soon received the American Astronomical Society's Helen Warner Prize, which goes annually to the U.S. astronomer less than 35 years old who has performed the best research (in the opinion of the awards committee).

Before receiving the Warner Prize in 1960 Arp had been invited to join the staff of Caltech's Mount Wilson and Palomar Mountain Observatories—that is, to have the greatest possible access to what were then the world's largest telescopes. Working with those telescopes, and in particular with the 200-inch glass giant on Palomar Mountain, Arp took galaxy photographs that were unsurpassed for technical excellence. Twenty or 30 years ago, astronomical photography was still as much art as science; now, with the silicon chips in CCD detectors having replaced photographic plates and telescopes completely automated, much of the art has vanished. One of Arp's special interests concerned *peculiar galaxies*—those whose shapes deviated from the normal spirals and ellipticals. For the past 25 years, the basic reference work in this field has been Arp's *Atlas of Peculiar Galaxies,* which presents the 338 most striking of these objects, observed by Arp over a four-year period, mostly with the 200-inch telescope.

During the 1960s, as the newly discovered quasars attracted a flood of attention, Arp wondered how he might investigate these strange new objects. Unsurprisingly, since he was finishing his *Atlas of Peculiar Galaxies,* he decided to study whether quasars might prove somehow related to peculiar galaxies. Arp began with a basic question: Were any of the quasars close in space to any of the peculiar galaxies in his *Atlas?*

Like all astronomers, Arp could see only two dimensions: north-south and east-west on the sky. The third dimension, the distance outward from the Earth, must be estimated, not measured. Astronomers performed this estimate by using the quasars' redshifts. Such estimates rely on the acceptance of Hubble's Law, that all objects' redshifts are proportional to their distances. Arp did not doubt Hubble's Law, but he decided to keep an open mind and perform a statistical analysis to see whether quasars tend to appear *on the sky* close to peculiar galaxies, more often than a random distribution of quasars in space could explain (Figure 70). If they did, quasars must be associated with the peculiar galaxies *in space;*

otherwise, no good way exists to explain the association of quasars and galaxies as we see them.

When Arp began his investigations, only a few dozen quasars were known. But even those few dozen sufficed to convince Arp to conclude—as he has steadfastly concluded ever since—that *quasars appear much more often close to peculiar galaxies on the sky than chance can reasonably explain.* This assertion raised a host of controversy, which has never been completely resolved. Superficially, the problem of determining whether or not quasars tend to appear close to peculiar galaxies on the sky should prove easily resolvable by statistics. Astronomers would agree upon the peculiar galaxies in question and would see how many quasars had positions close to them, in accord with an agreed-upon definition of "close." Then they would compare this number with the number expected on the basis of a random distribution, given the number of quasars sprinkled all over the sky. If, for example, astronomers had found 4,000 quasars in all, then any region covering one four-thousandth of the entire sky should contain 1 quasar. If 2 appeared in that region, this might be a chance effect; even 3 might turn up there in a random distribution; but if 5 or 10 quasars appeared in one of these regions, it would be difficult to insist that this arose purely by chance.

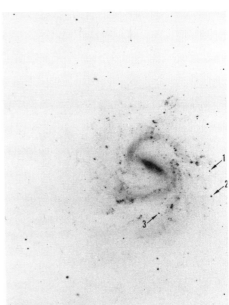

Figure 70. Halton Arp's photograph of the galaxy NGC 1073, printed as a negative to show detail, reveals three quasars (marked by arrows) close to the galaxy, either because of a chance lineup or because the quasars are close to the galaxy in space. (Courtesy of Halton Arp.)

Since the late 1960s, astronomers have debated Arp's suggestion that quasars are somehow linked with peculiar galaxies. Those who dispute Arp's assertion agree with him on one key point: His suggestion, if proven correct, would rock the world of astronomy.

Consider for a moment what Arp's theory implies. Arp claims to have found quasars associated with galaxies—quasars whose spectra show redshifts corresponding to velocities of recession enormously greater than those shown by the galaxies. The quasars' redshifts correspond to speeds of 10 percent, 30 percent, even 80 percent of the speed of light! No astronomer (including Arp) believes that a galaxy has ejected quasars from it at these speeds. For if the galaxy had done so, it would presumably have ejected *some* quasars in trajectories that approach rather than recede from us. The spectra of these approaching quasars would show a *blueshift* to higher frequencies, rather than a redshift to lower frequencies. No such quasars have ever been found. Hence Arp concludes that the redshifts of quasars do not arise from the Doppler effect; that is, astronomers are wrong to use quasars' redshifts as indicative of their recession velocities and thus of the quasars' distances from us.

But what would be wrong for quasars quite likely would be wrong for galaxies too. Most astronomers would agree that if Arp is correct, then our basic reliance on redshift as a distance indicator must be wrong. If Arp is right, Hubble's Law would be wrong, at least in part, because an association between galaxies and quasars with vastly different redshifts implies that the redshift does *not* provide an accurate way to estimate distances. One of two results must then follow. Either the redshift does *not* arise from the Doppler effect, or the redshift does arise from the Doppler effect—that is, from the galaxies' motions away from us—but the speeds of those galaxies are *not* correlated with the galaxies' distances. Both alternatives violate Hubble's Law.

Today only a few astronomers believe, with Arp, that quasars are indeed associated with peculiar galaxies—that the quasars and the galaxies in fact have the same distances and occupy nearly the same region of space. At least two reasons exist for this reluctance. First and most basic, astronomers have found evidence that at least *some* quasars do lie at the immense distances that their spectra indicate. This evidence consists of photographs that reveal faint galaxies in clusters surrounding some of the quasars. The galaxies in these clusters have redshifts that match those measured for the quasars—sufficient proof, to most astronomers, that Hubble's Law works perfectly well for the quasars in clusters of galaxies.

Secondly, astronomers meet extraordinary claims such as Arp's with the most basic scientific tool, skepticism. To a scientist, all "knowledge" remains open to question, but this emphatically does not mean that all knowledge is equally questionable. An assertion that contradicts the fundamentally accepted notions of astronomy requires far more, and better, evidence than one that makes only a slight modification in our understanding of the universe. Neither Arp, nor his supporters, nor his opponents reject this rule; if any of them did, we could simply rule the disagreement beyond the bounds of science. Precisely because both sides of the controversy agree on (at least most of) the rules, the ongoing disagreement concerning Arp's assertion has scientific validity.

Arp has squarely faced the challenge he poses to other astronomers: He accepts that if his data hold up, the central dogma of cosmology—Hubble's discovery of the expanding universe—becomes highly questionable. Small wonder, then, that astronomers would never easily accept Arp's quasar theories as correct. No one would lightly discard Hubble's Law, the big bang, and the ability to estimate the distances to faraway objects by measuring the redshifts in their spectra. In a movie, Arp would persevere until the day when his unorthodox ideas finally received recognition, when old ways of conceiving the universe were discarded and his research became the key to a new concept of the universe. In science, things rarely work this way.

If you feel that the scientific skepticism might be fun, then the next time someone presents you with a brilliant hypothesis—perhaps an explanation of why President Kennedy was murdered, or the effect that the planets' positions have on human lives—try asking yourself: What would make me reject this theory? If you answer "Nothing," then you erect a considerable gulf between your views and the scientific view of the world. And if you answer "Well, it may not be right, but I've heard a lot that makes it sound reasonable," you still maintain quite a distance from what a scientist would want to do: search for evidence that would either confirm or disprove the hypothesis. The writer Lewis Jones has referred to a "Grand Canyon of the intellect" that yawns between a scientific world view and other attitudes. You can determine on which side of the canyon you are standing by noting whether or not, in Lewis's words, you are used to asking: "How would I test that? What is the evidence for it? How likely is it that this was no more than a coincidence?" If you find yourself on the scientific side of the canyon, scientists salute you; if not, they might urge you to ask yourself whether it might not be worthwhile and fun to adopt a different vantage point, at least for awhile. You will give up the joys of believing that which it pleases you to believe, but in return you will gain the satisfaction of knowing why you think you know what you know.

Figure 75. In August 1989, *Voyager 2* found complete systems of rings around Neptune. The planet appears distended in this highly overexposed image. (NASA photograph.)

11. Exploring the Neighborhood

BENEATH THE SAN Gabriel Mountains in Southern California, the nerve center of the United States' exploration of the solar system embraces 175 acres, nearly a hundred buildings, 5,000 employees, and five decades of hard-working history. This is the Jet Propulsion Laboratory (JPL), whose name recalls its origins during the 1930s, when a Hungarian-born Caltech professor, Theodore von Karman, took some of his graduate students to what was then a desolate spot beyond the inhabited area of Los Angeles to engage in what one student called "rather odd experiments": the testing of rocket engines. Von Karman's research led to new advances in liquid- and solid-fueled rockets, as well as to the development of "jet-assisted takeoff" for propeller-driven aircraft, which proved highly useful during World War II and provided a crucial boost in aiding the exploration of Antarctica during the 1950s.

The U.S. Army had jurisdiction over JPL through the 1930s and 1940s, but late in 1958, two months after the U.S. Congress had created the National Aeronautics and Space Administration (NASA), the new civilian agency took over. For more than 30 years since then, JPL has been the primary center for the development of automated spacecraft. JPL built the first U.S. satellite, the 31-pound *Explorer 1* (launched on January 31, 1958); its scientists and engineers designed and built the *Ranger* and *Surveyor* spacecraft that landed on the moon; they engaged in the *Mariner* missions that flew by Mercury, Venus, and Mars, providing the first good views of those planets' surfaces and atmospheres; they carried out the enormously successful *Viking* mission to Mars in 1976; and they conceived and constructed the two longest-lived surveyors of the solar system, *Voyager 1* and *Voyager 2,* which successively and successfully examined the sun's four giant planets, Jupiter, Saturn, Uranus, and Neptune.

VOYAGERS THROUGH THE SOLAR SYSTEM

The *Voyager* mission to the giant planets grew out of a proposed super-mission called the Grand Tour. The idea for the Grand Tour—a visit to Jupiter, Saturn, Uranus, and Neptune, and their satellite systems—arose naturally from a cosmic happening, a relatively close alignment of the four giant planets that occurred during the 1970s and 1980s (Figure 71). Such alignments, even the merely approximate ones, occur only rarely, because each planet takes a different amount of time to orbit once around the sun.

Each of the giant planets, like the Earth and the other inner planets, moves around the sun in an elliptical orbit that takes the planet a few percent farther from the sun, or closer to it, than its average distance from our parent star. The more distant planets have farther to travel, and they move more slowly in their orbits than the closer planets to the sun. Hence they spend longer on each orbit: Jupiter takes 12 years; Saturn, nearly 30; Uranus, 84; and Neptune, 165. These widely varying orbital periods make it unlikely that you will find all four giant planets in a nearly straight line, but this situation occurred in the late twentieth century and provided the opportunity for the launch of a spacecraft to explore each of the four giant planets in turn, doing so far more easily than it ever could if the planets lay in entirely different directions outward from the sun.

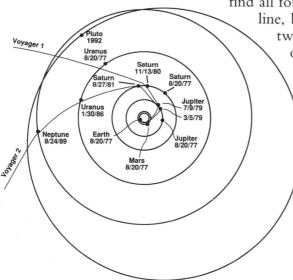

Figure 71. The trajectories of the *Voyager 1* and *Voyager 2* spacecraft took them outward, and in the case of *Voyager 2,* past the sun's four giant planets. (Drawing by Crystal Stevenson.)

To some, the situation called for exploitation of a different kind. In 1974, a book by John Gribbin and Stephen Plagemann called *The Jupiter Effect*—infamous among astronomers and geologists—predicted that the near-alignment of the giant planets would raise havoc on our planet in 1982. The authors of this book gave little emphasis to the fact that the alignment has occurred quite often throughout history, and this one was far from perfect. In the end, the chief seismic event arose not in the Earth's spin as the authors had suggested, but in their bank accounts. After the worst of the alignment had passed with little ill effect, the authors produced another book, *The Jupiter Effect Reconsidered,* which modestly noted that "most often [forecasts are], like the curate's egg, good in parts."

Between the publication dates of these two books, the *Voyager* spacecraft took advantage of the rough lineup of the outer planets to begin their epochal explorations. The original Grand Tour proposed by astronomers would have sent what might be called a luxury sedan of spacecraft past each of the four giant planets, capable of studying the planets, their atmospheres, and their moons in far greater detail than ever before revealed. Budgetary constraints pared the luxury sedan back to a good road car, and then to a stripped-down model capable of passing the most crucial road test: congressional approval. In order to save money, the two *Voyager* spacecraft were designed (during the period between 1972 and 1977) with sufficient fuel and durability to spend four years in space: enough time to pass Jupiter and Saturn, but not enough to reach Uranus or Neptune. The fact that the scientists subsequently found a way to send one of the two *Voyagers* to Uranus and Neptune, and to have the spacecraft function quite well during this 12-year journey, represents an accomplishment no one would have wagered on in 1977, when first *Voyager 2* and then *Voyager 1* left the Kennedy Space Center in Florida.

The two *Voyagers* reached Jupiter in 1979, one in March and one in July. Then, using Jupiter's gravity to change their trajectories, the spacecraft both went on to Saturn, where *Voyager 1* arrived in November 1980 and *Voyager 2* in August 1981. *Voyager 1* then headed outward from the solar system with no further planetary encounters, but *Voyager 2* went on to Uranus (January 1986) and finally to Neptune (August 1989). As *Voyager 2* neared its encounter with Saturn, the project scientists faced a crucial vote. In order to maneuver the spacecraft toward Uranus, they would have to forego a close encounter with Saturn's most mysterious moon, called Iapetus, a satellite that is extremely dark on one side but brightly reflective on the other. Knowing that no further missions to Uranus and Neptune were likely to be launched before the end of this millennium, they opted instead to gain the chance to look at the seventh and eighth planets of the sun.

ED STONE: THE MAN AT THE CENTER OF THE VOYAGE

At the center of the *Voyager* encounter with Neptune stood the man who has played a central role in the U.S. exploration of the outer solar system during the past decade: Ed Stone (Figure 72). Stone has more current job titles than most of us have job experience in a lifetime. Professor of planetary sciences at Caltech, he is also chair of the Division of Physics, Mathematics, and Astronomy. And he is Caltech's vice president for research, a position created when

Caltech became the prime mover behind the Keck Telescope now nearing completion on the Big Island of Hawaii. Finally, in 1991 he became the director of JPL itself. In the worlds of planetary exploration, Stone was a member of the U.S. government's Space Science Board from 1982 through 1985. He was, and is, the chief scientist on the *Voyager* mission—a position he has held since 1972, 5 years before the two *Voyager* spacecraft left Florida. In addition to being chief project scientist, Stone was also the principal investigator for the experiment aboard the spacecraft that measured *cosmic rays*—charged particles moving at nearly the speed of light. An ongoing effort since the dawn of the space age has been to learn more about just which particle types form the cosmic rays and what sources, such as exploding stars, produce them.

Figure 72. Ed Stone, a leader in the United States' effort to explore the outer solar system. (Photograph by Donald Goldsmith.)

Other principal investigators on *Voyager*—such as Brad Smith, the head of the *Voyager* Imaging Team—felt the full responsibility of leading a team of scientists through the *Voyager* trajectory and planetary encounters; Ed Stone had to do this with his left hand, while his right hand coordinated his own efforts with those of Brad Smith and the 10 other principal investigators.

Stone carries an inapt name for a man in ceaseless motion.

Born and raised in Iowa, the grandson of a Methodist minister and the son of a carpenter (who later became a building superintendent), Stone inherited all the midwestern virtues of hard work and careful attention to detail. In repose, Stone resembles a senator in deep cogitation, with a prominent forehead and a congressional dome; in speech, his statements are so quick and to the point that they might seem to come from a New Yorker rather than an Iowan. Now in his mid-fifties, Stone shows no sign of losing a step—steps he takes two at a time whenever he has the opportunity.

Ed Stone became deeply interested in science while still a boy. He attended junior college in Burlington, Iowa, and then, in 1956, went to the University of Chicago. Chicago was the place where Enrico Fermi and the other scientists and engineers had initiated the first controlled nuclear-fission experiment beneath the university's football stadium. Stone found his calling there, as well as his first key mentor: John Simpson, an expert in the nature and propagation of cosmic rays, who was one of the pioneers in constructing cosmic-ray detectors to fly aboard the first U.S. space probes. No one then (or now) knew for sure just what produces fast-moving cosmic-ray particles, so the challenges of detecting, identifying, and analyzing them could exert a keen grip on a scientist's mind. Since the particles move so rapidly that they would do considerable damage to our bodies, we may count ourselves fortunate that our atmosphere screens out nearly all of them; but once again, astronomers must rise above the atmosphere, by balloon, rocket, or satellite, if they hope to study this component of the universe.

Stone joined Simpson's group of research students even before he received his bachelor's degree, and worked on a balloon-borne cosmic-ray detector. He then graduated into the world of rocket- and satellite-borne cosmic-ray detctors; his Ph.D. thesis grew out of the results from the cosmic-ray detector built by Simpson's group and sent into orbit late in 1961 (the third year of the U.S. satellite launches).

The early 1960s were good years for young enthusiasts for the space program. Well before his Ph.D. was granted in 1964, Stone was at Caltech, which was hungry for cosmic-ray experts. New satellites were being designed as the previous generation was launched; by the start of the 1970s, the series of Orbiting Geophysical Observatories had been succeeded by the Interplanetary Monitoring Platform and then by the International Sun-Earth Explorer. Stone was involved in the cosmic-ray-detecting experiments aboard all of these, and thus the first decade of his career tabbed him not as a planetary scientist but as a cosmic-ray expert whose observations all came from just above the Earth's atmosphere. But the *Voyager* project came along and consumed much of Stone's time and attention for 18 years. If any one man deserves the credit for the incredibly successful mission of the *Voyagers,* that man is Ed Stone, who would be the first to point out that literally thousands of people devoted their considerable talents to make the modified Grand Tour happen.

FOUR PLANETS, MORE THAN 50 MOONS, AND A BUNCH OF RINGS

Although NASA avoided giving the mission of the *Voyager* spacecraft the name of Grand Tour, in the end that was just what the two *Voyagers* accomplished. The two spacecraft visited the sun's four giant planets (Jupiter and Saturn twice), discovered 25 new moons around them, sent back spectacular photographic images, used their spectrometers to spread the planets' reflected light into colors, thus revealing the composition of the planetary atmospheres and the satellites' surfaces, and made the deepest, finest exploration that humans have yet carried out of our immediate astronomical environment.

How far did the two *Voyagers* go? In terms of the Earth-sun distance (93 million miles), known in the trade as the astronomical unit (A.U.), Jupiter lies 5.2 A.U. from the sun, and hence anywhere from 4.2 to 6.2 A.U. from Earth (depending on the positions of Jupiter and Earth with respect to the sun). But a trip along the shortest possible trajectory would require too much fuel for the rocket that sends the spacecraft outward. Such a trip would fail to take advantage of the Earth's motion around the sun. Hence all planetary exploration flings a spacecraft either outward or inward along a path roughly parallel to the Earth's orbit. For the *Voyagers,* this meant that the trip to Jupiter covered about 7 A.U.

Because of the near-alignment of the giant planets, the journey onward from Jupiter to Saturn, which orbits the sun at a distance of 9.5 A.U., spanned only about 5 A.U., less than the trip to Jupiter. But the trip from Saturn to Uranus measured some 13 A.U., nearly twice as far as a voyage to Jupiter from Earth. From Uranus to Neptune took an additional 13 A.U. All these distances are immense, for 11 A.U. equals just over a billion miles. The increasingly immense distances between successive encounters meant that the time gap between planetary encounters increased from just over two years (Jupiter to Saturn) to four years (Saturn to Uranus) and to three and a half years (Uranus to Neptune). But the astronomers had time—for some of them, half a career's worth or more.

Two years after their launch, the two *Voyagers* reached Jupiter in March and July 1979. Monarch of the sun's planets, 11 times the diameter of Earth, Jupiter has a volume that could swallow our planet more than a thousand times, since an object's volume increases in proportion to the cube of its diameter (Color Plate 25). Like the other giant planets, Jupiter has no solid surface. An intrepid explorer approaching its surface would simply sink deeper and deeper into an ever-thickening, gaseous atmosphere. (Exactly this fate lies in store for part of the automated *Galileo* probe now on its way to Jupiter.) Thousands of miles down, the explorer would find that Jupiter does have a solid core—as if Jupiter wrapped a planet similar to Earth inside an enormous blanket of gas. The gases that form most of Jupiter, like those that comprise Saturn, Uranus, and Neptune, consist mainly of hydrogen and helium, the two lightest and most abundant elements. In their chemical composition, the giant planets resemble the stars far more than they resemble the Earth and the other inner planets.

WHY IS JUPITER SO DIFFERENT FROM EARTH?

All of the sun's planets formed within a rotating, pancake-shaped cloud of gas and dust, whose center ended up with most of the matter and became the sun, and whose outward parts agglomerated into the individual planets. As the sun contracted, it grew hotter and shone more brightly. Once nuclear fusion began within the sun's core, the sun achieved something like its present luminosity, heating the inner parts of the solar system far more than the outer regions. The additional heat made the material that was coalescing into planets dance more rapidly. This increased the likelihood that the inner planets would lose much of their matter before they could fully form. An additional assault on the planets-in-formation came from the stream of particles (typically atomic nuclei) that the newborn sun continuously ejected. We now call these particle streams the *solar wind*. The solar wind tended to push particles of dust and gas outward into space.

Thus the solar heating and the solar wind caused material to escape from the regions around the sun. The solar heating gave particles greater velocities and thus a greater chance at escape in their heat-induced dance of random motion, while the solar-wind particles pushed matter directly outward from the sun.

The sun's effectiveness in "clearing out" matter that would otherwise have joined the planets-in-formation varied dramatically for planets at different distances from the sun. Thanks to the heating and solar-wind effects, the parts of the disk of material that formed the inner planets lost nearly *all* their hydrogen and helium. Since these two elements comprised 99 percent of the total amount of matter that formed the solar system, all but one percent of the matter in the inner solar system when the sun turned on simply vanished, gone with the wind that had swept through the inner solar system. In contrast, the giant planets managed to capture and retain huge quantities of primordial hydrogen and helium, because their distances from the sun were 5 to 30 times greater than the Earth's. Since the effect of both the solar heating and the solar wind decreases dramatically with increasing distance from the sun, the two effects that caused a loss of the two lightest elements diminished nearly to zero.

Today the sun's four great planets remain gas giants that won the gravitational battle to retain their elemental birthright, even as Mercury, Venus, Earth, and Mars were losing their own struggles to retain hydrogen and helium (Color Plate 28). We live on the denuded husk of what could have been a gas giant if the sun had not begun to shine, but because it did, the solar system contains rocky inner planets as well as gas-giant outer planets.

JUPITER, SATURN, AND URANUS

Jupiter, lord of the planetary realms, has the most variegated colors of any planet beyond Earth (Color Plate 25). The explanation for these colors remains a mystery. When the *Galileo* spacecraft reaches Jupiter in 1995, it will send a piece of itself into Jupiter's ever-thickening veil of gas, returning messages about its composition that should settle this mystery of the colors' origin once and for all. From an analysis of the sunlight reflected from Jupiter, we know that most of the planet's outer layers consist of hydrogen, helium, and the simple chemical compounds that hydrogen forms with the next most common elements, such as carbon, nitrogen, and oxygen. (Helium stubbornly refuses to combine with anything.)

The compounds formed in the largest quantities—methane, ammonia, and water—provide no vivid colors, so Jupiter's orange, brown, red, and yellow hues must arise from less abundant compounds, which we have yet to identify. Whichever chemical explanation proves correct, Jupiter offers quite an atmospheric display: The colored layers show continuous changes, driven by the planet's rapid rotation (the same force that produces weather patterns on Earth) and by the release of heat from Jupiter's interior.

Most prominent of all Jupiter's atmospheric features is the Great Red Spot, a semipermanent cyclone, several times larger than the Earth, which was first observed three centuries ago. At nearly the same latitude as the Great Red Spot, Jupiter's atmosphere has formed three paler, smaller cyclones in which the gases rotate in the *opposite* direction of the Great Red Spot. One of the goals of the atmospheric scientists on the *Voyager* science team has been to understand the giant planets' atmospheres—and eventually our own—with sufficient insight to predict how patterns such as the Great Red Spot and the counter-rotating cyclones are born and die out. Since Jupiter has no solid surface, and no division into land and water, its atmosphere actually behaves more simply than our own and typically shows slowly changing bands of colors, parallel to the planet's equator. Nevertheless, the scientists' goal remains a distant one, both for Jupiter and for Earth.

In 1979, what most captured the attention of scientists and the public was not Jupiter's atmosphere but its moons. In orbit around Jupiter are 17 known moons (three of them discovered by the *Voyagers*), of which 4 are much larger than the others. These 4 Galilean satellites, named after Galileo's discovery of them in 1609, are each as large as the Earth's moon; the largest, Ganymede, is the largest moon in the solar system, one and a half times as large as our own moon. The four moons all orbit Jupiter in the same direction and in nearly the same plane, forming a miniature system of worlds whose formation must have followed the same general pattern as the solar system's. Each of the Galilean satellites has its own special characteristics: Callisto, the outermost, is the most heavily cratered object we know; Ganymede has a network of ridges and rills that suggest geological activity; and Europa has a smooth surface, probably composed of ice that has been repeatedly melted and refrozen, which may cover a liquid ocean beneath—an ocean within which primitive life forms have been speculated to exist. But the moon that received by far the greatest attention was the innermost large satellite, Io (Color Plate 26).

Io's claim to fame among all the moons of the solar system rests on its active volcanos—for many years the only active volcanos known to exist anywhere beyond the Earth (Color Plate 27). On Earth, volcanos occur because radioactive minerals heat the rock miles below the surface, keeping it nearly liquid. On occasion, the molten rock finds an avenue of access to the surface and oozes or spouts in fiery fury. Io too owes its volcanos to the heating of its subsurface layers, but the heating on Io arises from quite different causes. Io suffers from *tidal stress,* a continuous, constantly varying deformation that arises from the changing gravitational forces from the other three large satellites and from Jupiter itself. The tidal stress deforms and heats Io, as a paper clip heats up when you bend it repeatedly, though on a considerably larger scale. On Io, the constant frictional deformation heats the moon to the point where volcanos fling their sulfur-laden plumes hundreds of miles above the multicolored, continually changing surface. When the *Voyagers* first reached Io, Brad Smith (from the University of Arizona), the leader of the imaging team, stated "I've seen better-looking pizzas." For some, Io became—and has remained—the pizza moon.

Although Io's heating by tidal deformation had been predicted by Stanton Peale shortly before *Voyager 1* reached the Jupiter system, none of the *Voyager* scientists had been so bold as to predict that Io would have volcanos. The volcanos were discovered by Linda Morabito, a "navigator" of the spacecraft who used computer processing to enhance an image of Io, trying to see the stars in the background. Looking at the enhanced image, Morabito saw plumes extending above the moon's surface and correctly noted that they resembled volcanic eruptions. The *Voyagers* found at least nine separate volcanos on Io, which collectively make the satellite a place where you would get "not a weather report, but a geology report," to use a coinage from Rich Terrile, one of the members of Brad Smith's imaging team.

The *Voyagers* also discovered Jupiter's rings. To theorists who predict everything they can think of, the existence of the rings reminds us that nature has a continuing ability to amaze. Jupiter, like Saturn, turned out to have small particles of rock and ice in orbit around the planet. Unlike Saturn's broad, majestic rings, the rings of Jupiter are narrow and therefore difficult to see—but there they are, made of debris left over from the formation of the giant planet and its moons, the first indication that (as hindsight showed to be obvious) each of the four giant planets has systems of small particles that orbit in ringlike configurations.

In November 1980 and August 1981, the *Voyagers* came to Saturn. They photographed the famous rings of the planet in exquisite detail, revealing subtle, changing patterns in the motions of the ring particles (Color Plate 29). Spectroscopic analysis of the colors of sunlight reflected from the rings confirmed that most of the particles consist either of ice or of rocks coated with a layer of frost. The ring particles range in size from house-sized monsters (quite rare) to telephone-sized dangers (for those who sail unprotected through the rings) and to microscopic dust particles (Color Plate 30). Theorists had a fine time explaining the changing ring patterns, and a still better time working out the theory by which three small moons orbiting just inside and outside the rings "shepherd" some of the ring particles by gravitational attraction into special orbits.

Saturn itself, seen by the *Voyager* spacecraft two years after Jupiter, proved to be a paler, calmer version of the largest planet. The two spacecraft passed close by several of Saturn's 17 moons and photographed the crater-rich surfaces of all but the large and mysterious Titan. Once thought to be the largest satellite in the solar system (Ganymede turned out to be slightly larger), Titan remains the only moon with a thick atmosphere of its own, a nitrogen-rich soup that resembles the Earth's atmosphere more closely than any other planet's atmosphere. But a thick photochemical haze, something like Los Angeles in a bad dream, continuously blocks any view of Titan's surface. Hence *Voyager* found out little about Titan; planetary scientists continue to speculate that despite the tremendous cold on the surface (about −320 degrees Fahrenheit), lakes of liquid ethane and methane may exist there. In the quest to find the origins of life, Titan's surface may yet prove immensely useful as a giant natural laboratory, with a mixture of chemicals roughly similar to those present on Earth four billion years ago, about the time that life began. Because of this possibility, talk of Titan lights up the eyes of the leaders in the field of planetary exploration, who badly want to probe beneath the veil of this moon's hidden surface.

In November 1980, *Voyager 1* began its successful

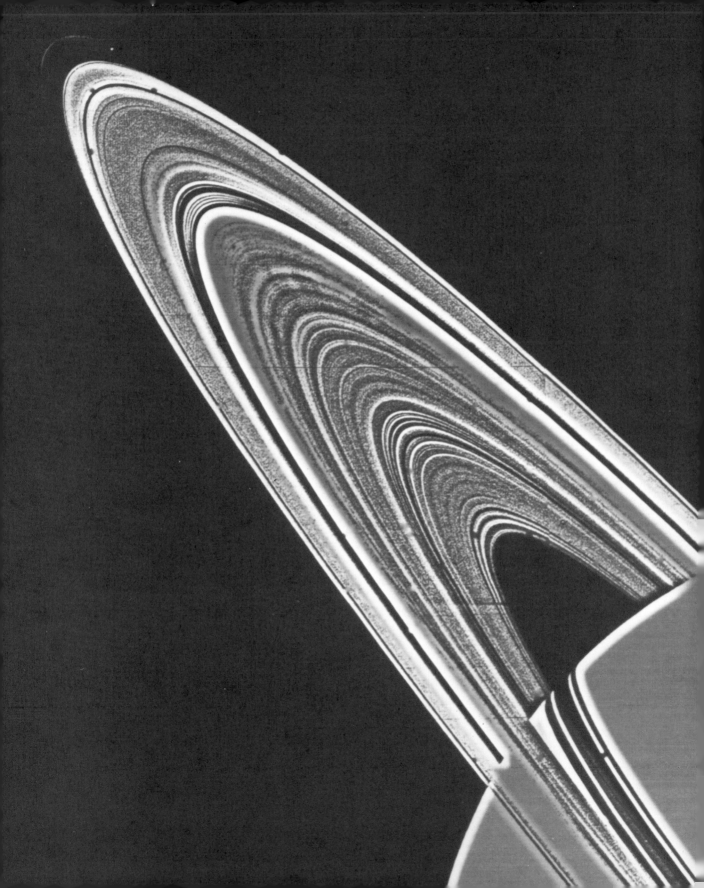

reconnaissance of Saturn and its moons (Figure 73). Even before then, NASA gave the *Voyager* scientists permission to consider taking a calculated risk with *Voyager 2,* which reached Saturn in August 1981. The scientists planned to use Saturn's gravity to change the spacecraft's trajectory, diverting it onto a path that would take it onward to Uranus and Neptune. The decision to take that step, which risked losing the *Voyager 2* spacecraft in a close encounter with Saturn, lay with the science steering group, composed of the 11 principal investigators and the team leader, Ed Stone, who had the largest single share in the decision process. Stone voted with the majority, who favored taking the risk. *Voyager 2* survived the turn, and just over four years later, in late January 1986, it sped by Uranus.

Since Uranus has more than twice Saturn's distance from the sun—nearly 20 times the Earth-sun distance—*Voyager 2* was now working at distances much greater than those ever attained by a spacecraft capable of sending photographs back to Earth. Not truly designed to survive so long or to communicate over such vast distances, *Voyager 2* by 1986 was growing creaky—"arthritic," the *Voyager* scientists liked to say—as its moving parts ran out of lubricant. At Saturn, a failure in the scan platform had limited the spacecraft's ability to direct its attention in new directions, yet the scientists had found a means to overcome this problem. *Voyager* was also growing low on the small amounts of fuel needed to make small adjustments in its trajectory and to change its orientation in space for the best views of the planets and moons that it passed.

Voyager's power supply, a small amount of radioactive plutonium, continued to supply the heat that generated the tiny amount of electricity—about the same as the light bulb in your refrigerator—that obtained the images and then sent them, in computerized form, across billions of miles of space for capture by Earth's most sensitive radio antennas. But *Voyager*'s brain, its on-board computer, underwent serious deterioration. Not much to begin with by standards of a dozen years later, the on-board computer has less memory than off-the-shelf models you can buy today. Hence any loss of memory might have doomed the spacecraft. The *Voyager* scientists not only overcame the problem but also invented a new way to send preprogrammed commands to

Figure 73. *Voyager 1* photographed Saturn's rings with a clarity that revealed complex, changing patterns in the distribution of the particles that form the rings. (NASA photograph.)

the spacecraft before its planetary encounter. These commands told it how to move during the crucial hours near the planet and actually yielded better images than the original design called for.

And so, even though creaky, senile, and low on fuel, but still energized and still receiving lively intelligence from its creators, *Voyager 2* passed by Uranus and its 5 known moons (*Voyager 2* found 10 more), sending pictures of all the objects that it saw. Uranus proved something of a media dud, pale in color and devoid of atmospheric features, but the moons were spectacular. Most spectacular of all was Miranda (named by its discoverer after a Shakespearean character in *The Tempest*), whose surface, only 400 miles in diameter, was revealed to be a jumbled mixture of strange terrains, with half-mile-deep fault scraps, parallel ridges and rills, and craters reminiscent of the Earth's own moon (Figure 74).

With the Uranus encounter over, *Voyager 2* was deflected by Uranus's gravity into a new trajectory and spent 1986, 1987, 1988, and the first half of 1989 covering the two billion miles that lay between Uranus and Neptune. By the summer of 1989, the *Voyager 2* spacecraft closed in for its last planetary encounter, with Neptune and its large satellite Triton. The three and a half years that the scientists had to wait for the next planetary encounter gave the observationally oriented astronomers time to reduce and study their data, and it gave the theorists an opportunity to theorize their hearts out about the coming encounter.

VOYAGER AT NEPTUNE

Voyager 2 performed flawlessly in its encounter with Neptune. The theorists enjoyed it, though not as much as the men and women who had designed the *Voyager* spacecraft's instruments and nursed them along through 12 years in space. On the night of August 25, 1989, those scientists basked in their hours of glory as *Voyager 2* sped first by Neptune (at about 1:15 A.M Pacific Daylight Time) and then by Triton some four hours later.

Neptune proved to be a lovely blue ball, lined by subtle, whitish atmospheric shading and dotted with what the *Voyager* scientists called the Great Dark Spot, a reference to Jupiter's Great Red Spot (Color Plate 31). *Voyager*'s instruments measured the speeds of the winds on Neptune and found the highest values in the solar system: 1,500 miles per hour. Like the Great Red Spot, the

Great Dark Spot varies its position with respect to the other atmospheric gases and is probably some sort of cyclone. In addition to the Great Dark Spot, astronomers saw smaller atmospheric features, including bright bands of cloud floating in the hydrogen-rich atmosphere, which proved capable of changing dramatically in less than an hour's time. *Voyager* also found complete systems or rings surrounding Neptune (Figure 75, p. 250).

Neptune has its appeal (especially to those who have devoted several years preparing for a few days' observation of the eighth

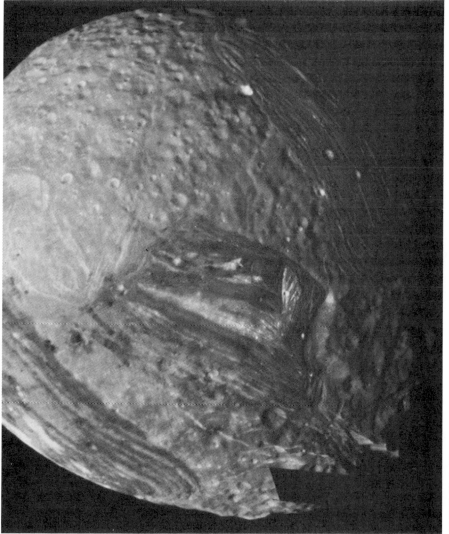

Figure 74. Miranda, one of Uranus's five larger satellites, revealed an amazingly varied terrain to *Voyager 2* in 1986. (NASA photograph.)

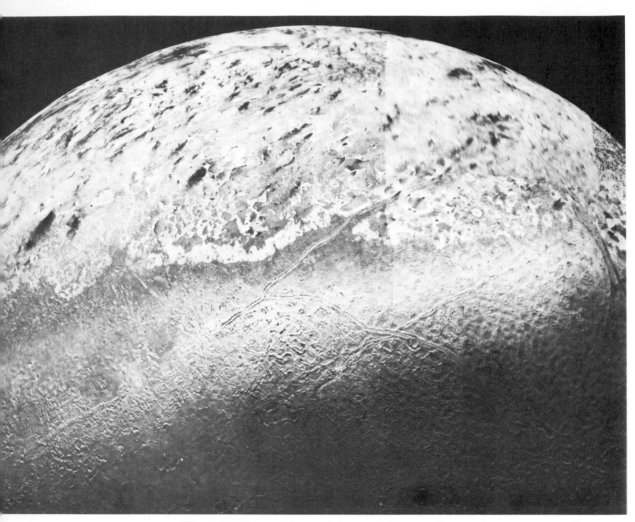

Figure 76. Triton, Neptune's large moon, turned out to have a strange and variegated terrain, perhaps largely covered by ice frozen to temperatures of −400 degrees Fahrenheit. (NASA photograph.)

planet), but Triton offers far more excitement—perhaps because we humans are partial to objects with solid surfaces. The *Voyager* encounter confirmed that Triton has a thin atmosphere, made mostly of nitrogen, making this the third moon in the solar system to possess a gaseous veil. The other moons with atmospheres are Io, whose volcanos continually replenish a thin, sulfur-laden haze, and Titan, with a much thicker atmosphere, made mostly of nitrogen like Triton's (and Earth's).

Triton's solid surface incorporates types of features seen by the *Voyagers* on a variety of other satellites, yielding a complex terrain that includes polygonal patterns of protruding ridges and incised grooves (Figure 76). Triton's crust may well consist mainly of familiar ice, but on the coldest sunlit surface in the solar system, at − 400 degrees Fahrenheit, ice on Triton's surface behaves differently than ice on Earth. Triton's southern hemisphere turned out to be *pink,* quite possibly because chemical reactions among fragments of nitrogen and methane are forming compounds that preferentially reflect this color of light. The south polar cap, plainly visible on the *Voyager* photographs, may be made mainly of nitrogen, which freezes at the unEarthly temperature of − 390 degrees Fahrenheit. *Voyager* also saw something completely unpredicted: geyserlike funnels that may be dust storms, or may be spouts of nitrogen gas undergoing a transition directly from the solid to the gaseous state.

In the entire solar system, the object most similar to Triton may well be Pluto, the sun's ninth planet and now the only one not visited by automated spacecraft from Earth. Although Pluto technically ranks as a planet and has a moon of its own (called Charon), Pluto has about the same size as Triton and nearly the same density of matter. Quite possibly both Pluto and Triton formed as the sort of objects that later agglomerated to form Uranus and Neptune (which each have about a thousand times the mass of Triton or Pluto). In that case, only cosmic luck has kept Triton and Pluto from joining their fellow "planetesimals" inside the giant planets—luck that has allowed us a closeup inspection of Triton, moving these past four billion years in its orbit around Neptune.

Voyager will never come again: You go only once for the first time into the outer solar system. NASA has the *Galileo* spacecraft under way to Jupiter (see chapter 14) and has plans for a return visit to Saturn and its moons. But for now we have only dreams of a return trip to Uranus and Neptune, or of the first encounter with Pluto—dreams that (if fully funded) the next generation of planetary astronomers will make into reality.

Figure 79. In 1976, the two Viking spacecraft took detailed photographs of the Martian surface at their landing sites. This photograph, taken by *Viking 2,* shows a coating of water-based ice only a thousandth of an inch thick on the surface that forms during the Martian winter. (NASA photograph.)

12. How Many Worlds in the Milky Way?

THE QUEST FOR extrasolar planets has a long history, most of it not only unsuccessful but futile. The crucial point of difficulty arises from the immense distances to other stars in the Milky Way. These stars, typically millions of times more distant than the sun's planets, lie so far away that even our best telescopes show them only as points of light. To see planets—if they exist!—around even the closest stars surpasses our present technological ability. Hence any search for *extrasolar* planets, that is, for planets around other stars, must use other means than direct vision.

To get a firm grip on the difficulty involved in finding planets around other stars, consider one of the two *Voyager* spacecraft on its journey outward from the solar system. The two spacecraft each travel at about 20 miles per *second*—72,000 miles per hour, just over a hundred times faster than a jet airplane. This speed enabled the *Voyagers* to escape from the solar system (as defined by the orbits of the nine planets) within less than 15 years after their launch. But the stars lie thousands upon thousands of times farther away than the planets.

To be precise, to reach the closest star to the sun, Alpha Centauri, you must travel 4.4 light years—26 trillion miles, equivalent to a billion trips around the Earth. If you pack yourself into a *Voyager* spacecraft, you can do this in about 40,000 years, about 4,000 times longer than the spacecraft took to reach Neptune. The distance the *Voyagers* covered to reach Neptune, somewhat over three billion miles, barely exceeds 1 part in 10,000 of the distance to Alpha Centauri. In other words, the distance to Alpha Centauri exceeds the distance to Neptune by the same factor that a trip to Europe exceeds a trip to the local shopping mall.

HOW TO FIND PLANETS AROUND OTHER STARS?

These enormous distances to other stars reduce them all to points of light and prevent us from seeing any planets, even those that are Jupiter-sized or larger, that may orbit these distant suns. Because we cannot see planets around other stars, any plan to find extrasolar planets must involve indirect methods—a detective hunt for worlds that are trillions of miles away. The indirect methods fall into two categories: We can look for the effects that planets produce on the *motions of stars* that we can see, or we can look for the effects that the formation of planets has left behind in the *surroundings* of stars.

THE EFFECT OF PLANETS' GRAVITY ON THEIR PARENT STARS

The first method relies on the fact that just as a star exerts gravitational force on any planets around it, the planets exert gravitational force on the star that they orbit. This statement reflects what physicists call Newton's third law of motion: Every action has an equal and opposite reaction. In gravitational terms, this means that the Earth, for example, pulls on the sun with exactly the same amount of force that the sun pulls on the Earth.

Why, then, does the Earth orbit the sun, rather than the other way around? The answer lies in Newton's second law of motion: When force is applied to an object, the object responds by accelerating in the direction of the force, but the amount of acceleration *decreases* as the object's amount of mass *increases*. An amount of force sufficient to drive a golf ball hundreds of yards down the fairway will barely accelerate a bowling ball. In the celestial realm, a star corrresponds to the bowling ball, and its planets correspond to golf balls. Each planet indeed exerts the same amount of gravitational force on its parent star as the star exerts on the planet. But the planet accelerates far more in response to the gravitational force from the star than the star accelerates in response to the same amount of force from the planet.

Nevertheless, the star does accelerate, and this could be the key to finding extrasolar planets. Like its planets, the star also moves in an orbit, but in a tiny one. Our sun, for example, performs an orbit as its planets move around it, in response to the combined gravitational pulls of all its planets. But this orbit spans only a few times the diameter of the sun—barely more than one one-thousandth of the distance from the sun to Jupiter.

However, an observer located a few light years from Earth could hardly hope to observe the sun's astronomically tiny orbit. Likewise, we on Earth cannot really hope to see any analogous changes in the positions of the closest stars—though measurements of stellar positions have become so precise that astronomers are almost in a position to do so. Within a decade or two, we may have telescopes in orbit that can make still more precise measurements and thus find the changes in stars' positions that arise from their planets' gravitational forces. For now, the best way to detect the effect of a planet's gravity on its parent star lies with observations of changes in the star's *velocity.*

The velocity changes arise from the star's motion in response to the planet's gravitational tug. This is the same effect that causes the star to orbit the center of mass of its planetary system, just as the sun makes its own small orbit. We can search for these velocity changes by studying the star's spectrum of light and using our knowledge of the Doppler shift, which changes all the colors of starlight if a star moves toward us or away from us. In the search for small velocity changes caused by possible planets, astronomers have a key advantage in comparison with their search for small changes in a star's position on the sky. The size of the changes in a star's observed *position* decreases as the star's distance from us increases. As a result, for faraway stars (and they are all far away), we cannot now detect these changes in position. But the amount of the changes in *velocity* does not diminish with distance. This means that although we could hope to find the changes in position only for the few stars closest to our own (and cannot quite do that with our present abilities), we can examine thousands of stars with a good chance of finding changes in velocity caused by the existence of planets.

How good are those chances? Imagine a planet with Jupiter's mass, orbiting its star at a distance equal to Jupiter's distance from the sun. Such a Jupiter-like planet would produce changes in the star's velocity through space of a few hundred yards per second. Any such changes would repeat in a periodic cycle as the planet orbits the star. Hence astronomers who search for other planetary systems by looking for velocity changes are searching for changes that repeat over time, presumably over a period of months or years, similar to the times that the sun's planets take for each orbit.

The two leaders in this search are Bruce Campbell, a Canadian astronomer at the Dominion Astrophysical Observatory on Vancouver Island, and David Latham, a Harvard astronomer. Campbell, in his early forties, has pioneered new techniques for measuring small changes in the velocities of stars. Campbell has found half a dozen candidates for stars with one or more planets in orbit around them. Astronomers take these candidates seriously, but because the velocity changes are so small, they are not ready to pronounce any one of them completely verified.

In contrast to Campbell, Latham has only one fine candidate, a star called HD114762, but it is the best of all. Latham once indulged in off-road motorcycle racing, but today, a group leader at the Harvard-Smithsonian Center for Astrophysics, he confines his biking to a speedy commute to Cambridge from his home in Concord, and to repeated trips to his "home" instrument, the 61-inch reflecting telescope in the rural town of Harvard, Massachusetts. This 60-year-old instrument, erected by Harvard astronomers in eastern Massachusetts in a highly optimistic mood about the weather there, has far fewer demands on its time than the larger, more modern instruments sited at observatories with clearer skies. For Latham this provides an ideal situation: He needs a telescope that can be used night after night to build up a data base that could reveal small, cyclical changes in a star's velocity as measured from Earth. Over the past 10 years, Latham and his associates have observed dozens of stars, and they have found one that clearly has a companion.

This star, named HD114762 from its listing in the Henry Draper Star Catalog, resembles the sun in its overall characteristics and lies about a hundred light years from the solar system. From 60-odd observations made during a seven-year span, Latham has found that HD114762 changes its velocity by plus or minus 600 yards per second. More important, the velocity changes repeat in a cyclical manner, with a period of 84 days—almost the same time that Mercury takes to orbit the sun.

Because this star has a spectrum much like the sun's,

astronomers think that it has an amount of mass nearly the same as the sun's mass. Using Newton's second law, they can calculate the amount of force that is accelerating the star to produce the observed changes in its velocity. And then, using Newton's law of gravitation, they can estimate the mass of whatever causes these changes in the star's velocity. Latham and his colleagues set this estimate at 11 times Jupiter's mass—or more. The "or more" must be added because we cannot determine the orientation of the companion's orbit around the star, that is, we cannot tell whether we see the orbit face-on, edge-on, or with a tilt somewhere in between. The amount of this tilt affects the estimated mass that we derive from the observed changes in the star's velocity. But suppose that Latham and his collaborators have found a companion of HD114762 with 11 times Jupiter's mass. Would this be the first verified planet beyond the solar system?

BROWN DWARFS: PLANETS OR FAILED STARS?

Quite possibly not. Astronomers can estimate the minimum amount of mass that any star must have in order for it to *be* a star—that is, for its own gravity to compress its interior to the point that nuclear fusion begins at its center. This minimum amount of mass has yet to be determined with complete precision, but it lies somewhere close to 80 times the mass of Jupiter. In a sense, any object with less mass than this "must" be a planet, since it cannot be a star. However, a more exact look at the situation leads astronomers to define a class of objects called *brown dwarfs*. Brown dwarfs have too little mass to become stars, but—like stars in formation—they continuously contract under their own gravitation, growing steadily hotter in their interiors (but never reaching the point where nuclear fusion begins). Latham's companion to HD114762 almost certainly is such a brown dwarf, a sort of quasi-planet.

    Why make so much of the brown-dwarf definition? Isn't this a bit of fine hairsplitting that denies Latham rightful praise as finder of the first extrasolar planet? After all, Jupiter and the sun's other giant planets consist mainly of hydrogen and helium, as stars do, and are slowly contracting under their own gravitational forces.

Could they not also be called brown dwarfs, like the one that may exist around HD114762? A subtle but key difference exists in most astronomers' minds between brown dwarfs and planets. Planets are thought to form through the sticking together of countless smaller objects that formed as individuals in orbit around their parent star. But brown dwarfs, like full-fledged stars, are thought to form all at once, from a single clump of material within an interstellar cloud of gas and dust that contracts and grows denser.

If this is so, finding a brown dwarf amounts to only the discovery of a failed, would-be star and tells us little about the frequency with which stars have left behind true planets as they formed. Thus the search for extrasolar planets must—at least for the time being—use other indirect methods, methods that employ still more involved chains of reasoning than Campbell's and Latham's searches for changes in the velocities of stars.

SEARCHING FOR THE TRACES OF PLANET FORMATION

The second indirect method of finding planets is to search for clues *around* stars, in the form of material other than planets. Material involved in the formation of planets can be much easier to detect than planets themselves. The search for the relics of planet formation splits into two subsearches. One approach is to look for material that is *now* in the process of forming planets; the other is to look for debris *left behind* once planets have formed. Neither of these indirect methods can prove definitively that extrasolar planets exist; the best they can do—good enough in most astronomers' eyes—is to provide clear and cogent evidence for such planets.

Material that has formed planets, or remains in the process of forming planets, will be cold, just as the sun's planets (in astronomical terms) remain today. By "cold," astronomers mean that the material radiates no visible light. Nonetheless, such material, like human bodies and other objects at similar temperatures, does produce radiation with longer wavelengths—infrared and radio waves. Therefore, the search for material involved in planet formation relies heavily on observations in radio and infrared. Most radio waves penetrate the Earth's atmosphere and can be detected with ground-based telescopes, but observations of most infrared wavelengths require a telescope in space.

PRE-PLANETARY DISKS AROUND YOUNG STARS

Some of the most compelling evidence concerning the possibility of other planetary systems has recently emerged from observations made by radio astronomers. Cold gas and dust particles emit radio waves, the lowest-energy, longest-wavelength part of the electromagnetic spectrum. Radio astronomers can use their ability to see relatively cold gas with radio waves to find disks of material in orbit around young stars. During the past decade, the discovery of such disks has been made primarily by two astronomers who are long-time friends, Anneila Sargent and Steve Beckwith (Figure 77).

Anneila Sargent speaks with a fine Scottish accent that she acquired during her childhood on Scotland's Firth of Forth, a few miles from the town that produced Andrew Carnegie, whose wealth has so abundantly helped astronomy. At school during the late 1950s and early 1960s, Sargent profited from a traditional Scottish emphasis on education, combined with the reaction to the "Sputnik era." She found nothing unusual about her interest in science, either in high school or as a physics undergraduate at the

Figure 77. Anneila Sargent (left) and Steven Beckwith (right) use radio waves to examine the surroundings of young stars for possible planet-forming disks of material. (Photographs by Donald Goldsmith.)

University of Edinburgh, from which she graduated in 1964. Shortly before then, she attended a short astronomy course at the Royal Observatory at Herstmonceux, deep in the south of England. There she met Wallace Sargent, an Englishman from Lincolnshire who had recently obtained his Ph.D. in astronomy and had chosen Herstmonceux (so Anneila learned later) because he had heard that it had a higher proportion of women than any other astronomical institution. Wallace Sargent, impressed by Anneila, suggested that she go to graduate school in astronomy in the United States, either at the University of California at San Diego or at the University of Arizona—coincidentally, the institutions at which he was about to work.

Anneila went to U.C.S.D. and married Wal (as astronomers call him), who was then an expert on stars but later developed into an extragalactic astronomer at U.C.S.D. under the tutelage of Geoffrey and Margaret Burbidge, a remarkable astronomical couple (Margaret, an expert on observing faraway galaxies and quasars, was briefly the Astronomer Royal of England; Geoffrey has a long career as a theorist in which he has never hesitated to challenge the conventional wisdom of astronomy). After Wal obtained an assistant professorship at Caltech, Anneila shifted her graduate studies to that institution, but upon discovering that she would have to begin graduate studies all over again, she left graduate school with a master's degree and had two children.

A few years of child-raising made Caltech's graduate school look more appealing to Anneila Sargent than it had before. In 1974, six years after leaving Caltech, she reenrolled as a graduate student. Wal was quite supportive of this effort; as Anneila notes, "Somebody had to drive the kids"—and who better than the established professor with a secure job? Anneila became interested in probing the surroundings of young stars by using short-wavelength radio waves, a technology then in its infancy, so that the six-year hiatus proved accidentally quite helpful in Sargent's career. Sargent received her Ph.D. in 1977, spent three years at Caltech as a postdoctoral fellow, and then became a "member of the professional staff." She eventually began to ascend the ladder of Caltech's research faculty and has now reached the top rung. Her marriage to Wal endures, perhaps because "we never talk about astronomy." During her second graduate-student career, Anneila became friends with Steve Beckwith, and together the two astronomers have studied the surroundings of young stars with a marked degree of success.

Steve Beckwith, a tall, muscular, brown-bearded man from Milwaukee, went to Cornell as an engineering physics major. But in 1973, upon enrolling in graduate school in physics at Caltech, he decided that astrophysics offered the best scope to his talents, which concentrate on designing and building new experimental equipment. Infrared astronomy then lay at the frontiers of science, and sophisticated instruments capable of precise analysis of infrared radiation were only in development. Beckwith was attracted by the chance to make an individual contribution to infrared astronomy. This set infrared apart from particle physics, the other fundamental area of physics that attracted him, where experimental teams typically number many dozen. He devoted his graduate-school career to the construction and use of infrared detectors to study dense interstellar clouds in the Milky Way. Beckwith became fast friends with Anneila Sargent, who received her Ph.D. in the same year that he did, and after returning to Cornell as an assistant professor of astronomy (he is now a full professor at his alma mater), he developed an ongoing research collaboration with her to investigate star-forming regions and the surroundings of young stars, mostly by observing them with short-wavelength radio waves. "Anneila and I have a good resonance," he says, "and it helps to have personalities and a sense of humor that match well on a long observing run."

During the past seven years, Sargent and Beckwith have been observing not planets but the stuff from which planets are made. They have discovered that many young stars are surrounded by rotating disks of gas and dust. Sargent and Beckwith's observing program employed radio telescopes at the Owens Valley Radio Observatory, east of the Sierra Nevada Mountains in California, to map out cool material in the immediate surroundings of young stars. To choose targets for their radio observations, Sargent and Beckwith used lists of young stars compiled by astronomers who specialize in identifying such newborns, typically by spotting telltale features in the spectra of starlight. Such spectral features reveal the continuing expulsion into space of the remnants of the cocoons of gas and dust from which the stars formed.

Sargent and Beckwith concentrated on about 85 stars located within a particular region where stars are forming, one of the closest of these regions to the solar system. The region is called the Taurus-Auriga complex because the star-forming area spreads across these two constellations in our skies. The astronomers found that more than 40 percent of the newly formed stars radiate strongly at shorter radio wavelengths, called *millimeter waves* because they have wavelengths of a few millimeters. Since stars emit insignificant amounts of millimeter waves, Sargent and Beckwith concluded that the radiation must arise from cool material close to the young stars. The two astronomers mapped out the amount of radio emission arriving from different regions close to the stars. Their maps revealed that in most cases the millimeter waves come from regions that are roughly disk-shaped. In other words, nearly half of the young stars surveyed by Sargent and Beckwith show disks of cool matter around them.

These disks of matter strongly suggest that planets are forming around the young stars that the astronomers studied. But what makes Anneila Sargent and Steve Beckwith's results especially exciting to astronomers is their discovery that at least some of the disks are *rotating*. Sargent and Beckwith used the Doppler effect to measure the velocities at which the material in the disks around stars is approaching us or receding from us. For their best case, a star called HL Tauri, they found a trend: One side of the disk has a velocity of approach, and the other side has a velocity of recession, in comparison to the central star. Furthermore, the velocity varies along the disk exactly as it would in a system of planets, or in any material orbiting its parent star under the influence of that star's gravitational force. Sargent and Beckwith conclude that HL Tauri—and probably other young stars as well—have disks of cool, dusty matter in orbit around them: the stuff of which planets can be made.

HOW TO FIND BETTER EVIDENCE FOR PLANETS?

Sargent and Beckwith's results have revealed that many young stars form with disks of material that may well become planets. Can we do better at finding planets themselves, even if we can't see them directly? One excellent possibility for demonstrating a star that may have formed planets requires a trip to the Southern Hemisphere, to the world's driest climate.

The Atacama Desert in Chile is as dry a spot as you can find on Earth; some of its inhabitants, old though they may be, have never seen rain fall. In the Pacific Ocean just to the desert's west, the northward sweep of the Humboldt Current carries cold water past what would be tropical landscapes, were it not for the lack of moisture and the cooling caused by the ocean currents. To the east of the Atacama Desert lie the Andes Mountains, whose peaks, rising to more than 23,000 feet above sea level, receive the moisture wrung from the clouds after they float high over the desert. The central Andean foothills, at altitudes of a few thousand feet, are too low to receive the cloud-borne moisture but are high enough to provide astronomers with probably the finest observatory sites in the world—except for the Big Island of Hawaii.

Astronomers recognized the potential of the western foothills of the Andes during the 1960s. Two factors motivated their search for better observatory sites: a desire to find clearer skies, all the more important as light and air pollution steadily worsened in Europe and the United States; and a need for giant observatories in the Southern Hemisphere, capable of matching those in the northern and able to observe the third of the sky that never rises above the horizon for mid-northern latitudes. Although observatories had been built in South Africa and Australia, these could never serve as the great centers of observation that astronomers needed, simply because neither of these countries has a world-class site. Australia has only modest mountains, often lacking (in most seasons) the crisp, clear weather that astronomers crave. South Africa fares even worse in offering good sites for observations and, as the 1960s passed, began to look politically dubious.

So the astronomers went to Chile. There, where the Andes hem the country into an east-west width that averages only 60 miles but allow a north-south extent of nearly 2,000 miles, they found the clearest skies for the most nights of the year anywhere on the globe. These favorable conditions extend northward into Peru, where Harvard University had built a small observatory during the late nineteenth century; but they reach their very best clarity a few hundred miles to the north of Chile's capital, Santiago. During the mid-1970s, three giant observatories sprouted in the Andean foothills: A consortium of European nations built an observatory, the National Science Foundation built one, and Caltech built its own.

As the three Andean observatories came into being, the sleepy seacoast town of La Serena, 150 miles north of Santiago, became one of the key transit points for observational astronomers. A typical observing run in Chile takes an astronomer from Europe or North America on a journey of 6,000 to 10,000 miles for four or six or (with extreme luck) eight nights on a telescope. If these nights are cloudy or otherwise unfavorable, that counts as bad luck and nothing else. With the observing (or nonobserving) done, the astronomer must reverse the journey and fly home, perhaps to return six months or a year later for further observations.

PROSPECTORS FOR PLANETS

Brad Smith and Rich Terrile have used the 101-inch DuPont reflector at the Las Campanas Observatory about once each year for the past seven years. Despite their friendship and mutual interest in the search for worlds beyond the solar system, Smith and Terrile are a study in contrasts (Figure 78).

Smith is a quiet, heavyset bear of a man now nearing 60. Born and raised in eastern Massachusetts, he discovered astronomy at the age of nine, when his grandmother gave him a book on the subject. As an adolescent, Smith regularly visited the Harvard College Observatory and was befriended by some of the astronomers there, including Fred Whipple, a famous expert on planets. Smith concluded, from Whipple's Model A Ford and the patched elbows on his jackets, that astronomy offered little in the way of income, but his fascination persisted.

When Smith graduated from Northeastern University with a degree in chemical engineering, he was drafted into the U.S. Army. Just at that time, he read an article in *Scientific American* announcing that the Army Map Service was looking for astronomers to help make precise observations of the moon. Smith wrote to the man in charge and, after his basic training, was assigned to this project. He then learned that Clyde Tombaugh, who had discovered the planet Pluto in 1930, was engaged in a classified project to search for small, undetected natural satellites of Earth. In those pre-Sputnik days, such hypothetical satellites had military significance, as indeed they might today if they existed. Smith spent the remainder of his army career working at the Lowell Observatory in Arizona on a systematic search via photography for possible Earth satellites.

Lowell Observatory had been founded in the last decade of the nineteenth century specifically to study the planet Mars. Percival Lowell, the observatory's founder, was the last of the great amateur astronomers. A member of the famous Lowell family of Boston and independently wealthy, Lowell used his observatory to

Figure 78. Brad Smith (left) and Rich Terrile (right) relax at the moment of learning that *Voyager 2* has successfully crossed Neptune's ring plane. (Photograph by Donald Goldsmith.)

study Mars. He became convinced that he had observed networks of canals—proof that an intelligent but water-hungry race was transporting the precious liquid from the Martian polar caps to the hotter, drier equatorial regions of the planet. Lowell Observatory was a fitting place from which to observe the close approach of Mars to the Earth in 1956. Smith was entranced; for him, it would be astronomy from then on. He enrolled in graduate studies in physics at New Mexico State University, Tombaugh's home institution and a developing center for planetary astronomy. By the mid-1960s Smith was a member of its faculty.

Smith's career took off after Robert Leighton from Caltech visited New Mexico State to discuss Mars, the special focus of Smith's astronomical observations. Leighton was a member of the science team for the *Mariner 4* spacecraft, which first photographed Mars from close by in 1965. From this visit, Smith developed a working relationship with Leighton and with his Caltech colleague Bruce Murray, who would later become the director of the Jet Propulsion Laboratory. Smith became the deputy leader of the imaging team for the *Mariner 9* mission to Mars, which took much-improved photographs of the red planet in 1971. These missions dissipated once and for all any lingering belief in the Martian "canals," which must have been optical illusions, caused when the brain of Percival Lowell (and others) linked together irregular surface features, dimly glimpsed through our fluctuating atmosphere, and made order out of chaos by "seeing" a reticulated web of fine lines.

From the *Mariners* grew the *Viking* mission, which sent two spacecraft to orbit Mars in 1976 and to send landers onto the planet's surface (Color Plates 32 and 33). Smith was a key member of both the *Viking* imaging team and the group that had to search for landing sites—a difficult and stressful job, since direct guidance of the spacecraft to a landing was impossible (radio signals took 18 minutes to make the trip from Earth to Mars) and a boulder only the size of a wastebasket could destroy the spacecraft! Thanks to skill and luck, the team succeeded. The two *Vikings* landed on Mars, studied its atmosphere, photographed their surroundings, and scooped soil samples into an amazing automated, miniaturized laboratory for analysis (Figure 79, p. 268).

To the public—and to many of the scientists as well—the heart of the *Viking* mission lay in the continuation of Percival Lowell's quest, the ongoing search for life on Mars. The results initially proved tantalizing, because they seemed to show the same effects that microorganisms in the soil would produce, but after careful analysis, the *Viking* biologists concluded that *Viking* did *not* find life in or on the soil at the two landing sites. To this day, a small minority asserts that the *Viking* evidence points to the existence of microorganisms in the Martian soil, but if this is so, the organisms' metabolism does not correspond to what we would expect on a cold, dry planet.

Most experts agree that the most intriguing place to search next for life on Mars would be the fringes of the polar caps. There water, judged essential to Martian life on most models, continually evaporates and refreezes. But this alternating freezing and vaporization at the polar fringes produces crevasse-ridden terrain that ranks among the most treacherous on Mars. Hence such explorations will be difficult. Astronomers would dearly love to return to the red planet with an automated "Mars Rover," or even with a joint Soviet-U.S. manned effort.

Fifteen years after the *Viking* landings, Smith remains the sort of man who could watch worlds nearly collide without visible perturbation. His sidekick is another sort of person: In contrast to Smith's lack of visible excitement, Rich Terrile radiates a happy, nervous enthusiasm for whatever life brings his way. Now nearing 40, Terrile was born in New York City to parents from Argentina who in turn had Italian ancestors. Raised in the streetwise ways of the borough of Queens, he learned early not to accept whatever was told to him as gospel.

Terrile found an early interest in science, which his parents welcomed, and which his third-grade teacher unwittingly encouraged at a key moment in his education. As Terrile tells it, the teacher had a mechanical model in which the Earth circled the sun and the moon circled the Earth (so far, so good). The moon model was half black and half white, accurately portraying the fact that the sun always illuminates *half* of the lunar sphere. But the teacher insisted (incorrectly) that the *dark* half of the moon was completely "unknown." Young Rich already knew, however, that although one side of the moon indeed always faces away from the Earth, this "unknown" side is *not* simply the dark side of the moon. Instead, each half—the half facing the Earth as well as the half facing away—alternates between dark and light as the moon orbits around us. Terrile saw that the teacher had grossly oversimplified the situation. He made sure he was right and confronted her. Before long, the teacher acquiesced, though not with good grace, and Terrile had a good lesson in how to conduct a scientific discussion.

Despite his interest in science, as a teenager Terrile displayed many of the tendencies that mark certain males' transition to adulthood. "I used to hang out with thugs," he remarks with some exaggeration. After graduating from high school, Terrile attended the then-new campus of the State University of New York at Stony Brook, on Long Island. "I was never a great brain," he recalls. "I had to buckle down in college." He did so sufficiently to graduate summa cum laude, an intense, dark-haired young man who pronounced his name as Ter-real. By the next summer, Terrile had left for graduate studies at Caltech, working mainly with Jim Westphal on the construction of an advanced infrared-imaging system. He received his Ph.D. in 1978, with a thesis on what his and other infrared observations of Jupiter and Saturn could tell us about the structure of the cloud layers in those planets.

Soon after graduation, Terrile was hired by the Jet Propulsion Laboratory to help coordinate observations of Jupiter made from ground-based observatories with those that the *Voyager* spacecraft would obtain in 1979. Brad Smith, the leader of the *Voyager* imaging team, made Terrile an unofficial and then an official member of the team and later began a collaboration with him on the search for extrasolar planetary systems.

Smith and Terrile dream of attaining a goal long cherished by astronomers: finding the first planets known to orbit other stars in the Milky Way. They hope to discover them, or at least evidence for their existence, through careful observations made in Chile. Not content even with this search, Terrile has a far more ambitious, long-term dream: a spacecraft sent into orbit to find extrasolar planets by detecting the submillimeter (long-wavelength infrared) radiation that the planets emit. Such an effort lies decades in the future.

THE BETA PICTORIS DISK: OUR BEST EVIDENCE FOR OTHER PLANETS?

For now, Smith and Terrile's attack on the problem of finding extrasolar planets must use far more subtlety than a simple attempt to look for planets around other stars. During the past eight years, Smith and Terrile have pursued their search for extrasolar planets as an additional effort beyond their "ordinary" work with the *Voyager* mission (and, for Smith, beyond his faculty duties at the Universities of Arizona and Hawaii). They have found intriguing evidence for a planetary system around a nearby star. Though indirect, this evidence is highly suggestive to astronomers who follow Smith and Terrile's observation and reasoning.

Unlike radio or infrared astronomers, who can hope to find material that does not radiate visible light, Smith and Terrile set out to search around stars in precisely that type of radiation—visible light—which stars emit in quantity. Their secret weapon has been a specialized instrument designed to overcome, at least in part, the fact that a star shines far more brightly than any planets that may orbit around it. And Smith and Terrile had an advantage. They knew the likeliest stars on which to train their weapon: those stars found to be sources of infrared emission by the Infrared Astronomy Satellite (IRAS).

NASA launched the IRAS in 1983 to observe the heavens at four different infrared wavelengths, all of which are blocked by our atmosphere. IRAS carried a modest reflecting telescope, along with a detector system capable of recording infrared radiation—and this meant having a system kept at temperatures close to absolute zero. Cooling the detector is essential; otherwise the infrared emitted by the detector itself would completely overwhelm the relatively weak infrared radiation from cosmic sources many light years away.

IRAS worked like a charm, but it lasted for less than a year as a functioning observatory before the coolant inevitably evaporated. Nevertheless, 1983 was quite a year for infrared astronomy. For the first time, we obtained a map of nearly the entire sky at four different infrared wavelengths (Color Plate 2).

The astronomers found tens of thousands of individual sources—most of them cool stars—and are still working hard to extract more information from the data, now stored on computer files and known as the IRAS catalog.

The most promising IRAS sources are those whose radiation appears to arise from dust particles warmed to temperatures roughly similar to those on Earth. Modern theories of planetary formation include the notion that planets formed from such dust particles, which orbited the star-in-formation and slowly agglomerated to form larger and larger objects. In other words, planets arise from myriad dust particles around stars. If this theory is correct, the existence of dust particles around stars should be a good sign of planetary formation at work, now or in the past.

The theory implies that dust particles are the tip-off to planet formation. Knowing this well, Smith and Terrile chose to study those stars from which IRAS revealed the infrared radiation characteristic of dust particles. Since stars themselves have temperatures sufficiently hot to destroy such particles, the infrared found by IRAS was presumably arriving from material close to but not inside the stars—material that would repay closer inspection if such could be made.

The two astronomers therefore went to Chile half a dozen times, equipped with a *coronagraph,* an instrument that could be mounted at the business end of the 100-inch reflecting telescope to place a tiny "mask" in the path of the light, blocking the light from a distant star to create a miniature, artificial eclipse. And there, in the cool, clear night skies above the coastal desert, Smith and Terrile obtained electronically processed images that revealed disks of material around several nearby stars, and in particular, around the star Beta Pictoris, about 50 light years from the solar system.

This by itself would have been impressive but hardly big news; Smith and Terrile would have *photographed* the sorts of disks that Sargent and Beckwith had "seen" by the dozens through their radio observations. What makes Beta Pictoris unique—and arguably the best candidate for a possible nearby planetary system—is what lies in the center of the disk, the part *covered up* by the mask of the coronagraph.

How can this be? If Smith and Terrile couldn't see this region, how could their observations have revealed the possible existence of a planetary system there? The answer lies in the chain of evidence and in the degree of confidence that it inspires.

First of all, Smith and Terrile did see a disk of material

around Beta Pictoris (Color Plate 34). This demonstrates that dust-rich matter lies close to the star. It also implies that this matter moves in orbit around the star, for if the matter were not orbiting the star, either the star's gravity would have long ago pulled the matter inward, or the matter would have been blown outward by streams of particles ejected from the star. Secondly, the IRAS satellite, which could not observe fine detail, could effectively measure only the *total* amount of infrared radiation from the region that surrounds and includes Beta Pictoris. These IRAS observations revealed the total amount of infrared emission from all the material in the disk (Beta Pictoris itself radiates relatively little infrared). The IRAS measurements included the part of the disk closest to the star, which was masked by the coronagraphic disk in the visible-light studies. The masked region spanned about the same size as Pluto's orbit around the sun; that is, it included the region that would contain all of the planets' orbits in the solar system.

Now comes the chain of reasoning: Smith and Terrile found that the density of dusty material in the disk around Beta Pictoris increases from the outside of the disk inward toward the star (until you encounter the edge of their coronagraphic mask). If they hypothesize that the density of material goes on increasing at much the same rate all the way inward to the surface of the star itself, they can calculate what the total infrared emission would be from all the dusty material. This calculated amount far exceeds the total infrared emission observed by the IRAS satellite. Hence, Smith and Terrile conclude, their extrapolation cannot be correct: The density of dusty material does *not* keep on increasing but in fact must decrease in the regions close to the star. Otherwise the disk would produce more infrared than IRAS saw. In short, the IRAS results plus Smith and Terrile's observations together imply that the center of the disk of material around the star must be mostly, or entirely, devoid of dust.

Quite a line of argument! To astronomers the links seem fairly tight. We see Beta Pictoris surrounded at relatively large distances by dusty material, but the infrared totals tell us that behind the coronagraphic mask, the inner portions of the disk around the star must have little or no dust. Putting numbers to the observations, Smith and Terrile conclude that the outer parts of the disk extend to a distance from the star equal to about 10 times Pluto's distance from the sun, but within a distance from Beta Pictoris approximately equal to Neptune's distance from the sun, the amount of dusty material decreases dramatically.

Smith and Terrile suggest that Beta Pictoris offers us a view of the debris left over from planet formation—and the crucial absence of dusty material within a region about the size of the sun's planetary system. An astronomer who accepts the evidence for a cleared area around the star can easily accept as quite possible, but not proven, the notion that this clearing arose from the formation of planets. When our solar system formed, the region within Neptune's distance from the sun underwent such a "clearing out," as the inner planets and the giant planets each accreted from smaller collections of dusty, dirty snowballs. Far beyond the planets' orbits, billions of comets, each an accretion of dust and ice, still circle the star with which they were born. Do we have reliable evidence of planets around Beta Pictoris—a star whose age we simply do not know but can estimate as something less than a billion years?

A skeptic might reply that the evidence for planets around Beta Pictoris consists of an unseen but guessed-at *emptiness,* a "hole in the middle" of a dusty doughnut. Even if this hole does exist, the formation of a planetary system would provide just one possible explanation. Other reasons might well exist for the existence of cleared regions at the centers of disks of dusty material around stars. For example, the "stellar wind" of particles ejected from the young Beta Pictoris might have cleared out the regions close to the star without any help from planet formation.

At least two conclusions about the surroundings of Beta Pictoris remain perfectly tenable: We have found either planets by deduction or a dust-laden disk that demands better observations before yielding its secrets to Earth-based observers. A proper scientific attitude requires a balance between the two. We may note that Beta Pictoris offers highly suggestive evidence for a planetary system within 50 light years of our own, and that we could profit mightily from better telescopic observations, perhaps from a space-borne observatory, to see whether or not the disk around Beta Pictoris does indeed show a cleared area at its center. Even then, since (as always) we cannot hope to see the planets themselves, our hopes of concluding that planets exist around another star must continue to rely on a chain of reasoning. Like the rest of us, Smith and Terrile are not delighted with the present state of affairs. Someday we may have a fully functioning telescope in space, free from the atmospheric blurring inevitable at any ground-based observatory, that may reveal our first images of planets like our own, in orbit around distant stars.

Figure 83. Joseph Weber of the University of Maryland, the first physicist to construct a gravity-wave detector almost capable of finding gravity waves, is shown here with the detector during the late 1960s. (Courtesy of Professor Joseph Weber.)

13. The Wave of the Future?

"ALBERT, IF YOU'RE not too busy, perhaps you wouldn't mind taking out the garbage?" When Leonid Grishchuk's wife Tanya starts to call him Albert, he knows that her patience with his cogitation may be reaching its limits. At Moscow State University, Grishchuk ranks as an expert on Albert Einstein's general theory of relativity, but at home—a three-room apartment on the top floor of a sixteen-story building, one of a dozen in a block of identical apartment buildings—he is valued for his more human side.

Leonid Petrovich Grishchuk has a highly intelligent face, somewhat long in the jaw and crisp in the mouth, framed above by receding brown hair, with soft Russian eyes that roam the horizon and exude an overall look of quiet patience (Figure 80). Grishchuk, a well-muscled man of 49, stays fit by playing energetic soccer with younger friends, but his mind finds its freedom in the field of general relativity and quantum cosmology. He is an expert in the arcane subject of *gravity waves*—ripples of space, predicted by Einstein's theory of gravity, that should arise from cosmic events of great violence but which have yet to be detected at all. Within the small circle of those who theorize about gravity waves, Grishchuk is best known for his calculations concerning primordial gravity waves, the waves produced when the universe was born. If Grishchuk is right, we may be closer than most astrophysicists believe to the day when we can detect these waves and can use them to learn secrets of the early universe barely guessed at today.

Grishchuk was born in Zhitomir, in the heart of the Ukraine, on August 16, 1941—a fateful year for the world, with fatal repercussions for his family. Grishchuk's father, Peter Fomich, had been trained as a priest; he married after the Russian Revolution

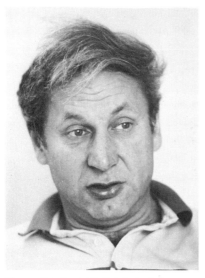

Figure 80. Leonid Grishchuk is a Soviet expert on gravity waves. (Photograph by Donald Goldsmith.)

and became a teacher, continuing to perform his priestly functions when allowed to do so. On June 22, 1941, the Nazi army invaded Russia. Countless thousands of Soviet citizens were immediately arrested and deported without explanation, Grishchuk's father among them, never to return. He left behind a daughter and four sons—and a wife seven months pregnant with his last child, Leonid Petrovich.

Grishchuk has no memories of his first three years, during which the Ukraine remained under Nazi occupation. Despite the hardships that confronted a widow with six children, Grishchuk's mother—aided by the oldest boys—managed to help all six to grow up and obtain college or equivalent degrees. Leonid, the youngest by a full 11 years, showed an early aptitude for science and mathematics. Though his high-school teachers provided little inspiration, his books did. Grishchuk remembers one in particular, for its title—

Rozhdenie Mirov (*The Birth of Worlds*)—now accurately describes his daily theoretical work. Today Grishchuk is the Soviet Union's leading theorist on gravity waves, especially concerned with the question of how the birth of the universe might have produced detectable amounts of these mysterious ripples in space.

Toward the close of his high-school career, Grishchuk won the mathematics prize for the Zhitomir region. He chose to attend Moscow University, then as now the center of Soviet education, where he has been an undergraduate, a graduate student, then a candidate for the higher degree that the Soviets call the *aspirantura,* and finally a professor.

As an undergraduate, Grishchuk concentrated on mathematical physics. Among the best of all the Soviet students, he stood out as exceptional. Once enrolled in graduate school, Grishchuk's abilities brought him into contact with the professor who had the greatest influence on his career, and on Soviet astrophysics in general: Yakov Borisovich Zel'dovich.

Zel'dovich ranks among the outstanding physicists of this century. Born in 1913 of a Leningrad family, he distinguished himself as a physics student during the early 1930s; in 1939 he helped formulate the theory that describes nuclear chain reactions in what would later be called an atomic bomb—which Zel'dovich helped the Soviet Union to develop shortly after World War II ended. Soon after that, Zel'dovich became part of the Soviet hydrogen-bomb program and made crucial scientific contributions to its success. But in the early 1960s, at just about the time that Grishchuk finished his undergraduate work, Zel'dovich felt that he had had enough of bomb-making and became a professor at Moscow State University. When you go to Moscow today, scientist after scientist will tell you how Zel'dovich (who died in 1987) encouraged and inspired them to dig deeper for the answers to fundamental physical questions. Most of all, Zel'dovich tried to explore the early moments after the big bang that began the universe. Of all his "converts" to this effort, one of the most outstanding is Leonid Grishchuk.

By the time that he finished graduate school in 1967, Leonid had met his wife-to-be, Tanya, a student of crystallography. Marriage to Tanya removed an obstacle to Grishchuk's immediate career development: He had been offered a faculty position at the university but did not have a *propiska*—a permit—to live in Moscow. (Soviet authorities deal with the overcrowding caused by desire to live in the Soviet capital by rationing these permits.) Tanya, born and raised in Moscow, had such a permit, and one permit suffices for a couple.

But no one would suppose that Tanya and Leonya Grishchuk married for official benefits alone. The pair may exchange an occasional verbal barb—especially well-crafted on Tanya's part—but they clearly enjoy each other's company. This statement carries special weight when you live, as the Grishchuks do, in a three-room apartment with two daughters and a son-in-law.

In such a situation, an ability to get along is essential, and it may prove useful if you have a mind capable of using Einstein's general theory of relativity to soar from the petty annoyances of daily life into the far reaches of the universe. Leonid Grishchuk has been intimate with Einstein's theory for more than two decades. His first major work dealt with the question of whether Einstein's theory of relativity inevitably leads to what mathematicians call *singularities,* places where all the normal rules of physics fail to describe reality. Grishchuk showed that singularities are indeed unavoidable and promptly found himself in a dispute with the authorities—in this case, only the scientific authorities. He now recalls this dispute as good training for a young theorist: You must learn to stand up for what you believe you have proven.

GRAVITY WAVES AND EINSTEIN'S
THEORY OF RELATIVITY

Much of Grishchuk's work in theoretical astrophysics has centered on a single, subtle phenomenon: the gravity waves produced by the birth of the universe. In order to understand Grishchuk's passion, one must therefore begin by understanding gravity waves.

Gravity waves are ripples of spacetime (Color Plate 36). This was a simple concept, to Albert Einstein. The rest of us must try to see space and time as Einstein did, or if we can't do that, to sneak up on Einstein's vision, attempting to read over his shoulder and understand how and why gravity waves emerge from Einstein's general theory of relativity. His theory, which deals with the effects of gravity, can be summarized (much as Milton's *Paradise Lost* may be summarized as Satan vs. God) in two phrases: Matter creates gravity that bends space, and space tells matter how to move.

Einstein perceived that the best way to conceive of gravity would be to think of it not as affecting objects *in* space, but rather as *affecting space itself* (Color Plate 35). Other types of forces—such as electromagnetism—are not so simple that we can use this concept, but gravity is: If we think of gravity as a force that bends space, we can see that in response to this force, objects simply follow what would ordinarily be straight lines—lines that now curve because they pass through curved space. The planets orbit the sun, for example, because the sun's gravity bends space, dimpling it inward much as a heavy shot-put dimples a rubberized floor. The planets, responding to the "curved" surface, then roll around and around the dimple. Other objects, not possessing the proper paths to orbit indefinitely, may roll right in to the sun.

For Einstein, this realization that gravity bends space marked a key moment in his path toward the general theory of relativity. Here "general" means "including situations in which gravity is present." In 1905, Einstein had published the four epochal papers that included, among other items, the possibility of converting mass into energy and the *special* theory of relativity. "Special" meant that Einstein was first considering idealized situations in which gravitational forces do not exist. Crucial though the special theory has proven to be in our understanding of the cosmos, the general theory has far greater importance: It deals more directly with the "real" universe, where gravitational forces emphatically *do* exist.

Einstein worked on his general theory from soon after 1905 through 1915, when he arrived at a satisfactory understanding and published his results in the *Zeitschrift für Physik*. At the beginning of this period, Einstein's new-found fame among physicists took him to new jobs in Zurich and Prague; toward the end, now a distinguished professor in Berlin, Einstein was able to work almost without distraction, for the First World War had begun and many of his students and colleagues were swept into Germany's war effort.

Einstein's spectacular theoretical results therefore received small notice from the world at large. Eventually, three and a half killing years after it began, the war came to an end. Kaiser Wilhelm took a night train to Holland; the Weimar Republic came into what proved a precarious existence; and Albert Einstein's university colleagues resumed their normal routines. Even then, they had little to say about the general theory, until the theory received a verification that caused worldwide attention.

One result predicted by Einstein's general theory of relativity is that *gravity bends light*. This follows directly from the proposition that gravity bends space and that light travels through space as directly as possible. In the absence of significant amounts of gravitational forces, light waves travel in straight lines, but in the presence of gravity, the light rays deviate slightly from straight-line trajectories (Figure 81). As discussed in chapter 1, the amount of

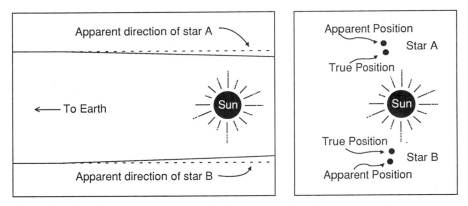

Figure 81. Einstein's general theory of relativity predicts that since gravity curves space, the path of any light ray must curve as it passes close to any object with mass. Thus starlight passing by the sun will be bent by the sun's gravity (left). We can observe this bending during a total eclipse of the sun (right), comparing the stars' apparent positions then with the positions measured when the sun no longer lies in that direction in the sky. (Drawings by Crystal Stevenson.)

this deviation depends on the object's mass and on the distance at which the light rays pass by the object.

In Einstein's day, the only hope for measuring such gravity-produced deviations involved the sun, which has by far the largest mass of any object in our vicinity. Einstein, who knew this quite well, had calculated that a light ray—perhaps from a distant star—that just grazed the sun's surface would be deviated by a small angle: 1.75 seconds of arc. A light ray that did not pass so close to the sun would be bent by a lesser amount. For example, a light beam whose trajectory brought it to within a distance of twice the sun's radius from the sun's center would be deviated by only 0.875 second of arc, half the amount predicted for a sun-grazing ray of light. But how could astronomers ever overcome the sun's glare to observe any such bending of light rays? The answer came in 1919, with a total eclipse of the sun.

Historically, the prediction of eclipses has been one of the astronomers' basic tasks, and indeed the oldest astronomical record in existence describes two Chinese astronomers, Hsi and Ho, who were apparently executed for failing to predict the total eclipse of the sun in 2137 B.C. Long before the twentieth century, similar encouragement had inspired astronomers to learn the complete art of eclipse prediction. They not only knew that an eclipse of the sun occurs about twice a year somewhere on Earth, but could also calculate with extreme accuracy the track of the moon's shadow across the Earth's surface. Hence the astronomers had easily predicted, well in advance of the date, that on May 29, 1919, the track of a solar eclipse would cross Brazil and the tiny island of Príncipe, off the northwest coast of Africa. Now, for the first time, astronomers had the chance to use the eclipse to test the new theory of gravity. In a burst of international cooperation, the British seized the opportunity and made Einstein world famous.

Astronomers from England organized two expeditions to view the eclipse, from Sobral in northeastern Brazil and from Príncipe. Their chief goal was to secure photographs of the region of the sky around the sun during the few minutes when the moon's disk completely covered the solar disk. During the eclipse, only the relatively dim light of the solar corona would appear, allowing the astronomers to photograph the brighter stars visible close by the sun. Weather favored the observations: Neither site was hindered by clouds at the time of total eclipse, and both yielded high-quality photographs. The astronomers carried their plates home, developed them, and compared the stars' positions on the plates with the positions of stars on other plates, taken at a time when the Earth's motion had moved the sun away from the region of the sky photographed during the eclipse. The results were beyond doubt: To within the astronomers' margin of error, the stars' positions had been shifted by the sun's presence, in just the way and by just the amount that Einstein had predicted. In his easygoing way, Einstein reacted to the British announcement by sending his mother a postcard that began, "Good news! The British expedition has confirmed my theory." But his life, and the world of physics, would never be quite the same.

Like Lord Byron just over a century before, Einstein awoke to find himself famous. To be sure, he was already well known in the world of physics. Now he was besieged by the world press, which, partly because the postwar spirit welcomed a German theory confirmed by an English expedition, promptly lionized him. For the rest of his life, Einstein was the world's most famous scientist—a role for which he had no good prior models, since the modern mills of publicity had just begun to grind their daily grist. Fortunately for himself, and for science, Einstein had the right mixture of humor and humility to carry this burden successfully.

Einstein had a fine time in the Berlin of the 1920s. He enjoyed both his academic life and the occasional dinner with important people; he attended most of the physics seminars and asked penetrating questions; he visited physicists around the world and charmed them easily, occasionally speaking French and English with more felicity then he admitted. Einstein's first marriage ended in divorce, and after 1921 Einstein saw little of his two sons (one of whom became an engineering professor in Berkeley, while the other was an institutionalized schizophrenic). After being awarded the Nobel Prize in 1923 (the prize money, already anticipated several years before, had been promised to his first wife as a sort of alimony), Einstein entered a second, happy marriage with his cousin Elsa. The Einsteins had a pleasant apartment in Berlin and a small home in Caputh, on one of the small lakes nearby that make summer in the Mark of Brandenburg especially enjoyable. And there, in the heart of Weimar Germany, where Bertold Brecht and Kurt Weill dominated the theater, where the Bauhaus architects created a new building style, where European culture found its center, Einstein continued his work.

THE SEARCH FOR A UNIFIED FIELD THEORY

And what was Einstein working on during the 1920s? Now that gravity was, so to speak, wrapped up, he concentrated on a still more ambitious project: to see whether, and how, both gravity and electromagnetism could prove to be aspects of a single type of force, deriving from what Einstein called a *unified field theory*. Although at various times he thought he had "got it," or at least part of it, in retrospect his efforts came to naught. But as Einstein remarked, unlike younger physicists, he could risk spending years on speculative endeavors that might lead nowhere.

On January 30, 1933, when Adolf Hitler came to power in Germany, to begin his "Thousand-[actually Twelve]-Year-Reich," Einstein was in California. He never returned to his native land. Instead, he decided to move to Princeton, New Jersey, where he became the leading scholar at the newly established Institute for Advanced Study. Although Einstein had German-speaking colleagues there, and although his English became quite fluent, he never again indulged in group conversations about physics with the zest of his Berlin days. Einstein's wife died in 1936, but he lived until 1955, continuing to spend his major efforts on his search for a unified field theory. Today, scientists recognize not two but four types of forces: gravity, electromagnetism, strong interactions, and weak interactions. The latter two types appear only at the size scale of atomic nuclei, and Einstein never thought of them as equal in importance to gravity or electromagnetism.

Only within the last two decades, long after Einstein's death, have physicists begun to make serious progress toward his goal of a unified field theory—a theory that would explain all four forces as parts of a single type of force. Theorists now feel rather confident that they can view electromagnetism and weak interactions as aspects of a single, *electroweak* force, and they have high hopes of achieving a grand unified theory that will unify strong interactions with the electroweak force. Finally, some day they hope to have a complete "theory of everything," one that would indeed meld all four forces into one.

In hindsight, Einstein's greatest achievements by far all came before his fortieth birthday, in the year that the British eclipse expeditions confirmed his general theory of relativity by showing that gravity bends light. The general theory of relativity has held up startlingly well against all later tests. The most accurate of these, which measure the bending not of light but of radio waves, have confirmed Einstein's theory to the satisfaction of all who work in the field of relativity and have disproved alternative, more complex theories.

THE DIFFICULTY OF DETECTING GRAVITY WAVES

With Einstein's theory now so well established, no one seriously doubts the existence of a crucial effect predicted by the theory but never observed: gravity waves. Einstein saw that if an object with mass—the sun, for instance—bends space into a sort of dimple, then the *motion* of any object with mass would move that dimple in space from place to place. This would produce a changing distortion of space, and this in turn would create a *ripple,* a moving wave in the fabric of space. (Actually, since relativity adds time as a fourth dimension to the three dimensions of space, the ripple occurs in the fabric of space-time. We need not worry here about time as the fourth dimension, though the concept has funded many a science-fiction novel.)

Einstein realized that the ripple created by the motion of mass will spread outward through space in all directions much as electromagnetic waves spread outward from a source. If this is so, then any other mass, quietly minding its own business in space, would be set in motion as the ripple passed by, much as the leaves in a pond bob up and down in the ripples produced when a stone falls into the water. The waves would be weaker at greater distances, just as a star appears dimmer to an observer farther from it. Einstein showed that a gravity wave would have an unusual effect on the objects it encountered: It would make them grow alternately longer and shorter as the waves passed by. Physicists eventually determined that the best way to detect gravity waves would be to suspend two large masses with extreme care and to monitor the distance between them precisely. If the distance grows alternately longer and shorter, the repetitive changes would provide evidence of a passing gravity wave.

But gravity waves are incredibly weak—a cosmic featherfall

in a violent universe. Einstein's theory predicts that stronger gravity waves arise from the swifter motion of larger masses. Today, thanks to increasing knowledge of the cosmos, we can imagine more violent motion of much larger masses than Einstein dreamt of. But even so, we can calculate that even the collapse at the end of a star's life that forms a black hole—the violent inrush of more mass than our sun contains—produces a gravity wave too weak to be detected with our present instruments.

Why is this so? What makes gravity waves so weak that an entire star's collapse can yield no detectable gravity waves? The answer lies in the inherent weakness of gravity itself, by far the weakest of the four types of force.

The assertion that gravity is weak may seem untrue in light of the fact that gravity dominates the motions of stars and galaxies, and indeed will decide the question of the ultimate fate of the universe. When physicists assert the weakness of gravity, however, they refer to what happens at the most elementary level of the cosmos: the interactions among particles believed to be fundamental in creating the universe. At the particle level, the weakness of gravity becomes obvious. In a hydrogen atom, an electron orbits a proton because of the electromagnetic force, not the gravitational force, between the two particles. The electromagnetic force between a proton and electron exceeds the gravitational force between them by more than a trillion trillion trillion times! Gravity could never hold electrons in orbit in an atom. Still less could gravity bind together the protons and neutrons in an atomic nucleus (the primary role of the strong interaction), or cause the decay of radioactive nuclei into other types of nuclei (one of the roles of the weak interaction). On the level of elementary particles, gravity plays no part: These particles would behave exactly as they do if gravity did not exist.

Gravity shows its stuff in the larger world, the world that consists of immense numbers of elementary particles. The strong and weak interactions operate only over minuscule distances, approximately the size of an atomic nucleus, and have zero effect over larger distances. Hence any object much larger than an atomic nucleus effectively feels only two types of forces: gravity and electromagnetism. And although electromagnetic forces inherently far outmuscle gravitational forces, they have a key property that proves ruinous in the competition with gravity: They can both attract *and* repel. This means that in a large object, made of large numbers of both positive and negative electric charges, attractive and repulsive electromagnetic forces tend to cancel one another and therefore produce a zero net force. In contrast, gravitational forces, always attractive, simply increase as an object's mass increases.

Although human beings exert gravitational forces on one another, these forces are close to zero—a tribute to the inherent weakness of gravity. Even the trillion trillion elementary particles in each of us cannot amount to much gravitationally. Only when we encounter objects roughly the size of planets (or at least of their moons) do we meet anything whose gravity must be taken seriously. Each planet contains trillions of trillions times *more* elementary particles than we do.

This overview of the force of gravity may help to emphasize the difficulty of detecting gravity waves—the ripples in space caused by the motion of masses, the sources of gravitational force. These ripples make objects move with respect to one another as the waves pass by, but by only incredibly small amounts. We can far more easily produce detectable effects with electromagnetic waves, which arise from the motion of electrically charged particles, and we do so routinely to create radio and television broadcasts. When electromagnetic radio waves strike an antenna, they induce small motions in the charged particles within the antenna—motions that allow us to detect and analyze the waves. But although gravity waves produce analogous motions, the motions are tiny almost beyond imagining. Because these motions are so small, we have yet to detect with certainty a single gravity wave. This fact has left gravity-wave astronomy in a peculiar state.

In 1917, with Europe still deep in the First World War, Einstein wrote a paper entitled "Cosmological Reflections on the General Theory of Relativity," in which he showed that his theory predicted the existence of gravity waves but that these waves would be so weak as to be undetectable. From that day to now, gravity waves have remained undetected. But the few years left in the second millennium of the Christian calendar offer the possibility of finally opening the universe to the new observational method that Einstein envisioned. Gravity-wave astronomers seek to observe the cosmos in an entirely new way: not with the electromagnetic waves that have brought us so much information, not with the neutrinos that have just begun to let us peer into the stellar hearts of darkness, but with a completely different "channel" of information, through the shaking of space itself.

Gravity-wave astronomy shows how, in many cases, theory precedes and leads experiment. Some natural phenomena—day and night, tornados, eclipses, and the like—are sufficiently obvious to even the most cursory "experimenter" as to call for explanation. Other phenomena are not: When Albert Einstein first noted that his theory of relativity implies the possibility of gravity waves, he also saw that the technology of his era could not possibly detect them.

During the long sweep of the twentieth century, the technological abilities of human society have steadily improved. During the past few years, physicists and astronomers have gradually become aware that we may indeed stand on the verge of developing the ability to detect gravity waves. Indeed, nearly every astrophysicist who studies the subject believes that gravity waves have been detected *indirectly,* not through the motions that gravity waves induce but through other effects. We know that certain *pulsars,* rotating neutron stars that blink on and off with impressive regularity, belong to *binary systems.* In these systems, the pulsar and a relatively ordinary star orbit around one another. Einstein's theory predicts that this orbital motion should produce gravity waves, and that these waves should continuously carry off some energy from the binary system. As the system loses energy, the stars move closer to one another and orbit more rapidly. By studying the motions of pulsars in binary systems, astronomers have observed this effect and have seen the orbital motion change in precisely the way that Einstein's theory predicts. In this sense, gravity waves have been confirmed by indirect observation.

Direct observation of gravity waves that could reveal strange objects solely by the gravity waves they produce continues to elude astrophysicists, but not for long. Since the mid-1960s, theorists and experimenters have inspired one another—the experimenters with stunning new ideas about how to construct more sensitive gravity-wave detectors, the theorists with new insights into possible sources of gravity waves that might make detection an easier proposition.

KIP THORNE AND THE SEARCH FOR GRAVITY WAVES

At the center of today's effort in gravity-wave astronomy stands—as often in science—the California Institute of Technology (Caltech). Teamed with the Massachusetts Institute of Technology (MIT), Caltech has a project under development to secure the first observations of gravity waves. The original driving force

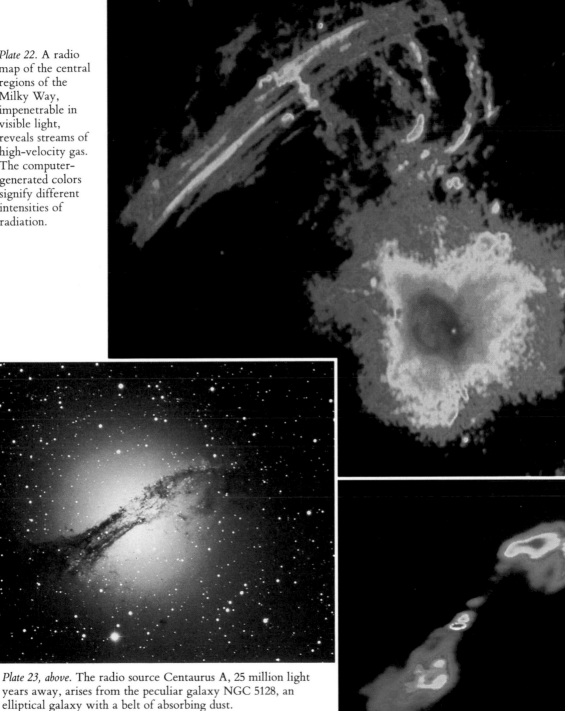

Plate 22. A radio map of the central regions of the Milky Way, impenetrable in visible light, reveals streams of high-velocity gas. The computer-generated colors signify different intensities of radiation.

Plate 23, above. The radio source Centaurus A, 25 million light years away, arises from the peculiar galaxy NGC 5128, an elliptical galaxy with a belt of absorbing dust.

Plate 24, right. A radio map of the region surrounding Centaurus A reveals that the radio-emitting regions, more than a million light years across, extend symmetrically on both sides of the visible galaxy, which fits easily into the small dot at the center of the map.

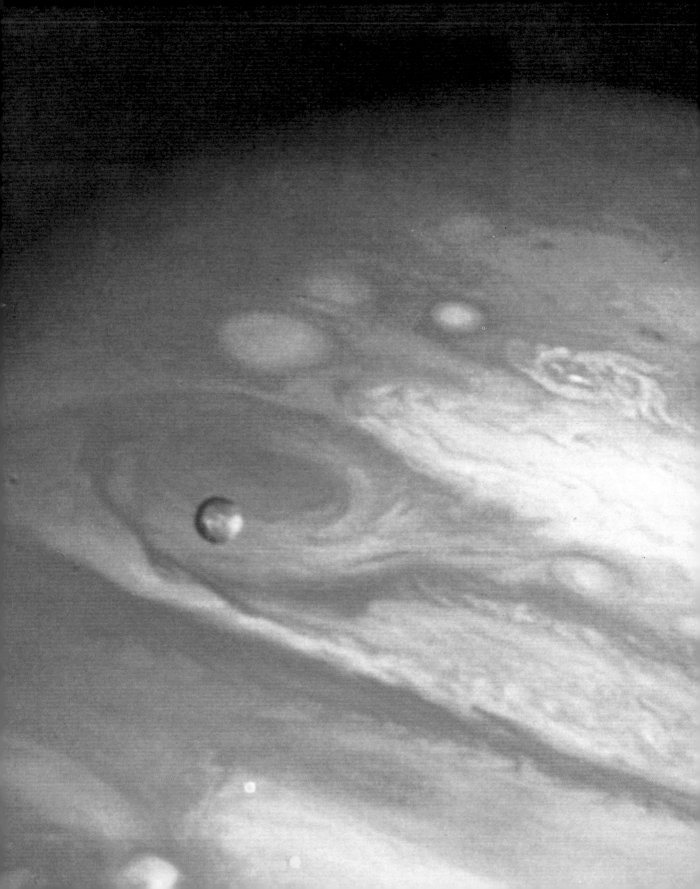

Plate 25. In 1979, *Voyager 1* photographed Jupiter's southern hemisphere with a resolution of about 250 miles. The Great Red Spot is prominent at the left center, with Jupiter's innermost large moon, Io, directly in front. At the right center, Jupiter's moon Europa, whose icy crust may cover seas of liquid, is visible.

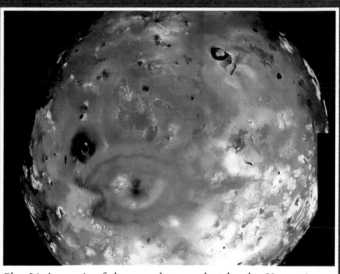

Plate 26. A mosaic of close-up photographs taken by *Voyager 1* reveals the pockmarked surface of Jupiter's moon Io, such as Pele at left center, where sulfur compounds provide visual excitement and active volcanos continually resurface the satellite.

Plate 27. This photograph of part of Io's surface reveals features as small as one mile across. The active volcanic vent at the lower right provides fresh material from beneath Io's crust.

Plate 28. Four billion years ago, half a billion years after the sun and its planets had formed, a huge impact with an asteroid formed the Mare Imbrium basin on the moon. This artistic representation shows the event as it occurred, while upon the Earth immense volcanos created an atmosphere of methane and ammonia.

Plate 29, above. In 1981, the *Voyager 2* spacecraft sent back this spectacular image of Saturn and its rings. Three of Saturn's moons can be seen below the planet, while a fourth casts its shadow as a black dot on the planet's atmosphere.

Plate 30, right. If one could pass through the plane of Saturn's rings, one would encounter hosts of objects ranging in size from that of a house down to sub-microscopic grains of dust as seen in this computer simulation. The combined gravitational effects of the material that forms the rings keep individual particles from straying.

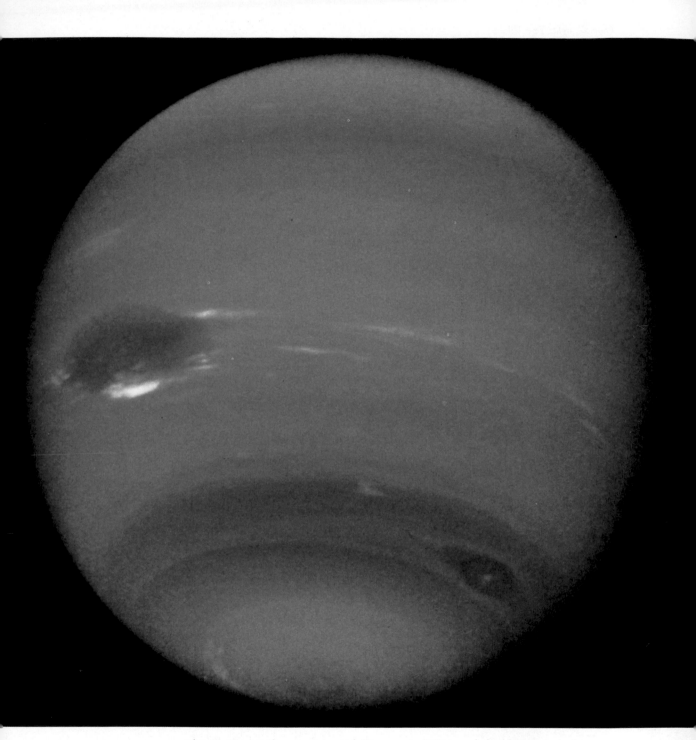

Plate 31. Voyager 2's encounter with Neptune in 1989 revealed a blue planet, whose coloration arises from methane in its atmosphere. In Neptune's southern hemisphere, the "Great Dark Spot" (left center) has about the same size as Earth, and is accompanied by whitish, wispy clouds.

Plate 32, right. The *Viking* spacecraft obtained this view of Mars's southern hemisphere, where the south pole has a thin coating of frozen carbon dioxide. The Valles Marineris, a chasm as long as the United States, can be seen at the lower right.

Plate 33, below. Mars's largest mountain, the extinct shield volcano called Olympus Mons, towers 16 miles above the Martian surface. This mountain, the largest in the solar system, spreads 300 miles at its base and has a summit crater or "caldera" 40 miles in diameter.

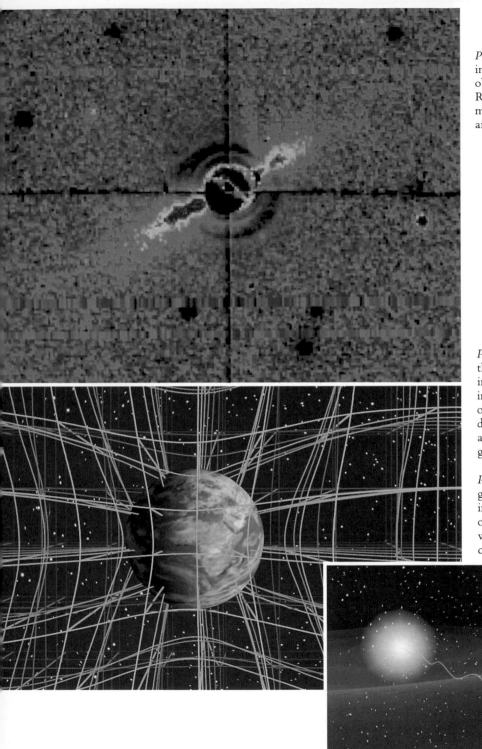

Plate 34, left. The processed image of Beta Pictoris obtained by Brad Smith and Rich Terrile shows a disk of material presumably in orbit around the star.

Plate 35, left. Einstein's theory of general relativity implies that we must imagine that massive objects, such as Earth, distort the fabric of space, as shown in this computer-generated rendition.

Plate 36, below. Einstein's general-relativity theory implies that the movement of massive objects in space will create ripples in space, called "gravity waves."

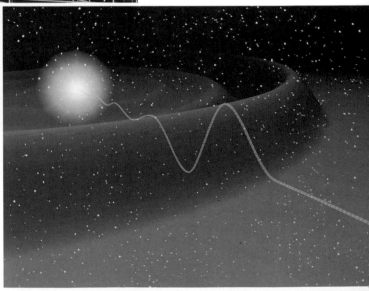

behind this project is a theorist, Leonid Grishchuk's
good friend Kip Thorne (Figure 82).

Thorne is one of a kind in the field of
theoretical physics, where many can lay claim to that
designation, though few so well. Born in 1940 into a
Mormon family whose ancestors went west with
Brigham Young, Thorne was the son of a soil
chemist and an economist, and the grandson of a
university professor, and grew up on hard work and
intellectual challenge. His best friend was a boy
named Merlin Olsen, the son of one of Kip's father's
agronomist colleagues at Utah State University. Olsen
became a big strapping fellow, a football star at Utah
State and in the professional leagues before
blossoming into an actor and football commentator;
in high school he and Kip were debate partners, a
formidable combination in both brains and
appearance. "In the midst of one debate, the opposing
team began to cry," Thorne recalls.

Figure 82. Kip Thorne is a leader in the effort to understand and detect gravity waves. (Photograph by Donald Goldsmith.)

By 1958, when the two friends graduated from
high school, Thorne was headed for Caltech. He had been
interested in astronomy from the age of eight, when his mother
took him to an astronomy lecture, and had begun to read books
about astronomy. Thorne had known for years that he wanted to
be a scientist—of a cerebral sort, unlike his experimentalist father.
Some budding astrophysicists build telescopes; Kip Thorne did
four-dimensional geometry. He recalls that "one of the most
wonderful experiences of my life was when I discovered that the
intersection of two planes in four dimensions is a point, not a line."
In adolescence, Thorne turned to books about relativity, especially
those by George Gamow. Years later, as a grown astrophysicist,
Thorne wrote Gamow a fan letter, saying that he had become a
relativity theorist largely because of Gamow's books, one of which
he'd read three times. Gamow sent Kip a copy of one of his
books—in Turkish, inscribed with the thought that this should
prevent Thorne from reading it for a fourth time.

On the bus to Caltech's freshman orientation program,
Thorne listened to his elitist fellow students discussing their IQs.
The lowest number mentioned was in the 150 range, whereas
Thorne's IQ had been rated at a mere 128. "The other students
were quicker," he says, "but they hadn't trained themselves as well
at figuring things out." Thorne is now convinced that a good

memory can be a great handicap to learning physics, or anything else, for it keeps you from learning how to think. Indeed, says Thorne, "the scientist with the worst memory I knew was Dick Feynman"—the Nobel Prize–winning physicist who was arguably the greatest all-around genius on the Caltech faculty.

Thorne's difficulties with the anticommunist loyalty oaths so prevalent in the 1950s and early 1960s led him into his first scientific research. He had worked for the Thiokol Chemical Corporation in Utah during the three summers preceding his junior year, but when the company sent him a new loyalty oath to sign for the summer of 1961, he refused and was terminated. Searching for a summer job at Caltech, he found Jesse Greenstein, who led him to examine the question of how electrons moving at nearly the speed of light in magnetic fields around stars could produce a particular type of radiation called *synchrotron radiation*. The summer's work produced Thorne's first scientific publication and convinced him that he could perform scientific research.

Kip Thorne had decided to marry his high-school sweetheart during the previous summer—his last in Utah—and had two children before the marriage ended in 1975. Ten years later, he married Carolee Winstein, a hard-working kinesiologist whose career often keeps her and Thorne apart for weeks or months on end—separations for which they compensate by celebrating their reunions with renewed joy.

Thorne recalls that the other Caltech students outgrew their fascination with relativity theory, but he did not. He was a convinced relativist by the time that he graduated in 1962 and moved to Princeton University for graduate study in relativity theory with John Wheeler, the man who named black holes. Under Wheeler's guidance, Thorne worked on the theory of objects that collapse under their own gravity. He received his Ph.D. degree after just three years of graduate work—close to the Princeton record—with a doctoral thesis that dealt with the mathematics of gravitational collapse in cylindrical systems, "which I never thought would really be relevant. But it turns out that much of what I did is now known as the theory of cosmic strings, and it took 20 years for the subject to become respectable."

During a postdoctoral year at Caltech, Thorne received a job offer from another institution that galvanized his alma mater into action and eventually led to his appointment, at age 27, as a tenured faculty member. Thorne has remained at Caltech for 23 years, working on the research that he chooses. At 50, his straight brown hair has turned partly grey (and his beard even more so), framing a large face with a prominent Roman nose and a massive forehead, creased by soft vertical lines, a face easily recognizable on a campus rich in deep, full-bearded thinkers. Seeking respite from administrative duties at Caltech, and a large block of time in which to work without interruption, Kip often retreats to a home on the Oregon coast that he, his wife, and his brother Lance (a master woodworking craftsman) have built.

During the 1960s and 1970s, gravity waves gradually drew Kip Thorne into their orbit. The science of gravity-wave detection began in earnest during the early 1960s with the efforts of a talented, lone experimenter, Joseph Weber of the University of Maryland. Weber took a cylindrical rod, two feet in diameter and five feet long, suspended it with extreme care, and monitored its movements with incredible precision, waiting for a gravity wave to perturb it ever so slightly (Figure 83, page 288). Thorne followed these experiments and was just daring enough to believe that they might succeed. He made calculations about the types of events that would produce gravity waves, seeking to find out whether existing detectors could detect them.

Thorne's interest in gravity waves repeatedly took him to Moscow during the late 1960s and early 1970s. Thorne had become friends with a Soviet theorist named Igor Novikov; through him, he met Yakov Zel'dovich, the kingpin of Soviet theoretical physics. Zel'dovich introduced Thorne to Vladimir Braginsky (the Soviet analog of Joseph Weber)—a highly creative experimenter who strove to find new and better ways to detect gravity waves. Stimulated by the low level of Soviet technology, Braginsky sought ever cleverer ways to find gravity waves. He made Thorne the "house theorist" of his experimental group to provide new insights into how the ripples in space could be felt. Kip Thorne traveled to Moscow for a month at a time, every other year, deriving intellectual stimulation in his interchanges with Braginsky and his colleagues.

DIFFERENT TYPES OF GRAVITY WAVES

Lacking any experimental detection of gravity waves, gravity-wave theorists have attempted to calculate the type of gravity waves that a particular kind of violent event—the collapse of a star's core, for example, or the merger of two black holes—will produce. Gravity waves come in various types, which differ in their *waveforms,* that is, in the shapes of the waves that emerge from a violent event of a given kind. They also differ in their wavelengths, the average distance between wave crests, and in the total amount of energy that the gravity waves carry off from the scene of cosmic violence.

If gravity waves are ever to be detected, theoretical calculations of their behavior may prove supremely important. Theorists must first deduce the types of gravity waves, and the strengths of those waves, that a particular type of astronomical event will produce. Only then could physicists know the chances of detecting such waves with experimental apparatus that might eventually be built. There would be no point in weaving a net for salmon if only minnows swim in the river; still less would it be worth the effort to make a net fine enough for minnows if salmon alone are there.

During the late 1960s, Thorne was almost the only highly qualified physicist who made serious calculations about gravity waves. He sought to answer questions such as: How strong an effect will gravity waves from the most violent events produce in a detector? Answer: According to the most optimistic estimates, they may move the detector by a distance equal to one one-thousandth of the diameter of an atomic nucleus. What will be the pattern of the gravity waves—what scientists call the waveform—that will be caught by the motion of the detector? Answer: Different types of events should produce different patterns. So, in theory at least, gravity-wave astronomers can someday determine what sort of violence produced the waves that shook the detector ever so slightly. What will be the *frequency* of the strongest gravity waves produced by a particular type of event? That is, how many times per second will the detector vibrate when the wave passes by? Answer: If astronomers can calculate the frequency of the strongest gravity waves from a particular type of event, actual measurement of the frequency at which the strongest gravity waves arrive would help to identify what type of event has occurred. For example, if two black holes that each contain a few times the sun's mass were to collide and coalesce, they would produce the strongest gravity waves at frequencies of several hundred oscillations per second. In contrast, the gravity waves that arise when a star falls into a supermassive black hole should be strongest for frequencies of about one oscillation per hour.

As the 1960s turned to the 1970s, Kip Thorne discovered

that he had plenty of company in this theoretical analysis of gravity waves—more company than he wanted, since he has something of a Daniel Boone approach to research: When a field of research becomes fashionable, with many scientists at work in it, Thorne feels it's time to move on to something else. Before long, on his third trip to Moscow, Thorne's ongoing interaction with the Braginsky group brought him into close contact with Leonid Grishchuk, who was then working on the problem of whether the early universe underwent significant perturbations of the sort that might form galaxies and galaxy clusters. Their friendship, which grew from their shared interest in theoretical astrophysics, has deepened through more than two decades. One key moment in the interest that Thorne took in Grishchuk's research occurred a few years after their first meeting, when Grishchuk made his key discovery about gravity waves from the early universe.

The big bang that began the universe was by far the greatest explosion of all time. This bodes well for producing detectable gravity waves, since more rapid motion of more massive objects lead to stronger waves. Working against any such detection is another fact. Any gravity waves that we might now observe from the big bang must have traveled an enormous distance—15 billion light years—just as the cosmic background radiation described in chapter 5 has done. And as the expansion of the universe has weakened the cosmic background radiation, so too would it have weakened the primordial gravity waves arising from the big bang.

But Grishchuk's calculations revealed something remarkable. Instead of weakening the primordial gravity waves, the early moments of expansion would have actually *increased the strength of these waves.* If this is so, the primordial gravity waves might be strong enough to detect today. Though Grishchuk had not previously been much interested in gravity waves, this discovery caused Grishchuk's interests to converge with Kip Thorne's. Grishchuk eventually replaced Thorne as the gravity-wave theorist for Braginsky. As their friendship developed, Thorne arranged for Grishchuk to visit Caltech for a semester during the late 1970s. Since then, a year has not gone by without significant interaction between the two. Unlike Thorne, who has concentrated on gravity waves generated by such "localized" violent events as the collapse of stellar cores, Grishchuk has an interest basically in only one source of gravity waves: the universe just after the big bang.

So far as these primordial gravity waves are concerned, Thorne and Grishchuk have a friendly disagreement, though not about Grishchuk's calculations. Thorne believes that the primordial gravity waves have the strength that Grishchuk predicts, but the disagreement deals with the likelihood of detecting those waves—a likelihood that depends on the strength of *other* sources of gravity waves. Such additional sources will interfere with our ability to see the primordial gravity waves, in the same way that daylight interferes with our ability to see the stars and planets.

What are the other sources of gravity waves, and how strong are the waves that they produce? Three of Grishchuk's students have shown that the chief competing source of gravity waves will be binary star systems, especially those where two stars orbit one another at distances only a few times the distance from the Earth to the moon. The essence of gravity-wave production lies in the fact that larger masses, moving more rapidly, and in closer proximity, produce the stronger gravity waves. Today we have only limited knowledge of the number of *close binaries*. (We would know far more if we could observe the gravity waves from them.) Using what we do know and can estimate about these binaries, Grishchuk's students have concluded that the total output of gravity waves from these star systems may be almost strong enough to overshadow the primordial gravity waves, much as sunlight scattered by the Earth's atmosphere keeps us from seeing stars in the daytime. Assessing the chances of finding gravity waves from the big bang in view of the competing gravity waves from close binaries, Thorne concludes that "it will be nip and tuck."

WHEN WILL WE FIND GRAVITY WAVES?: THE LIGO DETECTOR

For Grishchuk, primordial gravity waves remain the great goal of gravity-wave astronomy, but other astrophysicists will settle for more modest results. They hope to start with the detection of gravity waves from sources smaller and more localized than the big bang—for example, from the collision of two black holes in a distant galaxy, or the collapse of a star to produce a supernova explosion in a nearby galaxy. The possibility of detecting gravity waves from these "localized" sources now seems close to reality. The apparatus that may allow the first detection of gravity waves should be built by the late 1990s in the United States and perhaps in western Europe as well; in the Soviet Union, where technology

lags and gravity-wave research has even lower priority, no similar
plans exist. Thanks largely to Kip Thorne's persuasion, Caltech has
decided to devote substantial research funds—which in turn
prompted the National Science Foundation to commit far larger
refunds—to construct the Laser Interferometer Gravity-Wave
Observatory (LIGO) and to persuade an expert experimental
physicist and administrator, Rochus Vogt, to lead the LIGO project
to completion.

    As a theorist, Thorne is not the person to find gravity waves
by building LIGO: He only predicts them. The two men who in
addition to Vogt will directly participate in making LIGO a reality,
and should—with any luck—be the first to find gravity waves, are
Ron Drever and Rainer Weiss. Drever, whom Thorne persuaded to
come to Caltech from Glasgow, is a stout Scotsman who looks
ready to ship aboard a whaler (Figure 84) but in fact has led the
construction of a prototype gravity-wave detector in one of
Caltech's buildings. Weiss, a calmer, taller man who smokes a pipe
with enthusiasm (Figure 85), equals Drever in experimental
cleverness, but his institution (MIT) became the
junior partner to Caltech when the latter committed
four professors to the project to MIT's one.

    Between them, Drever and Weiss conceived
LIGO, which will eventually consist of two separate
detectors, located on either side of the North
American continent. At each site, two perpendicular
tunnels nearly three miles long will cross at one end
(Figure 85). Each tunnel will contain a metal pipe
that can hold a nearly perfect vacuum. At the far end
of each pipe will hang a quartz *test mass* fitted with a
superb mirror. A laser light beam will bounce back
and forth through each pipe, along both a north-
south and an east-west trajectory.

    As Einstein first calculated, gravity waves
interact with the matter they encounter in
unexpected ways. They produce no effect in the

Figure 84, top. Ron Drever, the chief Caltech experimenter in the
effort to construct the Laser Interferometer Gravity-Wave
Observatory (LIGO). (Photograph by Donald Goldsmith.)

Figure 85, bottom. Rainer Weiss of MIT, Ron Drever's counter-
part, provided key insights that helped to create the current design of LIGO. (Courtesy of the Massachusetts Institute of
Technology.)

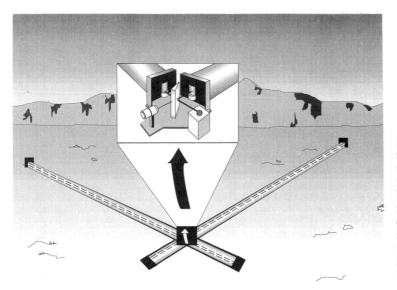

Figure 86. The LIGO detector system will have two perpendicular underground pipes, each four kilometers (2½ miles) long. A laser beam is split in two, and each beam is directed to a mirror at the end of each pipe. The laser beams are reflected back to the crossover point, where the patterns of the light waves are compared. (Drawing by Crystal Stevenson.)

direction parallel to the wave motion, but they do affect matter in the directions perpendicular to the motion. For these directions, gravity waves compress matter slightly in one direction while expanding it in the perpendicular direction, then alternate to reverse the compression and expansion, then repeat the original deformation. LIGO's two perpendicular trajectories will have exactly the same length. Thus in the absence of any compression or expansion, the two light beams should return to their starting point after exactly the same amount of time has elapsed. A gravity wave would make one laser beam have to travel a bit farther then the benchmark distance, and the other beam a bit less. Any detectable difference in the times of the laser-light trips up and down the two legs should therefore arise from, and should reveal, a change in the distance between one arm's test masses and the other's—perhaps the result of a gravity wave.

By building two LIGO detectors, the scientists can eliminate local sources of noise—a passing vehicle, a change in the weather, even a minor earthquake. Only if both detectors register an event simultaneously would the scientists assign a gravity wave as the explanation. Eventually, Ron Drever hopes to see at least four such LIGO installations around the globe. Then the experimenters could use the slightly different times of arrival of the gravity-wave disturbances at the various locations to pinpoint the direction from which the gravity waves arrive—that is, they would use the entire Earth as a gravity-wave telescope!

This sounds good, but can LIGO find gravity waves? To

detect gravity waves from a supernova, for example, we must hope to detect such stellar explosions in the Virgo Cluster, the closest large cluster of galaxies—or else wait dozens, even hundreds, of years for a closer supernova. But Kip Thorne's calculations show that a supernova explosion at this distance would produce a change of at most a million-billionth of a centimeter in the length of LIGO's pipes, and probably much less. We cannot hope to measure such a tiny change even with laser light reflected back and forth once through a three-mile pipe. But nearly two decades ago, Weiss saw that we *can* hope to detect this change if we reflect the laser light perhaps *one hundred* times back and forth through the pipes! Because each trip covers a slightly altered distance, the change in the distance covered during 100 trips will be 100 times greater than that in a single journey up and down the pipe.

To achieve these multiple reflections requires an incredibly careful alignment of a host of mirrors, so that the laser beam can make its hundreds of journeys, each of them nearly three miles long, and still produce a result in correct alignment. But Drever and Weiss believe that they can make this happen. They now have their prototype apparatus, with arms that are 130 feet in length, in operation in a basement at Caltech, and they hope to use what they learn there to build the two LIGO detectors. By the late 1990s, with any luck at all, the full system should be in operation. Then, shortly before the centenary of Einstein's great work, his theories may receive final vindication with the discovery of gravity waves.

DETECTING PRIMORDIAL GRAVITY WAVES FROM THE BIG BANG

Leonid Grishchuk still dreams of gravity waves from the big bang. He hopes to live to see a gravity-wave detector of much greater sensitivity than LIGO, capable of finding the gravity waves from the earliest moments after the big bang. Here, Grishchuk points out, the very weakness of gravity waves may prove an advantage. Precisely because gravity waves are so weak, they have passed through all of space, and 15 billion years of time, without being affected by intervening matter, though they have been weakened by the explosion of the universe in much the same way as the cosmic background radiation described in chapter 5. Finding these primordial gravity waves might reveal more about the big bang than any other scientific means of inquiry, known or speculative.

Grishchuk deals with the realm of *quantum cosmology,* the attempt to merge two tremendously successful views of the universe. One of these is cosmology, the study of the universe on the largest scales, which rests upon and embodies Einstein's general theory of relativity. The other is quantum mechanics, which deals with the realm of submicroscopic particles and how they interact. Quantum mechanics has proven overwhelmingly useful in describing atoms and atomic nuclei, and cosmology has done so in describing the universe at large. If we hope to describe the universe accurately, particularly in its earliest moments, when all of space had barely been born—when in fact neither space nor time can be clearly defined as anything like the space or time of today—we must certainly search, in the spirit of Albert Einstein's search for a unified field theory, for a view of the universe that *combines* quantum mechanics and general relativity.

Certainly we should search, but the trouble is that we don't know how. To be brutally frank, the best minds in the business can't come up with a coherent mathematical theory that incorporates both gravity, as described by general relativity, and quantum mechanics. The attempt to produce such a melding—a workable quantum cosmology—has frustrated the wisest heads, including Grishchuk's. Kip Thorne has not even tried, and Stephen Hawking, perhaps the greatest theoretical physicist of our generation, has not yet found a fully satisfactory solution to the problem of seeing how general relativity and quantum mechanics work together. "It's like mixing sand and water," Thorne says. "General relativity is the water, which bends with the curvature of the space around it; quantum mechanics is like sand, and describes the behavior of tiny particles. Put them together, and you can get quicksand, which resembles neither water nor sand; and it sucks you down as neither water nor sand can." Similarly, quantum cosmology is thought to resemble neither general relativity by itself, nor quantum mechanics by itself, but something different from both.

Today we have no complete theory of quantum cosmology to tell us how the early universe produced its gravity waves. We have half a theory though, thanks largely to the work of Stephen Hawking and his collaborator James Hartle; and Leonid Grishchuk is not afraid to use it to make predictions about primordial gravity waves, that is, gravity waves from the big bang. Grishchuk ranks among the most optimistic of theorists on the subject of detecting primordial gravity waves.

This detection involves two unknowns: How strong are the primordial gravity waves? And how strong are competing sources of gravity waves, which will interfere with our attempts to detect the primordial ones? To find primordial gravity waves will most certainly require some sort of space-based LIGO, a detector that reflects laser beams back and forth for *millions* of miles. The longer paths for the laser beams allow the detector to find gravity waves of much longer wavelength than those LIGO can detect. This capability is important because Grishchuk's calculations predict that among all the primordial gravity waves, the long-wavelength waves should be much stronger than the shorter-wavelength ones. Peter Bender, a physicist at the University of Colorado, has plans to create such a "space LIGO" system, and NASA has begun technology-development studies for this system. All those involved in such plans recognize, however, that the first step must be for LIGO to succeed.

Gravity waves now stand on the threshold of experimental confirmation, ready to pass from theoretical belief to verifiable reality. A century ago, Heinrich Hertz saw that the theory of electricity and magnetism implied the existence of electromagnetic waves; today we understand light as one form of Hertz's electromagnetic waves and routinely employ the other varieties— radio, infrared, ultraviolet, x rays, and gamma rays—to observe the universe. Once Einstein saw gravity waves as a theoretical by-product of his theory, engaging but undetectable; today physicists (and funding agencies) take gravity-wave detection seriously. Once we lived in relative darkness; today we have better and better ways to study the cosmos.

Albert Einstein said that what really interested him was whether God had any choice in making the universe—that is, whether only one universe, or one type of universe, is possible. Will gravity waves tell us the answer? What else will gravity waves show us? What will the next channel of information about the cosmos reveal? What will theorists and experimenters produce for our delectation and amusement? We cannot be sure, yet it is certain that a garden of cosmic delights awaits us.

Figure 87. An artist's conception shows the Hubble Space Telescope in orbit, 380 miles above the Earth's surface. (NASA artwork.)

14. Astronomy for the Twenty-first Century

IMAGINE A PLANET on whose surface life existed beneath a blanket of atmosphere so thick that despite their best efforts, the planet's inhabitants could never see outward into space. Its denizens, no matter how highly evolved, would miss most of what is glorious about the cosmos, which would remain forever shrouded from their view by their planet's opaque, protective atmospheric veil.

That planet is the Earth, so long as we attempt to observe the universe in radiation confined to the narrow wavelength bands of visible light and radio waves. Indeed we have used those channels of information open to us in studying the sun's planets, the Milky Way's stars, and the myriad galaxies that dot the cosmos. But by far the greatest challenge in astronomy consists of our basic inability to use most of the electromagnetic radiation to "see" anything, because our atmosphere blocks this radiation completely (see Figure 2, p. 5).

Happily, however, we live in the dawn of the new age of astronomy—the age of observations made from above the atmosphere. Within the next two decades, we should have true orbiting observatories, guided from the ground and capable of many years of observation, that can study the cosmos from beyond the opaque screen of our atmosphere. Although astronomers have other important goals for the final decade of this century and the first decade of the next, the effort to produce space-borne observatories ranks highest with nearly all such scientists.

THE FUTURE OF ASTRONOMICAL RESEARCH

Broadly speaking, during the next century astronomy will advance along four main lines. First and most important, astronomers will continue to send new and improved instruments into orbit above the atmosphere. Second, they will design and build improved detector systems, making better use of the radiation that reaches their instruments. Third, they will construct a new generation of telescopes on the surface of Earth, to complement and to follow in detail the revelations that will arise from their ongoing discovery programs. And fourth, they will send more sophisticated probes, possibly with humans aboard, throughout our solar system to continue to expand the results from the great explorations of the past 30 years. With this four-pronged effort, astronomers can reasonably hope to answer many of the great outstanding questions about the cosmos—and to uncover a host of new ones.

EYES ABOVE THE ATMOSPHERE

The loftiest goal of modern astronomy involves a plan to create observatories in space, free from the blurring and absorbing effects of our atmosphere. Only from space—from altitudes at least a few hundred miles above the Earth's surface—can we lift the atmospheric veil that has kept us from seeing the universe plain. Until then, we must look at the cosmos in visible light through a moving, blurring haze; we can capture only small parts of the ultraviolet, infrared, and submillimeter radiation that impinges on the Earth's atmosphere; and we can observe none of the x rays and gamma rays that may have traveled for millions of light years, only to be absorbed in the final stages of their cosmic journey. NASA, the Japanese Space Agency, and the European community of astronomers all have plans to put observatories in space, in order to allow us to view the cosmos in all the radiation that it produces.

NASA now has in operation or in plan five great observatories in space:

- the Hubble Space Telescope, launched in April 1990 to make ultraviolet and visible-light observations;
- the Gamma Ray Observatory (GRO), scheduled for launch in the spring of 1991;
- the Advanced X-ray Astrophysics Facility (AXAF), which should be launched during 1997 and should provide a significant improvement over the European ROSAT satellite, launched in 1990 to make x-ray observations;
- the Space Infrared Telescope Facility (SIRTF), which should achieve orbit by 1999 and should do better than a European infrared satellite called ISO, to be launched in 1992;
- the Large Deployable Reflector (LDR), designed to make submillimeter observations, truly a project for the next century.

The first of the great observatories, NASA's Hubble Space Telescope, has until now been a partial success and a partial failure. Launched in April 1990, the telescope turned out to have a primary mirror that had been mistakenly made with the wrong shape. Though this flaw may be corrected with redesigned instruments by 1993, until then the Space Telescope cannot obtain as sharp a view of the universe as scientists hoped, though computer processing can produce excellent images (Color Plate 4). It can, however, profit from its orbit above the atmosphere to make important ultraviolet observations. In doing so, the Space Telescope will blaze important trails in establishing the ability of space-borne observatories to study the cosmos (Figure 87, p. 312).

CONTINUED EXPLORATION OF THE SOLAR SYSTEM

Of the great planetary missions of the 1990s, two were launched in 1989—*Magellan* to Venus and *Galileo* to Jupiter. *Magellan* has mapped Venus with an advanced radar system to pierce her eternal veil of clouds. *Galileo* will reach Jupiter only in 1995, after a looping, six-year journey that takes it once past Venus and twice past the Earth, using the "slingshot effect" from these planets' gravitational forces (Figure 88). At Jupiter, *Galileo* will go into orbit around the giant planet, making detailed observations of its moon and of the

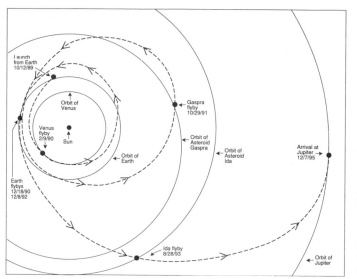

Figure 88. The *Galileo* spacecraft must take a long trajectory, sailing once past Venus (in 1990) and twice past Earth (in 1991 and 1992), in order to acquire enough speed from these deliberate planetary near-misses to proceed to its encounter with Jupiter in 1995. (Drawing by Crystal Stevenson.)

changing atmospheric patterns in Jupiter's cloud layers. Part of the spacecraft will then detach for a descent through the clouds to make on-the-spot measurements.

The third great NASA planetary probe of the 1990s will be the *CRAF/Cassini* project, two spacecraft that may be launched in 1996. One of the spacecraft will pass by a comet and an asteroid; the other will make detailed observations of Saturn and its moons, especially of the great moon Titan, considered the likeliest site for possible extraterrestrial life in the solar system.

OTHER WAYS TO OBSERVE THE UNIVERSE

In addition to launching space-borne observatories and sending probes through the solar system, astronomers hope to continue to build larger and better ground-based telescopes and to improve the detector systems for these telescopes and for observatories in space. NASA also has plans to make a serious search for other civilizations in the Milky Way, which may be detectable by the radio waves they use for their analogs of radio, television, and radar communications. Not all these plans will reach fruition, even in our great-grandchildren's time. But some will, and still more important, the discoveries we make will lead to ways now undreamt about to study the cosmos. As the twenty-first century unfolds, humanity (should we be wise enough to endure right through it) may yet find the answers to such mysteries as the formation of galaxies and the fate of the universe. If they do, it is easy to predict that still greater and deeper mysteries lie beyond.

Glossary

Absolute temperature scale. Temperature measured on a scale that begins at absolute zero (-459.67 degrees Fahrenheit) and uses the same degree units as the Celsius (Centigrade) scale.

Absolute zero. The lowest point on any temperature scale; the temperature at which all motion ceases: -273.16 degrees Centigrade or -459.67 degrees Fahrenheit.

Absorption. The blocking or elimination of electromagnetic radiation, typically by atoms, molecules, or dust grains in interstellar space, in the outer layers of a star, or in the atmospheres of Earth and other planets.

Absorption line. A small portion of the electromagnetic spectrum, usually in the visible light or ultraviolet regions of the spectrum, from which radiation has been removed.

Angular momentum. A measure of the amount of spin possessed by an object.

Angular size. The apparent size of an object, measured by the angle over which the object extends, measured in degrees of arc, minutes of arc, and seconds of arc. The sun and moon, as seen from Earth, each have an angular size of half a degree (30 minutes of arc).

Atom. The smallest unit of a chemical element, consisting of a nucleus of one or more protons and neutrons surrounded by one or more electrons in orbit around the nucleus.

Black hole. An object that exerts such enormous gravitational force that nothing, not even light or other forms of electromagnetic radiation, can escape from it.

Black-hole radius. The radius of an object to which it must be squeezed to become a black hole. This radius equals two miles times the ratio of the object's mass to the sun's mass.

Blueshift. A shift of all wavelengths and frequencies in the light from an object to shorter wavelengths and higher frequencies caused by the Doppler effect. A blueshift observed in the light from an object indicates that the object is approaching the observer.

CCD. Charge-Coupled Device. An electronic detector of electromagnetic radiation, based on silicon chips that respond to incoming radiation by producing an electric current. CCDs are replacing photographic plates as the best way to record the light from distant objects.

Celestial sphere. The sphere of the sky imagined by ancient Greek astronomers, centered on the Earth, on which the sun, moon, planets, stars, and galaxies could all be located at the same distance from Earth. In reality, astronomical objects have widely varying distances.

Celsius temperature scale. The scale of temperatures that registers the freezing point of water as 0 degrees and the boiling point as 100 degrees.

Center of mass. The point at which an object's mass can be imagined to be concentrated, in order to calculate the amount of gravitational force exerted on the object. A spherically symmetric object such as a cannonball has its center of mass at the center of the sphere. Irregularly shaped objects and groups of objects also have a center of mass. In these situations, the location of the center of mass can be found by locating the point from which, proceeding in any two opposite directions, the product of mass in that direction times the distance

317

from that point will be equal for the two directions. For example, the center of mass of a double-star system in which one star has 5 times the mass of the other lies on the line joining the two stars, but five times farther from the less massive star than from the more massive one.

Centigrade temperature scale. The Celsius temperature scale.

Comet. A fragment of primitive solar-system material, made of ice and dust, typically a few kilometers across, that moves in a huge, elongated orbit around the sun. Comets were the first objects to form as the solar system condensed from an interstellar cloud of gas and dust some 5 billion years ago.

Corona. The outermost parts of the sun (and other stars), millions of miles in extent, consisting of highly rarefied gas heated to temperatures of millions of degrees.

Cosmology. The study of the universe as a whole, and of its structure and evolution.

Dark matter. Matter of unknown form, deduced to exist by its gravity, and thought to comprise most of the matter of the universe.

Degree of arc. A unit of angular size equal to 1/360 of a full circle. Astronomers measure angular size by imagining themselves at the center of a circle (360 degrees) and determining the fraction of the circle that a particular object covers. The sun and moon each have an angular size, as seen from Earth, of half a degree.

Doppler effect. For any type of wave motion, such as the vibrations called sound waves, the change in frequency or wavelength that an observer notes when the source of the waves approaches or recedes from the observer, or the observer approaches or recedes from the source of the waves. During the early nineteenth century, the Austrian physicist Christian Johann Doppler first explained the effect for sound waves: When the source of waves approaches an observer (or the observer approaches the source), the waves are effectively compressed, producing a higher pitch (frequency) and a shorter wavelength. Similarly, velocities of recession lower the pitch and increase the wavelength of the observed waves. The same effect applies to light waves and other forms of electromagnetic radiation: Velocities of approach increase the observed frequencies and decrease the wavelengths, while velocities of recession decrease the observed frequencies and increase the wavelengths. The Doppler effect depends only on the velocity of the source of waves with respect to the observer, and not at all on the distance between source and observer. Greater velocities of approach or recession produce greater changes in the observed frequencies and wavelengths.

Doppler shift. The change in frequency or wavelength produced by the Doppler effect.

Einstein ring. The bending of the light from a distant source around an intervening object to produce a circle of light. This effect arises from the gravitational bending of light, first predicted by Albert Einstein, and has been observed in several cases where light from a tremendously distant galaxy has been bent from a straight-line trajectory as it passes around another galaxy that lies between ourselves and the more distant galaxy.

Electromagnetic forces. Forces that act between particles with electric charge, either as repulsive forces (between particles with the same sign of electric charge) or as attractive forces (between particles with opposite signs of electric charge). Certain types of elementary particles, such as electrons and antiprotons, each carry one unit of negative charge, while certain other types, such as protons and antielectrons, each carry one unit of positive charge.

Electromagnetic radiation. Waves of energy, consisting of massless particles called photons, characterized by a frequency (number of vibrations per second) and a wavelength (distance between successive wave crests). Human eyes have evolved to detect the type of electromagnetic radiation called visible light. Other types of electromagnetic radiation include radio waves, infrared, ultraviolet, x rays, and gamma rays.

Element. The set of all atoms with the same chemical properties and the same number of protons in each atomic nucleus. The nucleus, at the atom's center, consists of elementary particles called protons and neutrons. Carbon atoms each have 6 protons per nucleus; oxygen atoms each have 8 protons; and iron atoms each have 26 protons per nucleus. For a particular element, the number of neutrons in each nucleus specifies the atomic isotope.

Elementary particle. A fundamental particle of nature, such as an electron, considered to be an indivisible bit of matter.

Elliptical galaxy. A galaxy composed of stars whose distribution has an ellipsoidal shape, so that a photograph of the galaxy has the shape of an ellipse.

Energy. The capacity of a system, both actual and potential, to do work.

Fahrenheit temperature scale. The temperature scale, most commonly used in the United States but nearly unknown elsewhere, that registers the freezing point of water as 32 degrees and the boiling point as 212 degrees.

Frequency. The number of vibrations per second, usually measured in units of hertz (one hertz corresponds to one oscillation per second). The hertz honors Heinrich Hertz, a pioneer investigator of electromagnetic radiation.

Fusion. The joining of two atomic nuclei to create other types of nuclei, which typically reduces the total mass and therefore decreases the total energy of mass, which is measured by Einstein's formula $E = mc^2$. The decrease in energy of mass is matched by a corresponding increase in the total kinetic energy (energy of motion) of the particles emerging from the fusion.

Galaxy. A large group of stars, typically numbering in the billions, that are held together by their mutual gravitational attraction. Typical galaxies have diameters of about a hundred thousand light years.

Gamma rays. Electromagnetic radiation with the smallest wavelengths and highest frequencies of all types.

Globular star cluster. A spherical or ellipsoidal group of stars, usually 10 or 20 light years in diameter and containing several hundred thousand, or a few million, individual stars.

Gravitational arc. Part of an "Einstein ring."

Gravitational forces. One of the four basic types of forces (the others are electromagnetic, strong, and weak). Gravity is always attractive. For any two particles, the amount of gravitational force varies in proportion to the product of the two masses, and in inverse proportion to the square of the distance between the objects' centers.

Hubble's Law. The rule that summarizes our observations of the expanding universe: The recession velocities of the galaxy clusters that we observe equals a constant, called Hubble's constant, times the clusters' distances from us. Hubble's Law summarizes observations made by Edwin Hubble and others of galaxies as seen from Earth. If other observers throughout the universe likewise see galaxies moving away from them (this assumption is called the cosmological principle), then Hubble's Law implies that the entire universe is expanding.

Inflationary model. A mathematical model of the universe in which all of space undergoes enormous amounts of expansion during its first tiny fraction of a second.

Infrared. Electromagnetic radiation with slightly longer wavelengths and slightly smaller frequencies than the wavelengths and frequencies of visible light.

Interferometer. A device that uses two or more telescopes, and compares the signals detected by each, to observe sources of radiation with greater resolving power than one of these telescopes can.

Interstellar medium. The gas and dust between the stars, from which new stars are made.

Ion. An atom that has lost one or more of its electrons.

Ionization. The process by which ions are produced, typically by collisions with atoms or electrons, or by interaction with electromagnetic radiation.

Isotope. The subset of a given element that consists of those atoms whose nuclei all contain the same number of neutrons, as well as the same number of protons.

Kilometer. A unit of distance equal to 0.62137 mile.

Light year. The distance that light travels in a year, equal to 9.46 trillion kilometers or about 6 trillion miles.

Local Group. The small cluster of about 20 galaxies to which our Milky Way galaxy belongs.

Luminosity. The amount of energy produced each second by a star or galaxy. Unlike the apparent brightness of an object, the luminosity does not depend on the object's distance from an observer.

Magnetic field. A field of force in space, created by a magnet or by an electric current, that guides the trajectories of electrically charged particles by exerting an electromagnetic force.

Main-sequence star. A star in the prime of life, which is fusing protons into helium in its core at a constant rate and shining with a constant luminosity.

Milky Way. The galaxy to which our solar system belongs, whose central regions appear as a band of light or "milky way" that we can see from Earth in clear night skies far from city lights.

Minute of arc. One-sixtieth of a degree of arc.

Missing mass. An outmoded name for the dark matter in the universe.

Molecule. A stable grouping of two or more atoms, bound together by electromagnetic forces among the electrons and nuclei in the atoms.

Nebula. A diffuse mass of interstellar matter, often lit from within by young, hot stars that have recently formed from interstellar gas and dust.

Neutrino. A subatomic particle, either massless or with an extremely small mass, capable of penetrating large objects without interaction.

Neutron. A subatomic particle with no electric charge, one of the two basic constituents of an atomic nucleus.

Neutron star. A tremendously dense object, typically about a dozen kilometers across, formed from the central core of a collapsed star. Almost all the particles in a neutron star are neutrons produced when the core collapsed.

Nuclear fusion. The joining together of two nuclei to form other types of nuclei. Nuclear fusion typically reduces the total mass and increases the total kinetic energy of the particles emerging from the fusion. Stars use nuclear fusion to produce new kinetic energy from energy of mass at their centers, where the temperature is high enough for nuclear fusion to occur. These high temperatures arise from the pressure of the overlying layers, which squeeze and heat the gas at the center.

Nucleus (plural, nuclei). (1) The central region of an atom, containing almost all of the atom's mass, comprised of one or more protons and zero or more neutrons. (2) The central concentration of matter in a galaxy, typically spanning no more than a few light years in diameter.

Parallax. The apparent displacement in position of stars caused by the Earth's yearly motion in orbit around the sun; more generally, parallax describes the apparent change in an object's position caused by an observer's changing position. For example, looking at an object first with one eye and then the other produces a parallax effect. The amount of the apparent displacement caused by parallax is called the parallax shift. For the closest stars to the sun, the parallax shift arising from the Earth's motion in orbit around the sun equals a small fraction of a second of arc.

Parsec. An astronomical unit of distance equal to 3.26 light years, or approximately 19 trillion miles.

Planet. One of the nine largest objects in orbit around the sun; also, similar objects that may be in orbit around other stars.

Planetary nebula. A shell of gas surrounding an aging star. This gas has been expelled from the star itself; it is heated and partially ionized by the radiation emitted from the hot surface of the star. In a small telescope, a planetary nebula resembles the appearance of a planet.

Proper motion. A nearby star's motion in the sky, measured with respect to the sun, and caused by the fact that stars' orbits around the center of the Milky Way galaxy are not identical, so that the sun's neighbors move along slightly diverging or approaching trajectories as each star circles the galactic center.

Quasar. A quasi-stellar object, a source of visible light and radio waves. Quasars are almost starlike in appearance but actually rank among the most powerful and most distant sources of energy known to exist in the universe.

Radiation. See Electromagnetic radiation.

Radio. Electromagnetic radiation with the longest wavelengths and lowest frequencies of all types.

Red-giant star. A star that has passed through the major portion of its life, during which it fused hydrogen nuclei (protons) into helium nuclei at a constant rate, and has now swelled and cooled its outer layers while its central, nuclear-fusing core has contracted and grown hotter.

Redshift. A shift to longer wavelengths and lower frequencies, typically caused by the Doppler effect in a receding object.

Reflecting telescope. A telescope that employs a mirror as the primary means of collecting and focusing visible light or other forms of electromagnetic radiation.

Refracting telescope. A telescope that employs a lens as its primary means of collecting and focusing light.

Resolving power. A telescope's ability to reveal fine details in the objects it observes. A telescope of great resolving power can reveal two neighboring stars as individual sources of light when a telescope of lower resolving power will show only a single, combined source.

Seyfert galaxy. A spiral galaxy with an unusually bright, compact nucleus, named after the astronomer Carl Seyfert, who first systematically investigated this class of galaxies. The nuclei of Seyfert galaxies resemble quasars, but on a much reduced scale of energy and luminosity.

Solar sytem. The sun and the objects in orbit around it, which include 9 planets, nearly 60 known satellites of the planets, thousands of smaller objects called asteroids, and billions of comets.

Solar wind. Streams of charged particles expelled from the hottest, outermost layers of the sun, which pass the Earth and the other planets as bunches of electrons and ions, the latter typically nuclei of hydrogen, helium, oxygen, carbon, nitrogen, and neon that have lost one or more of the electrons that orbit each nucleus.

Spectrograph. An instrument that spreads electromagnetic radiation into its component frequencies and wavelengths.

Spectroscopy. The observation and analysis of the spectra of radiation from distant objects.

Spectrum (plural, spectra). The distribution of electromagnetic radiation over its component frequencies and wavelengths. In order of increasing wavelength and decreasing frequency, the spectrum of electromagnetic radiation consists of gamma rays, x rays, ultraviolet, visible light, infrared, submillimeter, and radio waves.

Spiral galaxy. A galaxy characterized by a flattened disk of stars, within which the youngest, brightest stars appear within spiral patterns called spiral arms.

Star. A self-luminous mass of gas held together by its own gravitation, at the center of which energy is released by nuclear fusion.

Star cluster. A group of stars born at almost the same time and place, capable of remaining a unit for billions of years because of the mutual gravitational attraction of the cluster's stars.

Strong forces. Forces that act between protons and neutrons, binding them together into atomic nuclei, and which are effective only at distances of 10^{-13} centimeter or less.

Supernova (plural, supernovae). An exploding star, visible for weeks or months, even at enormous distances, because of the tremendous amounts of energy that the star produces. Supernovae typically arise when massive stars exhaust all means of producing energy from nuclear fusion. In these stars, the collapse of the star's core results in the explosion of the star's outer layers. Another type of supernova arises when hydrogen-rich matter from a companion star accumulates on the surface of a white dwarf and then undergoes nuclear fusion.

Telescope. An instrument that collects and focuses electromagnetic radiation, typically with either a mirror (reflecting telescope) or a lens (refracting telescope). Telescopes are now often sent above the Earth's atmosphere, which absorbs most types of electromagnetic radiation. Modern telescopes use a variety of devices, such as CCDs, to record and analyze the radiation collected and focused by the telescope. These devices are superior to the human eye and photographic plates, and have therefore replaced them as recording instruments.

Temperature. The measure of the average energy of random motion within a group of particles. A home thermometer measures the temperature of surrounding gas or liquid by responding to the impact of molecules within the gas or liquid. Such impacts cause the liquid (typically mercury) in the thermometer to expand to a particular volume that indicates the temperature.

Ultraviolet. Electromagnetic radiation with higher frequencies and shorter wavelengths than those of visible light.

Visible light. Electromagnetic radiation with frequencies and wavelengths between those of ultraviolet and infrared, to which human eyes are sensitive.

Wavelength. The distance between two successive wave crests in a wave such as an electromagnetic wave.

White dwarf. A star that has completed the fusion of helium nuclei into carbon nuclei in its interior, in which the exclusion principle prevents any further contraction. Such a star slowly radiates away the energy stored while it is still performing nuclear fusion. It is typically a few thousand kilometers in diameter and of much lower luminosity than an active star.

X rays. Electromagnetic radiation with greater frequencies and smaller wavelengths than those of ultraviolet radiation.

Further Reading

1. Under the Dome of Heaven

Nathan Cohen, *Gravity's Lens* (New York: John Wiley & Sons, 1989).
George Field and Eric Chaisson, *The Invisible Universe* (Boston: Birkhauser Books, 1983).
Nigel Henbest and Michael Marten, *The New Astronomy* (London and New York: Cambridge University Press, 1983).
Philip and Phylis Morrison and the Office of Charles and Ray Eames, *Powers of Ten: About the Relative Sizes of Things in the Universe* (New York: Scientific American Library, 1982).
James Trefil, *The Dark Side of the Universe* (New York: Charles Scribner's Sons, 1988).
Wallace and Karen Tucker, *The Dark Matter* (New York: William Morrow, 1988).

2. The Dark Matter

Michael Disney, *The Hidden Universe* (New York: Macmillan Company, 1984).
Timothy Ferris, *Galaxies* (New York: Harrison House, 1987).
Lawrence Krauss, *The Fifth Essence: The Search for Dark Matter in the Universe* (New York: Basic Books, 1989).
Philip and Phylis Morrison, *The Ring of Truth* (New York: Random House, 1987).

3. We Are All Astronomers

Daniel Boorstin, *The Discoverers* (New York: Random House, 1983).
Will Kyselka and Ray Lanterman, *North Star to Southern Cross* (Honolulu: University of Hawaii Press, 1976).
Whitney's Star Finder (New York: Alfred Knopf, 1974).

4. Mapping the Universe

Marcia Bartusiak, *Thursday's Universe* (New York: Times Books, 1986).
Edwin Hubble, *The Realm of the Nebulae* (New York: Dover Books, 1958).
James Trefil, *The Moment of Creation* (New York: Charles Scribner's Sons, 1984).
Robert Wagoner and Donald Goldsmith, *Cosmic Horizons* (New York: W. H. Freeman & Co., 1982).
Charles Whitney, *The Discovery of Our Galaxy* (New York: Alfred A. Knopf, 1972).

5. The Afterglow of Creation

Richard Berendzen, Richard Hart, and Daniel Seeley, *Man Discovers the Galaxies* (New York: Columbia University Press, 1984).

George Gamow, *My World Line* (New York: Viking Press, 1970).

Edward Harrison, *Cosmology: The Science of the Universe* (London and New York: Cambridge University Press, 1981).

Edward Harrison, *Darkness at Night: A Riddle of the Universe* (Cambridge, Mass.: Harvard University Press, 1987).

Stephen Hawking, *A Brief History of Time* (New York and London: Bantam Books, 1988).

Steven Weinberg, *The First Three Minutes* (New York: Bantam Books, 1976).

6. Why Stars Shine

Jeremy Bernstein, *Hans Bethe: Prophet of Energy* (New York: Basic Books, 1980).

Katharine Haramundanis (ed.), *Cecilia Payne-Gaposchkin: An Autobiography and Other Recollections* (London and New York: Cambridge University Press, 1984).

Robert Jastrow, *Red Giants and White Dwarfs* (New York: W. W. Norton, Inc., 1979).

Robert Jastrow, *Until the Sun Dies* (New York: W. W. Norton, Inc., 1977).

Paolo Maffei, *When the Sun Dies* (Cambridge, Mass.: MIT Press, 1982).

7. Stars from Birth to Old Age

Carl Sagan, *Cosmos* (New York: Random House, 1980).

Lyman Spitzer, *Searching Between the Stars* (New Haven: Yale University Press, 1982).

8. The Stellar Explosions that Made Us

Donald Goldsmith, *Supernova! The Exploding Star of 1987* (New York: St. Martin's Press, 1989).

George Greenstein, *Frozen Star: Of Pulsars, Black Holes, and the Fate of Stars* (New York: New American Library, 1983).

Laurence Marschall, *The Supernova Story* (New York: Plenum Press, 1989).

Walter Sullivan, *Black Holes* (Garden City: Anchor/Doubleday, 1979).

9. Quasars and Peculiar Galaxies

James Cornell and Alan Lightman (eds.), *Revealing the Universe* (Cambridge, Mass.: MIT Press, 1982).

Richard Preston, *First Light: The Search for the Edge of the Universe* (New York: Atlantic Monthly Press, 1987).

10. The Beast in the Middle

Halton Arp, *Quasars, Redshifts, and Controversies* (Berkeley: Interstellar Media, 1987).

George Field, John Bahcall, and Halton Arp, *The Redshift Controversy* (Menlo Park: Addison-Wesley, 1973).

Wallace and Karen Tucker, *The Cosmic Inquirers* (Cambridge, Mass.: Harvard University Press, 1986).

11. Exploring the Neighborhood

Norman Horowitz, *To Utopia and Back: The Search for Life in the Solar System* (New York: W. H. Freeman & Co., 1986).

Bruce Murray, *Journey Into Space: The First Thirty Years of Space Exploration* (New York: W. W. Norton, Inc., 1990).

12. How Many Worlds in the Milky Way?

J. Kelly Beatty, Brian O'Leary, and A. Chaikin (eds.), *The New Solar System* (3d ed.) (Cambridge, Mass.: Sky Publishing Corporation, 1990).

Walter McDougall, *The Heavens and the Earth* (New York: Basic Books, 1985).

13. The Wave of the Future?

Ronald Clark, *Einstein: The Life and Times* (Cleveland: World Publishing, 1971).

Paul Davies, *The Search for Gravity Waves* (New York and London: Cambridge University Press, 1980).

John Wheeler, *Gravity and Spacetime* (New York: Scientific American Library, 1990).

Clifford Will, *Was Einstein Right?* (New York: Basic Books, 1986).

14. Astronomy for the Twenty-first Century

George Field and Donald Goldsmith, *Space Telescope: Eyes Above the Atmosphere* (Chicago: Contemporary Books, 1989).

Richard Lewis, *Space in the 21st Century* (New York: Columbia University Press, 1990).

For more information about astronomy, you may write to one of the following organizations:

Astronomical Society of the Pacific, 390 Ashton Ave., San Francisco, CA 94112

American Astronomical Society, Educational Office,
c/o Prof. Charles Tolbert, University of Virginia, P.O. Box 3818, University Station, Charlottesville, VA 22903

The Planetary Society, 65 North Catalina Ave., Pasadena, CA 91106

Color Photo Credits

Plate 1: Courtesy of Dr. Dale Cruikshank.

Plate 2: NASA photograph.

Plate 3: Photograph courtesy of Dr. Tony Tyson and Bell Telephone Laboratories.

Plate 4: NASA photograph.

Plate 5: Courtesy of Kleiser/Walczak Construction Company.

Plate 6: Computer graphic rendition by Digital Animation Laboratory, Inc.

Plate 7: Photograph copyright by the California Institute of Technology and the Carnegie Institution of Washington.

Plate 8: Photograph by Dr. David Malin, courtesy of the Anglo-Australian Telescope Board.

Plate 9: Courtesy of American Science & Engineering.

Plate 10: Photograph by Dr. David Malin, courtesy of the Anglo-Australian Telescope Board.

Plate 11: Photograph by Dr. David Malin, courtesy of the Anglo-Australian Telescope Board.

Plate 12: Photograph by Dr. David Malin, courtesy of the Anglo-Australian Telescope Board.

Plate 13: Photograph courtesy of the Palomar Observatory, copyright by the California Institute of Technology.

Plate 14: Photograph by Dr. David Malin, courtesy of the Anglo-Australian Telescope Board.

Plate 15: Photograph courtesy of the National Optical Astronomy Observatories, copyright by the Association of Universities for Research in Astronomy, Inc.

Plate 16: Photograph courtesy of Palomar Observatory, copyright by the California Institute of Technology.

Plate 17: Photograph courtesy of the National Optical Astronomy Observatories, copyright by the Association of Universities for Research in Astronomy, Inc.

Plates 18 and 19: Courtesy of the European Southern Observatory.

Plate 20: Photograph courtesy of Palomar Observatory, copyright by the California Institute of Technology.

Plate 21: Photograph courtesy of Palomar Observatory, copyright by the California Institute of Technology.

Plate 22: Courtesy of Professor Mark Morris, UCLA, and the National Radio Astronomy Observatory.

Plate 23: Photograph by Dr. David Malin, courtesy of the Anglo-Australian Telescope Board.

Plate 24: Courtesy of Dr. Jack Burns, Dr. Ethan Schreier, Dr. Eric Feigelson, and the Very Large Array.

Plate 25: NASA photograph.

Plate 26: NASA photograph.

Plate 27: NASA photograph.

Plate 28: Drawing by Don Davis, reproduced by courtesy of the artist.

Plate 29: NASA photograph.

Plate 30: Courtesy of Kleiser/Walczak Construction Company.

Plate 31: NASA photograph.

Plate 32: NASA photograph.

Plate 33: NASA photograph.

Plate 34: Courtesy of Brad Smith/Rich Terrile and JPL/NASA.

Plate 35: Image by Sidley/Wright, Inc.

Plate 36: Image by Sidley/Wright, Inc.

Index

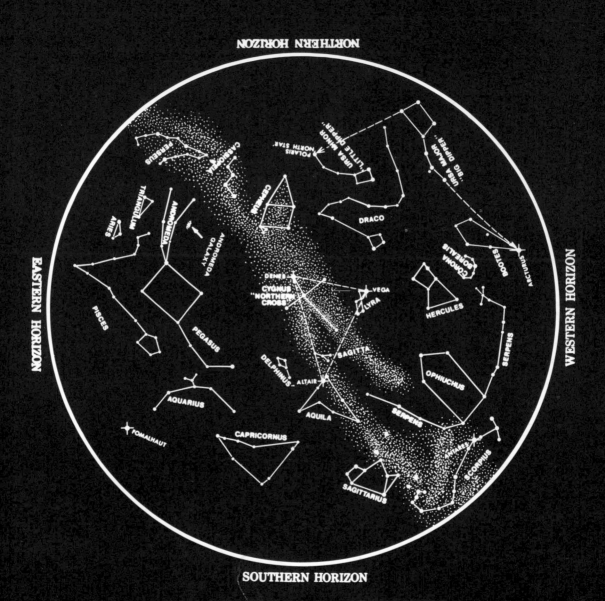

THE NIGHT SKY IN SEPTEMBER